Human-Powered Vehicles

Allan V. Abbott, MD
University of Southern California

David Gordon Wilson, PhD
Massachusetts Institute of Technology

Human Kinetics

Library of Congress Cataloging-in-Publication Data

Abbott, Allan V.
    Human-powered vehicles / Allan V. Abbott, David Gordon Wilson.
        p.   cm.
    Includes bibliographical references and index.
    ISBN 0-87322-827-8 (hardback)
    1. Human powered vehicles.   I. Wilson, David Gordon, 1928-
II. Title.
TL 154.A23   1995
629.04--dc20   95-10636
                                                        CIP

ISBN: 0-87322-827-8

Acquisitions Editor: Richard Frey, PhD
Developmental Editor: Rodd Whelpley
Assistant Editors: Jacqueline Blakley and Kent Reel
Copyeditor: Tom Plummer
Proofreader: Kathy Bennett
Indexer: Jacqueline Brownstein
Typesetter: Francine Hamerski
Text Designer: Judy Henderson
Layout Artists: Francine Hamerski and Tara Welsch
Photo Editor: Keith Blomberg
Cover Designer: Jack Davis
Cover Photograph: M.I.T. publicity photo, courtesy of Anne Maynard at M.I.T. Aero and Astro Department
Illustrators: Kent McDaniel and Paul To
Printer: Braun-Brumfield

Printed in the United States of America

10 9 8 7 6 5 4 3 2 1

Human Kinetics
P.O. Box 5076, Champaign, IL 61825-5076
1-800-747-4457

Canada: Human Kinetics, Box 24040, Windsor, ON N8Y 4Y9
1-800-465-7301 (in Canada only)

Europe: Human Kinetics, P.O. Box IW14, Leeds LS16 6TR, United Kingdom
(44) 1132 781708

Australia: Human Kinetics, 2 Ingrid Street, Clapham 5062, South Australia
(08) 371 3755

New Zealand: Human Kinetics, P.O. Box 105-231, Auckland 1
(09) 523 3462

To Colony for her loving patience

—A.A.

To Ellen Wilson, who greatly enjoyed her time with Colony Abbott when Allan and I were working on the book

—D.G.W.

CONTENTS

PREFACE

Human-powered vehicles have at some time touched the lives of all people. In many parts of the world people ride bicycles as their means of daily transportation. Other people rely on kayaks or other small human-powered boats for their livelihood. In industrialized nations human-powered vehicles are considered sometimes as toys for children and primarily as tools for sport or exercise. In these countries more dramatic innovation and progress have occurred in human-powered vehicles during the 1970s, 1980s, and now in the 1990s, than had occurred in all previous history. A human-powered aircraft was flown across the English Channel in 1979. In 1988, another human-powered aircraft retraced the course of the Greek legend Daedalus by flying 119 km (74 miles) from the island of Crete to the island of Santorin. The first human-powered hydrofoil watercraft flew in 1983 and has recently eclipsed the speed records of rowed racing shells. A four-man team in 1989 won the first Race Across America for human-powered vehicles in the astonishing time of 5 days 1 hour. A streamlined human-powered recumbent bicycle reached a speed over 68 mph (30.6 m/s) in 1992. These developments have stimulated groups and individuals all over the world to emulate and surpass these extraordinary performances.

This book reviews the history of human-powered water, land, and air vehicles and concentrates on the significant developments that have led to spectacular improvements in performance during the past two decades. Previously this information has been scattered widely in the world's literature and has never before been assembled into a single publication. This is the first comprehensive and up-to-date scientific and practical overview of all types of human-powered vehicles. The chapters are written by those people who have been responsible for the most recent innovations. The original stimulus for this book was the 1975 founding of the International Human Powered Vehicle Association (IHPVA) by Chester Kyle and Jack Lambie in southern California.

Coeditor Allan V. Abbott, MD, a family and sports medicine physician and professor at the University of Southern California School of Medicine, was the first president of the IHPVA. Abbott held the world paced-bicycle speed record (140.5 mph) at the time the IHPVA was founded and went on to pioneer in the development of streamlined recumbent bicycles and human-powered hydrofoils, setting several speed records in the process. Coeditor David Gordon Wilson, PhD, an engineer and professor at the Massachusetts Institute of Technology, is also a former IHPVA president. Wilson is well known to the cycling community for his book *Bicycling Science* (co-authored with Frank Rowland Whitt) and for his pioneering advocacy of recumbent bicycles. Abbott and Wilson have assembled a list of contributors that represents a who's who of leaders in human-powered boats, aircraft, and land vehicles.

This book is intended for inventors, teachers, students, hobbyists, and sports enthusiasts, yet it provides enough scientific detail to satisfy engineers and scientists. Because it covers scientific and practical aspects of human-powered water, land, and air vehicles, it will interest a wide range of readers and inventors from the boating, bicycling, and flying communities. This book also describes the performance capabilities of the "human engine" in sufficient detail so that human-performance engineers and exercise physiologists can use this as a reference in designing the next generation of human-powered vehicles.

The heyday of human-powered land vehicles occurred in the 1800s, when various bicycle and tricycle designs opened new possibilities for individual sport and travel. With the invention of the internal-combustion engine, much of the industrialized world's attention turned away from human-powered transportation and toward automobiles, powered aircraft, and other vehicles with powerful engines. Today, however, there is increasing concern over the negative impact on the environment of vehicles powered by internal-combustion engines, and there is increasing interest in economy and efficiency—in doing more with less. Against this backdrop, human-powered vehicles seem highly appropriate transportation choices.

The revolution in Western societies that accompanied the wide application of vehicles powered by internal-combustion engines has also changed our lifestyles so that the majority of us are couch potatoes or habitual loungers who never exercise. The negative consequences of having become a sedentary society (increased rates of heart disease, cancer, stroke, and arthritis, as examples) are now well understood. Industrialized nations are mounting efforts to encourage people to take up exercise programs. Human-powered vehicles can provide a purpose as well as a means for people to exercise.

I

HUMAN POWER:
AN INTRODUCTION

For hundreds of thousands of years, our human ancestors had no other choice for transportation—they had to walk. The last few thousand years saw the appearance of a few human-powered boats and, with the invention of the wheel, an occasional cart pulled by humans or animals. More recently, humans began inventing other devices to improve their use of muscle power. Machines were powered by hand cranks, arm or leg levers, treadmills, and most recently by leg cranking. It was not until the 19th century that real progress began with the appearance of the bicycle. Humans could transport themselves using their own muscle power much more efficiently than ever before.

The concepts of human-powered vehicles and of the human body as an engine arrived in the 20th century through a reconsideration of the following definitions:

Human—(Latin *homo*) of or relating to man and woman
Power—the amount of work (force times distance moved) done per unit time

Vehicle—a means of carrying or transporting something
Engine—a machine by which physical power is applied to produce a physical effect
Heat engine—a thermodynamic device that produces mechanical work, absorbing heat at high temperature and rejecting heat at a lower temperature

In the early 1900s the internal-combustion engine made many applications of human power obsolete. The application of human power for transportation and for useful work has been de-emphasized for close to a century, yet the technology of human power applications has continued to be developed for sporting applications. The present-day generation of human-powered machines offers greatly improved performance and encourages the human engine to perform to physiological limits. Thus, the designer of a modern, high-performance human-powered vehicle must understand the operation of the human engine through study of exercise physiology. Because most human-powered vehicles must operate for more than a few minutes, the physiology of endurance exercise is important.

Chapter 1, "Human Power in History," provides an overview of the evolution of humans as they became well suited for using their legs for traveling long distances by walking and running and their arms for fine manipulation and for carrying objects. The early, crude applications of human power to machines are described with examples of every major type of mechanism used to harness human power, the leg crank, or pedal, being the most recent.

Chapter 2, "The Human Engine," considers the portions of exercise physiology that are most important for the designers and operators of human-powered vehicles. All major factors that enhance and limit the performance of the human engine are discussed. Performance in endurance exercise requires an understanding of nutrition and hydration, oxygen consumption and power production, and temperature regulation.

Chapter 3, "Human Power Transfer to Modern Vehicles," concentrates on leg cranking. Leg cranking, or pedaling, and rowing are the means now most commonly used to power high-performance human-powered vehicles. Similar amounts of power can be transferred through pedaling and rowing; however, pedaling is the more efficient and has been applied more widely in recent years. The parameters of leg cranking have been extensively studied, and this chapter considers optimal pedaling rate, crank-arm length, seat-tube angle, seat height, foot position, and body position. The prospect of improving on leg cranking is discussed, although as the 20th century ends, all human-powered speed and performance records in single-rider land, water, and air vehicles were set by riders cranking circular chainwheels with only their legs.

1

Human Power in History

Allan V. Abbott
David Gordon Wilson

At the first mention of human-powered vehicles, most people today imagine a bicycle or perhaps a kayak. Yet studies of history and anthropology provide dramatically contrasting concepts. It is likely that crude land and water vehicles were constructed and powered by humans hundreds of thousands of years ago at the least, and perhaps more than a million.

The Evolution of Human Power

The early ancestors of today's humans adapted and evolved in ways that separated them from other animals. Three developments were particularly important: upright posture and habitual walking on two legs (about 4 million years ago), tool making (about 2.5 million years ago), and language (1 to 1.5 million years ago). These changes gave early humans an advantage as they adapted to their environmental circumstances; that is, natural selection favored these characteristics.

Upright posture and locomotion freed the upper extremities for a variety of carrying and fine manipulating activities, including tool making. By about 1.5 million years ago Homo erectus, the ancestor of Homo sapiens, had a completely modern skeleton and a physically active lifestyle. Homo erectus walked great distances and was a big-game hunter, a meat eater, and a user of fire.

Having developed the ability to make and improve tools, early humans designed vehicles to upgrade their ability to carry things. The term *vehicle* is defined simply as a means of carrying or transporting something. Thus, the first human to attach the kill to a tree branch and use the branch to carry the meat back home used a crude human-powered vehicle. The first person who straddled a floating tree trunk and paddled through the water using hands or a stick used a primitive human-powered watercraft. The endless possibilities of these primitive vehicles must have inspired the imaginations of early humans. Human prehistory must have been rich with human-powered vehicles long before the invention of the wheel.

Fossil records indicate that today's human species, Homo sapiens, appeared some 200,000 to 500,000 years ago; however, the earliest fully modern representatives of Homo sapiens appeared about 100,000 years ago. They traveled great distances by walking, migrating slowly throughout most of the world, where they established a variety of cultures with different emphases (Cavalli-Sforza, 1991). Throughout this long history, humans were their own primary source of power for all the work they did.

Early humans had become specialized for endurance running to facilitate tracking, chasing, and disabling swifter, smaller prey in the hot midday temperatures of the African savanna. This trend undoubtedly included development of a sweating apparatus that allowed improved dissipation of the heat generated by the body during rapid long-distance walking or running.

Humans have been hunters and gatherers throughout the vast majority of their evolutionary history (Malina, 1988). Because most of our basic physical and behavioral patterns are rooted in our evolutionary past, we are perhaps best equipped for the physically vigorous activities and lifestyle of the hunter and gatherer. Yet in spite of the spectacularly rapid rate of cultural change since the advent of agriculture (10,000 years ago) and the explosive cultural changes in the industrial era, there has been negligible change in the human physical structure over the past 100,000 years. Thus, the application of human power to tools, machines, and vehicles remains today more a matter of designing the machine for the human, rather than adapting the human to the machine. From this perspective, we should design human-powered vehicles that utilize primarily the work from those extremities that evolved to be the most powerful—the legs. Upper extremities are better suited for the more delicate activities of controlling the vehicle. Further, designs should allow body positions and motions of the legs and arms that approximate those occurring in walking and running, the activities human evolution favored to be the most efficient.

Applications of Human Power in History

The historical use of human muscle power not only was crude by today's standards, but also was inefficient for several reasons. First, the wrong muscles were often used. People were called upon to perform heavy tasks of digging, lifting, and paddling with the muscles of the arms and backs, rather than with the legs.

Second, the speed of muscle motion was usually too slow. People were required to heave and shove

with all their might, often moving only an inch or two. A modern parallel would be to force rowers to row boats with very long oars having very short inboard handles, or to require bicyclists to pedal using crank arms only two inches long.

Third, the type of motion itself was not optimal, even if it was carried out at the best speed using leg muscles. The length of stroke when paddling or rowing boats, for example, was not efficiently matched to the muscles of the arm, shoulders, and back.

Throughout history, human power has been applied to machines through only a small number of methods. A few examples of each of these mechanisms are described in the following paragraphs.

Pulling and Pushing

The simplest and undoubtedly the most ancient application of human power is through simple pulling or pushing. There is a seemingly endless list of examples. Chopping wood, digging with a shovel, and throwing a rock are examples of the application of human power in a variety of motions through the use of the arms. Modern wheelchairs utilize a variation of pushing with the arms pushing directly against the wheels. Another variation of direct pushing is the push-and-coast method used to propel early wheeled vehicles like the hobby-horses of the 19th century (see Figure 1.1) and still used today on skateboards and scooters. Still another variation is the unique pushing motion used in skating.

The rickshaw, or wheeled carriage in which one person pulls another, has been in use for hundreds of years. Millions of baby carriages and baby "joggers" are pushed today in a relatively efficient manner. Another contemporary example is a simple plow used in China. This plow is operated by two people, one pushing and one pulling. The wooden baseboard has a cast-iron share at one end. For this arduous task, both workers use their leg muscles, the most appropriate muscles for the duty. The motions are too slow to be efficient, and most of the other muscles and body frame are painfully strained to apply the force produced by the leg muscles.

Hand Cranking

Hand cranking is perhaps the most obvious means of obtaining rotary motion, and humans have been using it for centuries. The earliest known hand-cranked device was the bucket-chain bilge

FIGURE 1.1 Hobbyhorses were straddled and propelled forward with the rider's feet pushing directly against the ground. This Draisienne, invented by German Karl von Drais in about 1817, had front steering, like a modern bicycle, and apparently was the origin of the true bicycle.

From *Bicycling Science* by Whitt, F.R., Wilson, D.G., 1982, Cambridge, MA: MIT Press, p. 9. Reprinted with permission.

pump, found on two huge barges used by the Romans.

Agricola, a German physician (1494–1555), showed a complicated hand-cranked transmission for driving a similar bucket-chain water lifter (Agricola, 1950). A similar device is depicted in Figure 1.2. An endless-chain water lifter, different in two respects, was also used in China in much later times. Instead of buckets, the water was trapped by boards sliding in a trough. In addition, levers were attached to the cranks, with all the lost motion and top-dead-center problems they entailed. Presumably the levers were used to give a more comfortable working position for the ground-mounted trough.

Leonardo da Vinci (1452–1519) showed concern for the comfort of the user in his drawing of a textile winder with a handle at a convenient height and with a winder drum of a diameter giving a presumably near-optimum rate of action. Leonardo used gearing for the same reason in his design of a file-cutting machine, in which the crank was used to raise a weight at a speed to suit the operator and the weight subsequently delivered energy at an optimum rate to the drop-hammer cutter.

Hand-cranked mechanisms were designed for either low- or high-torque applications. Two more

modern examples of low-torque hand cranking are taken at random from the *Science Record* of 1872. The first is an air pump for an undersea diver. The second is a multiple stirrer for a nitroglycerin-manufacturing process in which the right hand turned a heavy and fluctuating load, while the left hand had to perform a difficult and hazardous control function. A high-torque application was the old hand wringer used to remove water from washed clothes.

Levers Actuated By Arms and Back Muscles

The earliest records of water vehicles are rock carvings and pottery decorations in the Nile valley dating from about 3300 B.C. They depict boats equipped with masts and sails as well as a line of rowers on each side (see Figure 1.3). Compared to the paddled log, these were highly sophisticated machines that utilized levers actuated by the rowers' arms and back muscles. It was not until the arrival of the sliding-seat scull in the 19th century that oars were moved also through leg action (Kemp, 1979).

Many lever-actuated machines were developed in ancient times. For example, air pumps for pipe organs designed by Ktesibios in Alexandria in the 3rd century B.C. utilized a rocking lever that could be operated with two hands.

In 1821, Louis Gompertz built the velocipede shown in Figure 1.4. The propulsion and steering were accomplished by swinging a lever over the front wheel. The lever carried an arc with a rack gear that engaged a circular gear, presumably on a freewheel, on the front hub. Some tricycles were designed for lever propulsion by the hands and the arms, with some power also supplied by the back muscles.

Capstans

The windlass, or capstan, where humans pushed levers attached to a spool on which is wound a rope or a chain, represented an enormous improvement over most earlier devices when maximum work output was to be given by human muscle power. As shown in Figure 1.5, the motions required, those of walking, must be at least reasonably efficient; the motion speed could be varied simply by using a smaller or a larger diameter winding spool. It seems likely, however, that slow, high-force pushing was used more

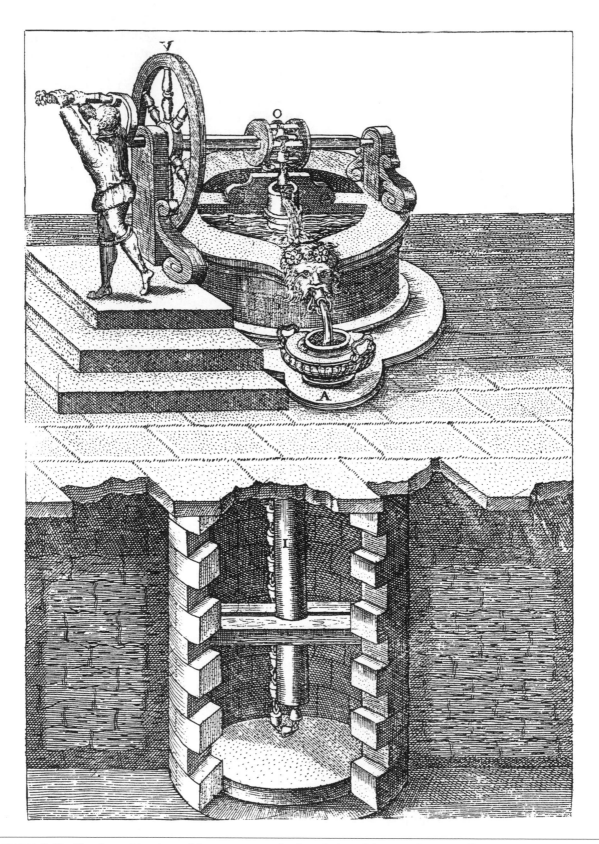

FIGURE 1.2 Hand cranking is used here to move a bucket chain to lift water from a well.

From *The Various and Ingenious Machines of Agostino Ramelli* (1588).

FIGURE 1.3 For centuries the rowed warship predominated as the fastest, most maneuverable warship in the Mediterranean. The most advanced of these boats had three banks of rowers on both sides (triremes) and well over 100 rowers. This 5th century B.C. stone carving is the best pictorial evidence of how a Greek trireme looked, with only the top bank of rowers visible. These rowers strained, using only the muscles of their arms and backs. Not until the 19th century A.D. invention of the sliding seat could rowers add use of the strong leg muscles. (Relief from Athens.)

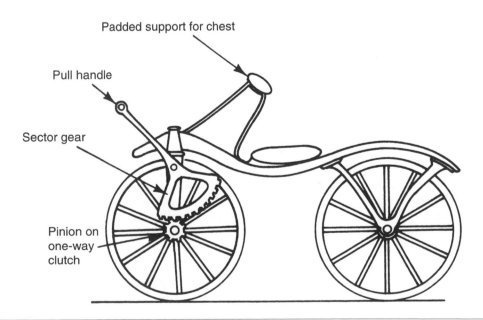

FIGURE 1.4 In 1821 Louis Gompertz fitted a swinging-arm ratchet drive to the front wheel of his steerable velocipede, an early example of arm-powered lever drive.

From *Bicycling Science* by Whitt, F.R., Wilson, D.G., 1982, Cambridge, MA: MIT Press. Reprinted with permission.

FIGURE 1.5 The windlass, or capstan, where humans push levers attached to a spool on which is wound a rope or a chain, represented an enormous improvement over most earlier devices when maximum work output was to be given by human muscle power. Here a capstan is used to lift water.

From *The Various and Ingenious Machines of Agostino Ramelli* (1588).

often than the fairly rapid and more efficient light-force walking.

Capstans have probably been in use almost as long as there have been ropes. A literally monumental use of capstans was in the erection of a 360-ton obelisk in the Vatican by Pope Sixtus V in 1586. Forty capstans, as well as 140 horses and 800 men, were used in a military-type operation.

Treadmills

Of the devices so far discussed, treadmills are the nearest approach to true pedal power. Varieties of treadmills were in use in Mesopotamia 1,200 years before the time of Christ. They continued in use in Europe at least until 1888, when the last treadmill crane on the lower Rhine ceased operation. Treadmills are still used in some developing countries.

Treadmills had the same advantages as capstans. The motion was walking, and the gear ratio could easily be adjusted to near optimum (but probably seldom was). Some treadmills shown in Agricola's book on mechanics and mining looked exactly the same as capstans, except that the radial handles were fixed and the circular walkway rotated.

A variation of the capstanlike treadmill had the rotating foot wheel inclined as shown in Figure 1.6. Rather than continually pushing on a bar to force the feet back, on an inclined treadmill a person moved as if climbing an endless ramp or flight of stairs. Body weight was usually enough to carry the wheel around and the horizontal bar was less for pushing against than for steadying the operator. One disadvantage of the inclined treadmill was that, whereas in a horizontal mill several people could all push at once as on a capstan, only one person could be located in the optimum position on an inclined treadmill.

Most treadmills were of the squirrel-cage variety, and, in fact, various animals from dogs to horses were frequently used in powering such devices as irrigation pumps or forge blowers. But when tasks requiring close control, such as lifting weights in a crane for building construction, were called for, humans were more usually employed. Some squirrel-cage treadmills are still installed in cathedrals and were in use until very recently (Matthies, 1992).

FIGURE 1.6 Treadmills had the same advantages as capstans. The motion was walking, and the gear ratio could easily be adjusted to be near optimum (but probably seldom was). Some treadmills were almost the same as capstans, except that the radial handles were fixed and the circular walkway rotated.

From *The Various and Ingenious Machines of Agostino Ramelli* (1588).

Leonardo da Vinci designed a treadmill to bend and cock four crossbows mounted radially on the inside of the wheel. A single archer loaded and fired each in turn. The wheel had unidirectional, comfortable-appearing steps on the outside of the wheel for several people to use when supplying the motive power. This must have been a superior position to being confined inside a wheel in an often cramped position. Leonardo took pains, too, to protect the workers as well as the archer with armor. Most of his designs were never actually constructed.

Legs on Treadles

Treadles use the action of the legs and feet to turn a wheel through levers. The application of leg muscles to treadles can be roughly divided into two categories: those where power requirements were low and the hands were required to perform an accurate task, such as in treadle sewing machines, and those in which maximum power output was desired, as in certain types of cycles.

Reciprocating treadles most often provided low-power energy. For example, a bowstring boring machine was used in the 14th century to drill pearls for necklaces. The Chinese used treadles to obtain continuous motion for cotton ginning and spinning.

The use of treadles for maximum power output principally has been in their application to cycles. Treadles were generally connected to cranks on the cycle driving wheel. The first pedaled bicycle, made by Kirkpatrick Macmillan from 1839 to 1842, was of this type (see Figure 1.7). Tricycles and four-wheelers often used Macmillan's system.

The American Star bicycle, with its smaller wheels, was introduced in the 1880s as a safer version of the "ordinary" or "high-wheeler" (see Figure 1.8). The American Star used a strap going from the foot levers to a spool on the wheel. The spool was mounted on a one-way clutch or freewheel, with a spring tending to wind up the strap. The rider could push down on the levers, alternately or together, to propel the bicycle forward. The diameter of the spool controlled the gear ratio, so that there was, in fact, no need for manufacturers to use a

FIGURE 1.7 Kirkpatrick Macmillan, a Scottish blacksmith, built a velocipede like this around 1839. This was the first known attempt to harness the power of the legs to turn the wheels directly. In this example of a treadle, the rear-wheel crank is connected with rods to swinging foot pedals.

From *Bicycling Science* by Whitt, F.R., Wilson, D.G., 1982, Cambridge, MA: MIT Press. Reprinted with permission.

FIGURE 1.8 The high-wheeler attained relatively high speeds as the result of the large front wheel, which increased the ratio of the distance covered to the rider's leg cranking. Modern safety bicycles use chain drive and various sizes of sprockets to precisely control this ratio.

From *Bicycling Science* by Whitt, F.R., Wilson, D.G., 1982, Cambridge, MA: MIT Press, p. 14. Reprinted with permission.

dangerous high wheel at all. The American Star was a promising development, but it was soon eclipsed by the small-wheeled, chain-driven, pedal-and-crank "safety" bicycle.

Leg Muscles Used in Cranking

Just as the high-wheelers were eclipsed by safety bicycles, so the lever propulsion systems which some of them used disappeared. During the 1890s the pedal-and-crank drive became almost universal. The essentials of the safety bicycle in almost all its aspects had been developed by the turn of the century—even derailleur gears had arrived—and it has reigned almost unchallenged since then.

One can believe, with the benefit of hindsight, that so obvious a system as pedals and cranks must have been used for muscle-power applications before the advent of the bicycle, but there is no known record of this. It is possible that the design of a cantilevered pedal with low-friction bearings to take the large forces that can be applied by a heavy, muscular person was too difficult, given the low-strength materials available earlier.

Once pedals and cranks had been developed for bicycles, however, they began to appear in many other applications. Pedaled racing boats were built that easily beat those crewed by trained rowers. Pedals were also applied to tools like lathes, saws, and pumps.

With the invention of the bicycle in the 1800s came a veritable avalanche of pedal and treadle machines. The bicycle influenced all aspects of life: work, sports, leisure, and transportation. Errand boys, police officers, and mail carriers discovered that the bicycle made them mobile and more efficient.

Women, so long tied to the home and garden, found some liberation in the two- and three-wheelers. And the sports world, which worshipped the speed of the trotter and race horse, turned to the bicycle racer, who promised undreamed-of speeds.

Resourceful Americans and Europeans tried to adapt the principle of the bicycle to all parts of the home and workplace. In one design, a velocipede powered a sewing machine. The patent office was alive with designs for countless applications for pedal power. One was for a railroad bicycle. All in all, at the turn of the century the bicycle seemed to present the possibility of humanizing the workplace and of relieving men and women of some of the drudgery associated with arduous tasks. If the bicycle represented a revolution of sorts, so did the manufacture of foot-power tools, which inaugurated in a small way the home workshop, where even the unskilled could perform certain machine tasks with accuracy.

In industrialized nations, interest and innovation in applications of human power continued to accelerate until the beginning of the 20th century. The internal-combustion engine and electrical power retired pedal-powered machines for the most part and bicycles to a lesser extent. Although technology has continued to be developed for human sporting applications, the application of human power for transportation and for useful work has been de-emphasized for nearly a century. However, decades of mechanization and pollution have led us to reconsider human muscle potential. A bicycle requires less energy per unit distance than does walking, running, travel by auto, travel by rail, or any other form of land transportation. Near the end of the 20th century, the most efficient type of human transportation on land is still the bicycle in its various forms (Brooks, 1989; Wilson, 1977). Ironically, as developing countries strain to give up their bicycles and human-powered equipment, industrialized countries are returning their attention to exercise machines and to human-powered vehicles.

References

Agricola, Georgius de Re Metallica (1950). (H.C. Hoover & L.H. Hoover, Trans.) New York: Dover. Original work published 1556.

Brooks, A.N. (1989). Energy consumption of high efficiency vehicles. *Cycling Science*, **1**(1), 6–9.

Cavalli-Sforza, L.L. (1991). Genes, peoples, and languages. *Scientific American*, **265**(5), 102–110.

Gnudi, M.T., & Ferguson, E.S. (1976). *The various machines of Agostino Ramilli: A classic sixteenth century illustrated treatise on technology.* New York: Dover.

Kemp, P. (1979). *The history of ships.* New York: Galahad Books.

Malina, R.M. (1988). Physical activity in early and modern populations: An evolutionary view. In R.M. Malina & H.M. Eckert (Eds.), *Physical activity in early and modern populations* (pp. 1–12). Champaign, IL: Human Kinetics.

Matthies, A. (1992). Medieval treadwheels: Artist's views of building construction. *Technology and Culture*, **33**(3). Chicago: Society for the History of Technology, University of Chicago Press.

Whitt, F.R., & Wilson, D.G. (1982). *Bicycling science.* Cambridge, MA: MIT Press.

Wilson, D.G. (1977). Human muscle power in history. In *Pedal Power.* Emmaus, PA: Rodale Press.

2

THE HUMAN ENGINE

Allan V. Abbott
David Gordon Wilson

In the developed world, for personal transportation, the human engine has largely been replaced by the internal-combustion engine. Thus, in considering the human as an engine, a comparison with the automobile engine seems appropriate. The automobile engine combusts gasoline with oxygen. The resulting expansion of hot gases pushes the pistons, producing mechanical power and much wasted heat. Power is tapped from the automobile engine and directed to vital ancillary components, such as the water pump to provide cooling, the alternator to provide electrical energy for ignition, and the oil pump to provide lubrication. The automobile engine is designed and constructed for performance and efficiency in specific applications. It can be stopped anytime for repairs. In contrast, the human engine uses various organic foods and oxygen as fuels. The human engine converts food through metabolism, a complex series of chemical reactions using oxygen, directly into mechanical power produced by muscle contraction which also produces waste heat. In the human engine, energy from food is also used for vital ancillary functions as will be described in this chapter. The efficiency or performance of the human engine is determined by genetics, physical conditioning, age, sex, nutrition, disease, and by the presence or absence of injury. The human engine can stop or die only once; thus, it must always continue "idling," even during sleep.

This chapter presents a simplified overview of the anatomy and physiology of the human engine, emphasizing those aspects which are most important in human-powered vehicles and giving extensive references for further study.

An Overview of Exercise Physiology

Even while at rest the human engine expends considerable energy; energy is used for digestion, absorption, and assimilation of food, for the function of glands, for maintaining appropriate electrochemical balance in cells, and for making chemical compounds. The food we eat is changed through a series of chemical reactions to an energy-rich compound, adenosine triphosphate (ATP), which is the basic fuel for cells. Some ATP is stored in muscles.

Human muscles may increase their energy requirements up to 120-fold during maximal physical activity (McArdle, Katch, & Katch, 1991). The limited muscle stores of ATP are capable of providing energy only for brief periods of vigorous activity. Muscles continually produce ATP to provide energy (metabolism), but must dramatically increase their metabolic rate to produce enough ATP for prolonged physical activity. The muscles are dependent on the respiratory (lung)

13

and cardiovascular (heart and blood vessels) systems to deliver oxygen and nutrients and to remove waste products. Exercise physiology is the study of these systems that allow humans to be physically active. A basic appreciation of exercise physiology is necessary to understanding the human-powered vehicle's engine.

Nutrition

The human consumes nutrients, which provide the biologic fuel for all functions in the form of carbohydrates, fats, and proteins. Carbohydrates comprise many forms of complex sugars, consumed as fruits, grains, vegetables, and simple sugars from sweets, such as candy. Carbohydrates make up about half of all calories in the typical American diet and are the major source of energy at rest and during exercise. Humans who are exercising heavily and regularly in such activities as running or cycling should consume about 60% of their calories as carbohydrates.

Fats, synthesized by both plants and animals, are divided into three groups: simple fats, which are either saturated (e.g., lard and tropical oils) or unsaturated (e.g., canola oil and corn oil); compound fats, which are simple fats in combination with other chemicals; and derived fats, such as cholesterol. In the human, fats provide the largest store of potential energy for work. In light-to-moderate exercise, fats can provide up to 50% of the energy used. As exercise is prolonged, fats stored in the body may provide more than 80% of the body's energy.

Proteins are found in the cells of all plants and animals; they are the building blocks for the synthesis of nearly all parts of the cell. Complete proteins of high quality are found in such foods as eggs and meat. Some of the body's proteins can break down to provide carbohydrate fuel for exercise, especially when the body's reserves of carbohydrates are low. Thus, it is necessary to maintain carbohydrate stores during training to avoid protein loss.

Vitamins are synthesized by plants and animals and do not supply any energy for exercise, yet they are essential for almost all body functions. They are provided in a well-balanced diet or through vitamin supplements. Minerals, found in nature in the water and soil, are absorbed by plants. Minerals are essential in regulating body functions, synthesizing the body's nutrients, and also in forming the structural components of bones and teeth.

The heat or energy available from both food and physical activity is commonly measured in units called calories. The unit of heat usually used in studies of metabolism is the kilocalorie (kcal)—the amount of heat needed to raise the temperature of 1 kg of water 1 °C. The kcal, equal to 4.19 kJ, is sometimes referred to simply as "a calorie." The most important factor determining the body's caloric need is the level of physical activity. Studies of nutrition have determined that the basic caloric intake for the healthy human should be divided approximately as 12% of calories from proteins, 30% or less from fats, and the rest from carbohydrates. Prior to heavy, prolonged physical exertion the human engine should consume foods that are easily digested, high in carbohydrates, and low in fats and proteins. Two to three hours should suffice for digestion and absorption of this "pre-event" meal.

Energy for Exercise

ATP, the energy used by working muscles, is produced through two energy pathways: the anaerobic (without oxygen) and the aerobic (with oxygen). Exercise is commonly described as anaerobic or aerobic, depending on the predominant source of energy the working muscles use.

The anaerobic pathway provides an immediate source of ATP for brief, intense physical exertion, such as running a 100-m sprint. Anaerobic pathways function in working muscles whenever the energy demand is greater than the supply of oxygen. ATP may be synthesized in the absence of oxygen by splitting another energy-rich compound, creatine phosphate (CP), or by the breakdown of carbohydrate through a chemical reaction known as glycolysis. Carbohydrates are the only food that can provide energy anaerobically for the formation of ATP.

Energy available from the anaerobic pathway rapidly decreases as exercise time increases. The ATP produced through the anaerobic pathway is only about 5% of the potential ATP that can be produced through subsequent aerobic reactions. In addition to the low ATP yield, the anaerobic pathway produces lactic acid, which accumulates during intense physical activity and results in rapid muscle fatigue.

Aerobic metabolism provides an additional means for producing large amounts of energy. Glycogen, fats, and proteins are broken down in the presence of oxygen to ATP, carbon dioxide, and water. More than 90% of total ATP production occurs via the aerobic pathway. Oxygen is critical to this process, and the body's ability to deliver it to muscles largely determines the level of prolonged exercise that can be performed (McArdle, Katch, & Katch, 1991).

Human Muscles

Human muscles have two basic types of fibers: red, slow-twitch fibers (Type I) and white, fast-twitch fibers (Type II). There is a great variability in the number of each of these fibers in different individuals. The ratio of muscle-fiber types is genetically determined and is not normally altered by physical conditioning. The metabolic capacity and performance of both fiber types can be improved by endurance-exercise training (Åstrand, 1986).

Persons with more slow-twitch than fast-twitch fibers usually perform better in endurance activities, which require aerobic metabolism. This is because slow-twitch fibers have a high oxidative capacity and produce much more ATP aerobically than fast-twitch fibers. On the other hand, athletes with more fast-twitch fibers are usually better at brief, high-intensity activities, which depend almost entirely on anaerobic metabolism. The metabolic capabilities of these fibers are also important in stop-and-go and change-of-pace sports such as basketball or football.

Body Systems in Exercise

Many body functions and systems work together to support metabolic demands on active muscles. These cause changes in heart rate, stroke volume, heart output, blood pressure, blood flow, oxygen difference between arteries and veins, and pulmonary (lung) ventilation; the result is increased delivery of oxygen-carrying blood to the active muscles.

Heart rate increases in a roughly linear relationship with work load or power output. The heart rate will stabilize within 2 to 3 min at a steady level of exercise, but it takes progressively longer to attain a steady-state rate as work loads increase. There is a limit to the maximal heart rate during maximal exercise. After a preceding warm-up period, the maximal heart rate for any specific activity can be measured immediately after or at the end of 2 to 4 min of all-out exercise in that form of work. The maximal heart rate decreases with age, and all-out exercise is not advised for adults older than ages 40 to 45 without medical clearance. The equation, maximal heart rate = (220 − age in years), provides an approximation of the maximal heart rate in normal healthy adults, but because of considerable individual variability (standard deviation $\sim \pm 10$ beats/min), this estimation should be used with caution in individuals. Although heart rate provides a good indication of the exertion level of any particular exercise for an individual, it is of limited value in predicting oxygen consumption or caloric expenditure among different types of exercise.

The stroke-volume (volume of blood pumped by the heart with each stroke or beat) response to exercise depends on hydrostatic-pressure effects. When at rest in the erect position, stroke volume is between 60 and 100 ml/beat in healthy adults. Increased heart muscle contractive force results in a more complete emptying of the heart with each stroke, thereby increasing stroke volume with exercise (Poliner et al., 1980). During exercise in the erect position, stroke volume will increase curvilinearly with the work load until it reaches a near-maximal value at approximately 50% of the individual's maximal capacity for exercise, increasing only slightly thereafter. The maximal stroke volume is about 100 to 120 ml/beat (Poliner et al., 1980).

Cardiac output generally increases linearly with increases in work load, from about 5 l/min at rest to a maximum of about 20 l/min during upright exercise. The two most important factors predicting cardiac output are body size and physical conditioning level. At exercise levels up to 50% of maximal capacity, the increase in cardiac output is the result of increases in both heart rate and stroke volume. At higher exercise intensities the increase results almost entirely from increasing heart rate (Poliner et al., 1980).

Blood pressure rises (systolic pressure) and falls (diastolic pressure) with each contraction of the heart. The systolic pressure increases linearly with increasing levels of exercise, typically reaching 190 to 220 mmHg. Diastolic pressures normally change little from rest to maximal exercise in the healthy adult. The difference between systolic pressure and diastolic pressure (pulse pressure) increases proportionally with exercise intensity.

The flow of blood changes dramatically during exercise. While at rest, roughly 20% of cardiac output goes to muscles; 80% goes to internal organs (kidneys, intestines, liver, etc.), the heart, and the brain. During exercise some arteries constrict, and others relax and become larger so that working muscles receive as much as 85% to 90% of cardiac output. Blood flow to the heart muscle is increased in proportion to the metabolic demands on the heart, whereas blood flow to the brain remains at resting levels. Blood flow to the skin is also greatly increased during exercise to dissipate heat. During maximal exertion the body can sacrifice circulation to the skin to meet the increasing metabolic demands of working muscles; increases in body core temperature and heat illness can result (Rowell et al., 1969).

Blood in arteries flowing to muscles carries more oxygen than blood in veins returning from muscles. The difference in oxygen content is the arterio-venous oxygen difference. As exercise intensity progresses from moderate to heavy, muscles extract more oxygen from the available blood. When the body is at rest, blood in arteries and veins carries about 200 ml and 150 ml of oxygen per liter of blood, respectively. As the work load approaches maximal levels, venous oxygen content decreases to about 50 ml/l blood, thus widening the arterio-venous oxygen difference from 50 to 150 ml/l, a threefold increase (Mitchell & Blomqvist, 1971).

Air movement through the lungs also increases dramatically during exercise. The volume of air inspired per minute increases from about 6 l/min at rest to over 100 l/min during intense exercise in the average sedentary adult male. This substantial increase in ventilation is accomplished through increases in respiratory rate and volume of air moved with each breath. The increase in lung ventilation is directly proportional to the increase in oxygen consumed by the body ($\dot{V}O_2$) and the carbon dioxide produced ($\dot{V}CO_2$). Lung ventilation is regulated primarily by the need for carbon dioxide removal. In healthy adults lung ventilation is not usually a limiting factor to aerobic capacity ($\dot{V}O_2$max) (McArdle et al., 1991).

Oxygen Consumption

The measurement of oxygen consumption is useful in many ways, including determining performance and efficiency of human-powered-vehicle engines. Human energy expenditure is often measured and described in terms of the amount of oxygen consumed ($\dot{V}O_2$); (see Figure 2.1). $\dot{V}O_2$ is usually described in terms of the volume of oxygen

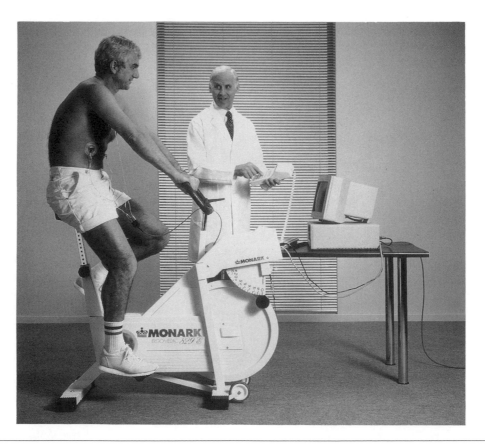

FIGURE 2.1 Human performance is usually measured indirectly through determination of the amount of oxygen consumed during exercise. During exercise, all of the expired breath is collected. Oxygen consumption can be calculated after determining the rate at which air is expired and its oxygen and carbon dioxide content.

consumed per unit of body weight per unit of time. The ability to consume oxygen varies with the capacity of the heart and lungs (centrally) and with cell metabolism and delivery of oxygen to muscles (peripherally).

For a typical 30-year-old man, dividing the resting oxygen consumption (about 250 ml/min) by body weight (70 kg), we derive the energy requirement at rest, which is 3.5 ml of oxygen per kilogram of body weight per minute (ml/kg/min). This energy requirement at rest is also referred to as one MET (metabolic equivalent). This expression of resting $\dot{V}O_2$ is independent of body weight and is relatively constant for all people. Multiples of this value, or METS, are sometimes used to quantify relative levels of energy expenditure. Both METS and $\dot{V}O_2$ are useful in describing the intensity of exercise (McArdle et al., 1991).

Maximal Oxygen Consumption ($\dot{V}O_2$max)

Increasing exercise work loads are accompanied by directly proportional increases in oxygen consumption. When the exercising human approaches exhaustion, the capacity to take in oxygen reaches its limit despite further increases in work load. This value is the individual's maximal oxygen consumption ($\dot{V}O_2$max). $\dot{V}O_2$max is generally the most accepted measure of endurance capacity of "physical fitness" (Taylor et al., 1955). During maximal exercise, healthy adults can typically increase resting $\dot{V}O_2$ levels 10 to 12 times. Some poorly conditioned people are unable to reach the plateau indicating $\dot{V}O_2$max because of physical fatigue and discomfort, which limits their work level.

Oxygen consumption can be determined by measuring the volume and oxygen content of expired air, corrected to standard temperature and pressure, dry (STPD), using this equation:

$$\dot{V}O_2 = \dot{V}_E \, (F_IO_2 - F_EO_2)$$

where $\dot{V}_E$ = expired measured volume/min, F_IO_2 = concentration of oxygen in the inspired air (normal room air is 20.93% oxygen), and F_EO_2 = concentration of oxygen in the expired air (Consolazio, Johnson, & Pecora, 1963). Maximal oxygen consumption may be described in liters per minute, indicating energy output and caloric expenditure for the total body (each liter of oxygen is equivalent to approximately 5 kcal). High absolute oxygen consumption is found in large persons simply by virtue of large muscle mass; therefore, this value (in ml/min) is generally divided by body weight (in kg) to permit comparison between larger and smaller individuals. $\dot{V}O_2$max, when expressed in milliliters of oxygen per kilogram per minute (ml/kg/min), is generally thought to be the best single measure of cardiorespiratory fitness or work capacity. A person's $\dot{V}O_2$max is decreased by disuse, disease, and aging; the disuse that accompanies a sedentary lifestyle greatly increases the rate of decline with aging. In addition to differences in body size, muscle mass, age, sex, habitual level of activity, physical conditioning, and athletic training also account for individual variations in $\dot{V}O_2$max (Mitchell & Blomqvist, 1971).

The maximal oxygen consumption can be increased by increasing the mass of muscle employed in performing the exercise task used to determine $\dot{V}O_2$. For example, the classic study of Taylor and associates (1955) showed that simultaneous running and arm cranking produced a significantly higher $\dot{V}O_2$max than running alone. Conversely, $\dot{V}O_2$max during arm cranking generally approximates only 64% to 80% of leg $\dot{V}O_2$max (Franklin, 1985). This is important when HPVs are powered by arms, by legs, or by both.

Several studies have examined the correlation between $\dot{V}O_2$max determined by leg exercise alone and $\dot{V}O_2$max of arm exercise. Bar-Or and Zwiren (1975) found that the correlation coefficient between arm and leg $\dot{V}O_2$max was only fair ($r = 0.74$), similar to the correlation obtained by Bouchard and colleagues (Bouchard et al., 1979), who compared the $\dot{V}O_2$max determined by arm-exercise testing in the standing position with the $\dot{V}O_2$max determined by four different leg exercise tests: cycling supine, cycling sitting, walking on a treadmill, and stepping on a bench. In summary, $\dot{V}O_2$max determined by leg or arm exercise alone generally provides at best a marginal estimate of reciprocal arm or leg aerobic capacity.

Even though young boys and girls show little difference in $\dot{V}O_2$max, Figure 2.2 shows there is considerable difference between the sexes after adolescence. Adult men have $\dot{V}O_2$max values roughly 15% to 25% higher than for women. It is not known whether these differences arise from cultural or from biological factors. The differences in mens' and womens' lifestyle and physical activity at the time of puberty is undoubtedly important. Additionally, women naturally have less lean-muscle mass and more body fat than men. Women also have lower hemoglobin levels and less blood oxygen-carrying capacity.

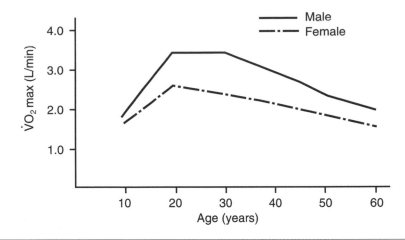

FIGURE 2.2   Both age and sex influence maximal oxygen consumption. Oxygen consumption peaks at about age 20 and declines gradually thereafter in most physically inactive people. In some healthy people who continue physical activity and training, the decline in oxygen consumption can be delayed as long as age 40. This figure shows the average adult male to have $\dot{V}O_2$max 15% to 20% higher than the average adult female.

In Western populations, a small annual decrease in $\dot{V}O_2$max begins in the early 20s. Physical inactivity and aging are responsible for most of this decline, with decreased lung and tissue gas exchange, reduced maximal breathing capacity and maximal heart rate, and less muscle mass. The major factor in this decline may result from sedentary living. In sedentary persons, there is a threefold greater decline in $\dot{V}O_2$max with age as compared with individuals who exercise regularly (Dehn & Bruce, 1972). In athletes the decline in $\dot{V}O_2$max may sometimes be delayed until after age 40 (Whitt & Wilson, 1982).

The extent of exercise-induced improvement in aerobic capacity generally shows an inverse relationship with age, habitual physical activity, and initial $\dot{V}O_2$max. Thus, young-to-middle-aged sedentary individuals tend to show the greatest percentage increase in $\dot{V}O_2$max with physical conditioning. $\dot{V}O_2$max also improves with increased frequency, intensity, and duration of conditioning exercise (McArdle et al., 1991).

In elite athletes, $\dot{V}O_2$max values range from as high as 94 ml/kg/min in a cross-country skier to the low 40s for some athletes participating in anaerobic-type sports (Franklin, 1985). Except for a few individual outstanding values, $\dot{V}O_2$max levels of 75 to 83 ml/kg/min represent the top of aerobic power for elite endurance athletes. These values have not changed in over 50 years of advancing training techniques, indicating that there is a definite limit to the capacity of the human body for endurance exercise (Saris, 1990). Nearly all world-class endurance athletes, including elite distance runners

and Nordic cross-country skiers, have a $\dot{V}O_2$max between 70 and 80 ml/kg/min, whereas many champion soccer players, cyclists, race walkers, elite swimmers, Alpine ski racers, rowers, and ultramarathoners have a $\dot{V}O_2$max of 60 to 70 ml/kg/min. In contrast, the reported $\dot{V}O_2$max of masters athletes, professional bodybuilders, basketball players, and volleyball players is between 40 and 50 ml/kg/min. Although strenuous physical training may produce a 25% or more increase in $\dot{V}O_2$max, it has become increasingly apparent that genetic background, rather than training, plays the primary role in producing a gold-medal winner in an Olympic endurance event.

Anaerobic Threshold

The anaerobic threshold (AT) is the peak work load or oxygen consumption at which oxygen demands exceed the body's ability to sustain aerobic metabolism. As work load demands increase above the AT, energy release from anaerobic metabolism must increase, resulting in increased blood lactic-acid levels. The AT signifies the onset of insufficient oxygen delivery to active muscles. During progressively more intense exercise, there is a disproportionate increase in CO_2 production ($\dot{V}CO_2$) and the movement of air through the lungs (minute ventilation) when the AT is reached. Traditionally, the AT has been determined by serial measurements of blood lactate during increasingly intense exercise. Now the abrupt increase in blood lactate can be determined by measurements of gas exchange (Davis et al., 1976). The gas-exchange AT can be determined by detecting the work rate or oxygen consumption just below the disproportionate increase in minute ventilation or $\dot{V}CO_2$ (Davis et al.) Conconi and associates (Conconi, Borsetto, Casoni, & Ferrari, 1988) have suggested that anaerobic threshold can be determined noninvasively, or without blood tests for lactate or gas exchange measurements. Conconi believes that there is an abrupt and detectable change in the slope of the increasing heart rate that accompanies gradually increasing exercise and that this abrupt change corresponds to the anaerobic threshold. The existence of this abrupt change of slope, however, is the subject of controversy at the present time.

Aerobic capacity is an important determinant of performance in endurance events. A more important determinant of endurance performance may be the percentage of $\dot{V}O_2$max that can be used in endurance exercise without significantly increasing blood lactate levels (Costill, 1972). The $\dot{V}O_2$max of distance runner Derek Clayton was 69.7 ml/kg/min. This was not particularly high considering that Clayton had one of the best marathon times in the world: 2 hours 8 min 33 s. This marathon performance was probably due to the fact that Clayton could use 86% of his $\dot{V}O_2$max aerobically while running continuously at his racing pace, a value considerably higher than that of the average elite marathoner (Costill, 1972). There is a good correlation ($r = 0.94$, $p < .01$) between the actual marathon time and the predicted marathon time, calculated from the treadmill velocity at the AT (Rhodes & McKenzie, 1984). This suggests that capacity for exercise at the AT is essential in determining endurance athletic performance. Recently the level of oxygen consumption at the AT was determined to be the best predictor of performance in elite cyclists (Coyle et al., 1991).

The effects of endurance-exercise training can also be determined by using the gas-exchange anaerobic threshold. Increases in both $\dot{V}O_2$max and in the percentage of $\dot{V}O_2$max at which the AT occurs have been demonstrated (Ready & Quinney, 1982). The AT can also be increased by exercise training, even when there is no improvement in $\dot{V}O_2$max (Denis et al., 1982). Although the AT may be a better measure of endurance fitness than $\dot{V}O_2$max, endurance fitness can also be defined and tested inexpensively in the field, such as by measuring the time to run a set distance or the distance run in a set time (Sharkey, 1991).

Metabolic Cost of Exercise

In developed countries the usual intake of calories in the form of food is about 2,000 to 3,000 calories per day per person. This is sufficient for light recreational activities. However, for intense, prolonged exercise the energy requirements may increase dramatically. In the 3,000-mile bicycle Race Across America, athletes ride for 20 hours a day or more and may eat in excess of 10,000 calories per day (Kyle, 1989). Cyclists in the Tour de France have been measured to ingest 6,067 calories per day over a period of one week (Saris, 1990).

The metabolic demands of various types of exercises are dependent on skill, efficiency, and individual motivation. It is possible to estimate the oxygen cost of a given activity during steady-state work. Although these estimates are equally accurate for men and women when the activities are performed in neutral surroundings, environmental factors such as wind, snow, or sand may decrease mechanical efficiency and increase aerobic requirements. For every physical activity an individual has a set of parameters that can be matched to minimize caloric expenditure: pace or rate of repetition, stride or length of the repeated motion, and force applied in each repetition.

Oxygen Cost of Walking. Walking on flat surfaces requires a linear increase in oxygen cost ($\dot{V}O_2$) for speeds between 50 and 100 m/min (1.9 to 3.7 mph), and exponentially thereafter (American College of Sports Medicine, 1986). Consequently, $\dot{V}O_2$ can be estimated with a reasonable degree of accuracy for walking speeds in this range. The oxygen cost of walking in m/min, equivalent to 0.1 ml/kg/min per m/min, is added to a resting component of 3.5 ml/kg/min or 1 MET, to obtain the total $\dot{V}O_2$:

$$\dot{V}O_2 \text{ in (ml/kg/min)} =$$
$$\text{m/min} \times \frac{0.1 \text{ ml/kg/min}}{\text{m/min}} + 3.5 \text{ ml/kg/min}$$

(Dill, 1965)

Oxygen Cost of Running. The $\dot{V}O_2$ for running increases linearly for speeds greater than 134 m/min (5 mph). However, for speeds between 100 and 134 m/min (3.7 to 5 mph) there is a gray area between fast walking and slow jogging where estimates of aerobic requirements are poor (American College of Sports Medicine, 1986). Running is a less efficient activity than walking, and the oxygen cost of running is about twice that for walking, or 0.2 ml/kg/min per m/min. This horizontal component is added to a resting component of 3.5 ml/kg/min to obtain the gross $\dot{V}O_2$:

$$\dot{V}O_2 \text{ in (ml/kg/min)} =$$

$$\text{m/min} \times \frac{0.2 \text{ ml/kg/min}}{\text{m/min}} + 3.5 \text{ ml/kg/min}$$

(Dill, 1965; Margaria et al., 1963)

Oxygen Cost of Leg Cranking or Bicycle Ergometry.
An ergometer is a mechanical device that measures work output; thus, ergometry is the technique of measuring units of work using an ergometer (e.g., bicycle or leg ergometer). Many sport-specific ergometers are in use today (e.g., treadmills, kayak ergometers, hand "grinders," and swimming ergometers). The bicycle, or leg-cranked, ergometer is commonly used and provides a ready measurement of the subject's power output (Shephard & Åstrand, 1992).

In most cycle ergometers, a flywheel is turned by the force of the rider's feet on the bicycle pedals and calibrated friction is applied to the flywheel. This friction force is assumed to be proportional to the force applied to the pedals. The power output (in watts) is calculated as the product of the force applied (N) and the flywheel circumference in meters (m), and the number of revolutions of the flywheel per minute, giving N • m/min, or power in W • 60. Since the work rate is independent of body weight, the absolute $\dot{V}O_2$ (i.e., ml/min) at any power output is comparable among individuals of different size (American College of Sports Medicine, 1986). However, a lighter person would have a greater relative $\dot{V}O_2$ (i.e., in METs or ml/kg/min) than a heavier person when exercising at the same work rate.

The $\dot{V}O_2$ for a person on a stationary cycle ergometer can be estimated with reasonable accuracy for work rates between 50 W and 200 W (300 and 1,200 kg • m/min)* (American College of Sports Medicine, 1986). The work associated with cycle ergometry is different from that of walking or jogging in that the horizontal component is largely eliminated because body weight is supported by a seat. However, the horizontal component is replaced by a vertical or resistive component

---

*The "kg" here is the old so-called "kilogram-force," or the weight of a kg-mass in standard gravity. 1 kg-force = 9.81 N.

where 1 W (about 6 kg • m/min) approximates an oxygen consumption of 12 ml/kg/m (Adams, 1967; Pugh, 1974). The resting component of oxygen consumption (corrected for body weight) is again added to obtain the absolute $\dot{V}O_2$ (in ml/min):

$$\text{Leg ergometry } \dot{V}O_2 \text{ (ml/min)} =$$

$$W \times 6.1 \times \frac{2 \text{ ml}}{\text{kg/m}}$$

$$+ (3.5 \text{ ml/kg/min} \times \text{body weight in kg})$$

Efficiency of the Human Engine

To determine the efficiency of any work-producing engine it is necessary to know the total energy input in the form of fuel and the energy output in the form of net mechanical work. For humans, it is impractical to attempt to calculate the total daily mechanical work output, because it is quite difficult to measure work output for most activities. However, there is one ultramarathon cycling event, the Race Across America, where this calculation is possible, because the athletes rest only about 2 hours a day. Dividing the total heat equivalent of the daily mechanical power to the pedals by the total daily energy input in the form of food calories and body heat consumed yields the net overall efficiency for the complete race—7 to 10 days. Using this method, net mechanical efficiencies from 16.9% to 20.3% have been calculated for three athletes during this race (Kyle, 1988). This efficiency includes the metabolic energy consumed during the brief rest periods (riders are off their bikes only from 1 to 2 hours per 24 hours). This overall thermal efficiency of human athletes is remarkably high considering the best economy-model automobiles at the present time have efficiencies between 15% to 20% (Brooks, 1989). This net efficiency is lower than efficiency during exercise because it incorporates all energy losses, including those from the process of converting and storing food energy.

A more common estimate of efficiency considers only the energy already stored in the body and uses oxygen consumption to calculate the energy liberated per liter of oxygen consumed. Knowing the ratio of carbon dioxide expired to oxygen consumed, the energy liberated in the muscles can be determined and an efficiency can be calculated based on the net mechanical power output measured by an ergometer. Because this does not include the energy losses in digestive and other processes, this so-called net metabolic efficiency is higher—from 21% to 24% (Åstrand & Rodahl, 1986; Pugh, 1974; van Ingen Schenau, 1983).

Training the Human Engine

A training program to improve the performance of the human engine must be appropriately designed to prepare for specific activities. A plethora of metabolic and physiologic changes result from athletic training. The major factors that affect training improvement are initial fitness level, frequency of training, exercise intensity, exercise duration, and type or mode of training. Intensity of training is most important. Muscles become stronger through overload training. A load of 60% to 80% of a muscle's maximal force-generating capacity is necessary to strengthen a muscle. For aerobic training, an activity involving repetitive activity of large muscle masses at an intensity that elevates the heart rate to 70% to 90% of maximum is most effective in improving fitness. A minimum of 30 min of exercise at this intensity performed at least three times a week is necessary to improve fitness. Training programs and methods differ widely (McArdle et al., 1991).

Exercise and Temperature Regulation

The amount of food energy that actually can be utilized to produce muscular work is a fraction of the total. To digest food and convert it into fuel for muscles (ATP), the multiple chemical reactions in the system and the cellular and muscular energy expended in the process cause heat to be generated. This is called the specific dynamic reaction of food and about 6% to 10% of the caloric content of food is converted to heat in the digestive process. Also, during digestion the metabolism is more active; this is equivalent to an increase of about 0.1 l of oxygen per min consumed (Guyton, 1986). In all, about 70% to 80% of the energy taken in as food ultimately results in internal heat production that must be dissipated by cooling (Pugh, 1974).

Core temperature of the body normally increases slightly during prolonged exercise. Maintaining the proper operating temperature of the engine of a human-powered vehicle is more critical than in any other powered vehicle. A drop in deep-body, or core,

temperature of 10 °C and an increase of only 5 °C can be tolerated; greater changes can result in death.

The core temperature is the result of a balance between the production and the removal of body heat. Heat is produced as a result of the reactions of energy metabolism. During vigorous exercise the metabolic rate can increase 25 times, which could potentially increase core temperature by about 10 °C every 5 min! Heat is also absorbed from the environment by solar radiation and from objects that are warmer than the body. Heat is lost from the body to the environment through several mechanisms, described in detail in the following paragraphs.

Adjustments in the circulation of blood provide the fine tuning. Heat is conserved by rapidly shunting blood to the core, using fat layers below the skin and other portions of the body's shell as insulation. When internal heat increases, blood vessels near the skin dilate and warm blood is channeled to the body shell. This facilitates sweating.

Exercise in Cold Environments

Cold environments cause constriction of blood vessels near the skin; this immediately reduces the flow of warm blood to the body's cooler surface and redirects it to the warmer core. Skin temperature falls and core temperature is maintained by the excellent insulation of the skin and subcutaneous fat. The heat generated through exercise is sufficient to maintain a constant core temperature in an air temperature as low as –30 °C (–22 °F) without extra clothing. If the human is not generating sufficient heat by exercising, metabolic heat is generated through shivering. The rapid transfer of heat through water makes heat loss during immersion in water as cool as only 28 to 30 °C particularly stressful.

Exercise in Warm Environments

The human body has evolved an elaborate heat-regulating system, designed primarily to dissipate heat to the environment during exercise in warm weather. Body heat may be lost by radiation, conduction, convection, and evaporation.

The radiation of heat results from electromagnetic heat waves, which are constantly emitted by objects. This radiation is how the sun's rays warm the earth, and it does not require air or molecular contact with the warmer object. Humans are usually warmer than their environment; thus, the net exchange of radiant heat energy in general is from the human to nearby cooler objects. When the objects in the environment are warmer than the skin, radiant heat energy is absorbed from the surroundings. The human body can absorb about 100 W of radiative energy from direct sunlight. In direct sunlight, light-reflective clothing can lower sweat losses and improve cooling in exercisers. Aluminized fabric is the most light-reflective material for clothing, followed by white fabric. The right fabric can reduce water losses, as compared with bare skin (Kyle, 1991).

Conduction involves the direct transfer of heat through a liquid, solid, or gas from one molecule to another. The vast majority of core body heat is transported to the skin by circulating blood; however, a tiny amount of heat is conducted directly through the deep tissues to the skin. Heat loss by conduction involves the warming of air molecules and cooler surfaces that are in direct contact with the skin. Heat loss through conduction depends on both the temperature difference between the skin and surrounding surfaces and on the thermal qualities of surrounding surfaces. A swimmer, for example, can lose a great deal of heat through conduction to cold water. This is illustrated by placing one hand in room-temperature water. The hand in the water feels much cooler than the hand in the air, even though the water is the same temperature as the air. Water can absorb several thousand times more heat than air can, and it conducts heat rapidly away from the warm body.

The rate of heat loss by conduction is also affected by movement of the air (or water) around the body. Convection involves the transfer of heat through movement of air or fluid. If air or water movement is slow, the air next to the skin is warmed and acts as insulation. This reduces further conductive heat loss. If the air that has been heated by the body is continually replaced by cooler air, heat transfer increases as convective currents carry away the heat. Air currents at 2 m/s, or about 4 mph are up to 16 times as effective for cooling as air currents at 0.5 m/s, 1 mph. Thus, even relatively small amounts of air flow inside a human-powered vehicle fairing can result in significant cooling.

Under ordinary conditions, evaporation is the most important means of dissipating heat to the air. Water is vaporized from the skin surface and from the moist inner surfaces of the nose, mouth, and lungs (respiratory passages). For each liter of water that vaporizes, 580 kcal (2.43 mJ) are extracted from the body and transferred to the environment.

Sweat glands are distributed throughout the surface of the body. When stressed by heat, these glands secrete large quantities of weak salt solution (0.2% to 0.4% NaCl). Up to 3.5 l of sweat can be produced per hour in exercise in the heat. The evaporation of this sweat thus cools the blood circulating near the skin. Additionally, about 350 ml of water that is not sweat "seeps" through the skin daily to evaporate, and about 300 ml of water evaporates daily from the moist mucous membranes of the respiratory passages.

The effectiveness of heat loss by conduction, convection, and radiation decreases as the temperature of the environment increases. When ambient temperature exceeds body temperature, heat is actually gained by these mechanisms of thermal transfer. In such environments (or when conduction, convection, and radiation are inadequate to dissipate a large metabolic heat load), the only means for heat dissipation is by sweat evaporation. Only a small amount of additional cooling is provided by the vaporization of water from the respiratory tract. As we have all experienced, the rate of sweating increases directly with the surrounding temperature.

Heat loss through sweat evaporation from the skin depends on three factors: the surface exposed to the air, air temperature and humidity, and the convective air currents about the body. Relative humidity is a critical factor determining evaporative heat loss. Relative humidity is expressed as a percentage and refers to the partial pressure of the water vapor present in the air compared with the partial pressure of water vapor in the same air at a given temperature when it is saturated. Relative humidity is commonly measured by comparing two thermometers: One has a "wet bulb," moistened by a water-soaked wick, and the other has a "dry bulb." When the relative humidity is 100%, the two bulbs indicate the same temperature. As the relative humidity decreases, the evaporation from the wet bulb increases, resulting in proportionally lower temperature readings on the wet bulb thermometer.

The vapor pressure of moist skin is about 40 mmHg. When humidity is low, relatively high air temperatures can be tolerated. When relative humidity is high, the vapor pressure of water in the air approaches that of the skin, and evaporation is greatly reduced. Insufficient evaporative heat loss through sweating under conditions of high humidity can lead to overheating and dehydration.

Integration of Heat-Loss Mechanisms

As in a liquid-cooled automobile engine, the circulation of liquid (blood in the human engine) is vital for temperature control. The heart rate and output of blood from the heart increase and blood vessels near the skin enlarge to divert blood to the skin and away from the core. This is manifested as a reddened face and skin on a hot day or during vigorous exercise. As much as 25% of total blood flow can be diverted to the skin. This increases the thermal conductance of tissues near the skin and improves radiant heat loss to the environment, especially from the areas which sweat most—the hands, forehead, ears, forearms, and legs below the knees. The blood is cooled at the skin and returns to the exercising muscles to pick up additional heat.

With the onset of vigorous exercise, increased sweating can begin within 1.5 s and after 20 to 30 min reaches an equilibrium according to the work load. In prolonged exercise a balance between heat production and heat loss is maintained when cooling by sweat evaporation is combined with a large blood flow to the skin. Within an hour of hard exercise in the heat, the loss of water can be great enough to hamper the heat-loss mechanisms, sweating is reduced, and the function of the heart and circulation can be severely impaired. Water loss by an intensely exercising athlete can be as much as 3 l per hour and can average nearly 12 l (26 lb) per day. After several hours of intense sweating, sweat glands can fatigue, ultimately leading to a loss of control of core temperature. Marathon runners, for example, can lose more than 5 l of water during a 26-mile run. This can be as much as 6% to 10% of their body weight.

Body-water loss equivalent to as little as 1% of body weight is associated with an increase in core body temperature compared to the same exercise with normal hydration. Core temperatures can, however, increase during intense exercise from a normal of 38 °C to as high as 41 °C without ill effect. Only about 1.5 l of water loss are tolerated by adults without an abnormal physiologic response. When water loss reaches 4% to 5% of body weight there is a definite impairment in physical work capacity; there is also an increase in heart rate, a decrease in sweating, and an increase in core temperature. A well-hydrated human engine always functions better than a dehydrated one.

If a human intends to do prolonged exercise in the heat, performance can be improved by drinking 400 to 600 ml of cold water 10 to 20 min before exercising. Hyperhydration prior to exercise in the heat delays the development of dehydration, increases sweating during exercise, and decreases the rise in core temperature. This does not replace the need for frequent replacement of liquids during exercise, and it is not as effective in maintaining tem-

perature as consuming an equal volume of water during the exercise. However, in intense physical exercise like running, it may be impossible to maintain complete fluid balance because only about 800 ml of liquids can be emptied from the stomach each hour during vigorous exercise. This is insufficient to match a water loss that may average 2 l per hour.

The ideal drink for consumption during prolonged exercise is the subject of much recent research. Liquids which are drunk at body temperature are emptied more slowly than are cool liquids (e.g., at 5 °C). The rate of stomach emptying increases with the volume of liquid in the stomach, up to about 600 ml. The optimal drinking of fluids during prolonged vigorous exercise is thought to be about 250 ml (8.5 oz) of cool fluids at 10- to 15-min intervals. Stomach emptying is also slowed if the fluid contains excessively concentrated simple sugars (glucose, fructose, or sucrose) or excessive salt.

Recent studies indicate that it is possible to delay fatigue by 30 to 60 min during prolonged (2 to 4 hours) intense activity by drinking carbohydrate-containing solutions throughout exercise. Ingesting 200 to 300 ml of a drink containing 5% to 10% glucose will meet this need and delay fatigue. Such carbohydrate solutions are also now thought to be as effective as plain water in preventing dehydration and overheating during exercise in the heat. Glucose, glucose polymers (solutions of maltodextrins), and sucrose appear to be equally effective in improving performance. In contrast, fructose cannot be rapidly metabolized and when consumed during exercise does not delay fatigue. Solid carbohydrate supplements can also improve performance, but must be taken with adequate water to replace losses (Burke, 1990; Coggan, 1990).

During prolonged exercise in a cool environment, fluid loss from sweating may not be great. A reduction in gastric emptying and fluid uptake can be tolerated and a stronger sugar solution (15 to 30 g per 100 ml water) may be beneficial. Under these conditions, it may take 20 to 30 min for the carbohydrate to reach the muscles after it enters the stomach. The trade-off between the composition of the fluid ingested and the rate of gastric emptying must be evaluated on the basis of environmental and metabolic demands.

Because sweat is lower in salt and electrolyte concentration than body fluids, it is much more of an immediate concern to replace water than to replace salts. Most sport drinks contain acceptably small amounts of salt. Studies with animals indicate that a small amount of salt in drinking water increases rehydration (Nose et al., 1986). In humans,

HEAT, HYDRATION, AND HUMAN PERFORMANCE DURING THE *DAEDALUS* FLIGHT

Probably the most rigorous evaluation of human performance, heat dissipation, and hydration during prolonged human-powered vehicle operation was performed prior to the 119-km flight of the *Daedalus* human-powered airplane. This distance was more than three times longer than Bryan Allen's 35-km crossing of the English channel in the *Gossamer Albatross*, which set the previous record for human-powered flight. The flight was predicted to last 4 to 6 hours, and the pilot would have to produce 3.5 W/kg of mechanical power continuously just to keep the aircraft aloft. At an efficiency of 24%, this was calculated to require a continuous $\dot{V}O_2$ of 45 ml/kg/min, which in turn would require an outstanding performance from an Olympic-caliber athlete; an average young male might be expected to have a $\dot{V}O_2$max of about 50 ml/kg/min and to maintain a $\dot{V}O_2$ of only about 30 ml/kg/min for an extended period.

Bussolari and Nadel (1989) calculated that a 68-kg pilot with a mechanical efficiency of 24% would produce about 900 W of metabolic power during steady flight. About 225 W would be used as mechanical work to power the aircraft, and the remaining 675 W would need to be dissipated (the pilot was in an enclosed cockpit). They assumed the pilot's skin temperature was 33 °C, the cabin temperature was 28 °C, and the total heat transfer area (exposed skin) was 1.2 m^2, for a heat-transfer coefficient of 10 W/m^2 °C. They calculated that 60 W of heat would be dissipated through radiation and convection, leaving 615 W to be dissipated through evaporation of sweat, with an estimated 900 ml of water lost per hour through perspiration.

Twenty-five outstanding cycling athletes were recruited for extensive testing. Their range of maximal oxygen uptake was 59 to 86 ml/kg/min, and their range of mechanical efficiency was 18.0% to 33.7%. The 11 athletes with the best performance were subjected to a 4-hour endurance test at 70% of their maximum power output. The final five averaged $\dot{V}O_2$max of 69.9 ml/kg/min, could produce an average 3.72 W/kg at 70% of maximum, and had an average mechanical efficiency of 27.5%. The athletes were also tested in both the standard upright and the semirecumbent cycling positions. There were no differences in $\dot{V}O_2$max or efficiency between the two positions.

Finally, Bussolari and Nadel developed their own rehydration drink for the athletes to consume during the 4- to 6-hour flight. A formula was developed from their calculations and tested with the athletes in a 6-hour laboratory simulation. Their conclusion was to rehydrate the pilot at the rate of 1 l per hour with a fluid drink containing 10% glucose and 18 milliequivalents of sodium per l. This approach was so successful that at the end of the nearly 4-hour flight on April 23, 1988, pilot Kanellos Kanellopoulos showed no signs of impending fatigue. His heart rate was monitored by telemetry and never exceeded 142 beats per min.

similar benefits seem to exist (Nose et al., 1988). For a fluid loss of less than 2.7 kg (6 lb) in adults, electrolytes are readily replenished by adding a slight amount of salt to the food.

Complications From Excessive Heat Stress: Heat Illness

When the normal signs of heat stress (thirst, tiredness, grogginess, and visual disturbances) are not heeded, a series of complications termed *heat illness* can result. The major forms of heat illness are heat cramps, heat exhaustion, and heat stroke. Immediate cooling and rehydration is needed.

Heat cramps can occur during intense exercise, most commonly in the calf muscle. This type of heat illness is probably due to an imbalance in the body's salts as a result of sweating. Body temperature may be normal. Heat cramps are prevented by providing large amounts of water and by increasing the daily intake of salt at meals several days before heat stress.

Heat exhaustion is often reported during the first heat waves of the summer or during the first hard training session on a hot day. Heat exhaustion usually develops in unacclimatized people and is believed to be caused by inadequate adjustments in blood circulation and by dehydration as a result of sweating.

Heat stroke requires immediate medical attention. It is the result of a failure of the heat-regulating mechanisms brought on by excessively high body temperatures. Sweating usually ceases, the skin becomes dry and hot, and body temperature rises to dangerous levels (41 °C and higher). If the victim has been exercising intensely, sweating may be present. Untreated, heat stroke progresses, and death ensues due to collapse of blood circulation.

Cooling the Human-Powered-Vehicle Engine

From the preceding discussion, it is obvious that the design of HPVs must provide cooling for the human engine. Nearly all HPVs operate with the human engine surrounded by air, so the HPV designer is dealing with an air-cooled engine. There are a few human-powered submarines where the engine is submerged in water, with breathing being provided by scuba gear. Cooling in these vehicles is equally important, but the excellent heat-conducting property of water facilitates cooling. With appropriate water temperatures, a swimmer can keep cool more easily than a runner. The swimmer uses a smaller proportion of the cardiac output to dissipate heat and a larger proportion to transport oxygen to the muscles than a runner.

When exercising in air, the movement of air past the skin is the single most important factor that facilitates cooling, assuming that air temperature and humidity are held constant. When a human is tested on a bicycle ergometer (a device for measuring stationary power output) for a sufficiently long period that the aerobic muscle actions predominate, for each milliliter per second of oxygen absorbed by the lungs about 4.5 W of power is produced by the legs. Laboratory experiments on the calorific ("heating") value of blood sugars and other chemicals oxidized by absorbed oxygen show that for the same flow, the heat output would be about 18 W. The efficiency of muscle action is, therefore, roughly 25%.

Most of the 75% of the energy that does not appear as power at the pedals is dissipated as heat. The evaporation of perspiration can dissipate enormous heat: 2.42 kW per gram of perspiration per second. Thus, it is important for exercising humans that their perspiration evaporate and not just drip off. Fast-moving air evaporates water far more quickly than slow-moving air. As a consequence, a pedaler on a stationary ergometer drips sweat profusely at a work rate of 0.5 hp (373 W). At 27 mph (12.1 m/s)—a speed corresponding to 373 W—a riding bicyclist is cooled far more effectively by sweat evaporation.

Most of the information on human power output has been obtained by careful experiments, most often with test subjects on ergometers. Most ergometers are pedaled in the same way as bicycles; other types are rowed or walked. Exercise physiologists can take careful and often precise measurements of human work output using ergometers in their laboratories. However, we must keep in mind three reservations about ergometers.

1. People vary widely in performance, and unless many are tested (as has been seldom the case) the data cannot be generalized to everyone.
2. Pedaling or rowing an ergometer usually feels stranger than riding a novel type of bicycle. It may take a month of regular riding before one becomes accustomed to, and efficient with, a novel bicycle. Subjects are seldom given the opportunity to adapt for more than a few minutes (occasionally, a few hours) to working an ergometer.

3. Most of the energy put into bicycling and a fair proportion of that put into rowing a boat goes into air friction. The heat transferred from a hot body to a cooler airstream is largely proportional to air friction. Subjects pedaling ergometers are seldom given equivalent cooling, and their maximal output is therefore likely to be limited by heat stress. (There are exercisers on the U.S. market in which most of the power is dissipated in fans, thus simulating the effect of wind resistance, but the air flow is usually not directed at the pedaler.)

The air blast generated by bicycling is of such magnitude that it bears little resemblance to the drafts produced by the small electric fans sometimes advised for cooling pedalers on ergometers. As a consequence it can be said that under most conditions of level cycling the bicyclist works under cooler conditions than an ergometer pedaler. At high speeds, most of the rider's power is expended in overcoming air resistance. At 20 mph (8.94 m/s)

about 0.2 hp (149 W) is dissipated in the air. The cooling is a direct function of this lost power. Even if the little fans often used for ergometer experiments ran at this power level, the cooling effect would be much less than that for the moving bicyclist, because little of this power is dissipated as air friction around the subject's body.

Many cyclists can exert 0.5 hp (373 W) for periods of up to an hour. That corresponds to a speed of about 27 mph (12.2 m/s) when cycling on a conventional bicycle. At that speed the heat flow from the moving bicyclist is about 707 W/m² (see Figure 2.3). If the cyclist exerts 0.5 hp (373 W) pedaling on an ergometer, all the heat lost by convection and evaporation in moving air—all of the heat in excess of 325 W/m²—must be absorbed by the pedaler's body. Thus, the ergometer pedaler with a body area of 1.8 m² absorbs (707 − 325) × 1.8 = 688 W if the small heat losses through breathing are neglected. If the pedaler weighs 70 kg and has a specific heat of 3.52 kJ (0.841 kcal) per kg per degree C, 0.84 kcal/kg °C or 3.52 kJ/kg °C, and if a

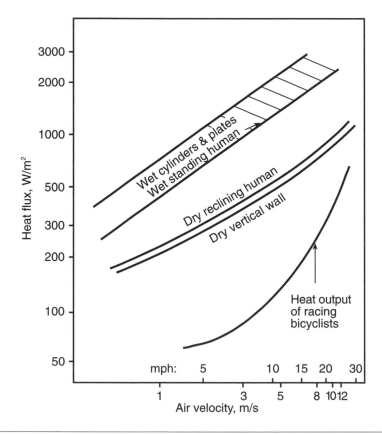

FIGURE 2.3 Heat loss from human and other objects is affected by air flow. Here, convective and evaporative heat flows are plotted against air velocity. We assume surface temperature 35 °C, air temperature 15 °C, relative humidity 80%, cyclist's body surface 1.8 m².

Adapted by D.G. Wilson from *Bicycling Science* by Whitt, F.R., Wilson, D.G., 1982, Cambridge, MA: MIT Press.

rise in body temperature of 2 °C is acceptable before physical collapse, the tolerable time limit for pedaling is calculated to be about 12 min (Whitt & Wilson, 1982).

Highly trained racing bicyclists attempting to pedal ergometers in one study at a power output of 0.5 hp (373 W) had a common range of endurance of 5 to 15 min (Whitt, 1982). Hence, the above estimates have some validity. The fact that the same racers were capable of outputs of nearly 0.5 hp (373 W) in 1-hour time trials demonstrates vividly the value of flowing air in prolonging the tolerable period of hard work. From Figure 2.3 it can be seen that a racing bicyclist producing 0.6 hp (450 W) evolves heat at about 850 W/m². According to the "wet standing human line," such a heat rate could be absorbed by air moving at about 3 m/s (7 mph).

Chester Kyle and co-workers at California State University (1974) carried out extensive trials with streamlined enclosures for riders of various machines. An interesting outcome was that, even in short rides, a streamlined casing that was skirted almost to ground level caused the rider to grossly overheat—almost certainly because of a lack of air flow through the enclosure. This problem seems to have been appreciated even with the earliest bicyclist fairings developed in the early 1900s. The *Gossamer Albatross* was the first human-powered airplane to fly across the English Channel. Its pilot, Bryan Allen, also suffered from overheating because of limited through ventilation and insufficient water during the nearly 3-hour flight.

Conclusion

Given a basic understanding of exercise physiology, it is possible to anticipate or calculate the needs and performance of the engine of a human-powered vehicle. This was illustrated by the carefully planned *Daedalus* flight, in which efficiency and consistent power production were essential.

Much heat must be dissipated during prolonged operation of any HPV engine because it is only 20% to 25% efficient. This is a different problem for HPVs that operate in cold weather or in water than for those in warm conditions, but all HPVs must be carefully designed to maintain proper temperature of the human engine. The heat-removal capacity of the air around a moving bicyclist at most speeds on the level is such that much more heat can be lost than the amount produced by the rider's effort. Hence, if an HPV has a streamlined enclosure or fairing, only a portion of the air moving around the HPV is needed for ventilation, which should be variable so the rider can remain comfortable and efficient under different conditions.

References

Adams, W.C. (1967). Influence of age, sex, and body weight on the energy expenditure of bicycle riding. *Journal of Applied Physiology, 22,* 539–545.

American College of Sports Medicine. (1986). *Guidelines for graded exercise testing and exercise prescription* (3rd ed.). Philadelphia: Lea & Febiger.

Åstrand, P.-O., & Rodahl, K. (1986). *Textbook of work physiology.* New York: McGraw-Hill.

Bar-Or, O., & Zwiren, L.D. (1975). Maximum oxygen consumption test during arm exercise: Reliability and validity. *Journal of Applied Physiology, 38,* 424–426.

Bouchard, C., Godbout, P., & Mondor, J.C. (1979). Specificity of maximal aerobic power. *European Journal of Applied Physiology, 40,* 85–93.

Brooks, A.N. (1989). Energy consumption of high efficiency vehicles. *Cycling Science, 1,* 6–9.

Burke, E.R. (1990). Sports drinks. *Cycling Science, 2*(1), 14–17.

Bussolari, S.R., & Nadel, E.R. (1989). The physiological limits of long-duration human power production: Lessons learned from the Daedalus project. *Human Power, 7,* 19.

Coggan, A.R. (1990). Carbohydrate feeding during prolonged cycling to improve performance. *Cycling Science, 2,* 9–13.

Conconi, F., Borsetto, C., Casoni, I., & Ferrari, M. (1988). Noninvasive determination of the anaerobic threshold in cyclists. In E.M. Burke, & N.M. Newsom (Eds.), *Medical and scientific aspects of cycling* (pp. 79–91). Champaign, IL: Human Kinetics.

Consolazio, C.F., Johnson, R.E., & Pecora, L.J. (1963). *Physiological measurements of metabolic functions in man.* New York: McGraw-Hill.

Cooper, K.H. (1968). A means of assessing maximal oxygen intake: Correlation between field and treadmill testing. *Journal of the American Medical Association, 203,* 201–204.

Costill, D.L. (1972). Physiology of marathon running. *Journal of the American Medical Association, 221,* 1024–1029.

Coyle, E.F., Feltner, M.E., Kautz, S.A., et al. (1991). Physiological and biomechanical factors associated with elite endurance cycling performance. *Medicine and Science of Sports and Exercise, 23,* 1, 93–107.

Davis, J.A., Vodak, P., Wilmore, J.H., et al. (1976). Anaerobic threshold and maximal aerobic power for three modes of exercise. *Journal of Applied Physiology, 41,* 544–550.

Dehn, M.M., & Bruce, R.A. (1972). Longitudinal variations in maximal oxygen intake with age and activity. *Journal of Applied Physiology, 33,* 805–807.

Denis, C., Fouquet, R., Poty, P., et al. (1982). Effect of forty weeks of endurance training on the anaerobic threshold. *International Journal of Sports Medicine, 3,* 208–214.

Dill, D.B. (1965). Oxygen used in horizontal and grade walking and running on the treadmill. *Journal of Applied Physiology, 20,* 19–22.

Franklin, B.A. (1985). Exercise testing, training and arm ergometry. *Sportsmedicine, 2,* 100–119.

Guyton, A.C. (1986). *Textbook of medical physiology* (7th ed.). Philadelphia: Saunders.

Kyle, C.R. (1988). The mechanics and aerodynamics of cycling. In E.M. Burke & M.N. Newsom (Eds.), *Medical and scientific aspects of cycling* (pp. 235–251). Champaign, IL: Human Kinetics.

Kyle, C.R. (1989, May). The human machine. *Bicycling,* pp. 196–200.

Kyle, C.R. (1991). Ergogenics for bicycling. In D.R. Lamb & M.H. Williams (Eds.), *Perspectives in exercise science and sports medicine: Vol. 4. Ergogenics: Enhancement of performance in exercise and sport* (pp. 373–419). William & Brown.

Margaria, R., Cerretelli, P., Aghemo, P., et al. (1963). Energy cost of running. *Journal of Applied Physiology, 18,* 367–370.

McArdle, W.D., Katch, F.I., & Katch, V.L. (1991). *Exercise physiology, energy, nutrition, and human performance.* Philadelphia: Lea & Febiger.

Mitchell, J.H., & Blomqvist, G. (1971). Maximal oxygen uptake. *New England Journal of Medicine, 284,* 1018–1022.

Nose, H., Morita, M., Yowata, T., & Morimoto, T. (1986). Recovery of blood volume and osmolarity after thermal dehydration in rats. *American Journal of Physiology, 251,* R492–R498.

Nose, H., Mack, G.W., Shi, X.R., & Nadel, E.R. (1988). Role of osmolarity and plasma volume during rehydration in humans. *Journal of Applied Physiology, 65,* 325–331.

Poliner, L.R., Dehmer, G.J., Lewis, S.E., et al. (1980). Left ventricular performance in normal subjects: A comparison of the responses to exercise in the upright and supine position. *Circulation, 62,* 528–534.

Pugh, L.G.C.E. (1974). The relation of oxygen intake and speed in competitive cycling and comparative observations on the bicycle ergometer. *Journal of Physiology, 241,* 795–808.

Ready, A.E., & Quinney, H.A. (1982). Alterations in anaerobic threshold as the result of endurance training and detraining. *Medicine and Science of Sports and Exercise, 14,* 292–296.

Rowell, L.B., Murray, J.A., Brengelmann, G.L., et al. (1969). Human cardiovascular adjustments to rapid changes in skin temperature during exercise. *Circulation Research, 24,* 711–724.

Saris, W.H. (1990). The Tour de France: Food intake and energy expenditure during extreme sustained exercise. *Cycling Science, 2,* 17–21.

Sharkey, G.J. (1991). *New dimensions in aerobic fitness.* Champaign, IL: Human Kinetics.

Shephard, R.J., & Åstrand, P.-O. *Endurance in sport.* (1992). Oxford: Blackwell Scientific.

Taylor, H.L., Buskirk, E., & Henschel, A. (1955). Maximal oxygen intake as an objective measure of cardiorespiratory performance. *Journal of Applied Physiology, 8,* 73–80.

van Ingen Schenau. (1983). Differences in oxygen consumption and external power between male and female speed skaters during supramaximal cycling. *European Journal of Applied Physiology, 51,* 337–345.

Whitt, F.R., & Wilson, D.G. (1982). *Bicycling science.* Cambridge, MA: MIT Press.

3

HUMAN POWER TRANSFER TO MODERN VEHICLES

Allan V. Abbott
David Gordon Wilson

Throughout history human power has been applied to machines through relatively few methods (see chapter 1), many of which are impractical for applications in human-powered vehicles (HPVs). Today's human engines propel HPVs by pushing or pulling, by arm or leg movement of levers or treadles, or by arm or leg cranking. The simplest way for a human to move a vehicle is to either push or pull it, as in the case of carts, carriages, and rickshaws. In these vehicles performance is limited to walking or running speed. Most human-powered water vehicles are pushed directly with the aid of either poles or paddles or by levers or oars. The efficiency and practicality of rowing has made this for centuries the preferred method of powering the fastest human-powered boats. Today, however, all speed and performance records in single-rider water, land, and air vehicles of unlimited design are held by vehicles whose riders are cranking with only their legs. Leg cranking is the most efficient, and certainly the most studied of these methods; thus, the majority of this chapter is devoted to exploring the principles of power transfer through leg cranking.

The speeds for walking, running, skating, and bicycling at various levels of energy expenditure are compared in Figure 3.1. The world-record speed for conventional bicycling over 200 m is 19.8 m/s as compared with the peak speed in the 100-m dash final of the 1988 Olympic games of 12.0 m/s accomplished by Ben Johnson and Carl Lewis (Alexander, 1992). The greatest factor limiting top speeds of HPVs is the friction resulting from moving through air or water. Thus, the top performance of HPVs should be compared cautiously if they are operated in different environments. Rowing and cycling are discussed later in this chapter.

Measuring Human Power

Throughout most of history the performance of humans has been compared in competitions, but seldom measured against a general standard. During

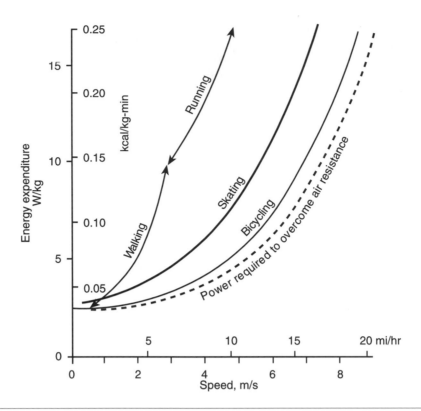

FIGURE 3.1 Speeds of walking, running, skating, and bicycling plotted against metabolic power requirements. The broken line represents the power required to overcome air resistance.

From *Bicycling Science* by Whitt, F.R., Wilson, D.G., 1982, Cambridge, MA: MIT Press. Adapted with permission.

the 20th century the measurement of human power has received increasing attention. Human power is measured today by two general methods: directly as mechanical power produced or indirectly as energy consumed in calories of food intake or in oxygen consumption ($\dot{V}O_2$) as discussed in chapter 2.

Human mechanical energy output is difficult to estimate or measure in most forms of exercise. In walking, for example, sophisticated mathematical calculations are required to estimate the effective mechanical energy output. The distribution between potential and kinetic energy of the limbs during a stride, and the energy lost in internal friction and the shock contact with the walking surface is uncertain. In cycling, the portion of the energy output that reaches the bicycle is much easier to determine, since it may be measured directly using an ergometer. The bicycle-human system forms perhaps the best combination for scientific analysis (Kyle, 1990).

Machine Versus Muscle Power

For a mechanical engineer, the measurement of power output from a continuously operating ma-

chine such as an electric motor is simple. The measurement of power produced by contraction of muscles, however, is complex. The maximal force produced by a muscle contracting against a nonmoving resistance may be quite different from the force produced by the same muscle moving a joint. This force also varies with the rate of movement of the joint. For example, the maximal power produced during knee extension occurs at a knee extension velocity of about 240°/s (see Figure 3.2). The range over which muscles contract is limited; every muscle contraction begins from a static start with time delays, accelerations, and rapidly changing forces; muscles produce work by moving joints, which move through constantly changing angles and leverage. Further, measurements of power produced by muscles are not made at the ends of the muscles, but rather at the "ends" of the human—the feet, hands, or back, for example.

Ergometers and Human Power Output

Human power output is measured with an ergometer. Ergometers have been built to measure power produced by many motions, including walking,

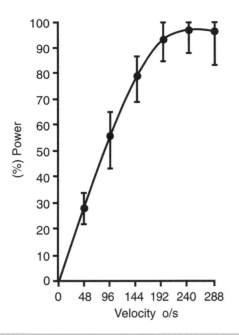

FIGURE 3.2 The maximal power produced by a muscle varies with the velocity at which the muscle flexes or extends the joint. In this study of knee extension of 15 subjects on a Cybex dynamometer, maximal power was produced at a velocity of 240°/s of knee extension.

From Perrine, J.J., 1986, The biophysics of maximal muscle power outputs: Methods and problems of measurement. N.L. Jones, N. McCartney, & A.J. McComas (Eds.), *Human Muscle Power* (pp. 15–25). Champaign, IL: Human Kinetics. Reprinted with permission.

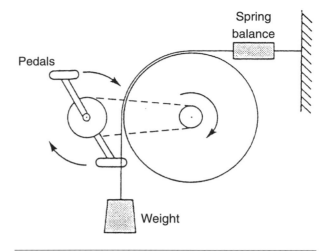

FIGURE 3.3 The power produced by a cyclist can be measured by an ergometer. In this simplified drawing of a cycle ergometer, a friction force is applied to the circumference of a flywheel, which is rotated by the cyclist's feet acting on the pedals. The brake is kept against the flywheel by the force of a weight, which can be increased or decreased. If there were no friction on the belt, as at rest, the force registered on the spring balance would equal the weight. The mechanical power needed to drive the flywheel is the friction force multiplied by the speed of the rim (rate of revolution of the flywheel times the circumference).

rowing, and arm cranking. The most common is the bicycle ergometer that is leg-cranked like a bicycle. The first mechanical cycling ergometer was built around 1880, and studies of human power output have continued since. A simplified diagram of an ergometer is shown in Figure 3.3. Cycling ergometers have been used to gauge human athletic ability and as training tools to measure the athlete's state of conditioning. A new generation of computerized electronic ergometers, such as the Schwinn Velodyne, may become an integral part of cyclists' training, allowing power, speed, cadence, heart rate, and other parameters to be displayed in real time. Several problems with using ergometers to measure human engine performance are discussed in chapter 2.

Maximal Performance Versus Time

Of prime importance to the HPV designer is the amount of power available from the human engine. The maximal power output of any working human begins at its highest level as muscles function anaerobically. As work continues, power falls rap-

idly over the first few seconds and minutes to a relatively steady state as anaerobic reserve energy is depleted and aerobic metabolism maintains the supply of energy. Even aerobically, work output continues to fall gradually with time because of fatigue. The maximal steady power that can be produced is shown as a function of duration of effort in Figure 3.4.

Human Power By Various Motions

The superiority of leg cranking has been demonstrated in several studies. Some of the best ergometer data were taken by Harrison with nine fit men, but not champion cyclists or rowers, ages 22 to 42 (see Figure 3.5). We judge these data to be good because the highest outputs—apparently those of Harrison himself—tend to form an envelope around the data of others. There are many reasons why the power outputs of people as measured on ergometers might be less than the peaks of which they could be capable on a bicycle or in a rowing shell; Harrison, who designed an ingenious ergometer capable of many different foot and hand motions that could also be used as a conventional bicycling ergometer, must have avoided most of the pitfalls.

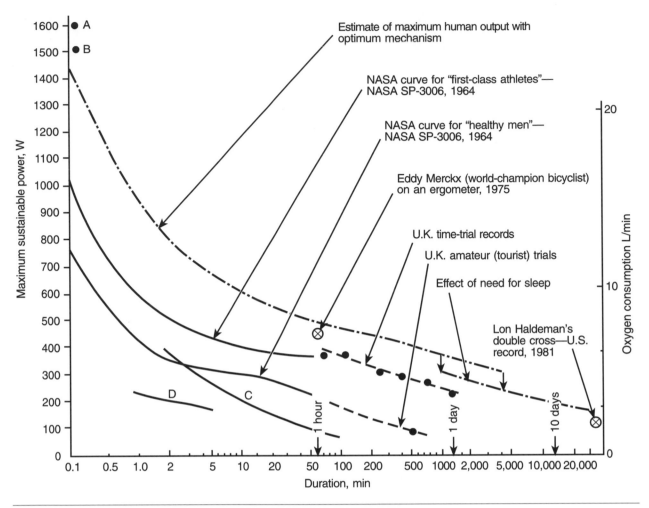

FIGURE 3.4 Maximal human power. Maximal human power produced by foot cranking decreases with time. The highest power (a) produced for a few seconds was by an Italian sprinter, Renzo Sarti, who produced 1,644 W for 5 s (Wilson, 1982; Point A from Dal Monte, 1989; Point B top cycling sprinters for 5 and 6 sec, from Kyle and Caiozzo, 1986; Curve C winch data from Trautwine, 1937; Curve D hand-crank data from Muller, 1965).

Harrison's power-output curves for linear ("rowing") foot motion (see Figure 3.5, Curves 2 and 4) are initially considerably below the cycling curve but approach it after 5 min. Rowing data taken on an ergometer have an additional reason for a diminished output: if the feet are fixed with respect to the ground, as they are normally fixed to the boat, the rower's body must accelerate and then use muscle energy to reverse the acceleration—a wasteful process. This occurs to only a minor extent in actually rowing a lightweight boat. A rowing shell is so light that the center of gravity of the rower's body is little displaced, and the boat is accelerated and decelerated quite strongly. This wastes some energy, but not nearly so much as in a stationary ergometer. A bicycle propelled by a rowing motion would also have a highly variable velocity. The variability would

be more pronounced if the feet were fixed to the bicycle and the seat were on a roller track (the usual arrangement in a shell) than if the seat were fixed and the feet were on a track. Likewise, in an ergometer one would expect the power output to be less when the feet were fixed to the stationary frame (as Harrison found) than if the seat were fixed and feet moved.

Of great interest are Harrison's results for what he called "forced" rowing. In normal rowing, the rower's body must decelerate and accelerate along with the oars at the end of each stroke. Harrison designed his ergometer so the mechanism defined the ends of the stroke and a flywheel conserved the kinetic energy of the moving masses. Perhaps the best way to describe the mechanism of this "forced" rowing ergometer is to imagine what would happen if the

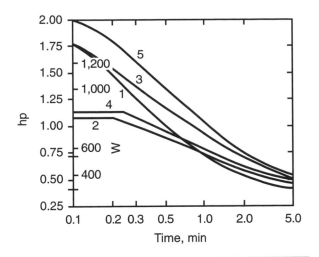

FIGURE 3.5 Human power by various motions: cycling (Curve 1), free and forced rowing with feet fixed (Curves 2 and 3, respectively), and free and forced rowing with seat fixed (Curves 4 and 5, respectively).

From Maximizing human power output by suitable selection of motion cycle and load, by Harrison, J.Y., 1970, *Human Factors*, **12**:3.

rower suddenly released the rowing handles: the mechanism would coast to a stop, with the handles continuing to move back and forth. With forced rowing and a fixed seat, about 12.5% more power for all subjects than with normal pedaling was obtained throughout the time period. This significant finding has yet to be translated into a practical mechanism for harnessing human power, despite several attempts.

More recently, Hagerman, Lawrence, and Mansfield (1988) compared the energy expenditure during conventional cycling ergometry and sliding-seat rowing ergometry. They studied 60 men and 47 women ages 20 to 74 who were healthy, but not trained athletes. The average maximal power output for men was significantly higher for cycling than rowing: 207 versus 195 W. A similar difference was also observed for women favoring cycling: 135 versus 126 W. Measurements of metabolic costs (VE, $\dot{V}O_2$, STPD, and heart rate) indicated that energy cost for rowing ergometry was significantly higher than cycle ergometry at all comparative power outputs, including maximum levels. Hagerman speculated that some of the difference may be due to involvement of a greater muscle mass in rowing and to some lack of familiarity with the rowing technique in these untrained subjects. It should also be noted that rowing a boat is more efficient than rowing a conventional ergometer, because of the kinetic energy that results from the boat's moving through the water.

Arm Power Performance

Wheelchairs have been propelled by arm power for hundreds of years. Maximal power output is somewhat less than half that from the legs, largely due to the limited muscle mass of the arms (Pivarnik, Grafner, & Elkins, 1988). Arm cranking produces power at about twice the efficiency as that in conventional wheelchair propulsion, with hands pushing directly against the wheels (Powell, 1994). Limited studies have suggested that the best crank-arm length for arm cranking is about 165 mm and that there is no significant difference in power produced with reciprocal cranking (as in a conventional bicycle) versus in-tandem cranking (one crank arm turned 180° so that both handgrips are aligned) (Powell, 1994). Power output for winching and hand cranking are also included on Figure 3.4. In 1992 the arm-powered 200-m land speed record was set at 13.7 m/s.

The question frequently arises as to whether or not one can add hand cranking to foot cranking and obtain a total power output greater than that which one would produce using either mode independently. Several studies have demonstrated that for short periods, combined arm and leg work produces 11% to 31% more power than with legs alone (Hagan, Gettman, Upton, Duncan, & Cummings, 1983; Nagel, Richie, & Giese, 1984; Powell, 1994; Reybronch, Hergenhauser, & Faulkner, 1975). Kyle and co-workers showed that, for periods of up to a minute, 11% to 18% more power could be obtained with hand and foot cranking than with the legs alone (Kyle, Caiozzo, & Palombo, 1978). The power was greater when the arms and legs were cranking out of phase than when each arm moved together with the leg on the same side. Whether or not this gain can be projected beyond the period of anaerobic work is not known. Strategies for combining arm and leg power in high-performance HPVs must consider the efficiency trade-offs between the small additional arm-power contribution versus the mechanical losses and the increased mass that are likely with a more complex drive train. For total-body conditioning and recreational uses, however, these efficiency concerns may not be critical (Powell, 1994).

The Transfer of Human Power Into Cycling Performance

In most circumstances the most effective way to improve cycling performance is by rigorous training (Spangler & Hooker, 1990). The physical condition of the human is the most important factor in improving endurance and in making a properly designed HPV go fast. The measurement of mechanical power output can most easily be made using an ergometer; however, as described previously, there can be problems with these measurements. During the last few years, electronic power meters have been designed that can measure the power at the rear hub of a bicycle being ridden on the road. These new devices will provide an entirely new perspective on human-powered-vehicle performance.

Most ergometer tests are made with subjects who are young, male, and near the championship class. One reason is obvious: Performance lower than that given by champions can be due to lesser ability or to any of the deficiencies in the testing method detailed previously. (Harrison's data are remarkable in recording high performance by nonathletes.) For a few seconds, some humans can produce surprising amounts of power. An Italian sprinter, Renzo Sarti, produced 1,644 W (2.2 hp) for 5 s (Dal Monte & Faina, 1989), Point A, Fig 3.4. Others have produced 1,500 W for 6 s, Point B, Fig 3.4, and world champion Eddy Merckx was measured to produce 455 W for 1 hour (Kyle & Caiozzo, 1986). Healthy, well-conditioned recreational cyclists can maintain this level of power output for only slightly over 1 min. Most trained, healthy people can produce over 700 W for a short period of time, and about 180 W for periods of 1 hour (Kyle & Caiozzo; Whitt & Wilson, 1982). The average cyclist can be expected to produce only about 50 to 75 W (about 0.1 hp) for longer periods of several hours. Thus, an HPV that is intended for use by an average person should be designed for continuous operation under power of about 50 to 150 W, with brief bursts of power up to 700 W.

Effect of Body Size

At higher speeds, energy in human-powered vehicles is primarily expended in overcoming air (or water) resistance. Swain, Coast, Clifford, Milliken, & Stray-Gundersen (1987) theorized that cyclists with large body size should have lower oxygen consumption ($\dot{V}O_2$) per body weight than would smaller cyclists because of the lower surface area (SA) per unit body weight (BW). They measured the oxygen consumption of cyclists of various body sizes while cycling in racing position on flat roads at 10, 15, and 20 mph. The large cyclists had 22% lower $\dot{V}O_2$/BW at all speeds than the smaller cyclists. However, SA/BW ratio was only 11% lower than that of small cyclists. The frontal area (FA) of these cyclists was determined photographically, and it was found that the large cyclists had a 16% lower FA/BW ratio than did small cyclists. They concluded that large cyclists have an advantage in terms of $\dot{V}O_2$/BW while cycling on level roads and that this advantage is principally due to their lower FA/BW ratio. Thus, it can be surmised that for maximum performance of land vehicles, body size should be considered.

Energy and oxygen consumption are compared with body weight and speed for bicyclists in Figure 3.6. Air resistance increases nearly proportionally with frontal area and proportionally with the square of the speed. As the body size increases, the frontal area increases roughly as the 2/3 power of the weight. The results of other studies have varied slightly from Figure 3.6, probably due to differences in the course and in the caliber of racing cyclists used in the tests (McCole, Claney, Conte, Anderson, & Hagberg, 1990; Pugh, 1974).

In land vehicles, rolling resistance is proportional to vehicle weight. However, aerodynamic drag is so dominant at higher speeds that small changes in rolling resistance due to the rider's weight and size are usually of little consequence. Body size and weight may be of greater importance in vehicles that receive dynamic support from air or water, such as airplanes and hydrofoils. In these vehicles, air or water resistance may vary more dramatically as a result of the effect of body weight on total vehicle weight. For water and air vehicles, power produced per unit of body weight is of greater significance than the weight of the rider alone.

Effect of Altitude

Numerous speed records on bicycles and human-powered land vehicles have been set at altitudes far above sea level. An increase in altitude is accompanied by a decrease in barometric pressure and in the partial pressure of oxygen. The reduced barometric pressure is of advantage in that air resistance is decreased. This advantage increases with the speed because the power lost to aerodynamic drag goes up with the cube of speed. The reduction of partial pressure of oxygen is, at the same time, a

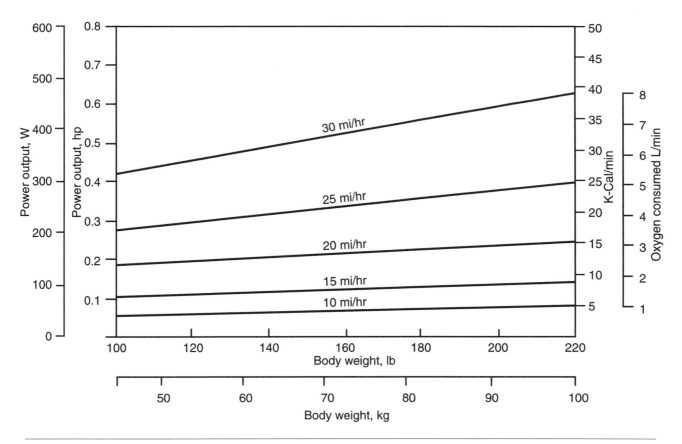

FIGURE 3.6 The effect of body weight and bicycling speed on power output, energy consumption, and oxygen consumption. The curves represent a cyclist of normal body type riding a racing bicycle in a crouched racing position at pedaling rates of 60 and 80 RPM. Although the energy required to travel at a constant speed increased with body weight, the muscle mass and therefore absolute power also increases, so one compensates for the other. These curves were developed by Kyle (1991) from work by Swain et al. (1987) and Sjogaard et al. (1982).

disadvantage to the human engine. As the altitude increases, the amount of oxygen available to the human decreases so that at 4,000 m, the $\dot{V}O_2$max is only about 78% of that at sea level. The highest competitive velodrome in the world is located at La Paz, Bolivia, at 3,417 m.

Although less oxygen is available for the human at high altitude, the reduction in air drag more than compensates for the loss of aerobic power. At the velodrome in Mexico City (2,230 m above sea level) the barometric pressure and partial pressure of oxygen are about 76% of that at sea level, whereas the $\dot{V}O_2$max of cyclists is about 91% of that at sea level. The human engine has several adaptive mechanisms that improve high-altitude performance, the most important of which is an increase in the oxygen-carrying capacity of the blood. High-altitude training and acclimatization are thus important for the human engine (Peronnet, Bouissou, Perrault, & Ricci, 1991). Generally, about 2 weeks are required for full acclimatization at an altitude of 2,300 m.

After that, about one additional week is required to fully adapt to each additional 610 m of altitude (McArdle, Katch, & Katch, 1991). The benefits of acclimatization are lost within 2 or 3 weeks of returning to sea level.

Impedance Matching and Optimum Pedaling Rate

For every application of human muscle power, there is an ideal *impedance match* of load and speed of motion that will optimize power production or efficiency. Impedance matching is perhaps best thought of in terms of the force a bicyclist can exert on the pedals. This force will be at a maximum when the pedals are held stationary. Now imagine that the pedals are rotated at increasing speed, perhaps by an electric motor, while the bicyclist tries to exert the maximum possible force on the pedals. As the speed increases the force will inevitably decrease, as shown in Figure 3.7. Eventually a speed is reached at which the bicyclist can keep up with pedal rotation, but cannot exert any force which, averaged around the pedal circle, is positive. We could call this zero-force point *shadow boxing* if we were dealing with the force exerted by the hands in cranking or in a linear motion.

The power delivered by the bicyclist is the product of the force on the pedals and the velocity. Therefore the power is zero at two conditions: when the velocity is zero and when the force is zero. At some point in between, the power goes through a maximum (Gregor & Rugg, 1986; Kyle & Caiozzo, 1986). Any mechanism is referred to as providing a good impedance match when the "driver," in this case the bicyclist, can operate at such a velocity that maximal power is produced. Bicycles along with most other HPVs allow the riders to choose a condition giving a good impedance match through variable-ratio gearing. HPVs that do not have to negotiate the equivalent of hills and mud or snow

generally are designed for just one impedance-match point. For instance, the builders of crew shells produce a good impedance match by having oarlocks—the pivot points for the oars—well outside the hulls so that appropriate combinations of force, stroke, and velocity are given at the oar handles.

In cycling, as in other sports, the rate of internal friction of movements of muscles, tendons, and cartilage, the rate of energy-wasting accelerations and decelerations of limbs, and other losses increase as cadence goes up. The maximum cadence varies among cyclists, but is somewhere around 200 RPM for trained athletes. Even at optimal pedaling rates, much of the total power generated by the leg is not available to turn the crank; approximately 25% of the power is wasted just in leg movement (Hull, Kautz, & Beard, 1991). Figure 3.8 shows that maximal power for brief periods of cycling occurs at 120 RPM or more for trained cyclists (Kyle & Mastropaolo, 1976). Kyle has plotted power output and pedal RPM from several studies (Kyle, 1991).

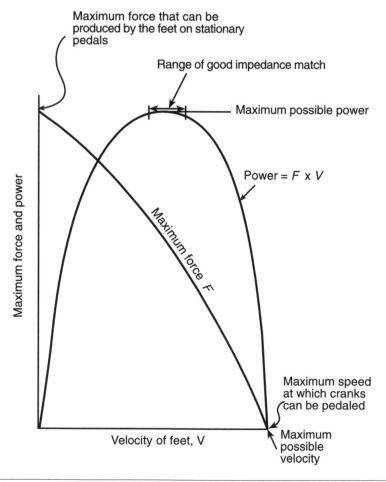

FIGURE 3.7 Impedance matching. For every application of human muscle power, there is an ideal impedance match of load with speed of motion. (Original illustration by David Gordon Wilson.)

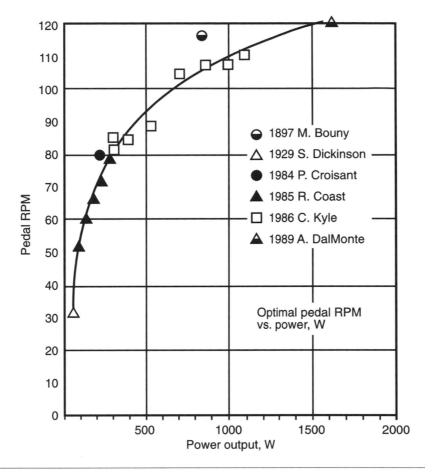

FIGURE 3.8 Maximum power output for a few seconds at various pedaling rates, plotted by Kyle (1991) from various studies.

Most studies of pedaling rate have dealt with relatively short-term exercise, usually of 6 min or less. Using trained bicycle racers, Coast, Cox, & Welch (1986) studied the optimal pedal rate over 20 to 30 min of cycle ergometry at fixed loads of about 85% of subjects' VO_2max. The researchers measured heart rate, work performed, perceived exertion, and blood levels of lactic acid, and they found pedaling rates between 60 and 80 RPM to be the most efficient under these conditions. Lactate levels and perceived exertion were lowest at 80 RPM.

Effect of Saddle Height

Changes in saddle height alter the angles of the knee and hip joints and alter the muscle lengths and the mechanical advantage of muscles as they move joints. Thus, the saddle height significantly impacts the performance of the rider. Saddle height in standard bicycles is usually measured as the distance from the pedal spindle to the top of the seat along the straight line of the crank and seat tube, with the crank at the bottom of the stroke oriented in line with the seat tube. Leg length is measured in two ways: from the symphysis pubis (the lower, forward bony part of the crotch) to the floor, or from the greater trochanter of the femur (the bony prominence that can be felt at the side of the hip joint) to the floor.

The saddle height for standard bicycles has been studied widely for many years. Using a single subject (a 39-year-old man) in 1937, Muller and Grosse-Lordemann found that more power was obtained when the saddle was raised by 40 to 50 mm (1.8 to 2 in.) above the "normal" height (that for which the heel can just reach the pedal with the leg stretched and the posture upright). On the other hand, Muller found minimum calorie consumption (or maximum energy efficiency) when the saddle was lowered 40 mm below normal. Nordeen-Snyder (1977) found the best metabolic efficiency at a height of 107% of the symphysis pubis-to-floor leg length. The efficiency curve is fairly flat near the optimal point, permitting reasonable variation before metabolic changes are noticeable. Thomas (Hamley & Thomas, 1967; Thomas, 1967a, 1967b) tested 100 subjects on a Muller ergometer and also found that maximum power output was obtained with the saddle set at a height about 10% greater than symphysis pubis-to-floor leg length. Gonzales and Hull (1989) calculated that a saddle height 97% of trochanteric leg length would minimize a cost function.

It is common for inexperienced cyclists to set the saddle height at lower than optimal levels. It is now generally agreed that the best saddle height is about 96% to 100% of the trochanteric leg length, or 105% to 109% of the symphysis pubis-to-floor leg length. Pedal design and shoe sole or cleat thickness can alter the effective seat height, and these factors have not been controlled consistently across studies. Further, these studies have examined saddle height only for the standard cycling position. The best seat-to-pedal distance for human-powered vehicles that use alternative body orientations and degrees of hip flexion is unknown.

Effect of Crank Length

The dominance of the design of the conventional safety bicycle has forced the length of the cranks to within narrow limits. With the saddle at the most efficient height above the pedals and with the pedals at a distance above the ground such that in turns (when the bicycle will be inclined toward the center of the turn) the pedals do not contact the ground, the saddle is at a height where the rider can just put the ball of one foot on the ground when stopped while still sitting on the saddle. The crank length is then chosen at a value at which almost all riders feel comfortable, normally taken as 165 mm (6.5 in.) or 170 mm (6.7 in.) for adult riders. Thus, the height above the ground of the bottom-bracket axle is fixed. Fitting longer cranks to conventional bicycles will reduce pedal clearance when cornering. Few riders of conventional bicycles, then, ever have an opportunity to try cranks longer than 170 mm, because a specially designed frame is necessary. (In this respect, recumbent bicycles have an advantage.) Most data on the effects of crank length have been taken on ergometers. Ergometer data can be regarded with suspicion, as we have implied; this certainly applies to data on long cranks.

Two people writing for a bicycling magazine in 1897 advocated shorter cranks (DeLong, 1978). One such writer, Perrache, experimented with 160-, 190-, and 220-mm cranks on a bicycle over a 5-km course and found that in maximum speed runs, he could get about 9% more power output with the 160-mm cranks than with the 220-mm cranks. We do not know whether the gear ratios were changed for different crank lengths. It would obviously penalize the use of longer cranks if the gear ratio were not increased to give approximately similar ratios of pedal speed to wheel-rim speed. It would also be a disadvantage if the rider was accustomed to using short cranks.

Muller and Grosse-Lordemann in 1937 tested the effect of crank lengths on an ergometer employing only one subject. Their approach was to set the power output the subject had to produce and to measure the maximum duration for which this output could be sustained. They also used three crank lengths: 140, 180, and 220 mm. In this case the subject was able to produce the most total work (that is, work for the longest periods) when using the longest cranks for all power levels. At the highest powers, the body efficiency (work output divided by energy input in food) was also highest when the longest cranks were used.

Harrison (1970) gave his five subjects an initial choice of crank length and found that they preferred the longer cranks (177 and 203 mm, or 7 and 8 in.). The subjects were not particularly tall. Harrison intended to take all tests at two different crank lengths; however, he found from initial tests that "crank length played a relatively unimportant role in determining maximum power output," and used just one (unspecified) length for most of his tests.

The former world champion Eddy Merckx used 175-mm cranks for his world's 1-hour record, and has used 180-mm cranks for time trials and hill climbs in the Tour de France. A strong advocate of very long cranks in the U.S., James Farnsworth, used them in achieving very fast climbs up Mount Washington.

Inbar, Dotan, Trousil, and Dvir (1983) studied the effect of crank length on power performance and found maximum power produced with 150-mm cranks for short-legged cyclists and 175-mm for long-legged cyclists (no RPM given). Hull, Gonzales, and Redfield (1988) calculated the stresses on leg muscles and joints, using a complex computer model. They found the lowest stresses (at 90 to 110 RPM) with 155-mm cranks for short men, 165-mm cranks for average men, and 170-mm cranks for tall men.

In summary, although there have been some fierce proponents and antagonists for longer cranks, crank length seems to be of minor importance for producing moderate power outputs through pedaling (Whitt, 1969). Cranks from 120 to 225 mm have been investigated, and crank lengths from 150 to 180 mm are optimum, depending on the size of the rider and the type of riding (sprinting, hill climbing, or touring) the cyclist is performing.

Pedaling Force

It is easy to calculate from the crank length and the pedaling speed in revolutions per minute how much thrust on the pedals is required for a given horsepower output. The peripheral pedal speed around the pedaling circle (or the vertical speed on the downward stroke) can be used in this equation:

$$\text{Thrust force (N)} = \frac{\text{Power (W)}}{\text{Pedaling speed (m/s)}}$$

Instrumented pedals that measure the forces during cycling have been in use for nearly a century. Bourlet (1896) discussed a pedal devised by Bouny that made it possible to measure the vertical and horizontal components of pedal thrust. There is a strong similarity between Bourlet's force diagram

and that shown in Figure 3.9. All of the studies with instrumented pedals have shown that cyclists using pedals with toe straps did not use them to pull upward during the rising stroke (Cavanagh & Sanderson, 1986; Faria & Cavanagh, 1978; Visich, 1988). There is a positive force during the entire circular pedal path with one leg helping lift the other. Pulling up on the pedals occurs only during hill climbing, accelerating, and sprinting, especially at low RPM and with large pedal forces.

Ergometer experiments (Whitt, 1971), conducted under constant-speed pedaling conditions to check the agreement between measured thrust and calculated thrust, have shown that at optimum pedaling speeds, measured thrust agreed with predicted thrust to a reasonable degree of accuracy, particularly for power outputs above 0.1 hp (74.6 W). At pedaling rates other than the optimum, the measured average vertical thrust on the pedal over its path was greater than that expected by amounts that could be predicted by oxygen-consumption tests from the lowering in pedaling efficiency. Hence it was concluded that, at other than optimum pedaling rates, thrust is "wasted" somewhere in the system. At 60 RPM, measured pedal thrusts are near

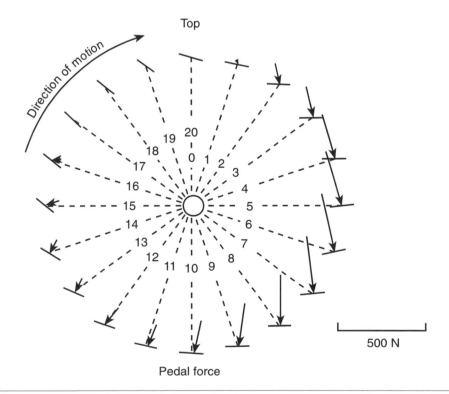

FIGURE 3.9 Resultant pedal forces. The arrows indicate the direction and magnitude (the longer the arrow, the greater the magnitude) of the resultant force applied to the pedal during steady-state cycling.

From The biomechanics of cycling: Studies of the pedaling mechanics of elite pursuit riders, by Cavanagh, P.R., Sanderson, D.J., 1986. In E.R. Burke (Ed.), *Science of Cycling*. Champaign, IL: Human Kinetics. Reprinted with permission.

those expected from the ergometer power requirements.

Several researchers have recently studied pedal forces with the hope of improving performance and efficiency (Cavanagh & Sanderson, 1986; Hull et al., 1988). A variety of pedaling techniques seem to work well for different cyclists. Negative or neutral pedal and muscle forces and joint movements may serve a very useful biomechanical purpose, and although no one now knows the answer to this question, it is likely to be one of the most productive areas of future research (Kyle, 1990).

Patterson and Moreno (1990) measured bicycle pedaling forces as a function of pedaling rate and power output. Recreational cyclists pedaled at 100 and 200 W at rates of 40 to 120 RPM. The pedal force averaged over the crank cycle was lowest at 90 RPM, at 100 W. They concluded that pedaling at 90 to 100 RPM may minimize peripheral forces and therefore muscle fatigue, even though this rate may result in higher oxygen consumption. Optimal pedaling rates are higher for cyclists with slim legs and slower for large-muscled, heavy-bodied cyclists.

Alternative Pedal Motions

During the past century hundreds of patents have been issued to inventors attempting to improve the standard foot-crank drive system. Cable drives, cam drives, hydraulic drives, linear drives, elliptical chainwheels, and lever systems are but a few of the endless ideas. Despite their inventors' claims of improved performance, none of these has consistently won races against bicycles or HPVs that use conventional foot cranking. Perhaps this is so because humans adapt well to small changes in exercise modes and ultimately have about the same mechanical efficiency and energy consumption with almost any practical pedaling motion. A 1% or 2% improvement over the standard bicycle drive might be all that is possible (Kyle, 1990).

Effect of Elliptical Chainwheels.   Elliptical chainwheels can be fitted to normal cranks so that the pedal motion remains circular. One purpose is to reduce the supposedly useless time during which the pedals are near the top and bottom "dead centers." This topic has some similarity to that of long cranks, in that there are many strong opinions for or against elliptical chainwheels, but few reliable data. Four of Harrison's five subjects produced virtually identical output curves (power versus time) using circular and elliptical chainwheels (Harrison, 1970). One, apparently Harrison himself, produced

about 12.5% more power with the elliptical chainwheel. All preferred the elliptical chainwheel for low-speed, high-torque pedaling. The degree of ovality was not specified, but Harrison stated that high foot acclerations were required.

Ovality can be specified by the ratio of the major to the minor diameter. (An illustration in Harrison's paper shows a chainwheel of about 1.45 ovality, which is high.) In the 1890s, racing riders using chainwheels with ovalities of about 1.3 became disillusioned with their performances, and these chainwheels fell out of favor. In the 1930s the Thetic chainwheel, with an ovality of 1.1, became quite popular. With a Thetic-type chainwheel, no deterioration of performance, compared with that on a round chainwheel, was recorded, and a small proportion of riders improved their performances by a few percent. Experiments with chainwheels having ovalities up to 1.6 confirm that high ovality (perhaps 1.2 or greater) decreases performance (Whitt, unpublished).

Henderson, Ellis, Klimovitch, & Brooks (1977) compared round chainwheels with an elliptical chainwheel of 1.4 ovality using active, male noncyclists on an ergometer. They also compared different orientations of the ellipse to the crank and found the most efficient setting to be one when the major axis of the ellipse was about 75° ahead of the crank arm. They measured both metabolic costs and power outputs and found at best a 2.4% energy cost savings at moderate work loads, but cautioned that this advantage could not be extrapolated to maximum or heavy-work situations. Kyle (1982) found that with sprockets with ovalities of 1.1 to 1.6 there was little difference in maximal power output on an ergometer; however, in field studies sprockets above ovality 1.2 had slower acceleration and were inferior to round sprockets in 20-min time trials.

Mathematical and treadmill studies of leg muscle action and interactions were conducted by Shimano in Japan in the early 1980s and a computer model was developed. The result was the design of a variation of the elliptical chainwheel intended to reduce pedal force and increase pedal speed at points of high knee angularity, thereby increasing power output and reducing knee strain. This was just the opposite of what was intended with previous elliptical chainwheels, which decreased time at top and bottom dead centers. The result was the Biopace chainwheel, widely marketed in the late 1980s, especially on mountain bikes. Despite laboratory tests and claims by Shimano, this chainwheel has fallen out of favor and has been replaced with round chainwheels by virtually all competitive riders. The claimed performance advantages with the Biopace were difficult to appreciate under actual riding conditions, and many riders complained that spinning at high RPM was more difficult.

Kautz and Hull (1991), using instrumented pedals, studied an elliptical chainwheel with the major axis oriented 90° to the crank arms. They found increased total energy expenditure during one crank revolution, resulting from increased downward forces applied to the upstroke pedal as the leg was accelerated against gravity. The resulting negative work necessitated additional positive work.

Thus, in the mid 1990s, it is unusual to find any chainwheel shape in competitive or recreational cycling other than round. The subjective characteristics of alternative designs and their results in races seem to outweigh any advantages indicated by laboratory tests; in any case chainwheel designs other than round are decidedly unpopular.

Effect of Alternative Drives. Many forms of linear drive, in which the foot pushes on (for instance) a swinging lever, have been invented and reinvented. The possibility of a wide variety of gear ratios is attractive. Variable ratios are attained if a cable, for example, is attached to the lever so that its position can be varied, and the cable is then attached through a length of chain to a freewheel on the back wheel and to a return spring. The drive of the American Star bicycle of the 1880s was of this general type, although the gear was not variable. The overwhelming disadvantage of this type of drive is that the feet and legs must be accelerated and subsequently decelerated by the muscles in the same way as in shadow boxing (Wilson, 1973). Harrison found relatively low outputs for motions of this type.

Users of lever drives complain of the inability to use ankle motions for propulsion, as is possible with the common rotary drives. Some years ago in Germany a "foot cycle" was made for handicapped people. This machine, which could be propelled by the use of only ankle motions, demonstrated that the muscles of the lower part of the legs can also help the unimpaired bicyclist.

Cam drives (a cam is an elliptical shape that changes rotating motion into linear motion) were developed in the late 1970s and early 1980s by Lawrence Brown. First the BioCam, then the Selectocam, and then the Powercam combined the variable-gearing feature of linear drives with conventional circular foot motion and conservation of the kinetic energy of moving masses. Brown first achieved this by fitting a cam in the place of the normal chainwheel and having the cam operate the lever system. In later designs, as the cam rotated it advanced and retarded the chainwheel in relation to the crank. By choosing the proper cam shape, Brown improved on the elliptic chainwheel, making the foot and leg motion more suited to the optimum muscle action. Speed-distance records have been claimed for this drive system. This drive system had several claimed advantages, but these either were never substantiated or they did not meet the needs of the marketplace.

As of 1993, all speed and performance records in single-rider land, water, and air human-powered vehicles of unlimited design are held by vehicles whose riders were in semirecumbent conventional bicycling positions, cranking circular chainwheels with only their legs. Ultimately, mechanisms that give noncircular foot motions or nonconstant velocities, or both, and mechanisms that allow hands and feet to be used together, may be required if the absolute maximal power output is to be obtained.

Optimization of Power Transfer Through Biomechanics

In actual laboratory tests with cyclists, it is necessary to vary only one setting of the bicycle position at a time for any given measure or test. The number and variety of combinations that can be tested are limited by the physical structure of the ergometer and by the patience of the experimenters. Gonzales and Hull (1989) calculated the optimal values for minimizing stresses in cycling, considering five variables simultaneously: pedaling rate, crank-arm length, seat-tube angle, seat height, and longitudinal foot position on the pedal. They used a biomechanical model of the lower limb that treated the leg-bicycle system as a five-bar linkage corresponding to the thigh, shank, foot, crank, and bicycle frame. For an average rider (height 1.78 m, weight 72.5 kg) at 200 W, they calculated the minimum global stresses with a pedaling rate of 115 RPM, crank-arm length of 140 mm, seat-tube angle of 76°, seat-height plus crank-arm length equal to 97% of trochanteric leg length (distance from the floor to the greater trochanter while standing upright), and longitudinal foot position on the pedal equal to 54% of foot length. A sensitivity analysis of these variables showed that pedaling rate is the most sensitive, followed by crank-arm length, seat-tube angle, seat height, and foot position. The optimal crank-arm length, seat-height, and longitudinal foot position increase as the rider's size increases, whereas the optimal pedaling rate and seat-tube angle decrease as the rider's size increases. Although these calculations did not consider actual experimental power output or performance, they did emphasize the importance of tailoring the bicycle equipment to the individual.

Effect of Body Position, Configuration, and Orientation

For this discussion, configuration refers generally to the hip angle, or the angle formed between the trunk and the femur. Body position refers to the seat-tube angle, or the position of the rider's hips relative to the crank. Orientation refers to the angle of the rider's trunk relative to horizontal. Too (1990) reviewed the previous literature comparing upright versus supine orientation, upright versus prone orientation, and upright versus low sitting position, semirecumbent position, and stand-up positions. Although many studies had attempted to examine these orientations and positions, the studies were neither standardized nor consistently controlled for the multitude of possible variables, and it was difficult for Too to draw conclusions.

Effect of Configuration

Heil, Wilcox, and Quinn (1992) noted the trend among triatheletes (who use aerodynamic handlebars) in recent years to move the bicycle seat position forward so that the seat was located directly over the crank. Riders had reported that the more forward position of the seat improves both performance and hip extension and comfort. Heil studied changes of seat-tube angle (body position) in 25 trained triatheletes using aerodynamic handlebars on a cycle ergometer. The seat-tube angle is the angle between the seat tube and the horizontal, or level horizon, (to the rear of the bicycle) and is about 75° on a conventional racing bicycle. The subjects cycled at 90 RPM and at a workload of 72% of $\dot{V}O_2$max. Heil found that the subjects' $\dot{V}O_2$, heart rate, and perceived exertion were lower at the 90° (seat directly over the crank) and 83° positions, as compared with the conventional bicycle seat-tube angles. His results supported the use of steeper seat-tube angles when using aerodynamic handlebars in conventional cycling.

Abbott (1991) performed a smaller study of various angles of hip flexion, or configuration, on a conventional cycling ergometer using higher work levels. In this study six elite male cyclists performed at work loads approximating racing speeds and changed the position of the trunk from sitting fully upright, through intermediate configurations, and to the fully streamlined position in which the trunk is horizontal. The subjects maintained a fixed cadence of 90 RPM and a fixed work load that approximated 90% of $\dot{V}O_2$max. There were no significant differences in oxygen consumption in any of these configurations. In the fully upright position there was a small (4 beats/min) increase in heart rate, and the cyclists reported a subjective increase in work load, but no other differences were detectable in any of these positions.

Changes in Body Position, Configuration, and Orientation

Too (1990) examined the effect of changes of five body positions and configurations on cycling ergometry, while controlling for body orientation. Sixteen male subjects were tested in five seating positions (0°, 25°, 50°, 75°, and 100°), as defined by the angle formed between the bicycle seat tube and the vertical (see Figure 3.10). Rotating the seat to maintain a backrest perpendicular to the ground induced a systematic change in hip angle from the 0° to the 100° position. Too determined that for total work output and maximal aerobic energy expenditure, as well as for 30-s anaerobic power, performance in the 75° position was significantly greater than for all other positions (except for the 50° position, which was not significantly inferior).

Another investigation by Too (1991) examined the effect of systematic changes of body orientation on aerobic cycling performance while controlling for body position and configuration. Using the 75° position, 10 male subjects were tested in three different body orientations (60°, 90°, and 120°), as defined by the angle between the backrest and horizontal. To obtain the 60° and 120° orientations, the entire ergometer apparatus was rotated 60° forward and backward. No significant differences in maximal aerobic energy expenditure and total work output were found with these changes of body orientation.

Bussolari and Nadel (1989) tested several athletes to compare the upright and semirecumbent cycling positions in preparation for the 119-km *Daedalus* human-powered airplane flight from Crete. They

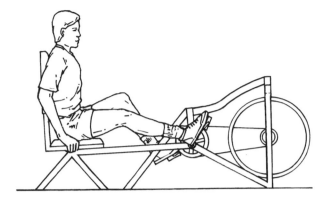

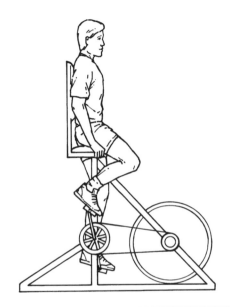

FIGURE 3.10 In a study by Too (1991), the total work output and maximal aerobic expenditure, as well as 30-s anaerobic power, was best in the 75° position—between the extremes of 0° and 100° illustrated here.

felt that the semirecumbent position had significant advantages because of the lower frontal area and the fact that the hands and arms had more freedom to manipulate the controls. However, they found no significant difference in either maximal oxygen uptake or mechanical efficiency between these two positions.

In summary, insufficient experimental data are available on the effects of body position, configuration, and orientation on performance of the human engine when leg cranking. A position with a seat angle of about 75° may be best (or 83° to 90° if aerodynamic handlebars are used on the conventional bicycle), and the orientation and configuration may not be critical as long as these do not differ dramatically from the standard cycling position. Almost without exception, today's racing cyclists have

done all of their cycling training in the standard racing bicycle position, and they can be expected to perform best in that position. The effect of prolonged training in other positions, configurations, and orientations is unknown.

Conclusion

Ergometers have been used extensively to study the power output of humans. Of the several mechanisms through which human power can be transferred to HPVs, leg cranking is generally both the most powerful and the most efficient. The optimal body position, crank length, and pedaling rate for leg cranking have been extensively studied. Despite many attempts to improve on the design of leg-cranked mechanisms, all present speed and performance records in single-rider water, land, and air vehicles of unlimited design are now held by vehicles whose riders are in the semirecumbent position, cranking in circular motions with only their legs. It is possible that future HPVs will find improved performance through mechanisms that utilize alternative motions of the legs, or perhaps through a combination of leg and arm power.

References

Abbott, A.V. (1991). The effect of hip flexion on cycling efficiency. *Cycling Science*, **4**, 12.

Alexander, R.M. (1992). *The human machine.* New York: Columbia University Press.

Bourlet, C. (1896). *Il nouveau traité des bicycles et bicyclettes, le travail.* Paris: Gautheir-Villars.

Bussolari, S.R., & Nadel, E.R. (1989). The physiological limits of long-duration human power production: Lessons learned from the *Daedalus* project. *Human Power*, **7**(4), 1–10.

Cavanagh, P.R., & Sanderson, D.J. (1986). The biomechanics of cycling: Studies of the pedaling mechanics of elite pursuit riders. In E.R. Burke (Ed.), *Science of cycling* (pp. 91–122). Champaign, IL: Human Kinetics.

Coast, J.R., Cox, R.H., & Welch, H.G. (1986). Optimal pedaling rate in prolonged bouts of cycle ergometry. *Medicine and Science of Sports and Exercise*, **18**(2), 225–230.

Dal Monte, A., & Faina, M. (1989). *Human anaerobic power output.* Paper presented at UCI Congress on the Medical and Scientific Aspects of Cycling, Abono Terme, Italy.

DeLong, F. (1978). *DeLong's guide to bicycles and bicycling*. Radnor, PA: Chilton.

Faria, I.E., & Cavanagh, P.R. (1978). *The physiology and biomechanics of cycling*. New York: Wiley.

Gregor, R.J., & Rugg, S.G. (1986). Effects of saddle height and pedaling cadence on power output and efficiency. In E.R. Burke (Ed.), *Science of cycling* (pp. 69–90). Champaign, IL: Human Kinetics.

Gonzales, H., & Hull, M.L. (1989). Multivariate optimization of cycling biomechanics. *Journal of Biomechanics*, **22**, 1151–1161.

Hagan, R., Gettman, L., Upton, S., Duncan, J., & Cummings, J. (1983). *Journal of Cardiac Rehabilitation*, **3**, 689–695.

Hagerman, F.C., Lawrence, R.A., & Mansfield, M.C. (1988). A comparison of energy expenditure during rowing and cycling ergometry. *Medicine and Science of Sports and Exercise*, **20**(5), 479–488.

Hamley, E.J., & Thomas, V. (1967). The physiological and postural factors in the calibration of the bicycle ergometer. *Journal of Physiology*, **191**, 367–374.

Harrison, J.Y. (1970). Maximizing human power output by suitable selection of motion cycle and load. *Human Factors*, **12**(3), 315–329.

Heil, D.P., Wilcox, A.R., & Quinn, C.M. (1992). *Cardiorespiratory and kinematic responses to seat-tube angle variation during steady-state cycling*. Unpublished manuscript.

Henderson, S.C., Ellis, R.W., Klimovitch, G., & Brooks, G. (1977). The effects of circular and elliptical chainwheels on steady-state ergometer work efficiency. *Medicine and Science of Sports and Exercise*, **9**(4), 202–207.

Hull, M.L., Gonzales, H.K., & Redfield, R. (1988). Optimization of pedaling rate in cycling using a muscle stress-based objective function. *International Journal of Sports Biomechanics*, **4**(1), 1–20.

Hull, M.L., Kautz, S., & Beard, A. (1991). An angular velocity profile in cycling derived from mechanical energy analysis. *Journal of Biomechanics*, **24**, 577–586.

Inbar, O., Dotan, T., Trousil, T., & Dvir, Z. (1983). The effect of bicycle crank-length variation upon power performance. *Ergonomics*, **26**, 1139–1146.

Kautz, S.A., & Hull, M.L. (1991). The relationship between mechanical energy expenditure and internal work during cycling. In *1991 Advances in bioengineering*. New York: American Society of Mechanical Engineers.

Kyle, C.R. (1982). Experiments in human ergometry. In A. Abbott (Ed.), *Proceedings of the First International Human Powered Vehicle Scientific Symposium*. Indianapolis: International Human Powered Vehicle Association.

Kyle, C.R. (1990). Patents on pedaling and peddling patents. *Cycling Science*, **2**, 2–21.

Kyle, C.R. (1991). Ergogenics for bicycling. In D.R. Lamb & M.H. Williams (Eds.), *Perspectives in exercise science and sports medicine: Vol. 4. Ergogenics: Enhancement of performance in exercise and sport*. William & Brown.

Kyle, C.R., & Caiozzo, V.J. (1986). Experiments in human ergometry as applied to the design of human-powered vehicles. *International Journal of Sports Biomechanics*, **2**, 6–19.

Kyle, C.R., Caiozzo, V.J., & Palombo, M. (1978, September). Predicting human-powered vehicle performance using ergometry and aerodynamic drag measurements (conference syllabus). *Conference on Human Power for Health, Productivity, Recreation and Transportation, Technology*. University of Cologne.

Kyle, C.R., & Mastropaolo, J. (1976). Predicting racing bicyclist performance using the unbraked flywheel method of bicycle ergometry. In F. Landry & W. Orban (Eds.), *Biomechanics of sport and kinanthropometry*, **6** (pp. 211–220). Miami Symposia Specialists.

McArdle, W.D., Katch, F.I., & Katch, V.L. (1991). *Exercise physiology, energy, nutrition, and human performance*. Philadelphia: Lea & Febiger.

McCole, S.D., Claney, K., Conte, J.C., Anderson, R., & Hagberg, J.M. (1990). Energy expenditure during bicycling. *Journal of Applied Physiology*, **68**, 748–853.

Muller, E.A. (1965). Physiological methods of increasing human work capacity. *Ergonomics*, **8**(4), 409–424.

Muller, E.A., & Grosse-Lordemann, H. (1937). *Der Einfluss der Tretkurbellange auf das Arbeitsmaximum und den Wirkungsgrad beim Radfahren*. Dortmund-Munster: Kaiser Wilhelm Institute fur Arbeitsphysiologie.

Nagel, F., Richie, J., & Giese, M. (1984). VO_2max responses in separate and combined arm and leg air-braked ergometer exercise. *Medicine and Science in Sports and Exercise*, **16**, 563–566.

Nonweiler, T. (1958). The work production of man: Studies on racing cyclists. *Proceedings of the Physiological Society*.

Nordeen-Snyder, K. (1977). The effects of bicycle seat height variation upon oxygen consumption and lower limb kinetics. *Medicine and Science in Sports and Exercise*, **9**, 113–117.

Patterson, R.P., & Moreno, M.I. (1990). Bicycle pedalling forces as a function of pedalling rate and power output. *Medicine and Science in Sports and Exercise*, **22**, 512–516.

Perrine, J.J. (1986). The biophysics of maximal muscle power outputs: Methods and problems of measurement. In N.L. Jones, N. McCartney, & A.J. McComas (Eds.), *Human muscle power* (pp. 15–25). Champaign, IL: Human Kinetics.

Peronnet, F., Bouissou, P., Perrault, H., & Ricci, J. (1991). The one hour cycling record at sea level and at altitude. *Cycling Science*, **3**, 16–22.

Pivarnik, J., Grafner, T., & Elkins, E. (1988). Metabolic, thermoregulatory, and psychophysiological responses during arm and leg exercise. *Medicine and Science in Sports and Exercise*, **20**(1), 1–5.

Powell, R. (1994). Arm power performance: Mechanics and physiology. In C.R. Kyle (Ed.), *Proceedings of the Fourth International Human Powered Vehicle Scientific Symposium*. Indianapolis: International Human Powered Vehicle Association.

Pugh, L.G.C.E. (1974). The relation of oxygen intake and speed in competition cycling and comparative observations on the bicycle ergometer. *Journal of Physiology*, **241**, 795–808.

Reybronch, T., Hergenhauser, G., & Faulkner, J. (1975). Limitations to maximum oxygen uptake in arms, legs, and combined arm-leg ergometry. *Journal of Applied Physiology*, **38**, 774–779.

Sjogaard, G., Nielsen, B., Mikkelsen, F., Saltin, B., & Burke, E.R. (1982). *Physiology in bicycling*. Ithaca, NY: Mouvement.

Spangler, D., & Hooker, G. (1990). Scientific training and fitness testing. *Cycling Science*, **2**(1), 23–25.

Swain, D.P., Coast, J.R., Clifford, P.S., Milliken, M.C., & Stray-Gundersen, J., (1987). Influence of body size on oxygen consumption during bicycling. *Applied Physiology*, **62**(2), 668–672.

Thomas, V. (1967, January). Saddle height. *Cycling*, p. 24.

Thomas, V. (1967, February). Saddle height: Conflicting views. *Cycling*, p. 17.

Too, D. (1990). Biomechanics of cycling and factors affecting performance. *Sports Medicine*, **10**(5), 286–302.

Too, D. (1991). The effect of hip position/configuration on anaerobic power and capacity in cycling. *International Journal of Sports Biomechanics*, **7**, 359–370.

Trautwine, J.C. (1937). *The civil engineer's reference book* (21st ed.). Ithaca, NY: Trautwine Co.

Visich, P.S. (1988). Physiological changes riding a bicycle ergometer with and without toe stirrups. In E.R. Burke (Ed.), *Medical and scientific aspects of cycling* (pp. 121–131). Champaign, IL: Human Kinetics.

Whitt, F.R. (1969, December–January). Crank length and pedaling efficiency. *Cycling Touring*, p. 12.

Whitt, F.R. (1971). A note on the estimation of the energy expenditure of sporting cyclists. *Ergonomics*, **14**, 419–424.

Whitt, F.R., & Wilson, D.G. (1982). *Bicycling science*. Cambridge, MA: MIT Press.

Wilson, D.G. (1982). Research needs for human-powered vehicles. In A. Abbott (Ed.), *Proceedings of the First International Human Powered Vehicle Scientific Symposium*. Indianapolis: International Human Powered Vehicle Association.

Wilson, S.S. (1973, March). Bicycling technology. *Scientific American*, pp. 81–91.

II

WATERCRAFT

Before the 19th century nearly all watercraft were designed to be poled, paddled, or rowed by humans. Wind and water currents were the only other sources of power available, and they were not always reliable. But during the 19th century two major advancements were made in rowing. The sliding seat allowed the rower to add the substantial power from the legs to that already in use from the arms, shoulders, and back. And the modern outrigger moved the pivot point of the oar outside of the boat, allowing narrower hulls and more efficient use of the oars.

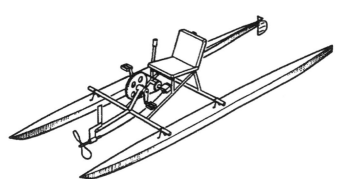

Until recently, the fastest human-powered watercraft have been the long, narrow oared shells, powered by crews of between one and eight rowers. The speed of modern racing shells with long, narrow hulls is limited primarily by skin-friction drag, by wave drag, and, to a minor degree, by air drag. The efficiency of rowing, or the power applied to the oar handles compared to that which propels the boat forward, is between 65% and 75%, whereas propellers can deliver power to the water or air with over 90% efficiency. Human-powered, propeller-driven hydrofoils have exceeded speed records set by rowed racing shells. Human-powered submarines and semiamphibious craft are also being developed.

Chapter 4 provides an overview of the history and various designs of human-powered watercraft and discusses the effects of different designs for supporting and propelling human-powered watercraft. This chapter considers the fastest rowed boat, the long, narrow racing shell and reviews the development of the more recent and faster human-powered hydrofoils. Submarines and semiamphibious craft are also discussed. Chapter 5, by Edward S. Van Dusen, a well-known rowing shell designer, details design and performance factors in high-performance racing shells. Alec N. Brooks, a fluid dynamics engineer and codeveloper of the first successful human-powered hydrofoil, delves into the science of hydrofoil design in chapter 6.

4

HUMAN-POWERED WATERCRAFT

Allan V. Abbott

Alec N. Brooks

David Gordon Wilson

People have used various human-powered boats for thousands of years. Humans have poled, paddled, or rowed a multitude of hull designs in a variety of conditions. The fastest was a long, narrow racing shell rowed by one to eight humans. Various submarines and semiamphibious craft have been developed in history and in recent years. Human-powered hydrofoils have recently set new speed records.

History

Some million years ago, primitive peoples learned that tree trunks and other floating objects had enough buoyancy to support a person's weight. They found that a tree stripped of its branches, instead of drifting aimlessly, could be given direction by movements of the feet. Thus, one of the earliest inventions was a human-powered vehicle—a watercraft.

This chapter is adapted from an article in *Scientific American*, Dec. 1986.

Through most of recorded history technological progress in human-powered boats was inspired by military purposes. Sophisticated and formidable human-powered vessels of war were used to do battle in the Mediterranean before the time of Christ. The early Greeks constructed *penteconters* with 25 oars on a side. These undecked, lightly constructed galleys were fast enough to overtake any other vessel. When penteconters proved too light for purposes of outright war, *biremes*, with two rows of oars on a side, became the warship of the Mediterranean. The most famous of the Greek warships, the *trireme*, had three rows of rowers on each side and up to 170 oarsmen, and it was stronger, heavier, and even faster. It measured about 40 m (130 ft) in length and had a beam of about 5 m (16 ft). The performance of the trireme was partly attributable to an innovation dating to the 6th century B.C., the outrigger planking, which was positioned laterally to the hull. The upper bank of oarsmen of necessity were positioned farther from the water than the lower ones. Their long oars (at least 4 m) passed through this outrigger and pivoted far enough from the oarsmen so that the blades could be swung more efficiently. These triremes are thought to have been capable of short bursts of speed up to 7 or 8 knots. (One knot, or nautical mile per hour is equal to about half a meter per second, or 1.15 mph.)

Before 1807, when the steam engine was used for the first time as practical power for a boat, designers could rely on only one source of power other than the wind or water current for propulsion—human power. Since the advent of steam and internal-combustion engines, modern human-powered watercraft have continued for only two purposes, practicality or sport. The majority of human-powered boats today are similar to the simple craft of thousands of years ago, and in underdeveloped portions of the world boats still are paddled or rowed about for utilitarian applications. It is the sporting and competitive applications of human-powered boats that have led to the recent technological advances in speed and efficiency.

The first recorded boat race took place in 1300 at a Venetian regatta among gondolas. To be sure, given the competitive human spirit, there were races as soon as two or more boats shared the same stretch of the Nile or the Tigris. In modern times, rowing was added as a sport at Oxford University in the 1790s, with eight-oared boats first used in 1815. The townsfolk of Henley-on-Thames, hoping to attract more visitors, started a regatta in 1839 as part of their annual market fete. They seem to have succeeded. From the beginning there was a Grand Challenge Cup for eight oars, and they added the Diamond Challenge Sculls for single scullers in 1844: these are now probably the most prestigious awards in rowing.

As a result of these competitions, the age-old technology of rowing and sculling evolved to give competitors more speed. The boats used in early competitions were relatively broad-beamed, stable wherries, constructed with overlapping laths of wood. This lapstrake construction is heavy, and it slowed the boats down because it is also less smooth. In early rowing boats the oarlocks, or pivot points for the oars, were mounted on the gunwales, or sides, of the boat. The width of the boats was determined by the need for stability and the need to position the gunwales 70 to 85 cm lateral to the seat to provide good leverage for the oarlocks and oars. The seats in 18th-century rowing boats were stationary, and rowers pulled their oars using only their arms and backs, facing opposite the direction they were traveling.

The modern outrigger—a tripodlike device attached to the side of the boat—was a major advance introduced in 1843. The oarlock is located at the apex of the tripod. Because the oarlocks no longer needed to be attached directly to the gunwales, boats could be narrower, which greatly reduced wave drag, and the oars could be longer, which in reasonably flat water allowed rowers to use a longer and more efficient stroke. But this stroke still used mainly the muscles of the torso and arms, and rowing was a heavy straining motion against a slowly moving resistance. The major turning point came in 1856 when a crude sliding seat was introduced, consisting of a sheepskin pad sliding on a greased panel. This allowed harnessing the powerful leg muscles as the seat slid fore and aft during the rowing cycle. The sliding seat on bearings was invented in the U.S. a year later.

Modern Watercraft

As Figure 4.1 shows, human-powered watercraft can be found around the world in a variety of shapes, construction materials, and propulsion devices. Some of the more sophisticated designs have the advantages of producing power by rapid movements of the legs, as on a bicycle. A champion cyclist can produce more than 2 hp (1,500 W) in a brief period of maximal effort. Power production over periods of more than 5 min drops to about 0.5 hp (370 W). The traditional rowing motion, with the rower sitting still and using only the muscles of the back, shoulders, and arms, produces considerably less power than the cycling motion. With the development of the sliding seat, which allowed rowers to use their leg muscles in the rowing action, the power level increased, rivaling cycling. The disadvantage of rowing is that with every stroke, the rower's arms and the oars must be accelerated and then decelerated by the muscles and, to some degree, water resistance. To a minor extent, the rower with a sliding seat also must accelerate and decelerate the body as the seat moves back and forth. However, because the racing shell weighs so little compared with the rower, the rower's center of mass is little displaced, and the boat is accelerated and decelerated quite strongly with each stroke.

The major technological advances that led to modern high speeds with rowed and sculled boats (one *rows* with two hands on a single sweep, and *sculls* with one hand on each of two sculls) were in place by 1857. Since then, development of boatmaking skills and materials has been more gradual. Wooden boats, made mostly of cedar, spruce, and mahogany, became ever lighter and were called "shells," probably because the wooden hull could

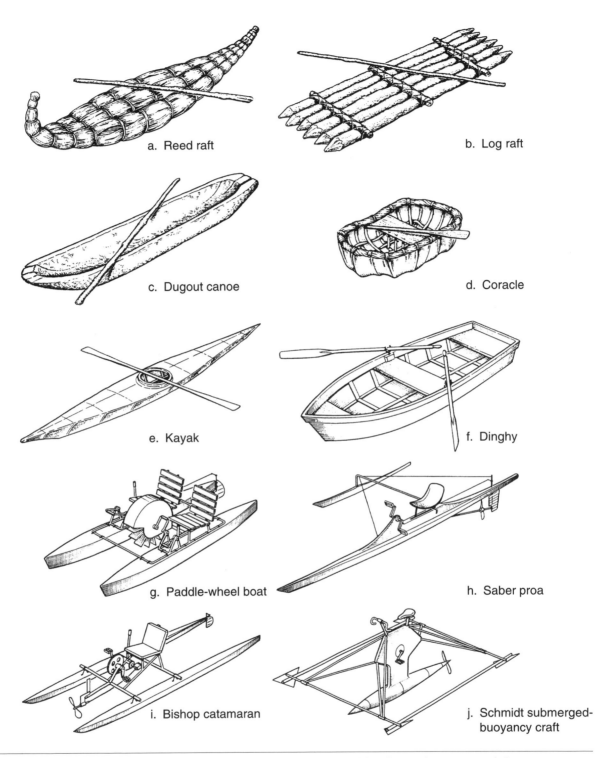

a. Reed raft

b. Log raft

c. Dugout canoe

d. Coracle

e. Kayak

f. Dinghy

g. Paddle-wheel boat

h. Saber proa

i. Bishop catamaran

j. Schmidt submerged-buoyancy craft

FIGURE 4.1 Human-powered watercraft can be found around the world today with a variety of shapes, construction materials, and propulsion devices. Relatively primitive craft are poled (*a* through *c*) or paddled (*d*, *e*) and are made of natural materials such as reeds, wood, and animal skins. More modern craft, made of wood, metal, and plastic composites, are rowed (*f*), an action that calls for the use of the arms, shoulders, and back, or are paddled using foot pedals, using the strong leg muscles (*g*). Pedal-driven-propeller boats (*h* through *j*) have the greatest propulsive efficiency of any of these methods. Recent novel designs intended for higher speeds reduce the drag these vehicles encounter. Theo Schmidt's experimental craft (*j*), for example, reduces the surface drag of the hull.

From Human Powered Water Vehicles by Brooks, A., Abbott, A.V., & Wilson, D.G., 1986, *Scientific American.* **225**(6), 120–130. Reprinted by permission.

easily be punctured with careless handling. Plywood, having layers of the thickness of veneers, came in use relatively recently with the development of good waterproof adhesives. In the 1950s, experimental shells were tried having at least the skin made of glass-fiber-reinforced plastic, and by the end of the 1960s commercially available composite-based boats had made a substantial penetration into the dominant position of wooden boats. Today the wooden shell is becoming a rarity. Sophisticated resins and aramid (Kevlar) or graphite-fiber reinforcement have brought the weight of the lightest "single" below 10 kg (22 lb). The length-beam ratio is about 30:1, and the length of a single is 8 to 10 m (26 to 33 ft), depending partly on the weight of the sculler and partly on fashion. If someone wins the Diamond Challenge Sculls or the Olympics in an unusual boat, scullers around the world order similar lines from the builders, craftspeople making boats singly or in very small numbers.

An unusual and innovative boat was rowed by Michael Kolbe to win the 1981 World Championships in Munich. Unlike conventional shells with sliding seats, it had a fixed seat—and a sliding frame supporting the riggers and "stretchers," or footboards. The rowing motion is the same with this arrangement as in conventional shells, but most of the rower's mass is on the fixed (rather than sliding) seat, greatly reducing the oscillations of the center of mass. This, in turn, reduces the oscillations of velocity of the hull through the water. (Conventional shells have a distinctive, jerky motion when rowed forcefully.) Because drag in the water is proportional to the square of the hull-to-water relative velocity, a fluctuating speed always produces more drag than would steady movement at the average speed. The drag reduction, though only slight, is enough to make a significant difference in the racing world. In 1982 five boats in the men's finals had fixed seats and sliding riggers. In 1983 all six finalists used sliding-rigger boats (the top U.S. rowers had boats made by Ted Van Dusen of Composite Engineering in Winchester, Massachusetts). After the 1983 World Championships sliding-rigger boats were ruled out of competition—an artificial restriction, many people think, limiting progress.

The length-beam ratio of the Western racing shells is rivaled by the "canoes," catamarans and proas of the southern Pacific peoples. Some of these are large enough to carry hundreds of warriors, paddling in superb rhythm and achieving high speeds, though not, apparently, rivaling the sliding-seat, eight-oared shells.

Racing shells, powered by one to eight rowers or scullers, were until recently the fastest human-powered watercraft. The fastest of the shells, powered by a crew of eight rowers, have achieved speeds of more than 12 knots over a standard 2,000-m course. Human-powered watercraft that are not bound by the arbitrary restrictions of officially sanctioned rowing events have recently surpassed this level of performance. Designers of these unconventional vehicles are dispensing with oars and taking full advantage of modern high-efficiency propellers. They are even dispensing with hulls as they explore innovative ways to reduce the resistance against motion, called drag, that water exerts on a moving boat.

Forces Acting on Watercraft

Regardless of its design—whether a crude flotation device propelled by underwater kicking, a wooden raft pushed along by poles, a dugout canoe powered by paddles, or a dinghy moved forward by sweeping oars—every watercraft must contend with four basic forces: weight, lift, thrust, and drag (see Figure 4.2). Weight and lift are the simplest forces to understand. Weight is simply the force of gravity pulling down on the craft and its operators. Lift is the force that acts upwards, resisting weight, and is equal to weight, because the vehicle is not accelerating vertically.

For most watercraft, lift is generated by displacement of water, or buoyancy, equal to the weight of the water displaced by the hull. In addition, many high-speed boats take advantage of dynamic lift, which is produced as a result of forward motion. Before the 1980s, human-powered watercraft were unable to successfully incorporate dynamic lift.

Drag is a force that acts in a direction opposite the direction of motion. Thrust, the force produced by the operator, acts in the direction of motion. If the craft is moving at a steady speed, thrust is equal to drag. In summary, at constant speed, lift balances weight, and thrust balances drag.

In designing for greatest efficiency, the most important objective is minimizing drag. One obvious way is to reduce the weight of the boat. The production of lift on a moving water vehicle almost always incurs a drag penalty. Minimizing the weight, and hence lift, lessens drag. Because the weight of the human operator is fixed, assuming that we start with a healthy, athletic person, weight reduction efforts must be applied primarily to the

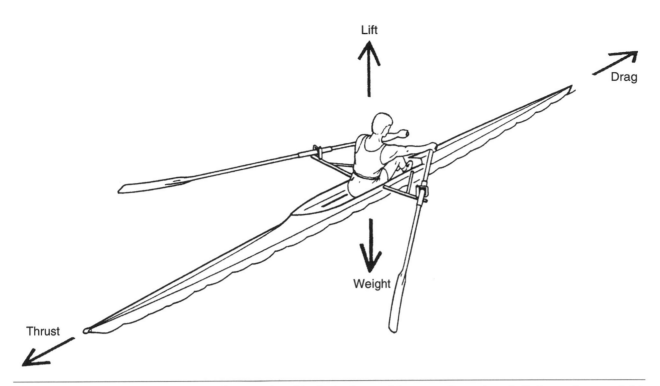

FIGURE 4.2 Four basic forces must be considered in designing such boats as the racing shell shown here: weight, lift, thrust, and drag. Weight is the gravitational force acting on the boat and the operator. Lift is normally generated by buoyancy, the upward force equal to the weight of the water displaced by the boat's hull. Thrust, in the case of human-powered water vehicles, is the force produced by the actions of the operator (shown here rowing) that propels the craft forward. Drag is the resistance to the boat's forward motion; it arises in most craft from the creation of a wake (wave drag) and the friction between the hull and the water flowing past it (skin-friction drag). When a boat has a constant speed, lift balances weight and thrust balances drag.

From Human Powered Water Vehicles by Brooks, A., Abbott, A.V., & Wilson, D.G., 1986, *Scientific American.* **225**(6), 120–130. Reprinted by permission.

craft. It is therefore desirable that the weight of the boat be only a small fraction of the operator's weight, similar to the relationship between the modern racing bicycle and its rider.

Assuming that the weight of the racing shell has been reduced to its practical minimum, a designer's attention must turn to other ways to minimize drag. Shells have what are called displacement hulls: virtually all of their lift is produced by the buoyancy of the hull. Displacement hulls have the unique property that their drag approaches zero as their speed through the water approaches zero. Thus, at very low speeds all displacement-hulled vehicles have extremely low drag and are among the most efficient of all vehicles. Racing shells, however, do not operate at low speeds.

As speed increases, the drag on a shell increases dramatically, due in part to the formation of waves. As the hull passes through the water, waves emanate from the bow and the stern. The energy required to produce these waves is manifested as wave drag. Wave drag increases rapidly with in-

creasing speed, but unevenly due to varying amounts of constructive and destructive interference of the bow and stern waves. At a speed called "hull speed," the bow is at the crest and the stern is at the trough of a single wave; the hull in its passage through the water has literally created a hill of water through which the boat has to push. At this point a great expenditure of power is needed to increase the boat's speed. The human power plant cannot supply the required effort, so hull speed acts as the effective speed limit of a human-powered, displacement-hulled vehicle.

Hull speed is proportional to the square root of the waterline length. Thus, long slender hulls are required for efficient, speedy displacement vessels. On the other hand, for a given amount of buoyancy, long, slender hulls have greater wetted surface area than short, wide hulls. The greater the wetted surface area, the greater the drag caused by the friction of the water as it flows past the surface of the hull. This type of drag is known as skin-friction drag. Hence, as slenderness increases, wave drag is decreased, but skin-friction drag then becomes a problem. The optimum hull slenderness minimizes the sum of wave drag and skin-friction drag.

Shells are designed to compete in 6- to 7-min races at power levels of about 0.5 hp (370 W) per rower. The resulting optimum length-to-width ratios of these sleek craft exceed 30:1. A single-person shell has a length of 8 to 9 m and a width of 250 to 300 mm or less. Interestingly, the drag of these slender hulls at racing speed is very unevenly distributed, with 80% due to skin friction and 20% due to wave drag. This unequal proportion results from the fact that at racing speeds, wave drag increases with speed at a much faster rate than skin-friction drag.

Given that skin-friction drag dominates the drag on a shell at racing speed, substantial drag reduction is possible if this drag component can be reduced. Skin friction arises from the thin, viscous layer of water, known as the *boundary layer*, that flows over the boat's hull. There are two fundamental types of boundary layers: *laminar*, in which the flow is smooth and steady, and *turbulent*, in which the flow is chaotic and unsteady. Laminar boundary layers have much less skin-friction drag than turbulent boundary layers. The boundary layer on a shell starts out laminar, but soon becomes physically unstable and turbulent, typically only a short distance back from the bow. Significant drag reductions are possible if transition can be delayed, effectively increasing the extent of laminar flow on the hull.

One method of extending the laminar boundary layer that is in use in some specialized underwater vehicles is the injection of long-chain polymers, sometimes referred to as "slippery water," into the boundary layer near the front of the craft. Race-sanctioning organizations are not likely to allow this practice in competition, if for no other reason than that it pollutes the water. A similar approach that might be allowed, however, would entail carefully cultivating a layer of naturally slimy algae or innocuous microorganism on the hull below the waterline.

Boundary-layer suction is another technique that has been used to stabilize laminar boundary layers. In this approach, fluid in the boundary layer is continuously sucked away through a porous hull surface, or through small slots. For shells, the suction might be achieved quite easily using a porous hull, allowing water to slowly leak in. A small pump would be used to occasionally pump the leaked water overboard. The added weight and complexity of such a design have never been shown to be advantageous.

The texture of the wetted surface of the hull can also play a role in reduction of skin-friction drag. Investigations under the auspices of the National Aeronautics and Space Administration have shown that a slick, waxed surface is not always best. Surfaces with very fine grooves running in the flow direction, called 'riblets,' have already shown drag reductions of 6% compared with smooth surfaces. Riblets have been tested on rowed shells by a group from the Flight Research Institute led by Doug McLean, an aeronautical engineer at Boeing. The group covered a single shell with an experimental plastic skin in which grooves had been formed. The spacing between the grooves was only 0.003 in. (less than 80 μm—finer than the groove spacing on phonograph records). Tests with a good rower indicated that the shell's maximum speed increased 2%. Although this may seem like an insignificant increase, it is tantamount to a four-boat-length advantage over a standard 2,000-m race. Encouraged by these initial results, the experimental skin was applied to the hull of the U.S. Olympic team men's coxed-four rowing shell. (A coxed boat is steered by a coxswain, who does not row, but calls out the rowing cadence.) The team made an excellent showing, taking a silver medal in the 1984 Summer Olympic Games; however drag-reducing hull coatings were subsequently prohibited by the La Fédération Internationale des Sociétés d'Aviron (FISA) (International Federation of Rowing).

Propulsion

Another essential ingredient in a high-performance human-powered boat is good propulsive efficiency: as much of the human's power output as possible must be converted to useful thrust. The efficiency of the propulsion system is defined as the ratio of useful power output (the product of the average thrust and velocity) to human power input.

Oars and paddles are basically drag devices; they generate their thrust by slipping backward through the water. This backward slipping represents an efficiency loss. The slip can be reduced by increasing the size of the oar blade, but only to a limited degree, due to practical constraints. The detailed physics of rowing is not entirely understood, but analysis by many researchers has placed the propulsive efficiency of rowing at between 65% and 75%. Thus, about two thirds of the rower's power output is delivered to the boat as useful work. The remainder goes into creating disturbances in the water.

Powered boats abandoned drag-device propulsion, such as paddlewheels, long ago. Instead, propellers are usually used. Propellers driven by human power have been successfully used for some time. In the 1890s, a three-rider propeller-driven catamaran was shown to be 13% faster than a triple-rowed shell over a 101-mile (163 km) course on the River Thames. During that period, human-powered propeller-driven boats were being developed for practical transportation purposes—they were much faster and less tiring than canoes or rowboats. These developments almost completely ceased when small gasoline-driven outboard motors were introduced.

A disadvantage of propellers is that they are susceptible to fouling with weeds and are subject to hitting the bottom in shallow water. Otherwise, propellers are especially suited for human-powered applications; the power level is quite low, which allows slender, high-efficiency propeller designs to be used. In addition, speeds are low enough that cavitation is not a problem. Cavitation, the formation of bubbles of water vapor, occurs when the absolute pressure on some part of the rotating propeller is reduced to below water's vapor pressure. Cavitation reduces efficiency and can cause excessive wear on blade surfaces. Propellers with efficiencies exceeding 90% are currently in use on several new human-powered watercraft. These are typically long, slender two-bladed propellers that are carefully designed for specific conditions.

Reducing Drag

Human-powered watercraft designers have attempted to minimize drag in novel ways. Theodore Schmidt, a Swiss engineer, experimented with a boat incorporating a submerged-buoyancy hull. This attempted to eliminate wave drag and greatly reduce wetted surface area, as compared with a rowing shell. The surface area of a shell is large because length and slenderness are required to reduce wave drag. Shorter, stouter hull shapes have less wetted area for a given buoyancy, but greatly increased wave drag. However, wave drag can be nearly eliminated by submerging the hull, with narrow struts extending upward to support the operator. In this case, the hull shape with minimum drag has a length of about three to four times its width.

With only one hull underwater supporting the rider, the configuration is like a unicycle—balancing would be difficult, if not impossible. Schmidt addressed this problem with limited success by stabilizing his single submerged-buoyancy hull with four small outrigger hydrofoils. A tricycle arrangement of three smaller submerged-buoyancy hulls could be used to provide stability, but would not be as efficient, because the surface area-to-displacement ratio gets smaller as displacement increases, and one big hull has less wetted surface area than three smaller hulls with the same combined buoyancy.

The balancing problem of a single underwater hull could be eliminated by placing the operator in the hull, in effect creating a submarine, but a streamlined hull big enough to carry a person displaces much more water and has more surface area than a hull that simply provides enough buoyancy to carry a person's weight. Although not optimum for human-powered transport near the surface of the water, the human-powered submarine can be a great improvement over a diver with swim fins.

Designs that employ dynamic lift to raise part of the boat out of the water can significantly reduce wetted surface area and the associated skin-friction drag. Although dynamic lift does exact a drag penalty, in many instances the reduction in skin-friction drag more than compensates for the drag produced by lift.

A common example of dynamic lift is planing: The bottom of the hull continuously deflects water downward, which produces lift as a reaction force. When a hull is planing, less buoyancy is required and the hull rides higher in the water, often right at the surface. Human-powered water vehicles that plane exist only in the imaginations of designers, although the concept is promising.

Hydrofoils

Dynamic lift can also be generated with hydrofoils. Hydrofoils are underwater wings that produce lift in the same way as airplane wings. The required size of a hydrofoil wing is quite modest. For example, at 9 knots, less than 0.1 m^2 (1 ft^2) of foil area is needed to produce enough lift to support a single rider above the water. A hydrofoil designed to produce the same lift at 18 knots would require only a quarter as much area. The small wetted area of hydrofoil wings results in minimal skin-friction drag. Hydrofoils, like airplane wings, incur drag, called *induced drag*, due to creation of lift. As the hydrofoil generates lift, it leaves behind a vortex wake, just as airplanes do. The energy needed to generate the vortex wake is manifested as induced drag.

PROPELLER DESIGN

by
Theodore Schmidt

Propeller design is complicated, and what is presented here is only an overview. Many variables influence each other: diameter, chord, pitch, planform, blade profile, and boat speed. Working with these variables is best done on a computer.

DIAMETER

The maximum efficiency obtainable by a perfect propulsor at a certain operating point is called the Froude efficiency. It tends toward 100% for large diameters, high vehicle speeds, and low operating loads. Propellers used at low speeds and high loads (e.g., for towing) benefit from large diameter as much as can be tolerated by the strength of the material used for construction and by operating limitations, such as shallow water depth. At high speeds a large-diameter propeller becomes inefficient because the increase in blade surface drag outweighs the high Froude efficiency, which may already be more than 99%. Many human-powered water propellers achieve their best total efficiency at a Froude efficiency of about 98%, corresponding to a 2% slip. Designing for this value at the desired boat speed will specify a good diameter to use. The diameters of today's highly efficient, two-bladed propellers for human-powered watercraft typically range between 30 and 45 cm.

CHORD

The chord, or blade width, and the number of blades must be chosen such that the blades operate at a sensible angle of attack. Many narrow blades may have less induced drag than a few wide ones, but wide blades operate at higher Reynolds numbers, and hence lower section drag, so the choice of blade number is not straightforward. (Reynolds number is a measure of the ratio of inertial forces to viscous forces.) Human-powered propellers are relatively lightly loaded and are usually two-bladed for practical reasons.

PITCH

A propeller can be thought of as a twisted wing, with the wing pitched, or angled, against the water (or air). Any good lifting surface propels most efficiently at an angle of about 45° to the direction of vehicle motion. Propellers with a very coarse pitch never reach this angle, whereas those with fine pitch have the 45° segments too near the hub to be of much use, as the outer portions of the blade do the most work. Fine-pitched propellers never stall and are good for conditions of low speeds and high loads, whereas coarse-pitched propellers may be nearly useless, but the latter have less drag and are efficient at high speeds. Good all-around practical propellers have pitch-to-diameter ratios of between 1:1 and 1.5:1 and high-speed racing propellers, up to about 2:1.

PLANFORM

The optimal planform, or chord distribution, is chosen such that the wash velocity through the propeller disc is as uniform as possible, that is, that the slip values of all blade segments are similar. This yields minimum induced drag; algorithms developed by Gene Larrabee and others to determine the optimal planform for a given operating point should be used if a racing propeller is to be optimized. The optimum planform can be approximated by a rule of thumb: make the widest part of the blade about where the 45°-angle condition is met and taper off gently toward the tip and hub, leaving the relatively unimportant hub segments wide enough for strength. This applies to high-aspect-ratio blades. Highly loaded low-aspect-ratio blades used in motor boats may be round or have skewed-back shapes designed to shed weeds or reduce vibration or cavitation.

BLADE PROFILE

The cross-sectional shape of the blade may be nearly any slightly cambered foil section. Highly cambered sharp-nosed sections should not be used on high-aspect-ratio blades.

BOAT SPEED

At low speeds the typical modern human-powered racing-boat propeller can produce only a little power before efficiency drops severely. At high speeds maximum efficiency is developed at high power levels. A propeller of fixed size and pitch is well adapted to those conditions and speeds for which it was designed, whereas for other conditions, such as accelerating or towing, variable pitch is helpful. Further technical discussions of the theory and design of propellers can be found in the following references:

REFERENCES

Larrabee, E. (1984). Propellers for human-powered vehicles. *Human Power*, **3**(2), 10.

Poole, P.K. (1991). A propeller design process for human-powered marine vehicles. *Human Power*, **9**(1), 6-16.

Schmidt, T. (1990). Propeller design. *Human Power*, **7**(2), 6–7.

A problem with human-powered hydrofoils is the need to reach the high speeds required for *take-off* (the point at which the hydrofoil wings generate enough lift to support the weight of the craft). Because hydrofoils produce zero lift at zero speed, another support system, such as a displacement hull, is required for the initial and final phases of a "flight." A wing sized for all-out speed may have to be moving through the water at 10 knots before it can generate enough lift to support the craft and rider; however, this speed may well be difficult to achieve while the craft is still supported by its displacement hull. A larger hydrofoil wing could reduce the takeoff speed, but the drag caused by the increased surface area would not allow the craft to go as fast.

Until the 1980s, all human-powered water speed records were held by displacement boats propelled by oars. With the goal of exceeding these speeds, two of the authors (Brooks and Abbott) in 1984 designed and built the *Flying Fish I*, the first hydrofoil capable of sustained flight on human power alone (Brooks, 1984). The sticky problem of initially getting the craft up to takeoff speed, which had plagued previous designers, was bypassed at first by eliminating the hull altogether. Flying speed was attained by catapult launching from a floating ramp, in a manner somewhat similar to that employed to launch jets from aircraft carriers. Using this launch method, Steve Hegg, an Olympic cycling gold medalist, pedaled the *Flying Fish I* in 1985 to a flying-start time of 6 min, 38 s over a 2,000-m course, eclipsing by 11 s the world record for a single sculler. The times, however, are not directly comparable, because the rowing record was set from a standing start.

The *Flying Fish I* achieves high efficiency by using long, slender wings supported by narrow vertical struts, and a high-efficiency, pedal-driven propeller. The main wing, which carries 90% of the weight, has large span (1.8 m) to minimize induced drag and a small chord to reduce wetted area and, hence, skin-friction drag. The smaller front wing is lightly loaded; its main purpose is to provide stability and control. It has an inverted-T configu-

ration, with active depth control. A small surface-follower (a spatulalike device) skates over the water surface and controls the depth by activating a small flap, like the elevator control on an airplane tail, on the front wing. The front wing strut doubles as a rudder and is connected to bicycle handlebars for steering. The craft is ridden very much as one would ride a racing bicycle, and the structure normally above the water is a modified bicycle frame.

The *Flying Fish II* (see Figure 4.3) was developed as a refinement of the first version, with lightweight catamaran floats added in the hope that takeoff could be made unassisted from standstill. This proved to be possible, and with practice, acceleration from standing start to fully foil-borne took only 3 s. Practicality also improved immensely, because the craft could "land" as well as take off—the catapult-launched *Flying Fish I* gave the rider a dunking whenever pedaling stopped.

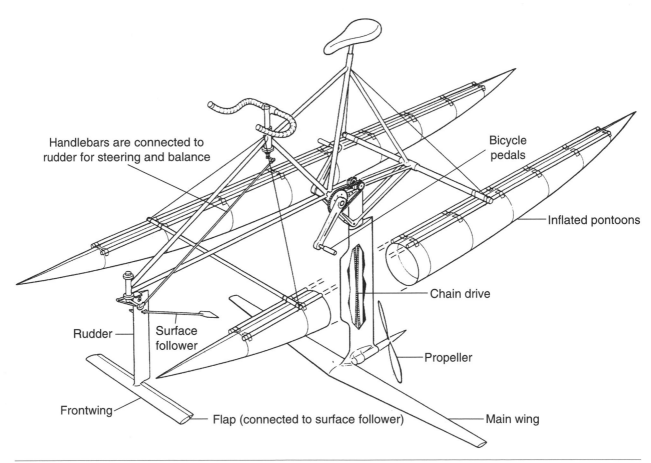

FIGURE 4.3 *Flying Fish II* is a human-powered hydrofoil designed and built by Brooks and Abbott. It is ridden and balanced like a bicycle. The craft, powered by a pedal-driven, high-efficiency propeller, takes off (the pontoons are lifted clear of the water) at 6 knots, and has a top speed of nearly 18 knots. The inflated pontoons support the craft at a standstill and at low speeds. This craft has completed a 2,000-m course approximately 1 min faster than a rowing shell.

From Human Powered Water Vehicles by Brooks, A., Abbott, A.V., & Wilson, D.G., 1986, *Scientific American*, **225**(6), 120–130. Reprinted by permission.

Aboard the *Flying Fish II*, Steve Hegg set a record time of 5 min 48 s over a 2,000-m course from a standing start, about 1 min faster than the single-rowing-shell record. In 1992, David Woronets, a champion cycling sprinter, raced the *Flying Fish 20* (a refinement of version II) through a flying-start 100-m course in 10.83 s, averaging a speed of 17.95 knots.

Several other hydrofoil designs have emerged in recent years. The highly successful *Hydro-ped* hydrofoil, designed by Sid Shutt in California, uses a semirecumbent rider position and a shaft-driven propeller (see Figure 4.4). The single hull permits good speed in the displacement mode and low-power takeoffs. Steering is via the forward vertical strut, which supports the front inverted-T foil. Shutt invented a forward surface-following skimmer, which directly controls the angle of attack of the front T-foil, thus controlling the depth of the foils while flying. The curved surface-piercing main hydrofoil provides roll stability and allows a variable hydrofoil area for efficiency at different speeds—a larger wing area at lower speeds and a smaller wing area for higher speeds (Shutt, 1989).

In the late 1980s, Parker MacCready developed a series of hydrofoil boats with flapping-wing propulsion (see Figure 4.5). This 45-lb version, the *Preposterous Pogo Foil*, is powered by bouncing up and down as on a pogo stick. The flapping of the main hydrofoil creates both forward propulsion and lift, like a bird's flapping wings. The foil angle is controlled by the pilot through a combination of springs and brake levers. The handlebars steer the front rudder, which supports the front foil that maintains depth (MacCready, 1990).

The fastest human-powered watercraft speed over a 100-m course was established by the *Decavitator*, pedaled by its designer, Mark Drela, from the Massachusetts Institute of Technology (Drela, Schafer, & Wall, 1991–1992). The *Decavitator* human-powered hydrofoil was designed specifically for reaching the fastest possible speed over short distances. It is propelled by a 3-m air propeller, connected via chain to bicyclelike foot crank (see

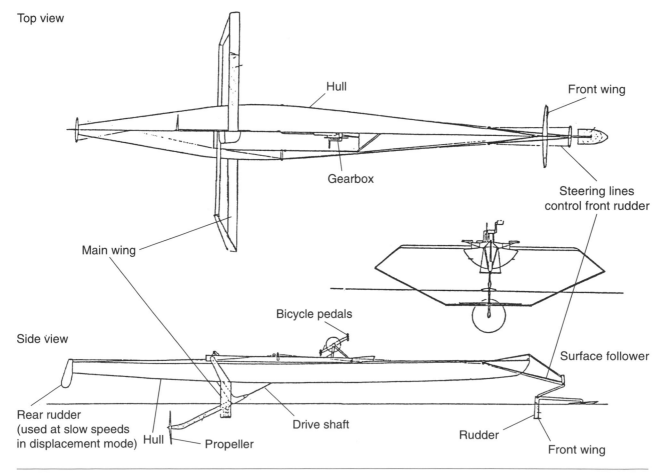

FIGURE 4.4 This hydrofoil, the *Hydro-ped*, is based on an efficient kayak hull for good low-speed performance. The upswept hydrofoil provided roll stability (drawing by Sid Shutt).

Figure 4.6). The air propeller eliminated the need for a wide underwater strut enclosing a chain or shaft drive system, thus reducing water drag. At low speeds the craft is supported by two 5.2-m displacement pontoons. When flying, the craft is steered via the vertical struts, which support inverted-T foils at the front of each pontoon. A surface-following skimmer on each front foil directly controls the foil's angle of attack, thus controlling the depth of the foils and providing roll stability. Two underwater hydrofoil wings, positioned directly under the rider, are used to take off at speeds of 9 to 10 knots. The larger of these wings is piv-

oted out of the water for highest speeds. In the fastest one-wing mode, the craft set an official speed record of 18.50 knots over a 100-m course in October 1991.

A technological revolution in human-powered recreational watercraft has begun. In the 1980s, the Laser company introduced the *Mallard*, a propeller-driven, semienclosed seaworthy "fun" boat designed by Garry Hoyt. Several new pedaled catamarans and proas (one main hull, with a smaller stabilizing outrigger) offer rough-water seaworthiness and impressive speed. Jon Knapp, of Saber Craft, manufactures a propeller-driven proa that is

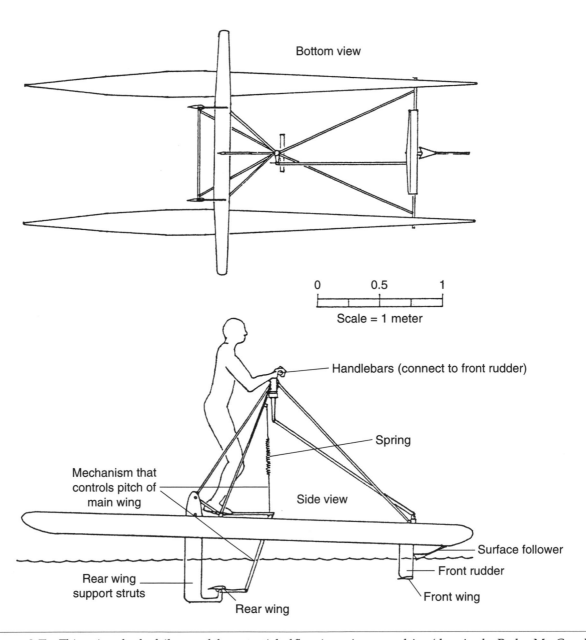

FIGURE 4.5   This unique hydrofoil proved the potential of flapping-wing propulsion (drawing by Parker MacCready).

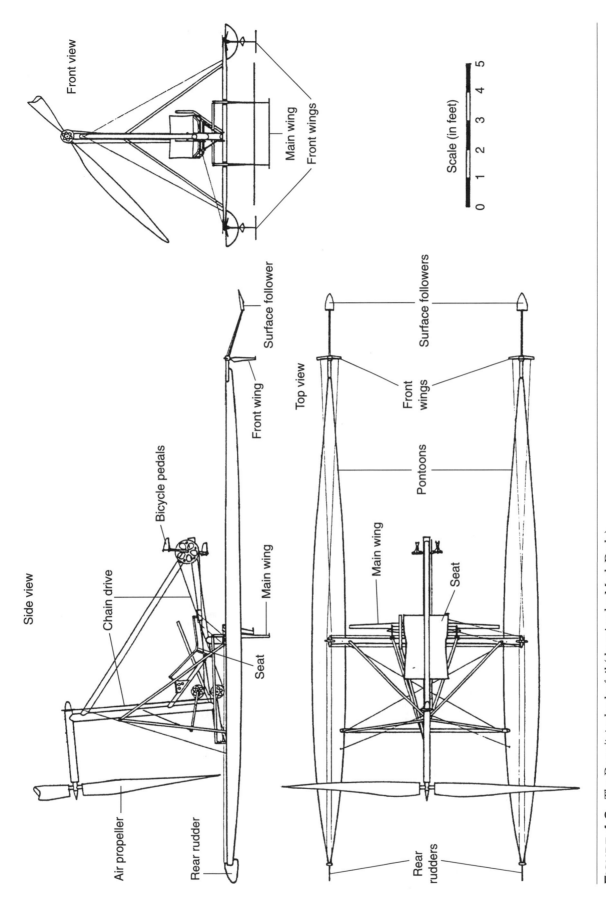

FIGURE 4.6 The *Decavitator* hydrofoil (drawing by Mark Drela).

faster than a shell in rough water, but unlike a shell, requires no special skills to operate. The *Dorycycle* (see Figure 4.7), a propeller-driven monohull craft designed by Philip Thiel, a Seattle-area naval architect, provides good seaworthiness and load-carrying capacity at speeds double that of the rowed dory from which it was derived. Thiel has also built a small propeller-driven, live-aboard canal boat for cruising the canals of France (Thiel, 1991).

Steve Ball, from San Diego, designed and built the unusual *Dragon Fly III* surface-effect craft in 1988, a catamaran design with a light rubberized canvas deck and water-contouring air-flow seals fore and aft. The cyclist's leg-cranking power is divided, about two-thirds to a 3.3-m air propeller for forward propulsion and one-third to a ducted fan, which provides pressure beneath the cushion area. This pressure lifts most of the displacement pontoons out of the water, thereby greatly decreasing the skin-friction drag of the hulls. On its first outing, this craft reached speeds of more than 11 knots (Hostetter, 1990).

Whether or not hydrofoils become popular for recreation, they have been used for the recent round of record breaking. The International Human Pow-ered Vehicle Association was formed to encourage competition of human-powered vehicles—on land, on sea, and in the air—without arbitrary design limits. Such competition has pushed the speed of human-powered hydrofoil craft toward its theoretical maximum of over 20 knots, faster than the speeds attained even by racing shells powered by eight athletic rowers. In 1989, the Du Pont company funded a $25,000 prize to be awarded by the International Human Powered Vehicle Association to the first single-person watercraft to exceed 20 knots over a 100-m course. If no vehicle had yet reached 20 knots, the Du Pont Prize was to go to the fastest vehicle at the end of 1992. In January 1993, the Du Pont Prize was awarded to the *Decavitator* for its fastest speed of 18.50 knots. The *Decavitator's* air propeller was ideally suited to take advantage of the small tailwind allowed by the Du Pont Prize rules.

Semiamphibious Craft

Most human-powered watercraft are somewhat restricted in their use because they are difficult to

FIGURE 4.7 The *Dorycycle* was designed by Philip Thiel to use low-tech components to apply pedal power and propeller propulsion to a traditional seaworthy watercraft. The *Dorycycle* weighs 1,300 N (300 lb) on a waterline length of 3.96 m (13 ft), and powered by a healthy adult travels at 4 knots in smooth water for about 1 hour (photo by Philip Thiel).

transport over land, requiring a car or train. Even inflatables or the ingenious folding canoes are too bulky to carry easily or take on a bicycle. Semiamphibious craft have been designed and built at least since 1913, when the German cyclist, Julius Bettinger, converted his bicycle for use on the water. Figure 4.8 shows that Bettinger's design attached a safety bicycle atop two catamaran pontoons. A simple reciprocating paddle mechanism was worked by the bicycle pedals. Other propeller-driven designs followed.

The Swiss designer Theodore Schmidt built several semiamphibious bicycle conversions. His *Amphiped* can be ridden on streets and to the water's edge with the disassembled water conversion attached. As shown by Figure 4.9, a simple framework supports the bicycle above the floats in such a way that the front wheel can be used to operate a front rudder via the handlebars. The front rudder works well as long as the boat's center of lateral resistance is well aft. This is achieved by using fixed rear skegs or by sitting to the rear, thus immersing more lateral area aft.

The propeller is driven by a bicycle chain, which is twisted 90° between the bicycle crank and the propeller sprocket. This drive, although somewhat noisy, is effective and compact. The *Amphiped* travels on water at 3 knots with little effort; 4 knots can be maintained, but 5 knots requires considerable effort. Several longer trips have been undertaken in the coastal waters of southern England, combining travel on water, by road, and by rail. Attempts to cycle from London to Paris with this vehicle have been foiled by bad weather.

Submarines

In 1620, Cornelius van Drebbel, a Dutch inventor, demonstrated the first known submarine, on the River Thames before King James I. This submarine was rowed, either just awash or just submerged, from Westminster to Greenwich. There was no provision for replacing oxygen for the rowers, who were in poor shape at the end of the short journey. Van Drebbel had many imitators in Europe, many of whom recognized the military potential of small submarines that might approach warships undetected and destroy them.

Two Americans, David Bushnell and Robert Fulton, are generally considered the fathers of the modern submarine. Both developed craft under the spur of war, and Bushnell's egg-shaped craft, the *Turtle*, (shown in Figure 4.10) was actually used in action in 1776. Fulton's *Nautilus* was an improved design built in 1800. Both were propelled by hand-cranked propellers and used the air trapped in the vessel to sustain the single pilot for relatively short periods of complete submersion. During the Civil War, the Confederate States built a series of hand-cranked submarines known as Davids (no doubt in comparison with the Goliaths of the Federal navy). As shown in Figure 4.11, these 15-m submarines, constructed from cylindrical steam boilers, were hand-cranked by eight men. The first sinking of a warship in action by a David occurred in 1864, when the Confederate submarine *H.L. Hunley* rammed a torpedo into the hull of the Federal *Housatonic*. The submarine apparently went down with the *Housatonic*, for the *H.L. Hunley* never returned (Kemp, 1979).

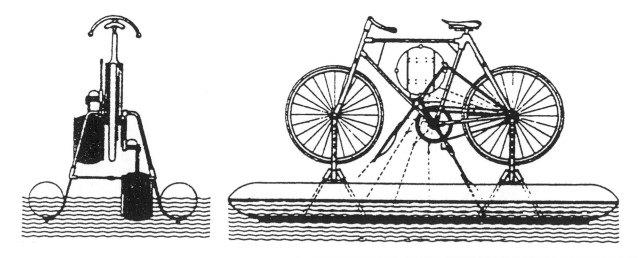

FIGURE 4.8 Semiamphibious craft have appeared occasionally since the early 1900s. Julius Bettinger, a German cyclist, attached a safety bicycle to catamaran pontoons in 1913. Power was delivered to the water through a reciprocating paddle mechanism attached to the pedals.

FIGURE 4.9 Theo Schmidt designed and built the *Amphiped*, which could be dismantled and carried aboard a conventional bicycle. At the water's edge, pontoons are inflated and a propeller drive is attached to the bicycle. The propeller is driven by the bicycle chain twisted 90°. The craft is steered by a rudder attached to the front wheel (photo by Theodore Schmidt).

Air-containing, or "dry," human-powered submarines had proven to be dangerous. No further examples of human-powered submarines are known until after scuba became available. In the early 1950s, a two-person human-powered submarine called the MiniSub (Figure 4.12), designed by Calvin A. Gongwer, was produced in small quantities by Aerojet General Corporation. The MiniSub was driven by twin 760-mm counterrotating propellers at the aft end of the hull. It reportedly could achieve a top speed of almost 6 knots with both people pedaling, about three times the speed a diver can swim underwater.

Several devices have been invented to improve a swimmer's efficiency underwater. A top speed of 5.5 knots is claimed for the Aqueon (see Figure 4.13), developed by Calvin A. Gongwer in California. The Aqueon provides thrust through a flapping hydrofoil powered by a diver's legs. Propeller-driven devices, cranked by a diver's legs, have also been developed (Levaseur, 1971).

In 1989, the H.A. Perry Foundation and the Florida Atlantic University sponsored the First International Human-Powered Submarine Race, held in Florida. Rules were somewhat stringent for the sake of safety; the required submarine was wet with two persons, a pilot and a propulsor ("stoker"), using scuba gear; the capability of rapid egress was required. Most designs used standard bicycle cranking to deliver power through a variety of drive-train and propeller mechanisms. Various leg-powered linear drive mechanisms also were tried. In the second human-powered submarine race in 1991, the entry from Florida Atlantic University (the F.A. U-Boat) reached the highest speed, 4.7 knots over 100 m from a standing start. In 1994 the F.A. U-Boat reached a speed of 5.94 knots over a 10-m course. In this craft (shown in Figure 4.14), both the pilot and propulsor face forward. The propulsor pedals a conventional bicycle crank connected to a single two-bladed propeller through a simple 3:1 gear box and shaft drive.

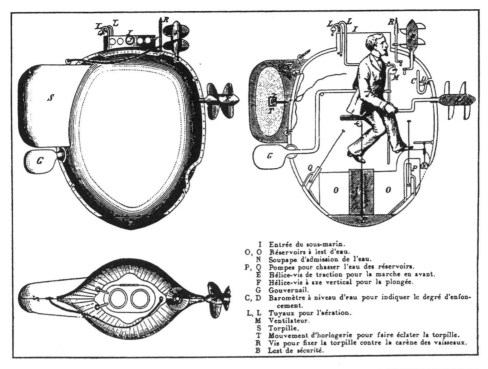

I   Entrée du sous-marin.
O, O   Réservoirs à lest d'eau.
N   Soupape d'admission de l'eau.
P, Q   Pompes pour chasser l'eau des réservoirs.
E   Hélice-vis de traction pour la marche en avant.
F   Hélice-vis à axe vertical pour la plongée.
G   Gouvernail.
C, D   Baromètre à niveau d'eau pour indiquer le degré d'enfon-
            cement.
L, L   Tuyaux pour l'aération.
M   Ventilateur.
S   Torpille.
T   Mouvement d'horlogerie pour faire éclater la torpille.
R   Vis pour fixer la torpille contre la carène des vaisseaux.
B   Lest de sécurité.

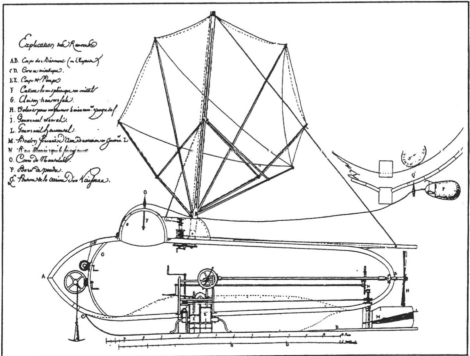

FIGURE 4.10 An American, Bushnell, built the *Turtle* submarine (top) in 1776 in an attempt to break the stranglehold of British seapower. Water ballast submerged the craft until it was just awash. It was moved forward with the horizontal screw. When near a warship at anchor, the craft was fully submerged using the vertical screw and was maneuvered beneath British warships in several unsuccessful attempts to attach time-delayed explosive charges to their hulls. The lower illustration shows Fulton's submarine, the *Nautilus*.

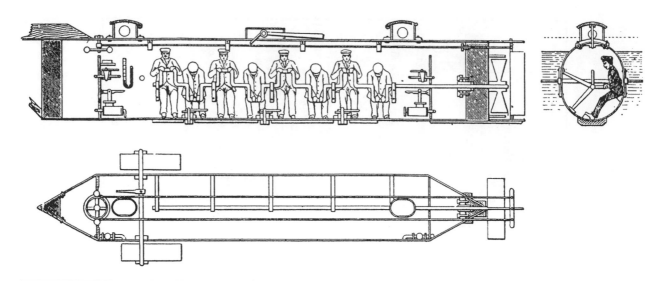

FIGURE 4.11 The human-powered submarine *H.L. Hunley* sank the Federal *Housatonic* in 1864 during the Civil War. Eight men cranked the propeller while a ninth operated fore and aft fins and ballast tanks to provide steering and depth control.

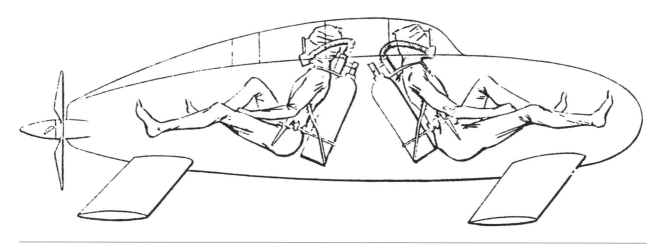

FIGURE 4.12 The two people in this 1950s wet submarine MiniSub used scuba gear and pedaled bicycle cranks that turned twin counterrotating propellers. It reportedly could achieve a top speed of almost 6 knots with both people pedaling.

References

Brooks, A. (1984). The *Flying Fish* hydrofoil. *Human Power*, **3**(2), 7–8.

Drela, M., Schafer, M., & Wall, M. (1991–1992). *Decavitator* human-power hydrofoil. *Human Power*, **9**(3, 4), 3–9.

Hostetter, D. (1990). *Dragonfly III. Human Power*, **8**(4), 5–6.

Kemp, P. (1979). *The history of ships*. New York: Galahad Books.

Levaseur, C. (1971). Diver's bike. *Official Gazette*, 884, U.S. Patent No. 3570436.

MacCready, P. (1990). Hydrofoil boats with flapping-wing propulsion. *Human Power*, **8**(1), 9–16.

Schmidt, T. (1988). Propeller design. *Human Power*, **7**(2), 6–7.

Shutt, S. (1989). Some ideas used on *Hydro-ped*: A hydrofoil pedal boat. *Human Power*, **7**(4), 5–7.

Thiel, P. (1984). The *Dorycycle*: Pedal power and screw propulsion in a traditional watercraft. *Human Power*, **3**(2), 4–5.

Theil, P. (1991). Pedal-power on the French canals. *Human Power*, **9**(1), 4.

FIGURE 4.13 The Aqueon provides thrust through a flapping hydrofoil powered by the diver's legs (photo by Calvin A. Gongwer).

FIGURE 4.14 This two-person wet submarine reached the highest speed of 5.94 knots over 10 m in 1994. This sub carries two forward-facing people using scuba gear; one pedals and the other controls the craft (photo by Alan Friedberg, Florida Atlantic University).

5

ROWING SHELLS

Edward S. Van Dusen

Both professional and interscholastic rowing became very popular during the end of the 19th century. This continued during the 20th century, when
the numbers and types of rowing craft proliferated.
Rowing shells can be differentiated according to
whether the crew use one oar, called a sweep, or
two oars, called sculls. Shells can also be differentiated according to the number of rowers in the crew,
and whether or not a nonrowing coxswain is required to steer the boat and to coordinate the efforts of the crew. In boats without coxswains, the
crew must steer by looking over their shoulders.

Although shells rowed by six rowers were once
popular for collegiate competitions, the current
Olympic fleet includes only single, double, and
quadruple sculling boats rowed without coxswains,
pair and four-oared sweep boats rowed without
coxswains, and pair, four-oared, and eight-oared
sweep boats rowed with coxswains. The dimensions
of Olympic shells and oars are shown in Table 5.1

Except for regulations stipulating the type of boat
and number of oarsmen required for a particular
race, until very recently there were only two rules
governing the use of rowing equipment in international competitions. The first rule requires that oars
pivot in oarlocks, rather than swinging freely like
paddles; the second rule requires that a white ball
40 mm in diameter be mounted on the bow of the
boat to minimize injuries during collisions and to
provide a reference point for judges during the start
and finish of a race.

The Fédération Internationale des Sociétés
d'Aviron (FISA) was formed to foster fair competition in rowing around the world. Prompted by fears
that modern technology would confer an unfair
advantage on more industrialized nations and that
the character of the sport might change from its
time-honored traditions, FISA drafted several new
regulations during the 1970s and 1980s. These
specify minimum weights for boats (based on the
lightest weights for wooden rowing shells), require
the use of fixed oarlocks to exclude the use of sliding-rigger boats, and prohibit the use of drag-reducing hull coatings. Outside the scope of FISA
regulations, the design of rowing shells and oars is
virtually unrestricted.

Modern Rowing Equipment

Despite the considerable latitude afforded by the
rules governing international rowing competitions,
the rowing shells used by different countries have
evolved to be very similar (see Figure 5.1). Modern racing shells are unusually long, slender boats.
They are fitted with a small sliding seat on wheels
that travels about 60 cm during a single rowing
stroke, and with track shoes fixed to an adjustable
footboard inclined about 40° from the horizontal.
The oars used to propel racing shells pivot in oarlocks mounted outside the boat. Forward motion

Table 5.1 TYPICAL DIMENSIONS OF RACING SHELLS AND OARS

RACING SHELLS

	1×	2×, 2–	2+	4×, 4–	4+	8+
Overall length (in m)	8.1	9.4	10.5	11.9	12.5	17.6
Waterline (WL) length (in m)	7.7	9.3	10.3	11.6	21.1	17.0
Waterline beam (in cm)	29.0	35.0	42.0	43.0	51.0	58.0
Draft (in cm)	11.0	14.0	13.0	17.0	17.0	18.0
Displacement (in kg)	110.0	200.0	270.0	400.0	455.0	860.0
Minimum weight (in kg)	14.0	26.5	32.0	50.0	51.0	93.0
Wetted surface (in m^2)	2.2	3.3	4.5	5.5	6.2	9.4
Metacenter above WL (in cm)	2.0	3.0	7.0	7.0	8.0	11.0
Seat above WL (in cm)	11.0	11.0	11.0	11.0	11.0	11.0
Scull length (in cm)	298.0	300.0		300.0		
Sweep length (in cm)		384.0	384.0	386.0	386.0	386.0

OARS

	Length	Width	Tip width	Area	Camber[a]	Angle[b]
Scull blade (in cm)	50.0	17.0	14.0	691.0	3.8	5.0
Sweep blade (in cm)	60.0	20.5	18.0	1,006.0	4.0	5.3

Note. The abbreviations 1×, 2×, and 4× indicate single, double, and quadruple sculls, respectively. The abbreviations 2–, 2+ indicate a pair, and the abbreviations 4+ and 8+ indicate a four-oared shell and an eight-oared shell respectively. A + indicates the presence of a coxswain; a – indicates the absence of one.

[a]The camber of an oar is the maximum distance from the pressure face of the blade to a straight line from the blade, where it meets the shaft, to the tip.

[b]The angle of an oar is the angle between the blade camber line and the shaft center line.

in rowing occurs as the oarblades are placed in the water and the boat is drawn past them. Smooth, powerful rowing requires excellent skill, balance, timing, and a lot of practice. The light, slender rowing shell responds to the slightest movement of the rower in ways that can slow the boat down. Crews not perfectly synchronized can waste considerable energy moving each other instead of moving the boat.

A typical rowing stroke consists of the catch, the drive, the release, and the recovery. At the start of the catch, the rower leans forward with knees flexed, arms extended toward the stern of the boat, and the oar shaft rotated about 50° fore of athwartships (the horizontal direction perpendicular to the boat's longitudinal axis or keel). At the catch, the vertical oar blade is dropped into the water. The drive begins only after the blade is buried in the water, to prevent slippage caused by air pulled down with the blade. During the drive the rower first extends the legs and back, and then flexes the arms to pull the boat past the oars. At the end of the drive the rower is leaning backward with hands and oar handles at the sides and the oar shaft rotated 40° aft of athwartships. The release occurs at the end of the drive when the oar blade is lifted vertically just above the water and feathered by tilting it 6° to 8° from the horizontal to reduce wind resistance. During the recovery, the sequence of legs, back, and arms used during the drive is reversed; the arms are extended, the back and legs are flexed, the oar blades are returned to a vertical position, and the rower is ready for the next catch.

The goal of rigging a boat is to adjust the relative position between the water, footboard, seat, and oarlocks to allow a particular athlete to row

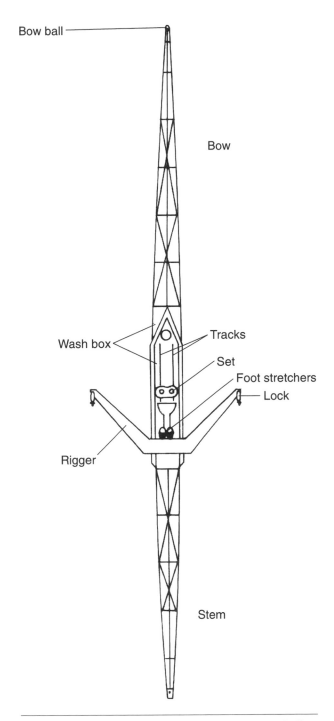

Bow ball

Bow

Wash box

Tracks

Set

Foot stretchers

Lock

Rigger

Stem

FIGURE 5.1 The design of a modern rowing shell.

surements and a rigid hull and riggers are important for correct adjustment.

Although racing shells are specialized to race on protected water, it is not uncommon for them to encounter wind and small waves. Rowers in shells rigged for maximum speed have trouble lifting their oars more than 30 cm above the water, so when the wave height exceeds 30 cm the oars will slap the waves on the recovery, making it difficult to balance the boat and to maintain a racing stroke rate. Because rowing shells generally span several waves, they slice through them smoothly under most conditions. Many shells are completely decked and fitted with small self-bailing cockpits so that they can safely survive conditions far worse than their skilled pilots would care to endure. Because running major rowing competitions involves a considerable amount of work for the organizers, and often a considerable amount of travel for the competitors, most rowing races are run on schedule, except when conditions are dangerous. The equipment and athletes must be ready to compete in all conditions likely to be encountered on a small lake or river.

Factors Influencing Rowing Shell Design

The physical challenge in rowing consists of maximizing useful human propulsion over the race distance, minimizing wasteful motion that may disturb water flow past the boat, and balancing a highly unstable craft. In stable boats, buoyancy and weight forces combine to cause a righting torque as the boat rolls. Rowing shells are highly unstable, however, and they can capsize if not actively balanced by the rowers. The constant series of adjustments required is much like trying to balance a pendulum upside down on your hand. The balancing feat requires great skill, and its difficulty is increased by the action of wind and waves.

Until very recently, rowing shells were designed empirically by craftsmen who understood rowing and were skilled in woodworking. Each new boat could incorporate innovations to be evaluated by trial and error according to success on the race course and feedback from the coach and crew. Considering the long history of rowing competition, the paucity of good scientific data on rowing shell performance is surprising. One reason for this lack of data is the difficulty of reconciling the goal of preparing a top athlete for competition with the development of reasonable scientific protocols for taking repeated measurements under controlled conditions. The interactions between the performance of

comfortably in a strong position, with minimal energy required to control the movement of the oars. The more relaxed the rower, the greater the percentage of energy available for propelling the boat. Discrepancies as small as 0.5° between the blade angles of the right and left oars can cause one oar to submerge more deeply than the other, pulling that side of the boat down and making the rower less effective. Discrepancies of several degrees are sufficient to capsize the boat. Precise meathe equipment and the skilled tasks performed by the athlete are so complex that it is nearly impossible to optimize one parameter without affecting several others. Moreover, the level of skill required by the athlete is so high that even small changes can require adjustment and additional training time before they become natural. By the time the required adjustments in style have been made, the athlete may have reached a different level of conditioning or changed training regimen. Some coaches have had considerable success based on their intuition, but intuitions are notoriously difficult to distill into information pertinent to engineers trying to design better equipment.

The task of improving rowing shell performance can be divided into two areas of research. The first is the study of methods for increasing propulsive power. For example, one method of increasing power is the development of an improved oar and rigger configuration that would permit the rower to develop more thrust by better matching the ability of the system to accept power at the force and velocity most efficient for the rower to produce. The second area of research is the study of methods for reducing energy losses in the system. For example, energy losses can result from the mechanical friction of the sliding seat or from aerodynamic or hydrodynamic drag.

The study of methods for increasing propulsive power is complicated, and is best analyzed using a computer-based dynamic model of the entire equipment-athlete system. Such a model is currently being developed at the Massachusetts Institute of Technology's Department of Ocean Engineering, but it will be some time before all the different subsystems are sufficiently well understood that confident predictions can be made. Therefore, this chapter will focus on methods for reducing energy losses in the existing propulsion system.

Resistance Encountered By Rowing Shells

The power generated by a rower is used to overcome the resistance of moving the boat through water and air once the boat is accelerated to racing speed. Wave drag, skin-friction drag, and air drag were introduced in chapter 4. Aerodynamic drag and hydrodynamic drag will be considered here.

Aerodynamic Drag

In still air at racing speed, the aerodynamic drag on a rower and shell is about 12% of the total drag;

hydrodynamic drag accounts for the remaining 88% of the total drag. I estimate that the aerodynamic drag on a typical single rowing shell traveling at 4.5 m/s is about 8 N; I have measured the hydrodynamic resistance on the same shell at 67 N.

Since aerodynamic drag increases at the rate of the velocity squared, it becomes significant even in only moderate head winds. It is surprising, therefore, that little has been done to reduce the aerodynamic drag on rowing shells. The total aerodynamic drag on racing shells can be broken down as follows: 5% drag on the hull, 8% drag on the riggers, 20% drag on the oars, and 67% drag on the rowers.

Aerodynamic drag on racing shells can be reduced when the standard round outrigger tubes supporting the oarlocks are replaced with streamlined aerofoil shapes. In 1986, a grant from the United States Olympic Committee (USOC) enabled us to develop a streamlined wing rigger that should improve speed by about 5 m over a 2,000-m race course.

Although most of the aerodynamic drag on rowing shells is accounted for by the rowers, the placement of fairings around the athletes probably is not feasible, because fairing would interfere with body heat transfer in this high-powered sport, and because fairings large enough to accommodate the required range of motion would adversely affect balance in crosswinds. Smooth, close-fitting clothing like the rubberized "skin suits" used in cycling and speed skating should confer a measurable advantage.

Hydrodynamic Drag

Hydrodynamic resistance is the most significant source of drag on displacement hulls, such as rowing shells. The total hydrodynamic drag on a rowing shell consists of approximately 92% frictional drag and 8% pressure drag.

Frictional drag (or viscous drag) is the force produced tangential to the surface of the hull by the viscosity of the water flowing past its surface. The water adjacent to the hull is called boundary layer, and the water touching the hull adheres to the surface of the hull no matter how slick its surface. A progressive shearing action takes place in the fluid until, at some distance from the hull, there is no detectable change in water velocity caused by hull movement.

Fluid traveling with the hull surface is considered to be in the boundary layer until it reaches speeds less than 1% of hull speed. The boundary layer is very thin at the bow of a rowing shell and reaches perhaps 50 mm at the stern. Because the velocity gradient across the boundary layer is much greater where the layer is thin, it follows that the viscous forces per unit area are much higher at the bow than at the stern. The total of the tangential forces summed over the entire surface of the hull is called viscous, or frictional, drag. Near the bow, flow in the boundary layer, parallel to the hull surface, is called laminar flow. At racing speed, the flow becomes unstable and breaks up into many small eddies, called turbulent flow, about 1 m back from the bow. Laminar flow, or flow parallel to the hull, is desirable because it has about half the drag of turbulent flow at any given place on the hull. A smooth surface and fluid pressure decreasing in the direction of the flow prolong laminar flow; a rough surface and an adverse pressure gradient hasten the transition from laminar to turbulent flow.

Pressure drag acts normal, or perpendicular, to the surface of the hull and results from the change in fluid pressure that occurs as the hull displaces the water in its path. Where the local surface of the hull is inclined to the direction of motion, a component of the pressure force acts in the direction of motion. When these components are summed over the entire hull, the result is pressure drag. The main manifestation of pressure drag is the surface wave pattern created by the moving boat. The force required to maintain these waves is called *wave drag*. Another form of pressure drag often occurs with blunt-shaped boats when the flow outside the boundary layer cannot follow the hull contours and this flow separates from the hull, leaving a large, turbulent wake. This type of drag is called *separation drag*, and it is a different phenomenon from the turbulent boundary layer previously described. Separation drag is likely to affect slender racing shells only when they are turning.

Even though hydrodynamic drag is the best-studied area of shell design, it is far from completely understood. One reason for this is the complicated motion of rowing. Because the rower weighs approximately six times more than the boat and travels back and forth on a sliding seat, the boat moves several times farther than the rower relative to the center of mass. As a result, the boat travels approximately 20% faster or slower than its average speed at different parts of the stroke. Since drag increases nonlinearly with speed, these variations always cause an increase in drag, relative to the amount of drag at the average speed. The skilled athlete seeks to adjust rowing style to minimize these speed variations. Measurements of rowing shells have shown that the shell travels slowest when the oars are about one-third of the way through the stroke. At this point, the boat is being pushed backward by pressure on the footboard, even though the center of mass is being accelerated. The boat travels fastest during the run, when it is coasting and the rower is in the recovery phase of the stroke, pulling the boat forward with the legs and getting into position for the next stroke.

Froude's Hypothesis of Drag

In 1868 William Froude postulated that the viscous drag on a ship's hull is similar to the drag on a flat plate with the same surface area and length as the hull and towed at the same speed. The pressure drag on the ship could be determined by subtracting the amount of viscous drag from the total drag. This formula is the basis of modern naval architecture, and it is a powerful tool, because it provides a method for predicting the performance of full-sized ships based on model tests. Unfortunately, viscous drag and pressure drag scale from models to full size by different similarity laws. Viscous drag scales by Reynolds number, $LV \div v$, where L is waterline length, V is the ship's velocity, and v is the kinematic viscosity. Pressure drag scales by Froude's number, which is $V \div Lg$, where V is the ship's velocity, L is the waterline length, and g the gravitational acceleration. The boundary layers on the model and the ship will be similar when the Reynolds numbers for the model and ship are equal; the wave pattern will be identified when the Froude's numbers for the model and ship are equal. In general, both these conditions cannot be met simultaneously, so model tests are scaled by Froude's number and the viscous effects determined by calculation. Scaling from the model to the ship is accomplished by scaling the pressure drag directly by the ratio of displacements and calculating a new viscous drag from known flat-plate tests. The interactions between the boundary layer and the pressure distribution around the hull are sufficiently strong that this method produces unacceptably large errors for racing shells, particularly because fractions of a second can make a big difference in Olympic competition. Hence, valid towing-tank studies of rowing shells must be run using full-sized hulls.

When a hull moves through water, a wave crest appears near the bow, followed by a series of troughs and crests. As the speed of the hull increases, the waves become longer and the second wave moves aft. Wave drag increases as the second wave approaches the stern. For many vessels, considerable power is required to accelerate beyond the speed the boat is traveling when the second wave reaches the stern (hull speed). Because hull speed increases with the square root of the waterline length, a long hull travels faster than a shorter one. If a hull is sufficiently slender, wave drag can be reduced to the point where only minimal energy is required to push the boat above hull speed. Racing shells are so slender that they are able to travel up to twice hull speed. When the length of the hull is increased, surface area and viscous drag are also increased. The minimum total drag for a rowing shell is achieved when the viscous drag exceeds 90% of the total hydrodynamic resistance.

Although the goal of rowing shell design is to find the hull form that minimizes the combined total of all drag components, there are several reasons why it is useful to know the breakdown of total hydrodynamic drag into its viscous- and wave-drag components. First, this information makes it possible to solve for the length and slenderness required for minimum total drag at a given speed and displacement; second, this knowledge makes it possible to determine the effect of shallow water on performance. Shallow-water effects become significant when the water depth is less than one-half of the wavelength. When shallow water is encountered, a series of waves of a given wavelength travel more slowly. A boat traveling in moderately shallow water has a wave pattern similar to the wave pattern it would have if it were traveling in deep water at a slightly higher speed. An eight-oared shell traveling at race speed in water 3.5 m deep will encounter wave drag about four times greater than it would encounter in deeper water. In water less than 1 m deep, the wave pattern changes completely, and drag may actually decrease. For this reason, FISA requires that international rowing courses be deeper than 3 m. It also follows that eight-oared shells designed for shallow water should be longer than eight-oared shells designed for deeper water.

Returning to Froude's hypothesis, we are trying to determine wave drag by subtracting a large calculated value from the total measured resistance. If we compare a range of hull shapes, we would expect wave drag to approach zero as hull shape approached the slenderness of a flat plate. For rowing shells, wave drag approaches zero only when the frictional drag is 5% to 10% higher than the frictional drag predicted by a flat plate of the same area and length. In 1989, this finding was confirmed by wave-energy measurements performed on a single shell at the David Taylor Research Center. An alter-

native approach would be towing the boat at such low speeds that wave drag is negligible and then comparing the frictional drag of the hull with that of a flat plate (see Granville, 1974; Todd, 1966). Unfortunately, drag force is so small at these speeds that measurement noise causes considerable experimental scatter. Results seem to suggest that drag is 5% to 10% higher on a rowing shell than on a flat plate. Since the wave drag on a shell is so small, this error in viscous drag produces an error of 100% in determining the wave drag.

The measured change in viscous drag is likely to result from a number of factors. The actual hull surface area increases 2% to 3% at racing speed as the waves move around the hull and the hull settles slightly in the water. The surface area of the hull is not rectangular like a flat plate, so some streamlines flowing along the surface are considerably shorter than the overall length. The surface near these shorter streamlines has a lower Reynolds number and a higher drag coefficient. The cross sections of a rowing shell are nearly semicircular, and transverse curvature increases the drag coefficient. This is apparent when one considers that the arc at the outside of the boundary layer is longer than the corresponding surface of the hull, so the momentum exchanged with the outer flow is concentrated over the smaller arc against the hull surface (Saunders, 1972). Finally, the air/water surface encourages the transition to turbulent flow, so it is likely that nearly all of the boundary layer around a shell is turbulent, because the shell's draft is so small.

At first glance, full-scale towing-tank resistance tests would seem to be a simple method for understanding racing shell performance, but these tests are not altogether straightforward. In general, towing-tank tests involve many considerations in addition to straight-ahead upright resistance in smooth water over a narrow speed range. Some of these are propeller interactions, heel, leeway, and seakeeping. Accuracy rates within a few percentage points are often adequate enough to ensure that the vessel will perform as intended. The difference in speed between the best and the worst racing shell entered in a major competition is probably about 3%. Resistance tests accurate to a fraction of a percentage point require extra care at every step of testing to yield meaningful results. The flexibility of long, slender rowing shells is a consideration in towing-tank tests, since the ballast used in the shells may deform them to a shape different from the one determined when the shell was out of water.

Results of Recent Resistance Tests

Although an excellent test of 3 eight-oared shells was performed by J.F. Wellicombe in 1967, so few racing shells have been tested that designers must study tests of higher-displacement ship forms for clues about the effect of variations in hull shape. The most complete of these studies was conducted by Taylor (1943), using 7-m models based on the British cruiser *Leviathan*, which had very low resistance over a wide speed range. In Taylor's test, hull shape was geometrically varied through an extensive range of characteristics.

In 1986, the USOC and Tracor Hydronautics sponsored resistance tests of full-sized shells. Figure 5.2 shows the resistance of a typical single shell at different speeds. Figure 5.3 replots the same results as a function of the total resistance coefficient, CT [$CT = RT \div (0.5\rho SV^2)$] versus Froude's number as a nondimensional speed so that the results can be more easily visualized. Here, RT is the total resistance, ρ the mass density of water, S the wetted surface area, and V the boat speed. An estimate of viscous drag is entered in the plot to show how the components of resistance vary with speed.

Application of Test Results to Shell Design

In the past, improvements in shell design were made slowly with difficulty and by trial and error, because refinements in one system often drastically affected the rest of the system. Today data from testing can be applied more scientifically to shell design.

Viscous Drag

A review of all the available data suggests that little can be done to reduce viscous drag, other than minimizing wetted surface area. Schemes for reducing drag by reducing the turbulence level in the boundary layer through chemical additives to the water or through carefully controlled surfaces such as the finely grooved Riblets are banned from competition by FISA.

Pressure Drag

Wave drag seems to be influenced primarily by the slenderness of the hull and the way the volume is distributed along the hull length. Even though pressure drag accounts for only a small percentage of the total resistance, minimizing its effect should yield a significant improvement in shell design. Fine ends require a larger maximum cross section to displace the same total volume. Increasing the maximum cross section works well at low speeds; reducing the size of the maximum section by filling out the ends works better at high speeds, because the water is not displaced as far when the boat moves through it. The curve of cross-sectional areas is the principal factor determining wave drag, and its optimum shape varies with slenderness and speed. This curve should change shape gradually to avoid abrupt changes in the fluid pressure along the hull.

Basic Hull Dimensions (Length, Breadth, Height)

Once the designer has selected the appropriate distribution of volume, the next step is to determine the beam and length of the boat. If semicircular cross sections are used to minimize the wetted surface area, the beam will be small, and the boat will be extremely unstable. The designer must decide how much instability the crew can handle. The best length for the hull can be selected from a series of trial designs to produce the minimum resistance. The need to reduce the pitching motion caused by the crew and sliding seats may lead to a slight increase in hull length. No single design works best for everyone. Athletes of different sizes and weights require differently sized boats, although weight variations of approximately 10% above and below the design displacement have little measurable effect on performance. Some athletes have above-average physical conditioning and below-average technical skill; for other athletes the reverse is true. A few athletes are above average in both conditioning and skill. For each athlete, the optimum trade-off between low resistance and stability will be slightly different. Although restricting international competitors to the use of a one-design boat has occasionally been suggested as a method for making rowing competition more fair, in fact it would simply favor a particular type of athlete.

Design of Topsides

Up to this point, we have discussed the best underwater design for maximum performance under

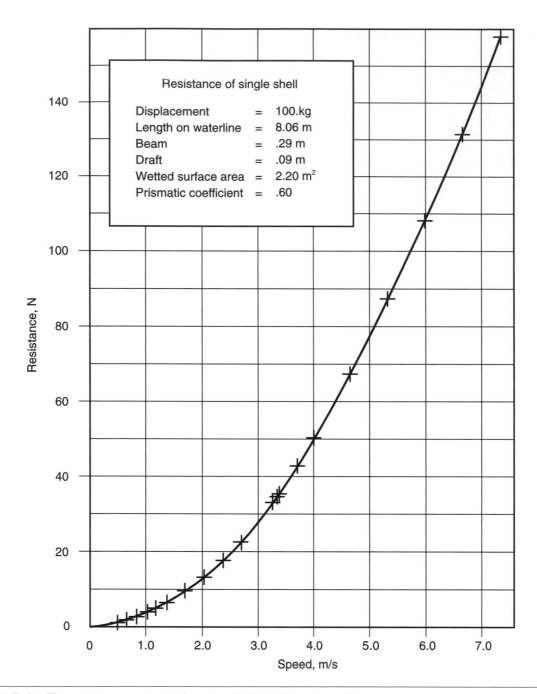

FIGURE 5.2   The resistance on a typical rowing shell at different speeds.

near-ideal conditions. Actual rowing conditions are seldom ideal, and the above-water shape of a rowing shell must be chosen for good handling characteristics under a variety of service conditions. The freeboard and reserve buoyancy must be selected to provide balanced performance. A shell with its decks awash in waves is slow; a shell with too much freeboard is blown around in the wind and is hard to handle. Topsides with flair add reserve buoyancy to handle big waves, but they have more added resistance when going through small waves. Under these circumstances, laboratory studies are no substitute for experience with a particular type of boat. An extreme design will do extremely well under some conditions and extremely poorly under others.

Handling Characteristics

In designing a rowing shell, some provision must be made for directional stability, so that little effort

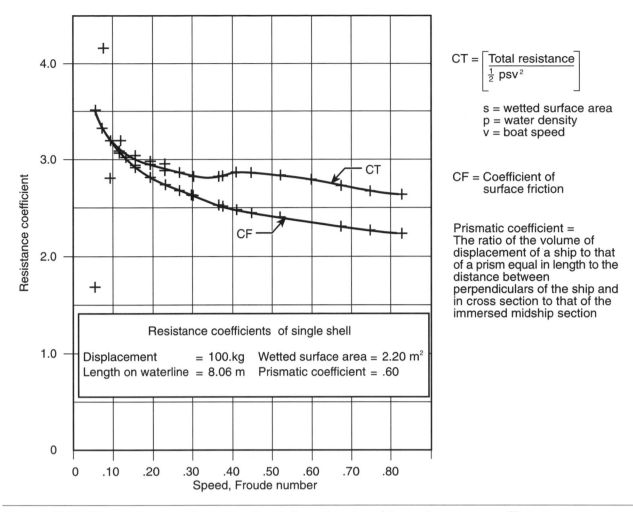

$$CT = \left[\frac{\text{Total resistance}}{\frac{1}{2}\,psv^2} \right]$$

s = wetted surface area
p = water density
v = boat speed

CF = Coefficient of
     surface friction

Prismatic coefficient =
The ratio of the volume of
displacement of a ship to that
of a prism equal in length to the
distance between
perpendiculars of the ship and
in cross section to that of the
immersed midship section

Resistance coefficients of single shell

Displacement   = 100.kg   Wetted surface area = 2.20 m²
Length on waterline = 8.06 m   Prismatic coefficient = .60

FIGURE 5.3   The resistance on a typical rowing shell as a function of the total resistance coefficient.

is required to keep the shell traveling in a straight line. No matter how slender a body of revolution, it will tumble in free fall unless some stabilizing surface is provided, like the feathers on an arrow. The most efficient method for increasing the directional stability of a rowing shell is to position a small fin near the stern. If the fin is just large enough to provide directional stability, the shell heads into the wind when it is rowed in crosswinds. This is undesirable, because the shell requires constant steering corrections. When the hull is traveling forward, it generates side force through lift, which, according to thin aerofoil theory, is centered approximately one quarter length back from the bow. The drag from the side wind acts near the mid-length, because the center of pressure of stalled flow is near the center of area. This turning moment must be balanced by additional foil area aft.

Hull Stiffness

Finally, we must consider the effect of hull rigidity on hydrodynamic resistance. When I designed my first single rowing shell, I estimated that it would have the same stability as the well-respected wooden shell I was rowing, but that it would also have 1% less resistance. I rushed to build a lighter foam-cored fiberglass prototype. When the 1% reduction in drag failed to materialize, I tried to determine the reason. The most significant difference between the wooden boat and the new design was that the bending stiffness of the new boat was less than half that of the old. This meant that the ends of the wooden boat bent up about 12 mm when I got in, whereas the ends of the fiberglass boat bent up over 25 mm. Because I had anticipated this flexion and built the hull curved so that it would straighten out to its designed shape in the water, this investigation yielded two additional sources of hydrodynamic drag. First, it is impossible to row without imparting some vertical motion to the hull. If the hull started flexing as a free beam, the pressure distribution caused by the motion could be analyzed as a fish-swimming motion. Flexing motion of the shell causes a drag force; however, there must be some width to the aft end to produce force—a fish with no tail cannot swim. The boundary layer does displace the outer flow, so even a double-ended boat acts as though it has some width, but the force I predicted was substantially less than the 1% drag decrease I was looking for. Another area of research was the effect of a vibrating surface on the boundary layers in air and water. An experimental study of the effect of engine vibration on the drag on aircraft found that vibration caused an increase in the turbulence and viscous drag of nearly the amount I was looking for. I concluded that I should learn to row as smoothly as possible and that I should build my shells with hulls as rigid as possible.

Rowing Shells as Human-Powered Vehicles

The rower's ability to use the oars to balance a highly unstable craft and to maneuver it under a variety of conditions has allowed rowing shells to evolve into highly specialized craft. Whitt and Wilson (1982) quote data showing that rowing produces the highest useful mechanical power output during exercises exceeding 1.5 min. For exercises of shorter duration, bicycle pedaling produces a higher useful mechanical power, because higher revolutions are achieved with less body motion. The motion of an oar blade in the water is semicircular. In the first third of the stroke, the oar moves away from the hull and the blade acts as an aerofoil. In the middle of the stroke, the oar moves rearward and the blade acts as a drag device. At the end of the stroke, it is unclear how much of the flow has reattached, and its efficiency in lift and drag is also unclear. Theoretical analysis of an unsteady flow near a free surface is extremely complicated, and all developments to date have been empirical. It appears that the efficiency of rowing is about 60%. The details of oar propulsion deserve far more analysis than they have received to date. A high-

efficiency propeller is about 20% more efficient than a pair of oars; this suggests that there is room for substantial improvement in oar design.

In comparing racing shells to other forms of high-speed human-powered watercraft, it is necessary to consider buoyancy and hydrodynamic lift as means of supporting the vehicle weight. In both planing and hydrofoil craft, lift is a function of speed; hence, both types of craft must be designed to operate within a narrow speed range. Performance below liftoff is quite unspectacular. Since the buoyancy of displacement craft is constant, they operate well at all speeds, but slender, high-speed craft cannot escape from their large wetted surface area, so they are capable of only small increases in speed from their current state of development. It is likely that the first human-powered hydrofoil craft to exceed the speed of a shell was able to do so more as a result of the increased propulsive efficiency of the propeller rather than as a result of the lift-to-drag ratio of the foils. As attempts have been made to travel substantially faster, smaller human-powered hydrofoils have been used with higher liftoff speeds and higher minimum energy requirements to fly. A top-speed vehicle makes brief sprints and then drifts around while the operator recovers. Although such feats of engineering are highly commendable, it will be along time before the versatility of displacement craft is replaced.

References

Granville, P.S. (1974). A modified Froude method for determining full-scale resistance of surface ships from towed models. *Journal of Ship Research*, **18**(4), 215–223.

Saunders, H.E. (1972). *Hydrodynamics in ship design*. New York: Society of Naval Architects and Marine Engineers.

Taylor, D.W. (1943). *The speed and power of ships*. Washington, DC: U.S. Government Printing Office.

Todd, F.H. (1966, April). The model-ship correlation problem. *Marine Technology*, pp. 152–157.

Wellicombe, J.F. (1967). *Report on resistance experiments carried out on three racing shells*.National Physical Laboratory, Ship Division.

Whitt, F.R., & Wilson, D.G. (1982). *Bicycling science*. Cambridge, MA: MIT Press.

6

THE 20-KNOT HUMAN-POWERED WATERCRAFT

Alec N. Brooks

The International Human Powered Vehicle Association (IHPVA) was founded to foster innovation in the design of human-powered vehicles. As a result of the IHPVA, land vehicle performance has taken a quantum leap in the last decade (see Part III). A similar revolution is underway in human-powered water vehicles. With the motivation provided by the Du Pont Watercraft Speed Prize, a new wave of watercraft has toppled records held by oared shells, with relative speed improvements at least as great as those seen for land vehicles.

Many of the new high-speed craft are hydrofoils. By literally flying through the water, hydrofoils eliminate the water drag of a hull. The required wing area for a fast hydrofoil is quite small—on the order of 0.5 ft² or less. This chapter discusses the design of human-powered hydrofoils, concentrating on wing sizing based on power available, minimum flight power, takeoff speed, and structural considerations.

Many hydrofoil configurations are suitable for human-powered applications. This chapter considers the Flying Fish configuration (see Figure 4.3), a single fully submerged main wing under the center of gravity and a small forward stabilizer wing

This chapter is adapted from an article in *Human Power*, Vol. 6, no. 1, 1987.

that carries little or no load. The main wing is supported at its center by a single strut that houses the drive mechanism to the propeller. Other more complex configurations (ladder foils, biplanes, multiple support struts, etc.) may prove to be better for really fast designs. The analysis ideas presented here can be readily extended to these cases.

The first known human-powered hydrofoil was designed by Brad Brewster (1979) as a bachelor's thesis project at MIT, but he did not pursue development because the V-foil configuration was predicted to have only moderate performance. He concluded that tandem fully submerged foils were the best approach, but that stability and control of this configuration could pose a highly complex problem. Dr. James Grogono, a hydrofoil sailing enthusiast in England, developed the first human-powered hydrofoil craft to successfully "fly" on its foils (Grogono, 1984)—a rowing shell equipped with a central fully submerged foil and a V-foil in front—but it had more drag with foils than without. David Owers, also in England, developed *Foiled Again*, a kayak outfitted with hydrofoils and propeller drive, with moderate success (Owers, 1985).

Allan Abbott and I developed the *Flying Fish* and *Flying Fish II* hydrofoils (Brooks, 1984; Brooks, 1985; Brooks, Abbott, & Wilson, 1986). The Flying Fish configurations are different from previous designs.

They incorporate tandem submerged foils, active depth control, and a standard cycling position. In 1986 the *Flying Fish II*, powered by Steve Hegg, set the single-rider standing start 2,000-m record with a time of 5 min 48 s (12.7 mph), about 1 min less than the fastest single-shell rowing shell. In 1992, David Woronets pedaled a modified version of the *Flying Fish II* to 16.8 knots (19.3 mph) over a 100-m course.

Another successful series of hydrofoil boats, dubbed Hydro-ped, has been developed by Sid Shutt (1989). Based on experience with hydrofoil sailboats, Shutt developed an effective forward-facing surface-follower, which controls the pitch attitude of the front wing. A similar device has been incorporated on the *Flying Fish II* and was also used on the *Decavitator* hydrofoil described in chapter 4.

Hydrofoil Drag, Propulsion, and Performance

Drawing on what we have learned designing the Flying Fish series, this chapter will explore the aspects of hydrofoil drag by examining the phenomena of induced drag, wave drag, profile drag, interference drag, spray drag, and air drag. Understanding these mechanisms for production of drag is important for the proper design of hydrofoils. Along with drag, the designer must also consider issues relating to power and speed goals for the watercraft, topics that are also covered in this chapter.

Hydrofoils Versus Airplanes

A hydrofoil boat is essentially like an airplane, except that the wings are in the water. Water is more than 800 times more dense than air, so we might expect larger drag. However, since lift and drag are both proportional to density, the drag of a hydrofoil wing should be no higher than for an airplane wing, relative to lift. The hydrofoil wing has 800 times as much drag per unit of area, but it needs only 1/800th the area of the airplane wing for a given speed and amount of lift.

A simple estimate of the speed attainable can be made based on the combined propeller and drivetrain efficiency, η, the power-to-weight ratio, P/W, and the lift-to-drag ratio, L/D:

$$V = \eta \cdot P/W \cdot L/D$$

For example, the Rochelt *Musculair II* human-powered airplane (Schöberl, 1986), which has a pro-

peller efficiency of about 82% (0.82), total weight (including pilot) of 172 lb, and L/D of 37, can fly at 47 ft/s, or 28 knots, with input power of 0.5 hp (275 ft-lb/s). The L/D of 37 is typical of a modern sailplane (L/D is equivalent to the glide ratio), but is extremely good for a human-powered airplane. Hydrofoils have sources of drag related to the air-water interface that airplanes do not have, and hence have lower L/D values than airplanes. These differences will be explained in greater detail in the following pages.

Even if a hydrofoil L/D of only 20 could be achieved, 13 knots would be possible on 0.5 hp, and 26 knots on 1.0 hp. It should be noted that for a given hydrofoil craft, the L/D is a function of speed, and above a certain speed it decreases with increasing speed. It is also more difficult to design a hydrofoil with L/D of 20 at 26 knots than at 13 knots. Although it is true that a wing alone optimized for 26 knots can have the same L/D as a wing optimized for 13 knots, the drag of the rider and framework in the air is higher at 26 knots, resulting in a lower overall L/D. High-speed hydrofoil craft can certainly benefit from lightweight aerodynamic fairings similar to those used on land vehicles, although safety in the event of capsizing must be addressed.

Induced Drag and Wave Drag

Like airplanes, hydrofoils have induced drag as a by-product of producing lift. Hydrofoil induced drag has the same functional form as airplane induced drag (D_i), but there is an additional multiplicative factor, f_i, to account for the proximity of the wing to the water surface.

$$D_i = q\, Cd_i\, S \text{ or } f_i\, W^2 / (\pi q\, b^2)$$

$$Cd_i = f_i\, C_L^2 / (\pi\, A)$$

$$C_L = W / (q\, S)$$

$$q = 0.5\, \rho\, V^2$$

Here, ρ is the density of water, V is the velocity, q is the dynamic pressure, W is the total weight, Cd_i is the induced-drag coefficient, C_L is the winglift coefficient, S is the wing area, b is the wingspan, and A is the aspect ratio (b^2/S).

Hoerner (1965) gives more information on the factor f_i, summarized as follows. If the wing is far below the water surface, f_i is equal to one, giving the same induced drag as an airplane. As the wing approaches the surface, a sort of "reverse ground effect" occurs, increasing induced drag because the wing has less fluid to act upon. When the wing is at the surface, the fluid volume around the wing is halved, and f_i reaches a limiting value of 2.

Unlike airplanes, hydrofoils can produce waves that cause an additional drag component, although experience with the *Flying Fish* suggests that wave drag is low. Except at very low speeds, near stalling, visible waves from the *Flying Fish* are very small. Hoerner (1965) also reports that shallow water depth can reduce or eliminate wave drag. In fact, wave drag vanishes at a critical speed, $V = (g H)^{0.5}$, where g is the acceleration of gravity and H is the water depth. At a typical hydrofoil speed of 12 knots (20.2 ft/s) the depth required is 12 ft. At much lower depth, wave drag is probably still negligible, and the induced drag may be decreased due to ground effect as the wing nears the bottom.

Profile Drag

Profile drag (D_p) is the drag of the wing and strut sections, and is of the same form as that for airplanes:

$$D_p = q\, Cd_0\, S$$

where Cd_0 is the profile drag coefficient and q is dynamic pressure. S is the reference area (usually span × average chord).

Selection of the proper foil section is critically important to achieving optimum performance. Circular-arc foil sections as used on large powered hydrofoils are not appropriate for human-powered applications. These are designed to minimize the pressure variation on the upper surface to minimize the possibility of cavitation. They do not have particularly low profile drag. Human-powered hydrofoils are not fast enough (yet) for cavitation to be a concern, so the foils can be standard airfoils as used on airplanes. For practical hydrofoil designs, it is usually desirable to have a low takeoff speed, hence high maximum wing lift coefficient (C_{Lmax}), and low drag at high speed, hence low Cd_0 at low values of C_L. These requirements are the same as those for sailplanes, which must circle slowly in updrafts and fly at high speed between updrafts.

The Reynolds numbers for human-powered hydrofoils (200,000 to 1 million) are too low to make use of full-scale sailplane airfoils. (Reynolds numbers are a measure of the ratio of inertial forces to viscous forces: $Re = V c r / m$, where V is the velocity, c is the wing chord length, r is the water density, and m is the viscosity.) However these Reynolds numbers are a good match to those of radio-controlled model sailplanes. Especially applicable is the F3B competition category, in which one of the events is a high-speed run. F3B competition has become increasingly fierce in recent years, and considerable analytical and experimental effort has gone into airfoil design. The HQ family of airfoils of differing thickness and camber (Althaus, 1985; Quabeck, 1983) have very good overall performance. HQ sections are used on the *Flying Fish II*. The 1992 version of the Flying Fish employs the Selig/Donovan 7084 foil section (Selig, Donovan, & Frasy, 1989).

Airfoil profile drag coefficients generally decrease with increasing Reynolds number. For model airfoils between Reynolds numbers (Re) of 200,000 and 600,000, the drag coefficient varies approximately as $Re^{-0.35}$. Obviously, performance will be better if, all other things being equal, the Reynolds number is increased. A property of water is that its kinematic viscosity (μ/ρ) decreases with increasing temperature. Thus the Reynolds number, and hence drag, can be minimized by operating in warm water. The drag reduction is modest, but could be enough to make a significant difference in record trials. Table 6.1 illustrates this phenomenon for a 3-in. chord section at 12 knots.

Table 6.1 DRAG REDUCTION ACHIEVED BY OPERATING IN WARM WATER

Temp (°F)	μ/ρ ft²/s (× 10⁻⁵)	Reynolds number	Section drag relative to 70 °F
50	1.41	359,000	1.10
60	1.22	415,000	1.05
70	1.06	477,000	1.00
80	.93	544,000	0.96
90	.83	610,000	0.92

Note: Figures in this table are based on a 3-in. chord section traveling at 12 knots.

A rule of thumb is that the profile drag coefficient decreases 1% for every 2 °F increase in water temperature. For simplicity, Reynolds number effects will not be included in the examples that follow. If these effects were included, the optimum spans and aspect ratios would be slightly smaller (i.e., larger chord), driven by the decrease in profile drag coefficient with increasing chord.

Interference Drag

Interference drag (D_{int}) is caused by the mutual interference of wings and struts at an intersection. There is no easy way to calculate interference drag. Hoerner (1965) presents some estimation techniques, based on test data. For a basic T-intersection of two foil sections, Hoerner gives the following:

$$D_{int} = q\,Cd_{int}\,t^2$$

$$Cd_{int} = 17\,(t/c)^2 - 0.05$$

where Cd_{int} is the interference drag coefficient, t is the average thickness of the intersecting struts, and t/c is the average thickness-to-chord ratio. This formula is only a rough guideline. Addition of good filleting, or staggering of the intersecting foils in a streamwise direction, can greatly reduce or eliminate interference drag. A practical solution for a human-powered hydrofoil is to cantilever the wing forward from the vertical strut.

Spray Drag

The vertical struts that support the hydrofoil create a spray of water at the point where they pierce the surface. Hoerner's (1965) discussion of spray drag (D_{spray}) indicates that it is primarily a function of the thickness (t) of the strut:

$$D_{spray} = 0.24\,q\,t^2$$

Thus the spray drag is roughly equal to the drag of a $t/2$-by-$t/2$ flat plate aligned perpendicular to the flow. It has been shown that spray can be reduced if the strut section has a sharp leading edge.

Aeorodynamic Drag

It is usually not necessary to consider aerodynamic drag on a human-powered watercraft, as the speeds are quite low. But in going for all-out speed air drag becomes significant, so aerodynamic streamlining should be added. A hydrofoil without aerodynamic streamlining is akin to a human-powered airplane without fuselage streamlining. Aerodynamic streamlining on watercraft has many practical problems, foremost of which is safety. Watercraft, especially hydrofoils, can, and do, capsize. A rider inside a streamlined enclosure may find it difficult to escape while submerged.

Propulsion

Virtually all of the new generation of high-speed watercraft are driven by propellers. It is generally accepted that propellers are more efficient than oars (albeit less practical in weedy lakes or shallow water). Air propellers have also been incorporated recently on Steve Ball's *Dragonfly II* hovercraft and Mark Drela's *Decavitator* hydrofoil.

Efficient water propellers for human-powered craft are different from propellers used on engine-powered boats. Slender blades and steep pitch are the rule for human-powered applications. One of the first applications of such propellers was on Calvin A. Gongwer's human-powered submarines in the mid-1950s. More recently, propellers optimized using the methods of Larrabee (1984) are used on craft such as the Knapp *Sea Saber*, the Owers *Foiled Again*, and the Flying Fish series. See chapter 4 for a more detailed description of propeller design.

Hydrofoil Design Considerations

In this section, the functional relationships of the various design parameters are given for craft based on the Flying Fish configuration. The goal of the design process will be to select the optimum wingspan and aspect ratio based on several design criteria. These criteria are: speed at design power, minimum power, takeoff speed, allowable bending stress in the wing, and wing tip deflection. To easily see how these factors interrelate, graphs showing constant values of the factors (contours) are plotted on axes of aspect ratio and wingspan. By overlaying these plots, we gain insight into various design trade-offs (e.g., how much can speed be increased by going from a fiberglass wing to a carbon-fiber wing?).

Table 6.2 lists the values of the variables used in creating the graphs in the following sections.

Design Power

The starting point for design of a human-powered hydrofoil is the design power level. It is determined to some degree by the duration of race or event for which the hydrofoil should be optimized. There are published curves (Whitt & Wilson, 1982) that show the attainable power output of various types of human power plants (from average people to world-class athletes) for different durations of

Table 6.2   VALUES OF THE FACTORS USED TO PLOT FIGURES 6.2 THROUGH 6.8 AND FIGURE 6.10

Symbol	Description	Value	Units
ρ	Density of water	1.938	slugs/ft^3
ρ_{air}	Density of air	0.00238	slugs/ft^3
C_{Lmax}	Max. wing lift coefficient	1.1	
W	Weight	190	lb
t/c	Thickness ratio	0.13	
l	Taper ratio	0.4	
η_{prop}	Propeller efficiency	0.85	
f_i	Individual drag factor	1.48	
Cd_o	Wing profile drag coefficient	0.008	
Cd_{strut}	Strut profile drag coefficient	0.0085	
S_{strut}	Strut area	0.46	ft^2
Cd_{fw}	Front wing drag coefficient	0.009	
S_{fw}	Front wing area	0.43	ft^2
Cd_{spray}	Spray drag coefficient	0.24	
t_{strut}	Strut thickness	0.0917	ft
Cd_{air}	Air drag coefficient	0.7	
S_{air}	Frontal area in air	7.0	ft^2
S	Main-wing area	variable	ft^2
b	Main-wing span	variable	ft

exercise. Table 6.3 lists the three combinations of power and duration that will be used for the design examples discussed later in this chapter.

Table 6.3   POWER AND DURATION COMBINATIONS ASSUMED FOR THE DESIGN EXAMPLES OF THIS CHAPTER

Duration	Power	Application
40 s	1.0 hp	100-m event
6 min	0.5 hp	2,000-m event
1 hour	0.25 hp	Recreation

Maximum Speed

The maximum speed occurs when the design power, reduced by propeller efficiency, is equal to the power required. The power required is the product of velocity and total drag. For simplicity, all of the drag terms not related to the wing are summed to give an equivalent drag area (S_{ref}). (The air drag term is multiplied by the air-to-water density ratio before summing.) The value of S_{ref} based on the data in Table 6.2 is 0.0158 ft^2.

$$P_{des}\eta_{prop} = V\{qCD_0S + qS_{ref} + f_iW^2 / (\pi qb^2)\}$$
$$= 0.5\rho V^3 (Cd_0b^2 / A + S_{ref})$$
$$+ f_iW^2 / (0.5\pi\rho Vb^2)$$

Minimum Power

A hydrofoil optimized for maximum speed at a given power may require high minimum power just to fly. This may be acceptable for an all-out racing machine, but for versatility or recreational use the capability to fly at a lower power may be desirable. Specification of minimum power as well as design power places a constraint on allowable designs and usually results in a penalty in speed at the design power.

Minimum power is found by setting the derivative (with respect to velocity) of the power equation equal to zero. This leads to

$$3\ \{0.5\rho V^2\ (Cd_0 b^2\ /\ A + S_{ref})\} = f_i W^2\ /\ (0.5\pi\rho V^2 b^2)$$

which can be solved for V, and then V substituted into the original power equation to get the minimum power level. Figure 6.1 shows contours of minimum power from .15 hp to .40 hp.

Takeoff Speed

Like the minimum power case above, hydrofoils optimized only for speed at high power may prove to have an uncomfortably high takeoff speed. Takeoff occurs when the wing generates lift equal to the total weight (W):

$$W = C_{Lmax} 0.5\rho V^2\ S$$

Solving for V:

$$V = \{2\ W\ /\ (\rho\ S\ C_{Lmax})\}^{1/2}$$
$$= \{2\ A\ W\ /\ (\rho\ b^2\ C_{Lmax})\}^{1/2}$$

It is seen that the takeoff speed varies as the square-root of the wing loading. With a wing loading of 130 lb/ft², the *Flying Fish II* is able to take off easily. Assuming a C_{Lmax} of 1.1, the corresponding speed is 7 knots. The 1992 version, *Flying Fish 20*, could just barely take off with a wing loading of 250 lb/ft². Contours of takeoff speeds between 4 and 12 knots are shown in Figure 6.2.

Bending Stress

The bending stress at the root of a thin, high-aspect, ratio hydrofoil wing can be very large. (It will be assumed that the wing is constructed as a solid mass of material: no lightweight core, etc.) From simple beam theory, the maximum bending stress (σ) is

$$\sigma = M\ /\ S_m$$

where M is the bending moment and S_m is the section modulus. Assuming an elliptical distribution of lift along the span, the resultant lift acts 42% of the semispan out from the root. This leads to a root moment of

$$M = 0.11\ W\ b$$

where b is the main-wing span.

The section modulus is a function of the thickness, chord, and distribution of thickness. For the HQ family of airfoils the section modulus is

$$S_m = 0.0746\ (t/c)^2 c^3$$

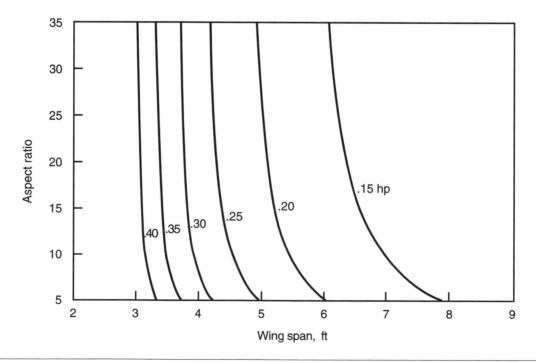

FIGURE 6.1   Contours of minimum power required to stay foilborne as a function of wingspan and aspect ratio.

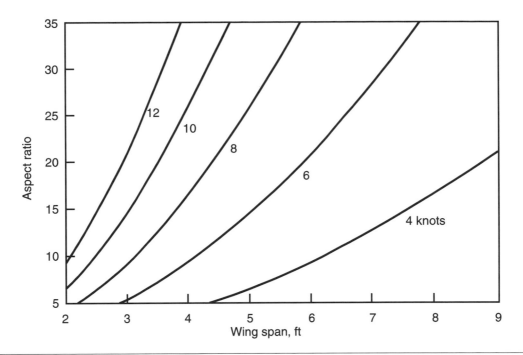

FIGURE 6.2 Takeoff speed contours, assuming takeoff at $C_{Lmax} = 1.1$.

The factor 0.0746 was calculated numerically for the HQ family of airfoils. (It doesn't change more than about 10% for other airfoils.) After including the effects of wing taper (λ is the ratio of tip chord to root chord),

$$\sigma = 0.11 \, W A^3 (1 + \lambda)^3 / \{8 \bullet 0.0746 \, b^2 \, (t/c)^2\}$$

Note that taper ratio and thickness ratio have a strong influence on the root stress. It is especially beneficial to taper the wing. Although an untapered, constant-chord wing may be easier to make, a tapered wing has much lower stress and is better hydrodynamically. For an untwisted, straight-tapered wing, a taper ratio of 0.4 is about optimum for achieving a nearly elliptical lift distribution. (Twist is not desirable if the wing must operate over a broad range of lift coefficients). A thickness-to-chord ratio of 13% is a reasonable compromise between low drag and structural considerations. Using these values, contours of root bending stress between 5,000 and 25,000 psi are shown in Figure 6.3.

Tip Deflection

High-aspect-ratio hydrofoil wings can have considerable deflection at the tip under load. Both translational and torsional deflections are important. If the wing is too flexible, the wingtips may rise up out of the water, or flutter, an aeroelastic (or hydroelastic) oscillation, may occur at high speed.

In airplanes, flutter is often disastrous, tearing the airplane apart. Flutter probably wouldn't structurally harm a human-powered hydrofoil, but it would ruin any chance of going fast, due to a large amount of extra drag. Flutter calculations were not made for any of the Flying Fish designs. The wings were designed with a somewhat-arbitrary tip deflection limit of 8% of semispan, and flutter has never been a problem.

Torsional deflections alter the spanwise lift distribution, causing increased induced drag. Torsional deflection depends on the torsional stiffness of the wing, sweep angle, the airfoil pitching moment, speed, and location of the shear center of the wing structure. Torsional deflections are beyond the scope of this chapter. It suffices to say that torsional deflections should be kept very small. The very thin wing on the 1992 version of the Flying Fish was fabricated of steel after an initial version of carbon fiber proved too flexible torsionally.

The normalized tip deflection, $\Delta = \delta / (b/2)$, can be calculated using elementary beam theory. The result is

$$\Delta = \delta / (b/2)$$
$$= f(\lambda, \text{loading}) \, W A^4 / (64 \bullet 0.037 \, E \, (t/c)^3 \, b^2)$$

where δ is the tip deflection, t/c is the ratio of foil section thickness to chord, and E is the modulus of elasticity of the wing material. The factor 0.037 is constant in the wing moment of inertia [$I = 0.037$

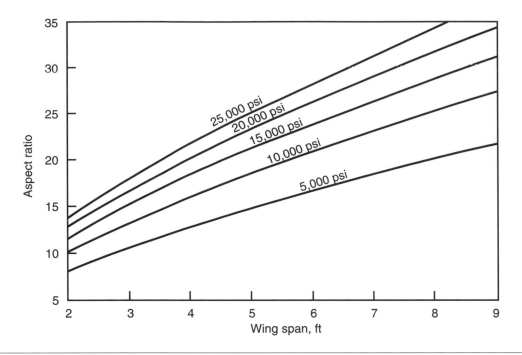

FIGURE 6.3   Root bending stress contours, assuming taper ratio of 0.4 and foil thickness-to-chord of 13%.

$(t/c)^3c^4$] and is accurate for the HQ family of sections; it is reasonably close for other airfoils. The function f, of taper and load distribution, is best calculated by numerical integration of the bending equations. Figure 6.4 shows contours of tip deflections between 4% and 20% of semispan. Figure 6.5 shows the effect of the material stiffness. Lines are shown for wood, fiberglass, aluminum, carbon, steel, and HM carbon (special high-modulus carbon) for equal deflections of 8% of semispan.

Design Examples

The graphs of the previous section can be used to evaluate the various tradeoffs involved in selecting wingspan and aspect ratio. It is not generally necessary to consider stress limits if deflection limits are also applied. The stresses at maximum deflections are almost always modest and are well below ultimate or yield strengths.

Three basic designs are considered here. All are designed initially with a maximum normalized wing deflection of 8% and a minimum power requirement of 0.2 hp to allow extended-duration cruising. The wing construction material is assumed to be either aluminum or carbon fiber-epoxy. The design first considered is for a recreational craft, with a design power of 0.25 hp and maximum takeoff speed of only 4 knots. The second is a competi-

tion craft designed for 2,000-m races, with a design power of 0.5 hp and maximum takeoff speed of 8 knots. The third is a racer for short 100-m sprints, with a design power of 1.0 hp and a maximum takeoff speed of 10 knots.

Figure 6.6 shows contours of maximum speed attainable for the recreational design. Constraint lines for takeoff speed, minimum power, and deflection are also shown. Taken together, the constraint lines form the boundaries of a region inside of which all constraints are satisfied. The best span and aspect-ratio combination inside the region is that which is on the highest maximum-speed contour contained in the region. If necessary, rough interpolation can be used to estimate the shapes of intermediate speed contours. It is seen that the best design point for this case has a maximum speed of about 7.6 knots, with a span of 9 ft and aspect ratio of 20 (the actual optimum is just off the edge of the graph). If the takeoff speed and minimum power constraints are removed, the maximum speed increases to 8.4 knots, the span decreases to 6.5 ft, and the aspect ratio increases slightly to 22. This design still has a modest takeoff speed of about 6 knots (this can be seen by overlaying Figure 6.2 on Figure 6.6 or by tracing additional takeoff speed contours onto Figure 6.6).

Figure 6.7 shows the results for the competition racing craft. The optimum design has a maximum speed of 11.7 knots. In this case, minimum power

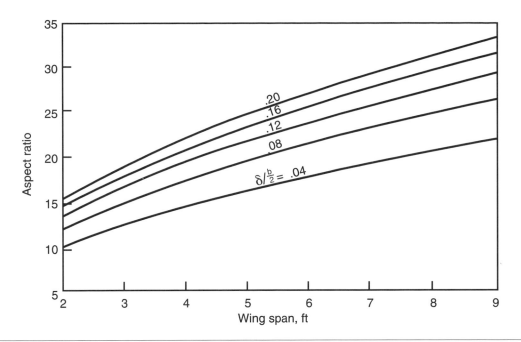

FIGURE 6.4 Contours of tip deflection normalized by semispan ($b/2$), assuming taper and thickness as in Figure 6.3, with material properties of aluminum or wet-layup carbon fiber.

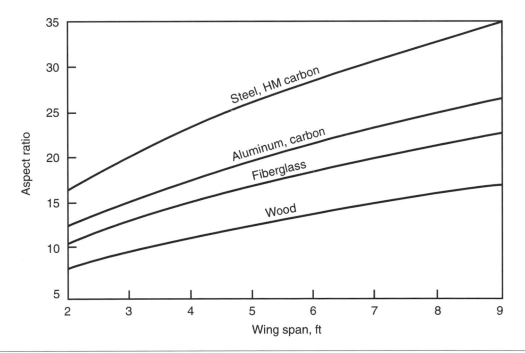

FIGURE 6.5 Effect of different wing materials for normalized tip deflection of 0.08.

and deflection are the limiting factors. If the minimum power and takeoff speed constraints were removed, the speed would increase only slightly to 11.8 knots (5 min 32 s for 2,000 m).

Results for the sprint craft are shown in Figure 6.8. The optimum design has a maximum speed of

15.3 knots. Without the minimum power and takeoff speed constraints, the speed increases to 16.0 knots.

Figure 6.9 shows the optimum planforms to scale for each of the three wing designs, both with original constraints and without minimum power and takeoff speed constraints. Table 6.4 gives a summary

.25 hp design

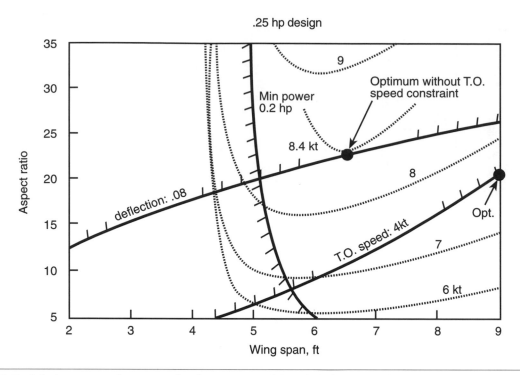

FIGURE 6.6   Maximum speed contours for the recreational (0.25 hp) design, with constraint lines.

.5 hp design

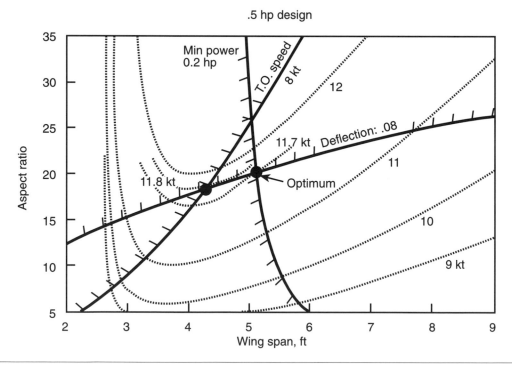

FIGURE 6.7   Maximum speed contours for the 2,000-m racer (0.5 hp), with constraint lines.

of the constrained and unconstrained speeds for the three designs.

The speed of the best 100-m sprint craft is still below the 20 knots goal of the Du Pont Prize. To increase speed further, the wing material could be changed to steel or high-modulus carbon to allow a higher aspect ratio, but this alone isn't enough. The drag of the craft must be reduced as well. With

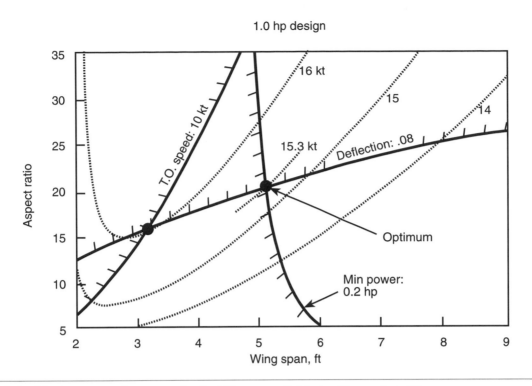

FIGURE 6.8 Maximum speed contours for the 100-m racer (1.0 hp), with constraint lines.

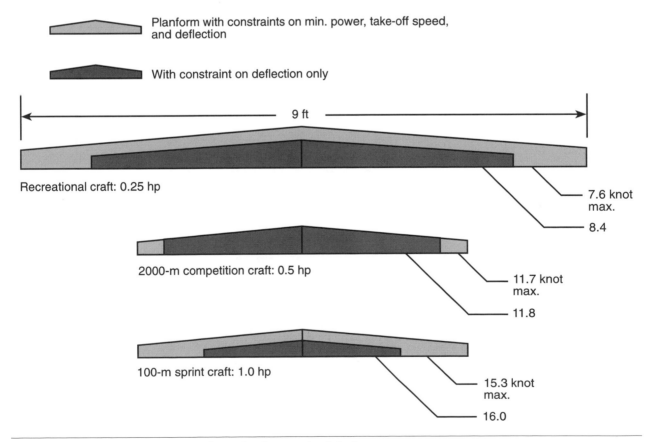

FIGURE 6.9 Optimum wing planforms for three optimal designs.

| Table 6.4 | SUMMARY OF THE CONSTRAINED AND UNCONSTRAINED SPEEDS FOR THE THREE DESIGNS | |

Design	Max. speed (knots)	Max. speed without min. power or takeoff constraints (knots)
Recreational craft	7.6	8.4
2,000-m competition craft	11.7	11.8
100-m sprint craft	15.3	16.0

the addition of an enclosed fairing, air drag could be cut in half. The main vertical strut could also be made smaller by about one-half to reduce spray and skin-friction drag. The area of the front wing could be made smaller, also by half. Figure 6.10 shows the results of these changes along with a deflection-limit line for steel or high-modulus carbon. A speed of 20.2 knots can be reached by this ultimate craft with a wingspan of only 2.5 ft and an aspect ratio of 18. The takeoff speed of 13 knots may prove to be an inconvenience, however! A

larger wing with just 20.0 knots top speed capability would have a slightly more reasonable takeoff speed of 11 knots.

Figure 6.11 shows a comparison of the power versus velocity requirements for the three original hydrofoil designs and the final, ultimate 20-knot craft. Also shown is the curve for a single rowing shell, based on the data of Rogen (1982), and assuming a rowing efficiency of 70%. Note that at low speeds, displacement hulls are as good as or better than hydrofoils.

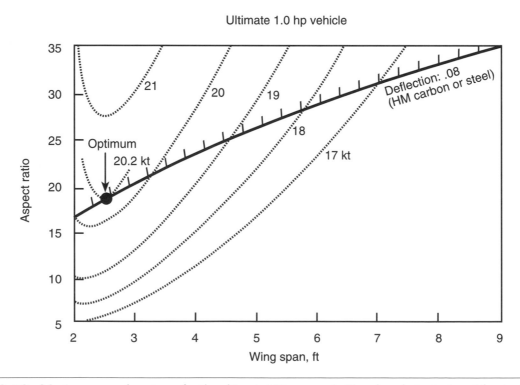

FIGURE 6.10   Maximum speed contours for the ultimate 100-m racer (with reduced air, strut, and front wing drag), with deflection constraint for high-modulus carbon or steel.

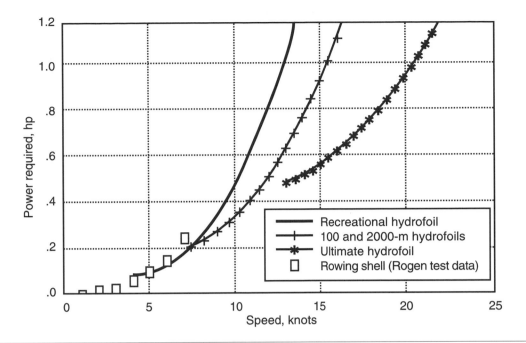

FIGURE 6.11   Power versus speed for the design examples and for a single rowing shell. Note that 2,000-m and 100-m designs are the same due to the minimum power requirement.

Conclusion

The examples in the previous section have just begun to scratch the surface of the kinds of trade-offs that are possible. By overlaying the graphs or tracing lines from one graph to another, one can explore many more questions and trade-offs such as these: How much is top speed reduced by having a low takeoff speed? How much faster at 1 hp is a craft optimized for 1 hp than a craft optimized for 0.25 hp? What is the trade-off in top speed from setting a low minimum required power? Is it worth the extra effort to make a wing out of carbon fiber instead of wood or fiberglass?

The 20-knot hydrofoil is certainly a possibility with today's technology. With time and healthy competition, the 20-knot barrier will surely fall.

References

Althaus, D. (1985). *Profilpolaren für den modellflug volumes I and II*. Villingen-Schwenningen, West Germany: Neckar-Verlag.

Brewster, M.B. (1979). *The design and development of a man-powered hydrofoil*. Unpublished bachelors thesis, Mechanical Engineering Department, Massachusetts Institute of Technology.

Brooks, A.N. (1984). The *Flying Fish* hydrofoil. *Human Power*, **3**, 2.

Brooks, A.N. (1985). Waterbike! *Bicycle Guide*, **2**, 3.

Brooks, A.N., Abbott, A.V., & Wilson, D.G. (1986). Human-powered watercraft. *Scientific American*, **255** (6).

Grogono, J.L. (1984). Human-powered flight on hydrofoils: A successful sculling craft conversion. *Proceedings of Conference on Human-Powered Marine Vehicles*. London: Royal Institution of Naval Architects.

Hoerner, S.F. (1965). *Fluid dynamic drag*. Brick Town, NJ: Hoerner Fluid Dynamics.

Larrabee, E.E. (1984). Propellers for human-powered vehicles. *Human Power*, **3**, 2.

MacCready, P. (1986). Features of flapping-wing propulsion. In A. Abbott (Ed.), *Proceedings of the Third International Human-Powered Vehicle Scientific Symposium*. Indianapolis: International Human Powered Vehicle Association.

Owers, D.J. (1985). Development of a human-powered racing hydrofoil. *Human Power*, **3**, 3.

Quabeck, H. (1983). *HQ profile für F3B, thermik, han, elektro- und gross-segler*. Baden-Baden: Verlag für Technik und Handwerk.

Rogen, B. (1982). Determination of drag force relationships and a drag coefficient for a rowing single scull. In A. Abbott (Ed.), *Proceedings of the Third International Human-Powered Vehicle*

Scientific Symposium. Indianapolis: International Human Powered Vehicle Association.

Schöberl, E. (1986). The *Muscalair 1* and 2 human-powered aircraft and their optimization. In A. Abbott (Ed.), *Proceedings of the Third International Human-Powered Vehicle Scientific Symposium*. Indianapolis: International Human Powered Vehicle Association.

Selig, M., Donovan, J., & Frasy, D. (1989). *Airfoils at low speeds*. Stokely.

Shutt, S. (1989). Some ideas used on Hydro-ped: A hydrofoil pedal boat. *Human Power*, **7**, 4.

Watson, B. (1982). Current trends in water power. In A. Abbott (Ed.), *Proceedings of the First International Human-Powered Vehicle Scientific Symposium*. Indianapolis: International Human Powered Vehicle Association.

Whitt, F.R., & Wilson, D.G. (1982). *Bicycling science*. Boston: MIT Press.

III

LAND VEHICLES

Throughout history, overland transportation has nearly always been by foot. It was not until the invention of lightweight wheels in the 19th century that human-powered vehicles (HPVs) became truly efficient. Even today, the majority of wheeled vehicles in the world—from rickshaws to bicycles—are human powered.

Bicycle use reached its heyday in the late 1800s, when it proved faster and more versatile than walking or using horse-drawn vehicles. The modern safety bicycle was invented in the 1880s, and its simple design remains basically unchanged today.

The persistence of the safety-bicycle design is not solely the result of design perfection: In the early 1900s the Union Cycliste International (UCI) banned from international competition anything other than the conventional safety bicycle. These rules were established when first streamlined bicycles and then recumbent bicycles began outperforming conventional bicycles. Although promoting the human athlete in international bicycle racing, the UCI rules inadvertently stifled bicycle innovation. Significant

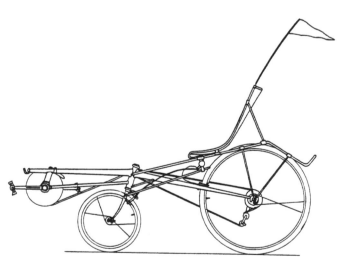

improvements in human-powered land vehicles had to await the formation of a new organization that sanctioned competitions with a minimum of rules on vehicle design. The International Human Powered Vehicle Association (IHPVA) started casually in 1974, became more formal in 1975, and established its full identity in 1976. Almost overnight new designs emerged and the record books were rewritten. Men and women all over the world found a new hobby, and thousands of human-powered-vehicle enthusiasts devote their energy to the new challenges that emerged.

Most human-powered land vehicles travel today on relatively smooth surfaces. However, the major commercial development of the last quarter of the 20th century has been the mountain bicycle, made popular by a group of enthusiasts in California. The rapid development of components and machines that allow riders to negotiate extremes of rough terrain has contributed not only to the health and fitness of an increasing number of devotees, but to the development of a wide variety of other HPVs. Gary Klein, designer and manufacturer of innovative bicycles, has suggested that the next logical extension for rough ground is a human-powered walking machine that could outperform mountain bikes in terrain that is too rough to be negotiated by wheeled vehicles. The all-terrain vehicle, or ATV, also encompasses machines that negotiate wide bodies of deep water in light-hearted competitions generally known as "kinetic sculpture races."

7

A HISTORY OF HUMAN-POWERED LAND VEHICLES AND COMPETITIONS

Chester R. Kyle

Over a century ago, an Englishman, John Kemp Starley, invented the modern bicycle (see Figure 7.1). Starley called the 1885 invention the Rover Safety Cycle and, except for the lack of a seat tube added in later models to make the typical diamond frame, it was nearly an exact prototype of a bicycle that you might buy and ride today. As with all new inventions it was preceded and followed by developments that inspired explosive and rapid progress in design. Seldom does an invention as complex as the bicycle spring from the mind of one inventor.

The rear-driving safety bicycle, which H.J. Lawson claimed to have invented in 1879 (Sharp, 1896) is generally credited to Starley (Roberts, 1990). He designed the improved Rover, and in turn Starley's Rover inspired other manufacturers. The first true diamond frame seems to have been introduced by Humber & Company of England in 1889 or 1890 when the bicycle as we know it was born. The Dutch utility bike, parked by the thousands at railroad stations in the Netherlands, could easily be mistaken for one of the early Humbers.

Early Cycling Aerodynamics

It wasn't long after the invention of the bicycle that competitive bike racers discovered the advantages of aerodynamics. By 1891 dropped handlebars were common, and the crouched racing position can be seen in photos dating from 1894 (Gronen, 1987).

Pacing

The most spectacular use of aerodynamics was in pacing. When cyclists join a pace line or are in the middle of a pack, they consume from 30% to 40% less energy due to the drop in wind resistance (Kyle, 1979). At speeds above about 4 m/s (8 mph) the wind drag is the dominant retarding force on a bicycle, and above 9 m/s (20 mph) it is more than 80% of the total resistance. So by drafting in the wake of another rider, a cyclist rides in a sort of an artificial tail wind. The closer the cyclist drafts, the greater the benefit.

FIGURE 7.1   John Kemp Starley's Rover Safety Cycle.

In the early 1890s bicyclists discovered that multiple-rider bicycles were far faster than solo cycles. For example, tandem bicycles can travel about 10% faster than standard bicycles, because the rear rider is drafting closely behind the front, and the combined wind resistance to the tandem and riders is about 30% less than to two solo cyclists. Cyclists soon began using multiple-rider bikes to pace single cyclists. A single rider could tuck in behind an "air plow" and sail along at 13 m/s (29 mph), which was about 2 m/s (5 mph) faster than without this help. It became popular to set point-to-point records and track-distance records using enormous four- to six-rider bicycles as pace machines. In 1897 Stocks of England covered a record 52.5 km (32.6 miles) in 1 hour behind a four-rider bicycle.

The British tire manufacturer, Dunlop (James Boyd Dunlop invented the pneumatic tire in 1888, making it for his son's bicycle), employed a whole stable of professional pacemakers who would travel to any location in Britain, as long as its expenses were paid by the record-seeking cyclist or sponsor. Several pace bicycles were used in rotation, switching off to achieve even higher speeds (see Figure 7.2). Because so many riders were involved, record setting became an expensive proposition with pace bicycles. In 1896 Dunlop charged £1 per pacemaker per day, equivalent to over $200 a day now. Not only were they expensive, but large teams were hard to manage. A better way was just around the corner.

In the mid-1890s, engineers began adding electric, steam, and gasoline engines on tandems for pacing single bicycles. On November 7, 1896 (in the British publication called *The Hub*), S.F. Edge, a spokesman for Dunlop, presented a view of the future:

Next year we will see our mechanical pacemakers at work. It is too early for me to divulge particulars concerning them; but anyway they will not be propelled by human muscles. True at first two, three or four men may be seated upon them, but this will simply be to provide wind shelter for the performer. Later on will come the most startling innovation; and you will then see at work our mechanical pacemakers fitted with windshields. The men going against time will ride drawn along in the vacuum created behind this shield that is being propelled round the track before him. No doubt the paths will have to be altered to be safer at the greatly augmented speed. But that is a mere detail. Then and then only, shall we be in sight of securing the fastest times that a human being on a cycle is capable of accomplishing.

This could have been a description of the technique used for every motor-paced bicycle speed record set since then.

These motor-driven pace machines were the first successful motorcycles (see Figure 7.3). Initially they still had cranks and pedals so that the riders could

FIGURE 7.2   World champion A.A. Chase in an 1896, 100-km paced record ride (27.82 mph).

From Gronen, W. *A history of bicycle racing and bicycles*. Reprinted with permission.

FIGURE 7.3   Albert Kocher at the Berlin-Friedenau track being paced by a motorized tandem bicycle. Notice the windshield.

From Gronen, W. *A history of bicycle racing and bicycles*. Reprinted with permission.

supplement the power furnished by the engine; soon, however, they became true motorcycles. By 1900 motor-paced cyclists were going over 65 km (40 miles) in 1 hour, or about 6.7 m/s (15 mph) faster than the best solo racing cyclist. At present this strange hybrid sport still survives in Europe. Bicycles paced by stayer motorcycles now cover over 60 miles in 1 hour.

Carried to its ultimate, wind shielding can result in extraordinary speeds. In 1896 "Mile-a-Minute" Murphy was the first man to exceed 60 mph on a bicycle. He rode on a board strip behind a special shielded railroad car. More recently, Allan Abbott, co-editor of this book, held the world motor-paced speed record at 62.8 m/s (140.5 mph) set in 1973 on the Bonneville salt flats, riding a bike of his own design behind a faired enclosure behind a race car. John Howard holds the current world motor-paced bicycle record of 68.07 m/s (152.284 mph) set in 1985 at Bonneville. By backing up until the trailing vortex creates an artificial tailwind, these drafting riders can extract energy from the wind stream. At this speed, overcoming the inertia force necessary to accelerate and pedaling against tire-rolling resistance forces would be impossible without added help for the human muscles.

The First Disk and Multispoked Aerodynamic Wheels

Streamlined cycling components were clearly described in 1896 by Archibald Sharp (1896) (see Figure 7.4). Figure 356 of his book shows a bicycle with a rear disk wheel and a front four-spoked aerodynamic wheel. Of these inventions, Sharp noted that it was claimed that the air resistance of these wheels was less than that of wheels with wire spokes. They were impossibly heavy, being made of pressed metal, which perhaps explains why they were never adopted in large numbers until present-day space-age materials made them practical. It is a little-known fact that devices to streamline airflow were used on bicycles long before they were widely adopted for aircraft.

During the 1890s, bicycles, motorized vehicles, and aircraft were in their infancy, undergoing almost simultaneous development. However, bicycles were king of the road, and they were a raging fad. Some of the world's best technological brains and efforts were concentrated on improving bicycles. The bicycle was the first inexpensive means of mass transportation, and it gave unheard-of mobility and freedom to millions of people in the 1890s. New cycling inventions made worldwide news. Bicycle

FIGURE 7.4   A disk and four-spoked aerodynamic wheel made by the Disk Wheel Company of England in 1896.

From Sharp, A. *Bicycles and tricycles*. Reprinted with permission.

racers were the heroes of the day; however, at the turn of the century they were soon displaced in the public's esteem by race-car drivers and airplane pilots. It is strange that the public can lavish such attention on those who can successfully manipulate simple mechanical transportation devices, but it happens over and over again (e.g., chariot drivers, sea captains, stage-coach drivers, and locomotive engineers) and it continues today with the fame of astronauts.

Early Streamlined Human-Powered Land Vehicles

In 1913 a Frenchman, Etienne Bunau Varilla, patented in Europe and America a streamlined enclosure for a bicycle (see Figure 7.5). He called this a "wind-dividing apparatus to be attached to transport vehicles with kinematic equilibrium, especially bicycles and motor-cycles with a view of diminishing the air resistance." He intended his fairing to "facilitate penetrating the air and to avoid the forming of eddies at the rear of a moving body."

This invention was first exploited by the French "hour specialist" Marcel Berthet, who built a torpedo-shaped shell of wood and canvas that completely enclosed the rider. Called the Velo Torpille, it had a mica window in front, and Berthet rode it in 1913 at 14.5 m/s (32.5 mph) for 5,000 m in a test at the Velodrome d'Hiver in Paris. This was 2 m/s (4 mph) faster than he could ride a standard bicycle over the same distance—12.7 m/s (28.5 mph). Inside the fairing was a standard stayer bicycle with a 27-in. rear wheel and a 24-in. front wheel. The small front wheel allowed cyclists to draft closer to benefit from the resulting lower wind resistance. This wheel-size combination is still common for present-day "funny bikes." (This epithet is applied to the bicycles allowed by the UCI to be introduced in the mid-1980s, having disk rear wheels, small front wheels, and forward-extended handlebars, allowing riders to take up a more streamlined posture.)

Berthet was asked to demonstrate his sensational vehicle at a Manchester Wheelmen meet in Britain in 1914. However, he showed up with a much smaller fairing, from which his head stuck out. The machine did not do well with gusty winds buffeting

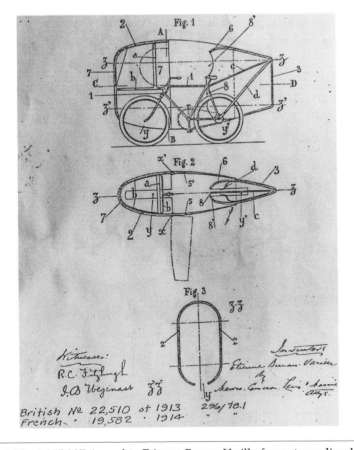

FIGURE 7.5 U.S. Patent No. 1,135,337, issued to Etienne Bunau Varilla for a streamlined bicycle.

it from every side, and the crowd was not impressed by his performance.

In Berlin on April 4, 1914, a match race was held on the Olympic track between Dutch champion Piet Dickentman and German champion Artur Stellbrink (see Figure 7.6). Stellbrink won when Dickentman crashed on the last curve. Dickentman's bike had covered wheel disks, and a wind gust forced the bike to swerve and crash—a common problem with disk wheels even today. Stellbrink covered 5,000 m in 5 min 23 s, an astounding 15.48 m/s (34.63 mph). This would translate into a 4-min 18-s 4,000-m pursuit time, fast enough to beat almost any world-champion four-man pursuit team of today.

In one of the most intense individual cycling competitions in history, between 1907 and 1914, Berthet and Oscar Egg, of Switzerland, traded the standard-bicycle world hour record six times. Grasping at any means that might gain an advantage over an arch rival, Berthet and Egg experimented with cycling aerodynamic devices, but unfortunately World War I cut short their competitive careers. Just before the war, in June 1914, Oscar Egg set a standard-bike hour record of 44.247 km (27.49 miles), which stood 19 years. In 1932, Egg invented a tail cone, the Velo Fusee, with which Francois Faure went 48 km in 1 hour, about 4 km

further than the standard-bike record (see Figure 7.7). Not to be outdone, Berthet returned to his early passion, the streamlined bicycle.

With the help of engineer Marcel Riffart and the aircraft manufacturer Rene Caudron, Berthet produced the Velodyne, one of the strangest pedal-powered machines created up to that date (Figure 7.8). He used a standard bicycle in a streamlined fairing that went nearly to the ground. A hole in the top permitted the head to stick out, or the rider could duck down behind a windshield and look through a small window in front.

Originally Berthet had intended to get a young professional to ride the Velodyne, but the competitive instinct was too strong and, at age 47, he once again began to train seriously. On September 9, 1933, he rode the strange machine 48.604 km in 1 hour, more than 4 km better than the official bicycle record. A few weeks later Berthet crashed at the half-hour mark during a second attempt. After recovering from his injuries, on November 18, 1933, he sped 49.992 km in 1 hour at the Montlhery motordrome. The attempt received worldwide publicity (see *Popular Mechanics*, December 1933), but the record was never recognized by any official cycling body and today Berthet's accomplishment has been all but forgotten.

FIGURE 7.6   Dutch champion Piet Dickentman (left) in the Brennabor Fish, and German champion Arthur Stellbrink (right) in the Goricke Bomb, at the Berlin Olympic Track, April 4, 1914. This was the first recorded streamlined bicycle race.

FIGURE 7.7 In 1932 Oscar Egg invented a tail cone for a bicycle with which Francois Faure went 48 km in 1 hour.

FIGURE 7.8 Marcel Berthet in the Velodyne, 1933.

The Velocar

In 1932 Charles Mochet of France introduced a supine recumbent bicycle, called the Velocar, that created a sensation in Europe. Ridden in a low easy-chair posture (see Figure 7.9), the bike had much lower frontal area and wind resistance than a normal bicycle. A professional cyclist of the second category, Francois Faure, was able to defeat all the first-category champions in Europe with the Velocar, and he managed to break most of the existing time-trial track records in the process.

By 1938, Mochet had constructed a completely streamlined enclosure for the Velocar, and Faure became the first person to break 50 km in 1 hour on an unpaced bicycle; his distance of 50.527 km broke Berthet's 1933 streamliner record. This recumbent pedal-powered streamliner and Mochet's earlier unstreamlined Velocar led to a furious debate among standard cyclists about whether recumbents were bicycles at all and whether they should be permitted in competitions. The UCI silenced the debate in 1934 by passing a series of rules against the use of recumbent bicycles. Earlier (in 1914) it had banned aerodynamic devices in racing. These actions essentially restricted bicycle design to minor variations of the traditional diamond-frame model of 1890. This is probably the major reason that recumbents have failed to gain public acceptance.

Actually the recumbent bicycle is an old idea. In chapter 8 Wilson discusses a series of recumbent bicycle designs spanning nearly 90 years. Despite the many obvious advantages of a recumbent over a standard bicycle (safety, comfort, stability, speed), the machine has never been popular, although numerous manufacturers have attempted to market this design over the years.

Modern Streamlined Human-Powered Land Vehicles

In the late 1950s, Oscar Egg tried to revive interest in streamlined bicycles by building the Sputnik (see Figure 7.10). By this time Egg's remarkable involvement with bicycle streamlining had spanned nearly 50 years. Egg leased the Sputnik to the Manchester Wheelers for a meet in 1958. With Frenchman François Lehaye riding the contraption, the Sputnik soundly defeated a crack four-man pursuit team, even though the door blew open and acted like an air brake. His time of 4:49.7 was 17 s better than the individual track record. G.H.

FIGURE 7.9 Francois Faure in Charles Mochet's Velocar.

FIGURE 7.10   Oscar Egg's Sputnik, 1958.

Stancer, promoter of the meet, could not afford to bring Lehaye and the Sputnik over the Channel again, so with the help of friends they produced their own version of Egg's machine.

In 1959 Harry Hardcastle, riding the Manchester Wheelers' Sputnik, caught a four-man team in the 4,000-m pursuit with the time of 4:26.2 (15 m/s; 33.6 mph). In 1961, John Carline of the Wheelers recorded a time of 1:36.4 for a flying-start mile (16.69 m/s; 37.34 mph). Because none of these times were recognized by the UCI, Stancer had a hard time knowing how to continue with the Sputnik; interest waned, so once again bicycle streamlining fell on hard times.

The California Streamliners

Southern California is the home of such timeless contributions to civilization as the supermarket, the shopping center, modern auto culture, smog, junk food franchises, surfing, creeping urban sprawl, and much much more. On the brighter side, southern California is also the home of modern streamlined bicycles. In 1973, concerning knowledge of bicycling history, Californians were in the dark ages, and therefore free to proceed without any concept of what was right or wrong.

At this time, I was a professor of mechanical engineering at California State University, Long Beach, when two senior mechanical engineering students, Doran Nadeau and Claude Crawford, approached me to settle an argument about bicycle tires. Nadeau claimed that sew-ups (tubulars) were superior, and Crawford said that clinchers (wired-ons) were just as good. A coast-down test in a 1/8-mile-long hallway was used to answer the question. By measuring the rate of deceleration of a gliding bicycle through a series of timing switches, we found that, indeed, Nadeau's sew-ups caused about 1 N (0.25 lb) less drag than Crawford's clinchers. But in this process we discovered that the wind resistance on a bicycle and rider was more than 80% of the retarding force at speeds over 20 mph.

The students suggested building an "aero-bicycle" by covering the wheels and frame with plastic sheet. They were delighted when the overall drag decreased by about 8% (Kyle, Crawford, & Nadeau, 1973). This meant that the frame's wind drag had decreased by about 25%.

About this time, Nadeau and Crawford graduated. I decided to build a completely streamlined bicycle. Using bent aluminum tubes for a framework, my wife, Joyce, covered it with heat-shrunk

Dacron aircraft fabric. The shape was based on an NACA-0020 airfoil. When tested in the hallway, the design achieved a 67% reduction in overall drag. In theory I calculated I could ride it at nearly 22 m/s (50 mph). Theory, however, is one thing and practice another; I finally rode the vehicle at a timed 18.5 m/s (41.5 mph).

Riding the vehicle gave the sensation of being inside a tightly packed suitcase—the fairing allowed only 12 mm (0.5 in.) of shoulder clearance, and the fairing came within 25 mm (1 in.) of the ground. It acted like a vacuum cleaner, sucking up dirt, leaves, and trash. I solved this problem by raising the skirt 150 mm (6 in.) from the ground and partly covering the bottom, but the streamliner still swerved with heart-stopping unpredictability in even lightly gusty winds. It wasn't the sort of HPV you'd like to pedal to the grocery store.

In a remarkable coincidence, in 1974 I ran into Jack Lambie at an American Institute for Aeronautics and Astronautics (AIAA) meeting on truck fairings, and he told me he was also building a streamlined bicycle. At that time, Jack was an aerodynamics consultant on truck fairings for AeroVironment of Pasadena, California. Neither of us had seen or heard of a streamlined bicycle be-

fore, and only about 20 of these had been built worldwide to date, so the chances of that meeting now seem almost vanishingly small. However, we organized the first scientific test session of streamlined bicycles in the California State University, Long Beach hallway, and Lambie's streamliner achieved about a 50% drag reduction because his fairing was wider and shorter.

The Founding of the International Human Powered Vehicle Association

I decided to see how fast my machine could go, and after months of practice on the runway of the Los Alamitos Naval Air Station, on November 11, 1974, U.S. Olympic cyclist Ron Skarin rode the streamliner 1 mile at 18.16 m/s (40.63 mph) and 200 m at 19.23 m/s (43.02 mph) (see Figure 7.11). The event got worldwide publicity, and it was only then that we learned of the long history of streamlined bicycles in Europe and of the UCI's rulings against them. Encouraged by the publicity, Lambie and I decided to organize what we ambitiously called the International Human-Powered Speed Championships. We wrote articles in *Bicycling* magazine and

FIGURE 7.11 The Kyle Streamliner, ridden by Ron Skarin, setting a world record for one mile at the Los Alamitos Naval Air Station in 1974.

Note. Photo courtesy of Chester Kyle.

Bike World and challenged all comers to a race. The first competition was held on April 5, 1975, at the Irwindale drag strip in southern California. The Speed Championships have been held every year since then.

About the only rules we had were that vehicles must have no stored energy of any kind and must be strictly human powered. Fourteen of the strangest vehicles ever designed showed up at the first race. Some were pedaled on the stomach (prone) and some on the back (supine), and one was steered like a skateboard. Testing had been minimal and crashes were frequent. One problem with our event is that contestants, who often seem to finish building their vehicles the night before the race, are surprised when they go through the speed traps upside down or sideways.

At the first Speed Championships, the winning speed for 200 m with a flying start was 20.06 m/s (44.87 mph), set by a streamlined tandem racing bicycle built by Phil Norton, a psychology teacher from Claremont, California. Mine was the winning single-rider machine, ridden by Skarin at 44.69 mph. Vehicles were allowed to accelerate for 610 m (2,000 ft) before going through a timed 200-m section. In the mid-1970s we founded the International Human Powered Vehicle Association (IHPVA) so we could sanction events of this type and recognize records set by machines that were not legal under UCI rules.

Successful Prone HPVs

Vehicle speeds have continually increased. At the second Championships in 1976, Allan Abbott, competing with a low recumbent bicycle of his own design, chose to make only one run and won at 21.4 m/s (47.8 mph) (see Figure 7.12). In 1981, riding an improved version of this prone machine, Abbott reached a speed of 23. 19 m/s (51.87 mph). Abbott's bicycle was extremely hard to balance at low speed, but above 7 m/s (15 mph) it was very stable. Apparently he had no qualms about flying along at 22 m/s (50 mph) head first, with his face about a foot from the pavement.

It takes nerve to ride a one-of-a-kind experimental HPV at high speed. But as far as I know, in spite of all the crashes, there have been no serious accidents in any of the competitions. The fairings usually protect riders from abrasion, and I have seen riders spill at more than 22 m/s (50 mph) and crawl out without a scratch.

Prone machines were often successful in the early years of the Championships. Paul Van Valkenburgh's hand-and-foot-powered four-wheeled cycle, the Aeroshell, won in 1977 at 22.07 m/s (49.38 mph). Gardner Martin's prone bicycle was the first single machine to exceed 50 mph, winning the single-rider category in 1979 at 22.73 m/s (50.84 mph) (see Figure 7.13).

Figure 7.12 Allan Abbott's winning prone streamlined bicycle, 1976.

FIGURE 7.13　Gardner Martin's prone bicycle, the first single HPV to break 50 mph.

In 1983, Steve Ball's ingenious hand-and-foot-powered linear-pedal-travel Dragonfly won at 24.55 m/s (54.92 mph) (see Figure 7.14). This cable-and-pulley-driven racer was so compact and low that the rider, Richard Bryne, had to use a periscope. It was probably the most complicated vehicle ever to compete successfully at the Championships. The prone-recumbent design seems very attractive because it puts the rider in a diver's position, the most streamlined of all human body positions, with the smallest frontal area. However, since 1983, few prone machines have competed, and none have been very successful. Riders who have tried the prone position are not impressed with the comfort, and it is difficult to support the rider in a practical fashion (Abbott, 1988). Prone machines have never been popular in competition.

Supine Tandems

In the early Speed Championships, multiple-rider machines got as much publicity as the single vehicles, and perhaps more. At Ontario in 1977, national team sprinters Jerry Ash and Gibby Hatton won on a standard streamlined tandem bicycle at 22.32 m/s (49.93 mph).

Also competing in that meet was a group of engineering students from Northrop University led by Tim Brummer, Chris Drieke, and Don Guichard. They built a clever supine tandem tricycle called the White Lightning. The mechanical design of this machine was superb: it had a solidly built drive train, a stable steering mechanism, and a light aluminum framework joined by epoxy-glued joints. However, the fairing was hastily formed and, as one spectator commented, it looked as if it had been put together with boxing gloves in the dark. White Lightning still managed to go 21.41 m/s (47.90 mph) for third place. I still remember Brummer's remark after the event: "Wait till next year: you guys may have the muscle, but we have the smarts." True to his word, the Northrop students spent hundreds of hours building a slick fairing for the tandem (based on an NACA 66-012 symmetric wing profile), and in 1978 they trounced the competition at 24.43 m/s (54.43 mph). Tim Brummer's chapter describes White Lightning and later vehicles.

In 1977, Allan Abbott had donated a $3,000 prize for the first human-powered vehicle to exceed 24.6 m/s (55 mph) under IHPVA rules. In 1979 White Lightning won the Abbott Prize on its first run at 24.96 m/s (55.85 mph) and received an honorary speeding ticket from the California Highway Patrol. In a later run it went 25.34 m/s (56.70 mph). In the 1980 Championships, the White Lightning became the first human-powered vehicle to exceed

60 mph (27.28 m/s; 61.04 mph), but lost to a sleek, new Vector tandem, which set a new world record at 28.13 m/s (62.92 mph) (see Figure 7.15). The rear rider in this tandem faced backward, making it very compact, with a much lower surface drag than any other tandem.

FIGURE 7.14   Richard Bryne in Steve Ball's linear-drive hand-and-foot-powered prone tricycle, 1983. Bryne had to use a periscope to see forward.

FIGURE 7.15   The Vector supine tandem tricycle, 1980. The rear rider faces backward.

Al Voigt's Vectors dominated totally for the next few years. The single Vector, ridden by Dave Grylls, set a world record of 26.32 m/s (58.89 mph) in 1980; this record stood until 1985, and to this date no multiple-rider vehicle has exceeded the 62.92 mph record set by the Vector tandem. During an hour time trial, Ron Skarin and Eric Hollander averaged nearly 50 mph for 1/2 hour at Ontario, and finally made 74.5 km (46.30 miles) in 1 hour. Later in 1980, the Vector tandem traveled on the Interstate 5 freeway from Stockton to Sacramento, California, at an average speed of 22.6 m/s (50.5 mph) for 68 km (42 miles). This lightweight fragile pedal-powered tricycle seemed totally out of place among the highway trucks.

Even though Voigt's Vectors never competed after 1982, the shape and design of the Vectors, with their rear drive wheel, two forward wheels that straddle the rider, plus their smooth and graceful aircraft shape, have fostered dozens of close copies in succeeding competitions.

The New Breed of Single HPVs

Starting in 1979, a new concept in HPV design began to take hold. Fred Tatch, riding a hand-and-foot-powered supine recumbent bicycle called the Manuped, won the 27-mile road race 2 years in a row on a twisting flat course at Ontario, the second year against the formidable Vector. It was no accident: the fairing was short and compact, and the bicycle was supremely maneuverable in the corners

and could accelerate like a dragster (see Figure 7.16). Tricycles like the Vector had to slow down in the turns to keep from rolling over, and the Vector skidded off the track upside down in the 1980 road race. Although the concept of combining arm and leg power is intriguing, Tatch's front-wheel-drive bicycle, invented by physicist John Thomas, was so difficult to steer that it took almost a circus performer to ride it. It was one of only three hand-and-foot-powered machines to win events at the Speed Championships: Van Valkenburgh in 1977, Tatch in 1979, and Ball in 1983.

Also in 1979, Danny Pavish, using Gardner Martin's Easy Racer supine recumbent bicycle as a chassis, designed a fairing shape that was to influence future HPV design. This shape consists of a low, narrow, rounded nose, tapering upward and back and reaching the widest point at the rider's shoulders. From this point, the contour tapers rapidly to a sharp trailing edge. Derivatives of this shape were used on the Avatar Bluebell, Lightning X2, Infinity, and Gold Rush, all of which have won the Speed Championships. The fastest bicycles in the world at present are the Cheetah (30.6 m/s; 68.4 mph), Gardner Martin's Gold Rush (27.28 m/s; 65.49 mph), and Tim Brummer's Lightning X2 (64.19 mph) (see chapter 9).

The Land-Shark shape (see Figure 7.17) and its relatives may have been originally based on wind-tunnel research, but the final versions were shaped by logic and pure eyeball intuition. There are two schools of thought in the design of HPV fairings:

FIGURE 7.16   Fred Tatch riding John Thomas's Manuped, 1979.

FIGURE 7.17 Danny Pavish's Land Shark, 1980.

the air-over advocates and the air-under advocates. The air-over advocates build a flat-sided fairing with a rounded body of revolution for the top and extend the fairing nearly to the ground so that very little air goes underneath (like the early White Lightning tandem). The idea is to avoid induced drag due to lift caused by trapping high-pressure, low-speed air underneath the vehicle. The air-under advocates raise the fairing up from the ground plane, round the bottom, and given the fairing a smoothly rounded three-dimensional shape. This permits air to circulate freely underneath. The theory is to give the air plenty of room so it won't interfere with the ground plane and cause induced drag.

Both types of vehicles have been almost equally successful. Don Witte's cleverly designed Allegro tricycle had a fairing that came within 12 mm (0.5 in.) of the ground. This vehicle, which had an ingenious front-wheel drive with front-wheel steering, broke the world record four times from 1985 to 1986, finally peaking at 28.15 m/s (62.98 mph). Witte was attempting to win the Du Pont Prize of $30,000 for the first human-powered vehicle to exceed 29 m/s (65 mph) under IHPVA rules. Gardner Martin's Gold Rush won the prize in 1986 on the high-altitude road near Mono Lake, California, with Freddy Markham riding.

The Gold Rush is presently the end of the evolutionary line stemming from the early Land Shark. The final version has a light Kevlar fairing and an overall length of about 2.4 m (8 ft), a width of 480 mm (19 in.), a height of 1,290 mm (51 in.), a frontal area of only about 0.46 m² (5 ft²), and a weight of about 13 kg (29 lb). It has set some notable records. In Michigan in 1989, Freddy Markham pedaled the Gold Rush 73 km (46.366 miles) in 1 hour, or 21 km (13 miles) further than the early streamliners of Berthet and Mochet. (The hour record was won by the UK's Bean in 1991.) The Gold Rush has also traveled faster on a velodrome than any other bicycle in the 4,000-m pursuit, with a time of 3:43.79 for an average speed of about 18 m/s (40 mph). Martin, of Watsonville, California, manufactures a street model of this recumbent called the Easy Racer. (The Cheetah set a new high-speed record of 68.4 mph, 30.6 m/s, in 1993.)

Practical HPVs and Other Notable Accomplishments

Tim Brummer, now an engineer from Lompoc, California, has designed a series of single-rider Lightnings that have proved that HPVs can be extremely effective on the road (see chapter 9). In 1984 his remarkable recumbent bicycle won the Speed Championships at 25.655 m/s (57.394 mph). Most HPV bicycle fairings are completely impractical: they require an assistant to help the rider in and to tape on the canopy. Then the assistant must hold the vehicle upright until it is pushed off. Brummer's Kevlar-honeycomb-Nomex fairing was uniquely designed for self-entry and self-starting. The front opened forward like a sports car hood, and trap doors in the bottom flipped open to allow the feet to balance at stops. In June 1985, this machine traveled 309 km (192 miles) from Seattle to Portland, averaging 11.4 m/s (25.5 mph) in 7 hours 31 min 42 s. This included stops and bumper-to-bumper evening traffic into downtown Portland. Long-distance Race Across America (RAAM) specialist Pete Penseyres rode the bike for Brummer.

For the 3 years from 1988 to 1990, another version of the Lightning won a 105-km (65-mile) road race in South Africa against some 11,000 racers, including most of the country's professionals and national team members. Ridden by amateur Lloyd Wright and prepared by IHPVA member John Stegmann, the Lightning averaged over 11 m/s (25 mph) in the races, covering a hilly, wind-blown, winding road course around the Cape of Good Hope, to finish minutes ahead of the closest competitors: tandem bicycles and professional cyclists in a pack. This model of the Lightning uses a front nose cone with a nylon spandex cover over a light aluminum framework. The rider's head sticks out, giving unobstructed 360° visibility, and the rider can also lower the feet at stops. The vehicle has a very small side area and seems to be easily rideable in fairly high winds.

Even more impressive was the Lightning's win in the August 1989 HPV Race Across America. A team of riders including Pete Penseyres relayed the spandex-faired recumbent bicycle 4,473 km (2,789 miles) from Los Angeles to New York in 5 days 1 hour to average 10.3 m/s (23 mph). They passed the rival Gold Rush team 200 km (125 miles) from the finish. The touring model of Brummer's supine recumbent is called the Lightning P-38, and it is manufactured in Lompoc, California.

International Competitions

When the International Human Powered Vehicle Association was organized, we had no idea whether the sport would in truth become international. It has. In 1978 Shinichi Toriyama held an event in Japan. The course was short and the speeds were slow, but enthusiasm was high. Since then competitions have been held in Canada (the Hull Festival) and England (organized by promoter Peter Selby), and Championships have been held in Europe for the past several years. There was even a 1989 race in Poland. Generally speeds have not been as high as in U.S. events, since good courses in Europe are scarce.

The European competitions have been dominated by a Vector prone-recumbent tricycle built by the famous bicycle historian Wolfgang Gronen. (Most of the early history of bicycle racing in this chapter derives from Gronen's research.) In a desire to contribute to cycling history himself, Gronen bought a new Vector from Al Voigt in 1983 and later modified the design and built several of his own. These machines, ridden by former West German sprint champion Gerhard Scheller, have set several IHPVA records. In 1987, Gronen and Scheller traveled to the high altitude (3,650 m; 12,000 ft) of La Paz, Bolivia, hoping to set an absolute speed record. They did not accomplish that goal, but they did reach 26.80 m/s (59.96 mph) for 200 m and set world records at 500 m (25.15 m/s; 56.26 mph), 1,000 m (23.58 m/s; 52.76 mph), the mile (20.88 m/s; 46.72 mph), and 100 km (18.23 m/s; 40.79 mph) (see Figure 7.18).

In Italy, Antonio Dal Monte, who designed Francesco Moser's hour-record "funny" bike in 1984, built a strange HPV for Moser in an attempt to win the Du Pont Prize. Moser pedaled the low-slung, carbon-composite-monocoque machine lying flat on his back and had to navigate using a tiny TV monitor operated from a forward-facing camera. In a highly publicized debut before dozens of reporters in 1985, the HPV wandered off course at low speed, due to a sloppy steering linkage. It later proved to have a resonant oscillation of the frame at about 18 m/s (40 mph) that caused it to weave at an ever-increasing rate at pedaling frequency, so it never surpassed this speed and the attempt was abandoned.

This illustrates one truth in building HPVs. Success seldom occurs on the first attempt: Several iterations, much practice, and continual refinement are usually necessary before one can surpass the others' accomplishments.

Conclusion

Human-powered vehicles can exceed the performance of standard bicycles on a smooth road under almost any foreseeable conditions. They take less energy, go faster, are safer and more comfortable, provide more weather protection, and even are more maneuverable than standard bicycles. Their advantages in human health and well-being

FIGURE 7.18 Gerhardt Scheller setting the 100-km record, 40.75 mph, in La Paz, Bolivia, September 1, 1987.

through exercise are obvious. However, HPVs have several handicaps, some of which are logical and some of which are not. HPVs usually cost more, are heavier, are harder to maintain, take up more space, are noisier, and are strange in appearance, prompting comments from passersby. Even alternative bicycles such as recumbents have some of these drawbacks. Considering everything, HPVs will probably remain a very minor part of the future transportation mix. However, the technology of lightweight high-efficiency, low-energy-consumption vehicles that has been developed for HPVs may have an important impact on future transportation.

Another facet of HPVs has already influenced hundreds of engineers, designers, and instructors. As an intriguing design project, an HPV is as exciting and desirable as anything ever invented. It is inexpensive and relatively fast and easy to build with minimum experience and few tools. The designers can be their own test pilots so that the success or failure of a design is immediately obvious. Working the bugs out of an HPV can be as much fun as building it in the first place. And riding it in competition can be the thrill of a lifetime. Thousands have gone through this experience in the Speed Championships.

For the past several years, the Western Region of the American Society of Mechanical Engineers (ASME) has sponsored an HPV race for student ASME chapters in western universities, and more than 100 vehicles have taken part in the races. Some of the best entries in the International Human-Powered Speed Championships come from these ASME contests or from other university design projects. As a teaching tool, an HPV design project is ideal. It includes aerodynamics, dynamics, strength of materials, construction techniques, shop practice, human factors, cooling, and, above all, planning, organization, and teamwork. And instead of being a dry theoretical design, the project can be tested in an exciting competition. If it were only for this development alone, the whole HPV movement, spanning nearly a century, would have been worthwhile. Etienne Bunau Varilla, Marcel Berthet, Charles Mochet, Oscar Egg, and the other HPV pioneers would have been proud.

References

Kyle, C.R. (1979). Reduction of wind resistance and power output of racing cyclists and runners traveling in groups. *Ergonomics*, **22**(4), 387–397.

Gronen, W. (1987). *A history of bicycle racing and bicycles*.

Roberts, D. (Ed.) (1990). The invention of the safety bicycle. (Available from the Veteran-Cycle Club, London, UK)

Sharp, A. *Bicycles and tricycles*. Cambridge, MA: MIT Press (originally published 1896).

8

THE DEVELOPMENT OF MODERN RECUMBENT BICYCLES

David Gordon Wilson

A *recumbent* pedaling position is one having the pedaling axis substantially in front of the rider. Further recumbents of the type where the rider is in a sitting position may be designated as *semirecumbent* and those where the rider is lying down, as *fully recumbent*. For this chapter, the boundary between semirecumbent and fully recumbent is set as a seat-back angle of 45° with the horizontal. Abbott defines four possible fully recumbent positions: the supine position with face upward; the prone position with face down; and on the right or left side, the right or left decubitus positions (Abbott, 1988). In general, full recumbents are used only for speed-record attempts, because of the position's inherent problems for both seeing and being seen. Technically speaking, the first pedaled bicycles were "recumbents," but this chapter briefly traces the development just of *geared* recumbent bicycles, from the first known examples that appeared in 1895 to the Cheetah of 1992. Case studies of the Avatar 2000 and of the Tour Easy and Easy Racer bicycles are covered in greater depth. Varia-

This chapter is adapted from SAE paper 8400021.

tions such as front-wheel drive and front-steering recumbents are introduced.

Recumbent bicycles have had many revivals. A recumbent called the Velocar disturbed the conventional bicycling world in the 1933 to 1935 period because it was used to topple most existing bicycle records, and it was ruled "not a bicycle." The latest revival of interest in recumbents has come about because of the formation of the IHPVA. Faired recumbent bicycles currently hold most of the world HPV records. Moreover, often the same recumbent bicycles that have won the Speed Championships have also been awarded practical-vehicle prizes. The recumbent bicycle, therefore, could have very wide application.

The Evolution of Safety Bicycles and the Upright Riding Position

Karl von Drais designed the first known bicycle (circa 1817) simply as a running aid, so it is difficult to define it as having a recumbent or upright sitting position. However, the designers of the first pedaled bicycles, Kirkpatrick Macmillan in about 1839 and Pierre Lallement in about 1865, used the recumbent position, probably because riders of what were then unusual machines wanted to start with their feet on the ground. However, the direct coupling of the pedals to the wheels meant that the effective gear ratio was, in modern terms, superlow. Gears and chains were not developed to the point where they could be used to improve the gear ratio (the impedance match). Accordingly, the pedaled front wheels of the Lallement bicycles were steadily increased in diameter until they were as large as could be comfortably ridden: the machine became the high-wheeler. The only way in which the high-wheeler could be both pedaled and steered was for the rider to be almost vertically over the front wheel. Riders were exhorted to "get over the work," that is, the pedals. When the development of improved chains and sprockets (circa 1884) allowed the development of the geared safety bicycle—so called because the high, precariously balanced riding position of the high-wheeler was extremely unsafe—the upright pedaling position, regarded as normal, was retained. Accordingly, when the recumbent bicycle reappeared in geared form, it was regarded as an aberration.

The Geared Recumbent's First 30 Years, 1895 to 1925

The modern safety bicycle had evolved almost to its present configuration by soon after 1890. The geared recumbent made by Challand in Ghent, Belgium, around 1896 (Salvisburg, 1897) was very close in design to one form of modern recumbent, such as the one shown in Figure 8.1. In Challand's recumbent the rider sat high, directly over the rear wheel, so that starting off from rest may have been difficult. A recumbent patented by Wales in the U.S. in 1896, incorporating hand-and-foot drive, positioned the back of the seat forward of the rear-wheel center, but still over the wheel. Another American recumbent was that produced by Brown (Dolnar, 1902), in which the rider's seat was entirely forward of the rear wheel and the front wheel was forward of the cranks (Figure 8.1), an arrangement now characterized as long wheelbase or LWB. It was received rather scathingly by the British bicycling press, although its virtues were grudgingly acknowledged.

Peugot produced a recumbent bicycle in France at an unfortunate time: 1914, the start of World

FIGURE 8.1   Brown's recumbent.

War I. Perhaps this machine had the greatest possibility of success of all unorthodox bicycles, because Peugot, a significant company, had a great chance of influencing the French-dominated Union Cicliste International (UCI). However, the war ended this effort. After the war Swiss engineer Paul Jaray, whose fame came from his work on the Zeppelins, made the J-Rad recumbents (see Figure 8.2) in Stuttgart in 1921, with limited success. They used a swinging-lever constant-velocity transmission having three ratios given by using pedals at different radii along the levers.

The Velocar

Later in the 1920s a class of cycle car racing became very popular in Germany, with the American-German sailboat researcher Manfred Curry taking a prominent part. In France a self-taught engineer, Charles Mochet, was making small motorized cycle cars (Schmitz, 1990). He also made a one-seat, four-wheeled pedal car for his son, Georges, who would "amuse himself by pedaling fast and passing ordinary bicycles with ease." Charles switched his production entirely to a two-seat, four-wheeled HPV that he called a Velocar. According to Schmitz it had free wheels, a differential, and a three-speed gear and was fast enough to pace bicycle racers on the track. Its instability on turns gave Mochet the

FIGURE 8.2 J-Rad, 1921 (from a photograph owned by the Veteran-Cycle Club, U.K.).

idea of "cutting the Velocar in half, figuratively" by building a recumbent bicycle for racing. The front wheel was steered "through a bevel gear connected to flat handlebars by a long horizontal tube." After it was finished in 1932 the champion professional, Henri Lemoine, rode it and found it comfortable and easy to pedal, but he did not want to switch to it.

One who did take to the Velocar was Francis Faure, a second-rank racing cyclist, who defeated the champion, Lemoine, in a 4-km pursuit race (see Figure 7.9). He also broke track records. A professional road racer, Paul Morand, won the Paris-Limoges race "going away" on the Velocar in 1933 (Schmitz, 1990). Mochet had written to the UCI in October 1932 to verify that the Velocar accorded with the UCI's racing rules. The then-existing UCI rules required that the crank axis be between 240 and 300 mm from the ground; that the vertical through the crank axis be no more than 120 mm from the nose of the saddle, between 580 and 750 mm from the vertical through the front-wheel axis, and no more than 550 mm from the vertical through the rear-wheel axis; that no power be obtained from hand motion; and that no means of reducing air resistance be used. The UCI met in some disarray and in 1934, after much controversy, passed rules that disallowed recumbent bicycles for officially sanc-

tioned racing and, therefore, the records that Faure and other had set (Abbott, 1988; Barrett, 1972).

The Velocar inspired several commercially produced recumbents, especially those built in Great Britain by Grubb. These had handlebars beneath the seat, an excellent design introduced in the last century for high-wheelers and known as Whatton bars, after their inventor. Neither the Whatton bars nor the Velocar-inspired recumbents became established. Nor did an interesting variation known as the Ravat Horizontal, sold in Great Britain as the Cycloratio, in which the pedals and cranks were over the front wheel. The present author would later unwittingly borrow this design idea. As the seat was partly over the rear wheel, this style could be called the high, short wheelbase. Another variation of this style was the 1939 Velocino in Italy and the Donkey Bike, built by Emil Friedman in Frankfurt, West Germany, in 1965. The front wheel had a diameter of only about 310 mm. A high, long-wheelbase recumbent using a steering wheel but otherwise being constructed of conventional bicycle components was the Moller Triumph (see Figure 8.3).

Oscar Egg, the renowned Swiss bicyclist who competed with Marcel Berthet for the 1-hour record from 1907 to 1914, when he set a record which was to last until 1933, built a streamlined recumbent bicycle, propelled via levers, with the intention of

FIGURE 8.3   Moller Triumph (from a photograph owned by the Veteran-Cycle Club, U.K.).

becoming the first bicyclist to exceed 50 km in 1 hour. Berthet had reached 49.992 km in November 1933 in a streamlined, regular (pacer) bicycle. But it was Faure and a streamlined Velocar who reached 50.537 km in 1 hour, in March 1939 (Schmitz, 1990).

The Postwar Doldrums

After World War II, the principal users of recumbents who received any notice were some in Great Britain still riding Grubbs and Dan Henry in the U.S., who designed and built a long-wheelbase (LWB) machine for his own use. The LWB design positions the rider entirely between the wheels. Henry used standard 27-in. wheels and designed very effective springing on both. Most previous recumbents were built with small front wheels, because in the long-wheelbase machines little of the total weight is carried by the front wheel, so that the small increase in rolling resistance (which is inversely proportional to wheel diameter and proportional to the normal load) is probably outweighed by a reduction in air drag at normal speeds. At the same time the bicycle mass and

length are decreased and the steering is likely to be more precise. In the short-wheelbase recumbent, the front wheel is made small because it is located under the legs or feet, which must be able to reach the ground.

The Evolution of the Avatar 2000

The Avatar 2000 was developed largely in ignorance of the foregoing history. To some extent we (David Gordon Wilson and Richard Forrestall) repeated what had been done before. However, had we known of the existence of previous recumbents, we might well have taken the same course, because little had been reported of either their deficiencies or their advantages.

The design evolved from many initial sketches and careful layouts on the drawing board. There was even some simple analysis. But progress mostly came from old-fashioned trial and error. This was not through laziness or lack of rigor. Any device that interacts closely with human beings—a nuclear-power-station control room, for instance—should be designed with great attention to detail and overall logic, but even so some major deficiencies become apparent only after a device is in use. A review of the stages we went through and the conceptual errors we uncovered may help others to avoid similar mistakes.

The first two recumbent bicycles in the series were made by H. Frederick Willkie II, who had been inspired by a design contest I organized and had requested a sketch of what he thought would be an advanced bicycle that he could build. Willkie called the first (1972) of the two bicycles Green Planet Special I (GPS I) and, unknown at the time to the designer and builder, it bore a strong resemblance to the Ravat. Willkie used the GPS I around Berkeley, California, reportedly achieving high speeds, but he found the rather crude seat jarring to his spine. It also seemed hazardous to have the handlebars and stem almost directly in front of his face, because of the risk of injury in an accident. Willkie asked the author to sketch a revised design.

The result was the 1973 Green Planet Special II (GPS II), in which the cranks were lowered as far as possible and the steering-head tube was brought back so that the front-wheel rim would clear the heels. This also permitted the handlebars, while fastened directly to the fork-steerer tube, to be under the thighs. Although Willkie used a hard, molded-plastic seat, he found that this machine was far more comfortable than GPS I, partly because it had a far more open angle between the torso and the line connecting the hips to the crank axis, allowing better breathing, and partly because he was now sitting more on his buttocks and less on his coccyx.

The 16 × 1-in. tubular front tire was, however, heavily loaded, with a typical life of less than 160 km (100 miles). The author bought GPS II from Willkie and brought the rear wheel about 300 mm (12 in.) forward to reduce the load carried by the front wheel, fitted a robust 16 × 1-3/8-in. wheel and wired-on tire, and experimented with many seat types and angles until he arrived at the approximate configuration shown on Figure 8.4 and a construction using 19-mm (3/4-in.) O.D. aluminum-alloy tube and a stretchable-canvas slung seat.

A large fiberglass trunk was also fitted. On this much-modified version of GPS II, renamed the Wilson-Willkie (WW), many thousands of miles were covered in great comfort and enjoyment, in summer heat and winter cold.

The sight of an obviously relaxed and cheerful rider on this unusual machine attracted media attention, and the bike was the subject of many newspaper articles and photographs, TV interviews,

FIGURE 8.4 Wilson-Willkie recumbent (from a photo by Mike Atlas).

talks, two school movies, and a nationally shown Mobil television commercial. It may have inspired a commercial recumbent of similar appearance but dissimilar details, known as the Hyper-Cycle, that was produced after this publicity.

The WW did have flaws, despite its delightful features. It was still heavy on the front wheel, causing even the wired-on heavy-duty tires to last only 1,000 to 2,000 miles (1,600 to 3,200 km). Spokes in the front wheel regularly broke. Snow at a depth of more than 3 in. caused front-wheel sliding. Heavy braking on the front wheel could cause the rear wheel to lift, and after an emergency stop the rider could end up standing in front of the now-vertical bicycle. On two occasions there were more dramatic stops when, in one case, the front-brake retaining nut shook itself off, and the brake fell out onto the tire, rotated around the rim, and became entangled in the spokes. The front wheel locked, the forks bent back, and the rider, travelling at about 12 m/s (27 mph), tumbled forward, feet over hands. Nothing more than abrasions and bruises resulted. This and the other spills confirmed the outstanding safety features of the recumbent design with below-seat handlebars.

Serendipity

One of the many pleasures of design and development is encountering serendipitous advantages. My initial interest in designing recumbents had been purely for safety: I had been saddened to read of many deaths and serious injuries to riders of regular bicycles who had been thrown over the handlebars by encounters with dogs, potholes, and anything that could jam the front wheel. I had expected that the result would be a compromised machine, with safety advantages, but with many other disadvantages. Yet, unexpected advantages kept appearing. It had not been expected, for instance, that it would be possible to pedal around corners without any danger of the pedals hitting the ground. The great sense of relief coming from a relaxed upper body and the ability to breathe deeply using the diaphragm was another pleasant surprise. When the brakes failed during a downpour on a high-speed descent down a hill with a sharp bend and a dangerous intersection at the bottom, it was an even greater relief to learn that one tennis shoe put flat on the road provided rapid and safe deceleration under full control.

Another unexpected finding was that the canvas seat acting over the full area of the back gave stiffness against pedaling thrusts, and relieved the hands and upper torso of any need to exert a reaction force, but the weight acting against the small area of the pelvic bones and buttocks was resiliently and comfortably sprung. The safety flag, easily installed on a recumbent bicycle, together with the brightly painted surfaces of the large trunk, made the vehicle far more visible to other road users than is a conventional bike not so equipped. The relaxed seating position at a level with that of the drivers of most private automobiles seemed to promote instant communication, and there resulted a higher degree of courtesy from other Massachusetts road users than had been thought possible. There was a remarkable absence of neck and eye strain, of nerve damage in the hands and crotch, and of back pain, compared with what is generally accepted in the conventional bicycle racing position.

Front Wheel Loading and Rolling Resistance

Through the interest of a potential manufacturer in an improved version of the Wilson-Willkie, the author met Richard Forrestall in his search for builders willing to work on what may have seemed the somewhat strange designs he was drawing. Forrestall and his partner, Harald Maciejewski, first built the Avatar 1000 (A1K) (see Figure 8.5), an improved version of the WW, in 1978. In this design the front wheel was moved forward about 250 mm (10 in.) from that in the WW to further reduce the

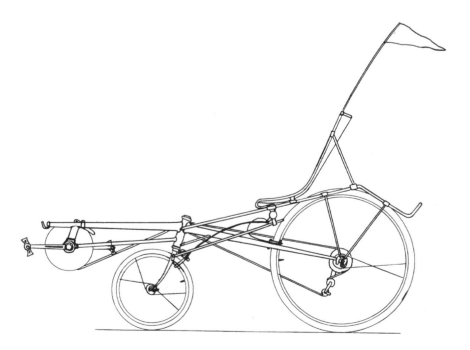

FIGURE 8.5 Avatar 1000.

load on the front wheel. This was done despite the potential interference between the heels and the front-wheel rim, because this could occur only at speeds below about 2.5 m/s (6 mph); at higher speeds, the maximum amplitude of front-wheel steering movements was too small for interference to take place. To retain the previously convenient and comfortable placement of the handlebars below the seat, a ball-jointed steering rod was used to connect the handlebars to the fork crown.

The A1K was a considerable improvement on the WW, and gave longer front-tire and front-wheel life. The learning period needed to become used to keeping the heels out of the way of the front tire at very low speeds was short. Only in extremely heavy braking did the rear wheel show any tendency to lift. Comfort, already impressive on the WW, was further enhanced with the reduction in front-wheel loading.

The rolling resistance is formally given as the force resisting forward motion divided by the vertical force, or load, on the wheel; it is termed the coefficient of rolling resistance (C_r). The C_r for bicycle tires on normal roads is between 0.0025 and 0.015. It is a function of the wheel diameter, being lower for larger diameters. It is also affected by tire suppleness, tubular tires being formerly more supple than clinchers. However, improved reinforcing materials, synthetic rubbers, and construction have brought lightweight clinchers in the 1990s almost to the C_r range of tubulars. Rolling resistance is also greatly affected by tire pressure. Approximate values taken from tests by Whitt (1982) for $27 \times 1\text{-}1/4$-in. pre-1980 tires for pressures of 2, 4, and 6 bar (30, 60, and 90 psig) are 0.008, 0.005, and 0.004, respectively. At 4 bar the C_r for a tire of $16 \times 1\text{-}3/8$-in. (and similar vintage) was approximately twice the value for the larger tire on a similar (in this case, "medium-rough") surface.

Thus, although rolling resistance is usually small compared with aerodynamic drag, it is far from negligible. Suppose, for instance, that the weight of a sprint-record machine, like the Cheetah or Gold Rush, plus the rider were 1,000 N (224.7 lbf) and that it were traveling at 30 m/s (67.1 mph). If the tires have a C_r of 0.005, the power lost to rolling resistance would be $1,000 \times 30 \times 0.005 = 150$ W, more than 0.2 hp. Reducing this C_r to 0.0025 through better tires and a smoother road surface could make a major difference when the rider's output at that point in a record run is probably well below 1 hp (746 W). Having most of the weight of the rider and vehicle over a large-diameter rear wheel also reduces rolling resistance. The small-diameter lightly

loaded front wheel, although having a higher coefficient of rolling resistance, probably allows a much greater reduction of aerodynamic drag than the increase of a rolling drag.

However, with the load on the front wheel, C_r was still higher than on a conventional bicycle. Table 8.1 shows approximate percentages of front-wheel and rear-wheel loading for conventional and some recumbent bicycles.

Table 8.1 FRONT-REAR LOADING DISTRIBUTIONS		
	Front	Rear
Three-speed (Roadster)	36%	64%
Ten-speed (Sports)	40%	60%
GPS II (estimated)	70%	30%
Wilson-Willkie (WW)	65%	35%
AVATAR 1000 (A1K)	62%	38%
AVATAR 2000 (A2K)	31%	69%

The higher loading on the smaller front wheel of the A1K, compared with the conventional bicycles (three speed or ten speed), inevitably leads to higher rolling resistance. There was no reluctance to load up the rear wheel, and interstate trips were confidently and comfortably undertaken loaded with camping and hiking gear. However, the performance on soft ground, in snow, and with a soft or flat front tire was poor: having so great a proportion of the weight over the front wheel meant that its tracking needed to be precise to give the rider good control. This weight distribution gave good slow-speed balancing on hard surfaces with a fully inflated front tire, but this was not enough compensation for the alarming loss of control when the front tire deflated or when snow or mud was encountered. (Other experimenters have reported improved performance using large-diameter mountain-bike tires.)

We felt that to improve on the A1K we should further decrease the loading on the front wheel. The weight distribution of conventional bicycles, with 35% to 40% of the weight on the front wheel, combined with the lower center of gravity given by the recumbent position, seemed desirable, giving good traction, excellent and safe braking, and easy balancing. For this the ideal front-wheel location would seem to be for the wheel to have a common vertical tangent with the front of the pedaling circle. To avoid the high pedaling position of the Ravat and the GPS I, a "squashed" pedaling path, for instance an elongated elliptical or a linear motion, would have to be used. We built and tested several lever transmissions that seemed in prospect to have many advantages over rotary cranking, but when tried out they had unforeseen disadvantages (see Figure 8.6).

The lever drives included a simple piston-crank mechanism, with the pedals taking the place of pis-

tons. The line of action of the pedals did not pass through the crank axis, giving a quick-return motion that seemed to have advantages. But the mechanism, designed as it must be to withstand high pedaling forces, weighed far more and had far more friction than the pedals it replaced. Reluctantly, we put the search for a lightweight, efficient mechanism to produce a linear or an elongated elliptical motion (possibly having ergonomic advantages) on a lower priority basis, and in 1979 we solved the

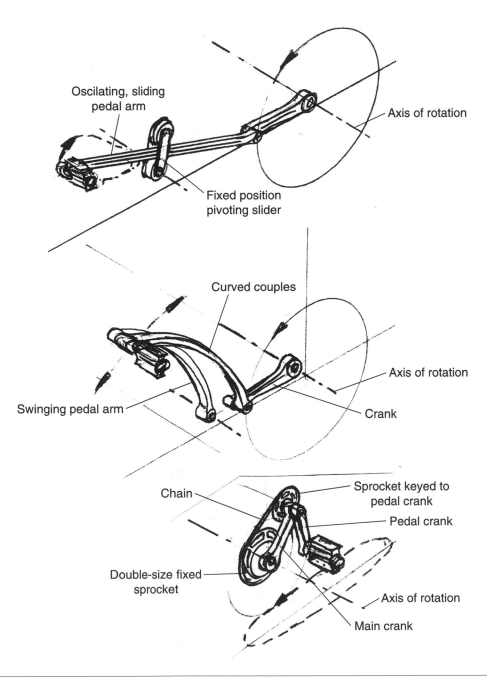

FIGURE 8.6 Lever transmissions giving elongated pedaling motion.

nose heaviness of the short-wheelbase recumbents by going to a long-wheelbase design. We called this the Avatar 2000.

Avatar 2000

Again, serendipity rewarded us. The sole "cost" to moving the front wheel forward appeared to be that the Avatar 2000 (A2K) (see Figure 8.7) became longer than the A1K, which was almost identical in length to a conventional bicycle. There was not necessarily an increase in mass, because although two frame tubes, the steering rod, and the brake cable become longer than in the A1K, the frame is much simplified, stresses are greatly reduced, and two idler cogs needed to route the chain over the front wheel in the A1K are no longer needed. In addition, the following advantages over the short-wheelbase A1K were found, some of them unexpectedly, to be added to the already listed advantages of the recumbent bicycle over conventional bicycles:

1. Tracking accuracy became very precise. Although all bicycles should go where the riders steer them, the outstanding ability of the A2K in this respect extended to ice and snow conditions, in which the light loading on the front wheel allowed it to climb over ice and snow ridges that would cause the short-wheelbase versions to skid. (It is not claimed, however, that recumbent tracking ability in ice and snow is better than that of the conventional bicycle, which is very good in this respect.)

2. Full braking on both wheels could be used at all times except on slippery surfaces. In normal circumstances a front-wheel skid cannot be induced. An early abnormal circumstance was when an improperly mounted tire pump broke loose from the top tube, fell onto the rider's right foot, and went through the spokes of the front wheel during a turn onto a busy street. The front wheel locked and skidded, but the feet could be immediately put on the ground and the rider remained seated on the bicycle. This type of accident on a conventional bicycle can result in very severe injury, often including skull or spinal fracture. In the case mentioned here, the pump was ruined, one front-wheel spoke was slightly bent, and the front-fork paint was chipped, but no other damage occurred, and the 35-mile run continued.

FIGURE 8.7 Avatar 2000.

THE TOUR EASY AND EASY RACER

As I've said before, any device that interacts closely with human beings should be designed with great attention to detail and to overall logic. The Easy Racer team offers the following pair of anecdotes to support its claim that its recumbent is a truly practical, primary mode of transportation. Elisse Ghitelman commutes year-round to her Massachusetts high-school teaching duties. She rides a 1983 Tour Easy, repainted bright red following the November 1990 birth of Jacob Allen, with whom she "cocycled" 2,129 miles during their first three trimesters together. Elisse's total distance traveled on the Tour Easy now exceeds 30,000 miles.

Don Gray started riding bicycles in 1988. In 1991, at age 50, he was the first-ever recumbent rider to complete the Markleeville Tour of the California Alps, covering 206.8 km (128.5 miles) and climbing 4,627 m (15,180 vertical ft) in just under 14 hours. There is a general belief that recumbents are no good on hills, which seems to be a generalization from the poor hill-climbing performance of one or two particularly poorly designed and poorly geared recumbents. But obviously, a stock Easy Racer without fairings can climb hills! Challenged by the loss of an arm as the result of a motorcycle accident, Gray chose recumbent cycling for his fitness program. Gardner Martin stresses the personal satisfaction he derives from the human dimension of Easy Racer riding: an ergonomically kind vehicle that fits the practical needs of a wide range of riders with fewer barriers of age, sex, or physical limitation.

In a recent road-test article in *The Recumbent Cyclist* newsletter, the editor, Bob Bryant, had this to say about the Tour Easy:

> "Born to be wild!" This is the tune I hear in my head every time I climb on board the Tour Easy. The upright handlebar steering is a confidence builder for first-time riders. It is also among the easiest of all recumbents to learn to ride. By "learn" we are only talking about a matter of a few minutes and almost anyone can be cruising in comfort. The lower bottom-bracket height is also easier to handle in traffic or for starts and stops. The low-slung trademark Tour Easy design is also among the fastest. I'm sure there are SWB riders who may beg to differ, but when riding the Tour Easy equipped with a Super Zzipper fairing, I found it significantly faster than any other stock recumbent. As a general rule recumbents with upright handlebar steering are faster due to less air drag from your arms, shoulders and handlebars sticking out the sides, as on an underseat-steering recumbent. The acceleration is excellent, as is the high-speed stability. My test bike and I went up to 52-mph down a local hill together. (Please, for you at home, do not try this.) The LWB design does not offer the perfect weight distribution: the front wheel can be lightly loaded. In my many miles on LWBs, especially the Tour Easy, this has never been a problem. The Tour Easy has perfect road manners. The LWB makes up for its lightly loaded front wheel with great stability in all situations.

Many people ask about steering with those long forks and handlebars. It is a bit tiller-like but nowhere near what you'd expect. After a few rides on the bike, you don't even notice. A real plus for the steering is that it is direct, with no rods, cables or linkages; this keeps the bike simple. This long-wheelbase bike glides along almost effortlessly. It also takes much less attention to the road than its SWB counterparts. Some like this and others do not. In all my Tour Easy miles the only real drawback is not in the bike itself, but in how to transport a LWB recumbent. . . . To sum it all up, a fellow rider described the Tour Easy to me as "the recumbent from which all others are judged." Now it is up to you to decide.

3. The high proportion of the weight distribution on the rear wheel gives outstanding rear traction in snow and ice and outstanding rear-wheel braking in all conditions.

4. Although the seat frame undergoes almost the same vertical accelerations as the rear wheel, the resilience of a fabric seat (in the case of the A2K it is nylon mesh with leather border and straps) in the vertical direction gives the effect of springing.

5. At speeds above 2 or 3 m/s the combination of rolling and air drag for the wheels alone is lower than for two large wheels, because of the low forces on the small front wheel. The rear wheel runs partly in the lee of the rider's body, reducing its air drag. The semirecumbent position gives a lower frontal area, of course, than does a conventional bicycle, because having the legs out in front more than compensates for the somewhat more exposed attitude of the torso and head.

6. A small but appreciated advantage of the long-wheelbase recumbent is that it can be carried around almost like a briefcase by holding the top tube just in front of the seat.

7. Another unexpected advantage was the ease in dealing with aggressive dogs, which are responsible for many deaths and injuries among bicyclists each year. When such a dog attacks, it has to do so running alongside in easy reach of the rider, who can easily discourage it by hitting it on or near the nose. Trying to do this from a conventional bicycle often leads to a loss of control and a dangerous fall.

The Racing Avatar and Modern Machines

The Avatar 2000 gained some publicity in Europe when the author took it to Velo-City, an HPV congress in Bremen in 1980, and it appeared on television. Richard Ballantine, a prominent author and publisher of bicycling books and magazines, later purchased an Avatar 2000, tested it, and gave it outstanding reviews. Derek Henden, a British amateur constructor employed by Xerox, borrowed it to find how its performance would be improved by a fairing. He used a narrower seat to reduce the frontal area and increased the gear ratio with a crossover drive (the chainwheel on the pedaled shaft is on the left and drives a smaller sprocket on the left side of a parallel shaft; the regular chainwheel(s) is (are) on the right side and drives the rear wheel) in the normally unused bottom-bracket tube beneath the seat. HPV racing in Britain had started, with Ballantine's encouragement, and the new vehicle, named Bluebell from the color of its fairing and running for the Nosey Ferret Racing Team, named for its sharp-nosed appearance, began winning (Wilson, Forrestall, & Henden, 1984). Henden borrowed ticket money from Ballantine to compete in the IHPVA International Human-Powered Speed Championships in Irvine, California, in October 1982.

For 2 years, 1980 and 1981, the Vector tricycles won all the major HPV races, setting records for the 200-m flying start as well as over many other distances. On its first appearance in 1982 at the International Human-Powered Speed Championships (IHPSC), the Bluebell beat not only the

Vector but also the Easy Racer recumbent bicycle in the 200-m top-speed event. The speed was not a record, but the course and conditions were different from those at which the previous records were set. The rider, Tim Gartside, was an Australian lawyer touring in Britain who had never raced previously.

In road racing also the three-wheeled Vector and its clones lost their dominance at the 1982 IHPSC. The two-wheelers reasserted their superiority as the Easy Racer recumbent bicycle pulled away from the tricycles for a solid win. The Bluebell was competitive in this event, but crashed in a fast corner. (This was a notable demonstration of the high level of safety of the recumbent design. Gartside ran into the chain-link fence at a speed approaching 22 m/s [50 mph] after the wind load on the banked fairing lifted the front wheel. He was strapped into the seat solely to allow him to push harder on the pedals. The combination of the feet-forward position, the fairing, and the straps enabled him to walk away from this spectacular crash with no more than bruises from the shoulder straps.) The battle continued on the velodrome, where the Vector produced a final win in the 4,000-m pursuit race, beating the Easy Racer by a fraction of a second. This was the first time on a velodrome for both rider and vehicle. Two weeks later Gartside in the Bluebell won over Vector and Easy Racer when both crashed. After the 1982 racing season, the Vector retired from racing. Two-wheeled recumbents have gone on to win almost all events through 1994.

One shouldn't try to make too much of individual wins. However, in HPV racing as in rowing, fashions follow winners. In 1981 and 1982 most challengers were building low tricycles inspired by the Vectors. Afterwards, there was a switch to short- and long-wheelbase recumbent bicycles. As Australian writer and racer Doug Adamson wrote in the December 1983 issue of *Bicycle Magazine*: "An interesting aspect of the [1983] speed trials was that half of the vehicles in the top ten were bicycles. Most previous thinking had concluded that low frontal area and increased stability of three wheels was the way to go for speed." Presumably as a result of the Bluebell IHPSC and European-circuit wins and of exposure of the Avatar 2000, on European television, several small companies in Europe and the U.S. began making machines that seemed to be inspired by the Avatar 2000—indeed, a few were almost indistinguishable from the Avatar 2000, even to its builders.

The Dominance of Gardner Martin's Easy Racer Team

Gardner Martin is a former automobile and motorcycle racer who was inspired to design improved bicycles by a 1974 *Bicycle Magazine* article by Chester Kyle, "Are Streamlined Bicycles in Your Future?" Martin entered the 1975 IHPSC with a very-low-frontal-area, flat-on-the-belly (prone recumbent) bicycle that earned the distinction of being the first vehicle to crash at an HPV speed meet. But by 1979 Martin had combined a refined vehicle with Olympic-class "Fast Freddy" Markham as rider to drive the vehicle, Jaws, over the 22 m/s (50 mph) mark, a first ever for a single-rider HPV.

In 1976 Martin started work on the laid-back Easy Racer design, partly because his wife, Sandra, objected to the impracticality and the hazard of the head-first prone recumbent for everyday use. Martin started by modifying an old tandem bicycle, removing the front seat, the rear pedals, and extending the handlebars. Gradually refined, this prototype became the Easy Racer and began winning road races and criteriums. Sandra and Gardner Martin proceeded to develop the Easy Racer into a vehicle that proved to be the world's fastest HPV bicycle, and yet, with minor changes, could be used for shopping and commuting. The Martins began marketing their everyday version under the name Tour Easy. In addition, with an openness that has been emulated by few others, they sold plans with which amateur builders could make their own Tour Easies, using two diamond-frames and standard parts.

Surprisingly, for some, even the "everyday" Tour Easies began winning races after fairings were installed, for example, setting a new record in the 4,000-m race at the Major Taylor velodrome and winning many road-race events. In 1982 and 1983 the first practical-vehicle contests were won by stock Tour Easies with partial fairings added. Beginning in 1983, Easy Racer's dominance was continually challenged, at times successfully, by Tim Brummer's beautiful Lightnings. Brummer tells his story in chapter 9.

The Easy Racer-Lightning rivalry intensified in January 1984 when the Du Pont Company offered $15,000 (plus interest) to the first single-rider HPV team to exceed 65 mph (29 m/s) over a 200-m run with a flying start. At least three vehicles comfortably exceeded 60 mph on several occasions, but the Gold Rush, an Easy Racer, (see Figure 8.8) was the first vehicle to achieve that goal. On a late evening in May 1986 the Gold Rush reached 65.484 mph on a state highway near Yosemite National Park. Now housed in the Smithsonian Institution, the original Gold Rush never raced again, but a regular-production aluminum-frame Gold Rush Replica went on to dominate IHPSC racing from 1986 through 1991, winning all top speed events, three times breaking the world 1-hour record.

In a dramatic 5-day race in the 1989 Race Across America, the Easy Racer and Lightning teams continued their competition. The Easy Racer team led for most of the way across the country in a street-modified Gold Rush Replica, only to have the Lightning team forge ahead decisively in Pennsylvania, where confusion over the route lost the Easy Racer team a great deal of time and poise.

Gardner Martin's success owes a great deal to dogged persistence, a drive for excellence, and a remarkable rider: "Fast Freddy" Markham. Markham has raced and won titles on Easy Racer designs since 1978 and as late as summer 1994 was the only bicyclist to win two gold medals in the Los Angeles Olympic Sports Festival on standard frames. Markham is the exception among world-class bicycle racers: most racers are reluctant to lose some undocumented degree of muscle training by pedaling a recumbent. Freddy Markham's three world-record 1-hour runs on Gold Rush serve notice that when more of the world's top racing cyclists switch to recumbents, single-rider speeds will continue to push the envelope.

Two points of coincidence between the Martin and Brummer teams are worth noting. One is that both teams used forward rather than under-the-seat handlebars to reduce frontal area and to suit riders who feel more comfortable pulling on something in front of them rather than on something underneath. The second point of coincidence: both shaped their fairings by eye, at least at first. The 2-year supremacy of the Vector design was earlier attributed partly to extensive aerodynamic analysis by computer and wind-tunnel testing, at a time when the back-yard mechanic was considered out of date.

As the speed competitions heated up in the early 1980s, designers agreed on the overriding importance of aerodynamically optimized fairings. However, some unpredicted aerodynamic benefits of the free-form Avatar Bluebell fairing contributed to its defeat of the Vector. The Bluebell was in turn beaten by the Lightnings and Easy Racers. The Lightning used a free-form fairing, whereas the Easy Racer

FIGURE 8.8 Easy Racer's Gold Rush (photo courtesy of Gardner Martin).

combined underwater-torpedo laminar-flow analysis with free-form canopy, fins, and contours. Will the next big increase in speed be made by the team that rigorously optimizes the fairing, perhaps including boundary-layer suction to induce low-drag laminar flow?

Front-Wheel-Drive Front-Steered Recumbents

The types of recumbent bicycles that have been made and raced since the earliest versions have been predominantly rear-wheel drive and front-wheel steered. There has been a perception that the long chain that results from this configuration is heavy, attracts dirt and deposits some on the rider's legs, and adds too much weight. Whether or not reality accords with perception is a matter of debate.

A frequently tried alternative configuration is to use front-wheel drive with front-wheel steering. This involves either the cranks turning with the front wheel and the leg thrusts affecting steering, or the chain, or other transmission element, twisting from a fixed pedaling position to the steered wheel. This technology is at present in a state of interesting flux. Eliasohn (1991) assembled and ed-

ited a review of several different variations of front-wheel-drive recumbents in the summer 1991 issue of *Human Power*. Front-wheel drive could be part of machines with all-wheel drive, considered by some to be highly desirable for off-road vehicles. Recumbent bicycles are, however, completely unsuitable as all-terrain vehicles, which rely to a large extent on the agility conveyed by a highly independent rider.

Conclusion

Recumbent bicycles, in the form of the Cheetah (see Figure 8.9), the Lightning, and the UK's Bean hold, at the time of writing (1994), HPV records, respectively, for the flying-start 200-m event (over 29.4 m/s; 68.4 mph), the HPV Race Across America (5 days and 1 hour), and the 1-hour distance (over 72 km; over 45 miles).

Recumbent bicycles are therefore currently the leaders in the HPV racing world. Through the awards they have received as practical vehicles they are to some extent front-runners for commuting and touring. Their users almost universally are extremely enthusiastic about their favorable attributes. Recumbents have attracted, however, nothing like the astonishing explosion of enthusiasm that has

FIGURE 8.9   The Cheetah, holder of the 200-m speed record (29.4 m/s, 68.4 mph) in 1993.

greeted the mountain bike. The recumbent's time could come. The increasing frequency of total traffic standstills in many of the world's major cities, coupled with increasing environmental concern, could result in increased support for human-powered travel. A vehicle that is far more comfortable, easier to pedal, and faster than the alternatives will achieve considerable success, if mass-produced (and mass-advertised) so that the costs come down and options increase. The recumbent bicycle awaits its hour.

Acknowledgment

I would like to thank Sandra and Gardner Martin for generously supplying me with material on the Easy Racer bicycles.

References

Abbott, A.V. (1988). Prone-position recumbent bicycles. *Human Power*, **7**(2), 1, 12–13.

Barrett, R. (1972, Winter). Recumbent cycles. *The Boneshaker*, pp. 227–243.

Dolnar, H. (1902, January 8). An American stroke for novelty. *The Cyclist*, p. 20.

Eliasohn, M. (1991). Front-wheel-drive recumbent bicycles. *Human Power*, **9**(2), 11–19.

Salvisburg, P. von. (1980). *Der Radfahrer in Bild und Wort*. Hildesheim and New York: Olms Presse. (original work published 1897)

Schmitz, A. (1990). Why your bicycle hasn't changed for 106 years. *Cycling Science*, **2**(2), 6.

Wilson, D.G., Forrestall, R., & Henden, D. (1984). Evolution of recumbent bicycles and the design of the Avatar Bluebell. Detroit: Society of Automotive Engineers. (SAE No. 8400021)

9

LIGHTNING PROGRESS: AN HPV DEVELOPMENT CASE HISTORY

Tim Brummer

The IHPVA, in existence since 1976, has held many competitive events for human-powered vehicles during its nearly 20 years. Events during the first 5 years concentrated mostly on top speed, probably because

1. everyone wanted to know how fast it was possible to go; and
2. the lack of experience with these new types of vehicles made designing and building them much simpler if it was not necessary to provide for easy rider entry, visibility, cooling, and maneuverability.

As the years passed and top speeds increased past 25 to 27 m/s (55 to 60 mph), more emphasis was placed on the practical aspect of HPVs, starting in the early 1980s. This was done by including closed-course road races and "LeMans starts." The first race for HPVs on open roads was held in 1985, from Seattle to Portland. The decade culminated with the HPV Race Across America in 1989.

Practical-vehicle contests were also held, although the execution and judging process of some contests were not to the liking of all contestants. The problem was, and is, that *practical* means different things to different people. In the arena of human-powered road vehicles, one person may put the ability to carry 500 kg (1,100 lb) high on the scoring list, whereas another feels that weather protection is more important.

So how is it possible to resolve these conflicting requirements when designing a practical HPV? In a free-market society, you don't: you let the consuming public do it for you! The major use of bicycles in the U.S. today is for recreation. This includes racing, century rides, and weekend trips. The second most prevalent use is for commuting. Thus, the designer of an HPV intended to replace conventional bicycles should keep these facts in mind, along with what the intended market is willing to pay.

I have been involved with HPVs since 1977. This chapter examines the performance advances of four of my vehicles over the 1980s. Although the machines featured did not win every race or set all the records, they did win a few and were always near the top in competitions. On that basis, they are representative of HPV trends and progress in general.

These vehicles are also compared with a top Union Cicliste International (UCI) bicycle. The UCI, the organization that sets rules for professional and Olympic bicycle racing, does not allow recumbents and fairings because of their speed advantage. As a result, the majority of bikes sold today are "UCI" bikes, because manufacturers build bikes that are similar to those that have, for instance, "won twenty Tours de France." This chapter discusses how HPVs have made great improvements in practicality so that for some uses they are now superior to UCI bikes.

Vehicle Descriptions

The Lightning series of vehicles reflected contemporary design philosophy. The first vehicle of the series, the White Lightning, was designed when it was thought that maximum speed would be reached in a vehicle with several riders in a prone or supine position. Vehicles of that period had up to five riders. After the best of the multiple-rider vehicles, the two-person Vector, had been beaten decisively by a single-rider recumbent bicycle, designers turned equally decisively in this direction. Later Lightning-series vehicles reflected this changed design philosophy.

White Lightning

WEIGHT: 80 lb (36 kg)

LENGTH: 20 ft (6 m)

WIDTH: 28 in. (710 mm)

HEIGHT: 30 in. (760 mm)

BUILT: 1977

RACED: 1977 through 1983

LAYOUT: Two riders in a supine recumbent position facing forward. Three wheels: two rear-drive wheels, front wheel steers. Standard six-speed rear cluster and circular cranks. The rear rider also had a set of hand cranks.

CONSTRUCTION: Bonded and welded oversize-aluminum-tube frame. Fiberglass-honeycomb fairing. Acrylic windshield.

White Lightning was first conceived in 1977 as a club project by students at Northrop University. Since this was during the early days of the IHPVA, the only design criterion was to run at the highest possible speed. The final result was a two-person, three-wheel vehicle 6 m (20 ft) long, only 760 mm (30 in.) high, and weighing 36 kg (80 lb). As it would be run only on a race track, the ground clearance was 13 mm (0.5 in.), the turning radius was 15 m (50 ft), and the visibility was poor.

White Lightning was the first vehicle to break 24.6 m/s (55 mph), thus winning the Abbott Prize; it eventually went over 27.3 m/s (61 mph). In spite of not being raced for more than 11 years, it still holds the 5-mile, 1/4-mile, and 600-m records. We also discovered it was very comfortable when compared to a standard bike, which led to the incentive of trying to build something similar, but able to be ridden on the streets.

Lightning X-2

WEIGHT: 40 lb (18 kg)

LENGTH: 92 in. (2.34 m)

WIDTH: 22 in. (560 mm)

HEIGHT: 52 in. (1.32 m)

BUILT: 1983

RACED: 1983 through 1986

LAYOUT: Single-rider, medium-wheelbase, semirecumbent bicycle. Standard circular cranks and drive train, 12 speed (see Figure 9.1).

CONSTRUCTION: Brazed 4130-steel frame. Aramid-honeycomb fairing. Acrylic windshield.

Numerous designs were investigated and a couple of prototypes were built during design of the X-2. The seating position was raised considerably, compared to the White Lightning, to have good visibility in traffic. This seat height and the desire for a light, compact, and maneuverable machine led to a two-wheel, medium-wheelbase design. The frame was built of 4130 steel, for ease of modifications, with a nylon-mesh seat. The fairing construction is similar to White Lightning, with aramid being substituted for fiberglass.

One innovation that caused considerable interest was the ability of the rider to get into the bike and ride off without assistance. Until the X-2, all riders of fully streamlined machines needed help from the pit crew to get in, to put the canopy in place, and to hold the machine upright until the rider had gotten started. Two design features were used to achieve this capability. First was the pair of

FIGURE 9.1   Lightning X-2.

landing-gear-style doors that opened when the rider put his or her feet down: Thus, the rider could stop or start without assistance. Once underway, the doors were closed by hand. The second feature enabled the rider to enter by stepping in from the side. This was achieved by hinging the entire nose section of the fairing so it tilted forward. The object was to develop an HPV that was not only fast but also could be ridden on the street without assistance.

The X-2 enjoyed considerable racing success. It was the world's fastest bicycle in 1983 and 1984; in 1986 it recorded a low-altitude speed of over 28.6 m/s (64 mph). It also won the Seattle-to-Portland challenge in 1985, with an average speed of 11.4 m/s (25.5 mph). This was the first HPV event staged in the U.S. on open, public roadways.

The X-2 was not a commercial success, however, due to the high cost of the honeycomb fairing and the door-operating hardware. The vehicle also was too bulky and too hard to park in city use, as well as being hot on climbs.

In 1986 the Lightning X-2 suffered major damage in a high-speed (28.6 m/s; 64 mph) crash while attempting to set a new top-speed record. In 1991 it was repaired and modified for the John Paul Mitchell Systems Challenge from San Francisco to Los Angeles. Ridden by Pete Penseyres, it won that competition in a time of 18 hours 4 min, setting a new record.

Lightning X-4

WEIGHT: 50 lb (23 kg)

LENGTH: 92 in. (2.34 m)

WIDTH: 22 in. (560 mm)

HEIGHT: 48 in. (1.22 m)

BUILT: 1985

RACED: 1985 through 1989

LAYOUT: Same as the Lightning X-2 (X-4 is shown in Figure 9.2).

CONSTRUCTION: Brazed 4130-steel frame. Skin-and-stringer fiberglass fairing, with a nylon-fabric middle section. Acrylic windshield.

The X-4 was similar to the X-2, but with a fairing built of conventional fiberglass and with the rider's head sticking out the top. The Lightning X-3, a paper design, was never built. The design objective for the X-4 was to make an HPV more practical and less expensive than the X-2. This design was not very successful, mainly because of the 23-kg (50-lb) weight. Although it was only 4.5 kg (10 lb) heavier than the X-2, the difference proved considerable when climbing hills. Also, when descending hills the safe speed limit was quickly exceeded.

FIGURE 9.2   Lightning X-4.

To simplify the design and reduce costs, a zipper was provided on the nylon part of the fairing for rider entry, and openings provided in the bottom to allow the feet to be put down. (These features were carried over to the following model.)

The X-4 never set any records or even won a race, which is why it is not well known. It was entered in a couple of local races, however, and finished in the middle of the pack. The X-4 was useful, in that the experience gained with this machine showed how not to make a practical HPV, and it led to the creation of the F-40.

Lightning F-40

WEIGHT: 32 lb (14.5 kg)

LENGTH: 84 in. (2.1 m)

WIDTH: 20 in. (500 mm)

HEIGHT: 48 in. (1.2 m)

FIRST BUILT: 1987

RACED: 1987 to present

LAYOUT: Same as the Lightning X-2 (Figure 9.3 shows the F-40).

CONSTRUCTION: Brazed 4130-steel frame. Lightweight fiberglass nose fairing. Remainder of fairing is spandex, stretched over a light-weight aluminum framework in the rear. Lexan windshield.

The latest Lightning design is a true production, street-usable HPV. Over 50 of these vehicles have been sold as of the end of 1993, with many of the owners using them for commuting. The nose section of the fairing is built from thin fiberglass, with the remainder being spandex stretched over a lightweight aluminum frame. Zippers are provided for entry, cooling, and for access to the rear storage compartment. This construction reduces the weight to 14.5 kg (32 lb) while maintaining the same air drag of the X-4.

The F-40 has also enjoyed some racing success on long-distance, demanding, open-road races. The most notable of these is winning the HPV Race Across America in a time of 5 days, 1 hour, for an average speed of 11.3 m/s (24.5 mph).

Performance and Cost Comparisons Between the Lightning Series and the Best UCI Bicycle

There has naturally developed a degree of friendly rivalry on the part of riders of recumbent bicycles and riders of UCI bicycles. Either type vehicle is

FIGURE 9.3 Lightning F-40.

seen to have advantages and disadvantages. This section compares such performance measures as top speed, cruising speed, and hill-climbing speed; such safety and handling characteristics as turning radius, visibility, and braking; and other attributes, such as cost and rider comfort.

Top Speed

As shown in Figure 9.4, putting a fairing on a recumbent bicycle results in a vehicle with a faster top speed than the best UCI bicycle ridden by the best cyclist in the world. Over the past ten years, the top speed attained by sprint champions on the best UCI cycle has increased only about 1 mph. Most of this has been due to better-trained athletes.

When compared to the speed increases made by HPVs in the past decade, the small progress made by UCI bicycles is indeed miniscule. When the first HPVs were raced at Ontario Speedway in California (which has since been torn down), speed increased by an average of 1.8 m/s (4 mph) every year. This rapid performance increase was the result of continuing vehicle refinements by the White Lightning and Vector teams. The vehicles would be modified and improved based on lessons and new ideas garnered from the previous year's race.

This continual performance improvement can also be seen in the yearly speed increase of the Light-

ning X-2 and F-40 vehicles. The X-2 eventually surpassed the best speed set by White Lightning, although the course used for this record was about 2 mph faster than at the old Ontario Speedway. The conclusion is that rapid advances in vehicle design and construction over a 6-year period have resulted in an HPV roughly as fast as the original vehicles, but with the additional capability of being operated on the open road and without need for a large ground crew.

The F-40 vehicle does not have as high a top speed as the previous machines, a result of trade-offs with such other design considerations as cooling and cost. As can be seen, however, this vehicle is still being refined in much the same pattern as the previous ones, so there is room for further improvement. Also, the current top speed of about 22 m/s (50 mph) is still much better than the best UCI bike's speed of 19 m/s (43 mph).

Cruising Speed

Cruising speed on level ground is a much more useful indication of performance than top speed. Whereas top speed can be held for only a few seconds and requires a power output of more than 750 W (1 hp), a top athlete can maintain 375 W (0.5 hp) for close to 1 hour. As shown by Figure 9.5, the UCI bicycle has made some improvements in

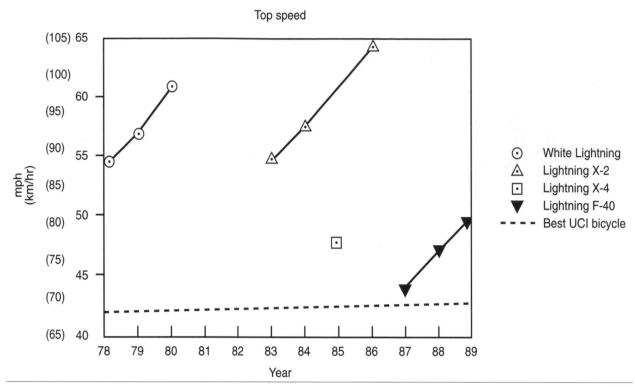

FIGURE 9.4   Top speed of Lightning and UCI bicycles.

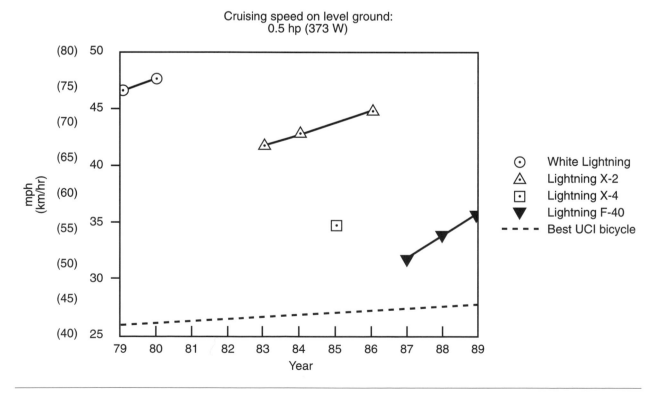

FIGURE 9.5   Cruising speed on level ground at 373 W (0.5 hp).

cruising speed over the past 10 years. This is due to the introduction of disk wheels, Scott-type handlebars, skin suits, and aero frames. These improvements have also resulted in much more expensive bicycles, and a slight decrease in some of the other performance factors as will be seen later.

The cruising speeds shown for the HPVs are similar to the previous graph for top speed. As time goes on, the speed for each vehicle increases due to continued development and modification. The speed for each successive vehicle, however, decreases due to trade-offs with other design considerations. In any event, the current F-40 vehicle is still much better than the best UCI bicycle, with a cruising speed advantage of about 3 m/s (7 mph). For those who don't think it is possible to cruise at 16 m/s (36 mph) on a bicycle, the fastest average speed for the Lightning F-40 team during the HPV Race Across America was at just this speed. This was when Bob Fourney rode 145 km (90 miles) in 2.5 hours across parts of Texas and Oklahoma.

Also of interest is the advantage White Lightning has in cruising speed over the X-2, although the top speed of these two vehicles is essentially the same. This is because the supine riding position of White Lightning limited the amount of maximum power that could be produced during sprinting, as compared to the X-2's more efficient position.

Climbing Speed

Climbing hills seems to be a major preoccupation with traditional bike riders, as can be inferred from the large amount of coverage devoted to the subject in cycling magazines. Thus, the performance of the HPVs compared with the UCI bike is shown in Figure 9.6 for an 8% grade, a fairly steep slope and the maximum specified for modern highways.

As can be seen, the UCI bike has an advantage on these steep hills, because its lighter weight overcomes the aerodynamic advantage of the HPV.

However, the progress made by HPVs in hill-climbing performance during the past decade has been substantial, especially when compared to the small progress made by UCI bikes. The UCI progress is mainly due to alternative frame materials that have produced slightly lighter and stiffer bikes. The improvements in hill climbing for HPVs is a result of reduction in weight, improved rider positions, and more efficient drive trains.

The hill-climbing speed of the early HPVs, such as that of White Lightning, could not have been maintained for a long period because of poor rider cooling. Current HPVs, such as the F-40, have much-improved cooling and thus can maintain the speed shown up the longest hills.

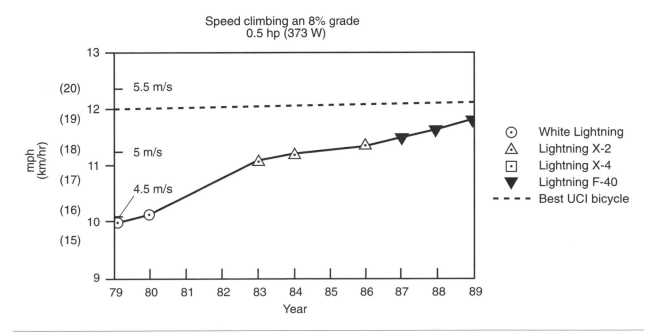

FIGURE 9.6 Speed climbing an 8% grade at 373 W (0.5 hp).

When comparing the hill-climbing graph with the graph of cruising speed, it can be seen that the HPV is faster on flat ground, but the UCI bike is faster climbing steep hills. Which machine is faster on medium-grade hills? If the grade is less than about 6%, the HPV has the advantage; the UCI bike has the advantage on steeper grades.

However, just because a UCI bicycle has an advantage in climbing steep hills does not mean it has an overall advantage in hilly areas. For every uphill there is also a downhill. Unless speed is limited on the downhill by numerous sharp curves, the HPV descends much faster and more than makes up the time lost in climbing.

Turning Radius and Handling

Turning radius is a parameter that can be measured; however, handling is more subjective. Therefore, Figure 9.7, the graph for turning radius and handling, uses a relative rather than a numerical scale. Although White Lightning was stable and responded well to steering inputs, it also had a 15-m (50-ft) turning radius that gave it a poor rating in this category. As can be seen, the successive Lightning designs exhibit improved turning and handling. This is due to shorter wheelbases and improved frame and steering geometry.

The current Lightning F-40 is similar to the best UCI bikes in responsiveness and cornering speed, as confirmed by John Schubert, writing in the May 1986 *Bicycle Guide Magazine*. He commented that "the Lightning will match any specialty criterium bike for steering quickness" (p. 66). The UCI bikes, with a shorter wheelbase, still have a slight advantage in minimum turning radius, thus achieving a slightly better rating in this category than the HPV.

Visibility

Visibility in this case refers to the ability of the rider to look out of the vehicle and to have an all-around view of the environment. This is again a subjective scale (see Figure 9.8), where excellent would be just standing in the middle of the road and being able to see up, down, and all around.

Early HPVs, such as White Lightning, had very poor visibility, limited to peering through a small windshield at the end of a long, tubelike fairing. The X-2 design was an improvement, with the windshield close to the rider. The X-4 and F-40 designs were better still, with the rider's head outside of the fairing.

These machines are in fact better than the UCI bike, because of the ability to have upward vision in the recumbent position. This is not possible with the head-down riding position needed on the UCI bike to reach optimum performance. Visibility on the UCI bikes has actually decreased as the riding position has become lower and more stretched out to lower drag and increase speed.

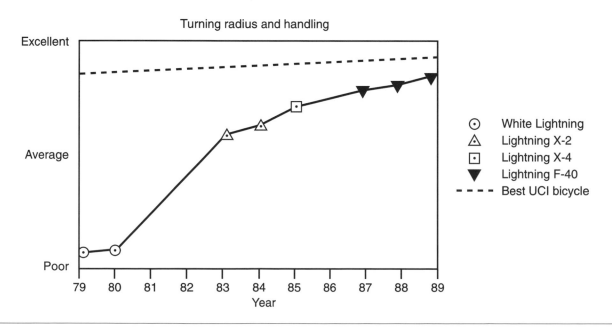

FIGURE 9.7   Turning radius and handling.

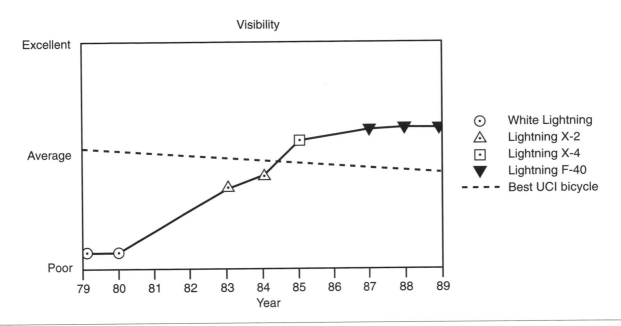

FIGURE 9.8   Visibility from Lightning bicycles.

Rider Cooling and Comfort

The latest HPVs, like the Lightning F-40, are more comfortable and at least as cool as UCI bikes. The semirecumbent seating position allows the use of a wide seat back and bottom, thus spreading out the load on the rider's tender parts. Also, neck, back, and arm strain is virtually eliminated by this position. In fact, a large percentage of recumbent-bicycle riders purchase these vehicles because they can no longer ride standard bikes due to physical problems, many of which have been caused by standard bikes. A subjective estimate of the improvement in rider cooling and comfort in Lightning recumbents is shown in Figure 9.9

How can an HPV with a fairing that blocks the cooling airflow be as cool as a bike without a fairing? There are a couple of ways. First, when an HPV is cruising at 13 m/s (30 mph), sufficient air leaks through the front-wheel slot and around the windshield to keep the rider from "cooking." If the speed drops, such as when climbing a hill, parts of the fairing can be opened up to admit more air, so that the cooling airflow is close to what it would be without a fairing.

Second, when the sun is intense, the fairing acts as a sunshade, lowering the amount of heat received from solar radiation. In the California desert during the HPV Race Across America (RAAM), Pete Penseyres noticed that one part of his arm was sweating profusely where the sun was shining on it through the head opening in the fairing. The rest of his arm, in the shade, was hardly sweating at all.

Thus, adequate cooling in a current HPV is achieved by varying the amount of cooling airflow in relation to speed and by having the fairing acting as a sunshade. As can be seen from the graph, much improvement has been made in cooling airflow since the days of White Lightning. Because the seating and comfort of the HPVs are essentially all the same, all of the improvements shown are due to cooling improvements. In contrast, the UCI bikes have experienced a slight decrease in cooling over the past 10 years, due to the use of aero helmets and skin suits.

Braking

Braking ability as displayed in Figure 9.10 refers to maximum stopping capability. The ability to stop in a shorter distance gives a better rating. Wet-braking performance is also a consideration. If a recumbent is properly designed, it is possible to use full braking power without the back wheel leaving the ground. UCI bikes cannot utilize full braking, because their high center of gravity causes the rear wheel to leave the ground. Thus, a recumbent can utilize increased braking power and stop in a much shorter distance than a UCI bike. As shown in Figure 9.10, all of the HPVs except for White Lightning have better braking than the UCI bike. The braking for White Lightning was limited because it had only two caliper brakes for two riders.

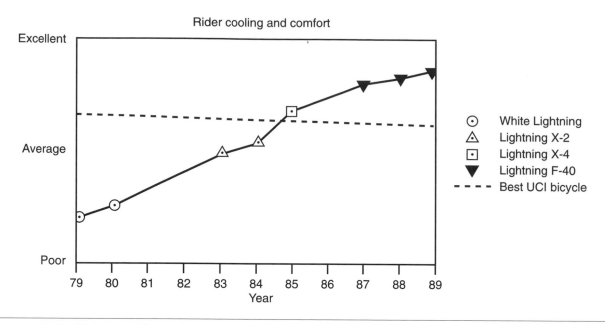

FIGURE 9.9   Lightning rider cooling and comfort.

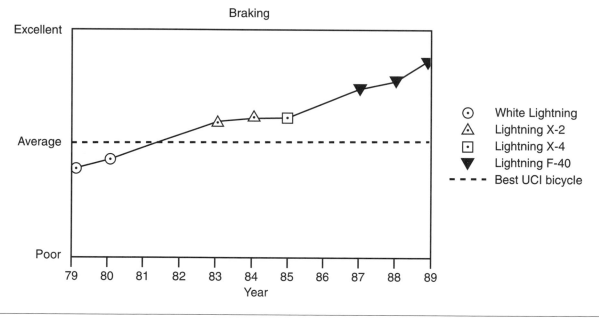

FIGURE 9.10   Braking.

The most recent F-40, as used on the HPV RAAM, employs hydraulic caliper brakes, which give superb dry braking and good wet braking. Pete Penseyres gave a demonstration of wet braking during the HPV RAAM when he was coming down a hill at 22 m/s (50 mph) in a rainstorm toward an intersection with heavy cross traffic. About 90 m (300 ft) from the intersection, the light turned red. Pete squeezed the brake levers for all he was worth, and after a few revolutions the rims were hot enough to boil off the water and give full braking power. He slid to a stop just at the crosswalk.

Cost

Cost is toward the top of many people's list of what makes a bicycle practical, especially when they have to pay for it! As shown in Figure 9.11, the price of HPVs has been reduced considerably over the past 10 years. HPVs such as White Lightning and Light-

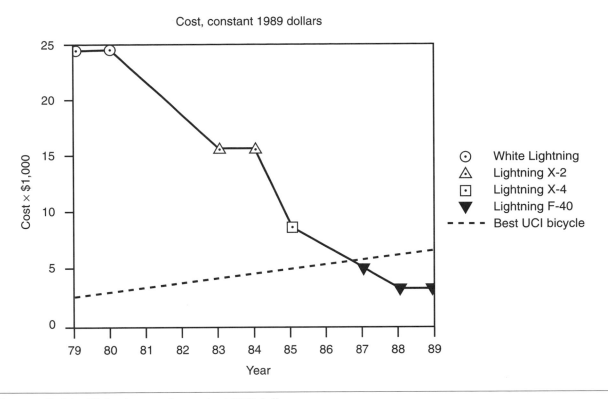

Cost, constant 1989 dollars

FIGURE 9.11   Lightning cost in constant 1989 dollars.

ning X-2 were hand-built, one-of-a-kind machines. The honeycomb-composite fairings and tooling costs, being absorbed by only one or two machines, made them very expensive.

The Lightning X-4 utilized some of the X-2 tooling with a less-expensive fiberglass fairing. Still, many hours were required for construction, making this machine fairly expensive, though half of the X-2 price. Simplifying the design and utilizing spandex for half of the fairing resulted in the F-40. The current price of $4,000 is more than that of most bicycles, but it is only 22% of the cost of the X-2, demonstrating the great advances that have been made in cost reduction.

In contrast, the cost of top UCI bicycles has risen considerably during the same time. Hand-built aero frames, tensioned disk wheels, and 200-psi Kevlar tires mean that only national or professional teams can afford these bikes. As a prime example, the time-trial bike Greg LeMond used to win the Tour de France in 1989 is worth $6,000. Thus, the restrictive UCI rules, while more or less making sure that competitions are between people rather than machines, have also produced a machine that is slower and less comfortable than an HPV, but much more expensive.

Neither the Lightnings nor, at present, any other recumbent bicycles are made in sufficient numbers to compete with mass-produced UCI type bicycles. In 1993, discount-store ten-speed bicycles could be bought for about $100 in the U.S., while the lowest cost recumbents were advertised at more than $300.

Analysis

Much progress has been made over the past 10 years in HPV technology. For the open-class racing HPVs, top speed has increased 15%. Even more impressive, this speed increase has been achieved by single-rider vehicles rather than the multiple-rider vehicles previously used. Some single-rider vehicles are also capable of being used in open-road racing events.

Another significant development is the advent of HPVs practical enough to be used on an every-day basis, and ridden wherever a standard road bike can go. These HPVs are almost as fast as the racing HPVs of 10 years ago, and they have better climbing, turning, handling, visibility, cooling, and braking characteristics. They also cost a fraction of the price of a record-setting machine.

This new type of practical HPV also shows the futility of trying to improve the existing standard racing bike under the restrictive UCI rules. Performance of the best UCI bicycles has increased only on the order of 5% over the past 10 years, yet they cost more than twice what the UCI bikes cost a decade ago. It is obvious that after 100 years of development, the performance curve for UCI bikes has reached the point of diminishing returns.

The best UCI bikes have an advantage over the practical HPV only in two areas: in extreme hill-climbing ability and in minimum turning radius. The UCI bike is at a disadvantage to the HPV in terms of top speed, cruising speed, visibility, comfort, braking distance, and cost for the same level of performance. The UCI bike also does not have the additional HPV attribute of being able to carry a useful load (such as for commuting) with little loss in performance, nor the additional weather and crash protection provided by a fairing.

The only major drawback to widespread substitution of HPVs for UCI bikes at present is cost. HPVs still cost more than all but the best UCI racing bicycles. The trend for the 1990s, however, is for large HPV cost reductions, and this should make HPVs much more attractive to the people who decide whether a bicycle is practical or not: consumers.

Although not examined in this chapter, HPVs are also on the verge of becoming practical alternatives to cars for commuting. How can a mere bicycle be faster and better than a car? First, consider that most cars on the freeway have only one person, the driver. Then consider that the average speed for the Lightning F-40 riding all the way across the United States was 11 m/s (25 mph). The average speed on the 405 freeway in Los Angeles during rush hour is only 8 m/s (18 mph). The current limiting factors preventing greater HPV replacement of cars are a lack of safe and efficient places to ride. If bicycles replaced cars on freeways, vehicle for vehicle, the roads would operate at far under peak capacity and traffic would indeed flow freely.

The Future

Although it appears that little can be done to significantly improve the UCI bicycle under current

rules, what are the prospects for further HPV improvements, particularly in practical HPVs? Improvements will not take place at the rate of the past decade, but improvements will continue to be significant. By extending the past trends for performance improvements into the future, and with more than a little speculation, I have come up with predicted performance for HPVs in the year 2000. For the racing HPV, top speed will be more than 33 m/s (75 mph), and the hour record will be more than 80 km (50 miles).

Even more significant, especially to society at large, will be the practical, or GT-class, HPV performance:

1. Top speed will be over 24 m/s (55 mph).

2. Cruising speed on level ground will be close to 18 m/s (40 mph).

3. Hill climbing will be equal to that for UCI bikes, perhaps through the use of a light, efficient linear drive that could give more power than a rotary drive.

4. There will be slight improvements in handling and visibility, compared to today's machines.

5. Further improvements in cooling and comfort may be expected.

6. A 25% improvement in braking performance, particularly in the wet, should be realized.

7. Retail prices will be less than $1,200 in 1990 dollars.

Of course, people who try to predict the future are usually off the mark, and that will probably be the case with these predictions. But, there are no great technological barriers to be bridged for these predictions to come true. The greatest unknown is the social acceptance, or need, for these kinds of vehicles.

Reference

Schubert, John (1986, May). Road test: Lightning F-40. *Bicycle Guide*, **3**(4), 66–68.

10

BICYCLE AERODYNAMICS

Chester R. Kyle

Bicycle racing has always been a measure of the excellence of both the athlete and of the equipment. A good example is the world hour record for conventional bicycles (see Figure 10.1). Since the record was first established in 1876, when F.L. Dodd of England went 25.598 km (15.91 miles) on a high-wheeler, the distance has nearly doubled. The period from 1876 to 1896 was a time of swift improvement in equipment that saw the introduction of the safety bicycle, the pneumatic tire, adjustable ball bearings, drop handlebars, and other innovations. During this period the hour distance record rapidly increased to nearly 40 km.

For the next 70 years improvements in the hour record were basically due to better training methods and better athletes. But in 1984, with the record ride of Francesco Moser, the advances again could be credited to better equipment. Radically redesigned by Antonio Dal Monte of Italy, Moser's "funny" bicycle used aerodynamics to break Eddy Merckx's record by nearly 2 km. Actually, without strict regulations that carefully define what kind of bicycle can be used, even Moser's hour record could be broken by more than 25 km.

In chapter 7 it was shown that completely streamlining a standard bicycle makes possible very high speeds, so that open races between streamliners and standard bicycles would be completely unfair. Above about 3.5 m/s (8 mph) the wind drag on a bicycle and rider is greater than the rolling resistance, and above 11 m/s (20 mph) wind drag is more than 80% of the total drag. It is a simple matter to decrease the dominant air drag by using even simple improvements. The question has been what should and what should not be permitted in competition.

Competition rules have attempted to tightly define what is permitted, but they have only partly succeeded. Aerodynamic refinements can sometimes be so subtle that they are hardly obvious, and the rules are usually several steps behind the improvements. This chapter discusses recent developments in bicycle aerodynamics.

The UCI rules specifically prohibit recumbents, aerodynamic devices, and the use of arm power. The UCI eliminated recumbents in 1934 by defining the distance between the seat, the bottom-bracket spindle, and the wheels. The organization controls aerodynamic devices and arm power with this simple 1914 statement: "Any circular propulsive action, alternating or otherwise, brought about by means of the hands or the use of protective shields, wind-breaks or any other means of reducing wind resistance shall be prohibited" (Schmitz, 1990). UCI eliminates monocoque (shelllike) frames by specifying a triangular frame and limiting the tubing size to a maximum diameter of 45 mm for round tubing, or to 45 mm × 75 mm for oval tubing. Wheel diameter must be in a range from 500 mm to 700 mm. In time trials, either one spoke (a disk wheel) or 16 spokes or more must be used, but disk wheels are illegal for mass-start races.

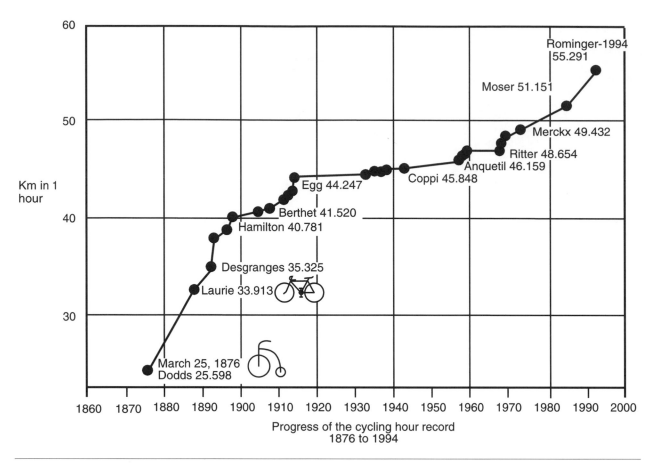

FIGURE 10.1 The hour bicycle record has progressed over the years.

Paradoxically, as can be seen from these above rules, the UCI does permit aerodynamic devices such as disk wheels and airfoil-shaped tubing, even though this apparently conflicts with the rules. Why is this? Beginning in 1975, the International Human-Powered Speed Championships demonstrated, with an avalanche of international publicity, that major increases in bicycle speed were made possible by the use of aerodynamics. The same sequence of events had occurred repeatedly since 1913, but this time it seemed to impress the right people. This was a major influence in starting the movement that has gradually modified the UCI's attitude toward changes in the traditional bicycle.

About 1976, at the world championships, slick skin-tight one-piece suits for cycle track racers were introduced to smooth air flow over the rider and "funny" bikes with aero tubes made their appearance. They were promptly outlawed by the UCI, but in 1978, for unpublicized reasons, the UCI technical commission relented and permitted skin suits and funny bikes. Accordingly, after 1978, bikes using airfoil-shaped frame tubing and wheel rims

became common at European time-trial races. In 1980 Shimano introduced a line of aerodynamically shaped components that have influenced the shape of all bicycle components since.

The present interpretation of the UCI rules seems to be that if a component or bicycle-frame element serves a traditional purpose, then the shape can be modified, within reasonable limits, to lower the aerodynamic drag. The UCI still prohibits the addition of obvious fillets, fairings, or other devices that are added only to decrease aerodynamic drag. The big breakthrough was when UCI declared the disk wheel legal in 1974. The only purpose of a disk is to lower the aerodynamic drag, but curiously the UCI permitted them in Moser's hour ride of 51.151 km (January 23, 1984, in Mexico City). With this ruling, the dam broke, and a flood of aerodynamic components is now in common use, including helmets, skin suits, clipless pedals, hidden cables, cranks, sprockets, frames, and handlebars.

In 1982, Ed Burke, technical director of the United States Cycling Federation, was asked by the USOC to organize a group of scientists and engineers to improve the U.S. Cycling Team's chances in the 1984 Olympics. I was asked to organize the cycling-equipment project. We decided to concentrate on time-trial bicycles. Ultimately, 30 volunteers, many from the IHPVA, donated more than four person-years of time to give the racing bicycle a face-lift. Don Guichard designed disk wheels, Paul Van Valkenburgh designed streamlined helmets, Jack Lambie performed aerodynamic testing and fabricated helmets, Bruce Sargeant did the electronic test instrumentation, Joyce Kyle fashioned prototype skin suits, and I was responsible for the overall frame and handlebar design. Allan Abbott, Paul MacCready, and Alec Brooks acted as consultants.

Our plan was to clean up and smooth everything aerodynamically so there would be no rough edges and air would flow around the bike and rider with a minimum of turbulence. We tried to create a system as slick as a jet aircraft. In 1983, we tested the prototypes in the full-scale wind tunnel at Texas A&M, and we achieved a 9-N (2-lb) drag reduction at 13 m/s (30 mph), compared with a traditional track bike and clothing. There was nothing standard on our bikes: everything was custom made. They had narrow headsets, narrow bottom brackets, narrow hubs with flush mounting bolts, special seat posts, and streamlined handlebars. The tubing was streamlined helicopter-strut tubing (Kyle & Burke, 1984).

Our group ended up building the wheels, helmets, cranks, sprockets, shoe covers, and pedals used on the medal-winning U.S. time-trial bikes in the 1984 Olympics. Mike Melton of Huffy built the frames using aluminum tubing based on our prototype design, and Pearl Izumi of Japan made the skin suits. The U.S. Cycling Team won nine medals in 1984, the first U.S. Olympic cycling medals since 1912. Since that time, nearly every time-trial record in the world had been broken with the modern funny bike (see Figure 10.2). Components similar to ours have been produced by dozens of manufacturers worldwide.

One result of our design efforts was that several new equipment rules were passed by the UCI. Equipment designed by our group was banned on seven occasions from 1984 to 1987. Many of our clothing items were outlawed: a face hood that filled in the chin cavity, a full-length skin suit, mittens that completely smoothed the airflow over the hands, shoe covers, and our preposterously long aero helmet, which led to the rule that restricts helmet length to 300 mm. Just after the Olympics, the 578-mm (22-3/4-in.) wheels we had used on our team time-trial bikes were banned, but after a storm of protest they were again permitted. This wheel size has been used for 75 years for "stayer" bikes, but the size had not been common on time-trial bikes. In 1986, Don Guichard and the author

FIGURE 10.2   This aerodynamic bicycle helped win gold medals for the U.S. Olympic cyclists in 1984.

designed a composite monocoque-frame bike for Du Pont with a very simple and efficient airfoil shape, to be used for the individual pursuit in the 1988 Olympics (see Figure 10.3). But this was immediately outlawed and led to the rule that specified a three-element triangular frame and placed limits on the size of the frame tubing.

We were responsible for eight or nine UCI rule changes. This points out the continual conflict between the coaches, athletes, designers, and manufacturers, on one hand, who want to achieve the best equipment possible, and the rule-making bodies, on the other hand, who want to make sure that any race is a fair contest among athletes and not a competition among equipment designers. Given the dynamics of competition, there will always be changes in equipment because rules will never be perfect.

The Aerodynamics of Time-Trial Bicycles

At racing speeds, the air drag on a bicycle is from 20% to 35% of the total air drag, the remainder being the drag of the human body. Standard bicycles have the higher drag, being about 35% of the total, whereas well-designed "aero" bicycles are only

about 20% of the total. Obviously, then, because the human body is two-thirds or more of the total drag the most important element in the aerodynamic design is the human body, and the most important factor is the riding position.

Riding Position and Handlebars

Figure 10.4 shows how the riding position affects overall drag. The best position aerodynamically is the hill-descent position, with hands in the center of the bars, elbows tucked in, chin on the hands, the crank at 90°, knees squeezing the top tube, and the back as flat as possible. The overall drag in this position is 30% less than when the rider is resting in an upright touring stance. Unfortunately, it is impractical to pedal in the hill-descent position. A practical pedaling posture, however, is to use "cowhorn" bars, with the rider in a full racing crouch. The resulting drag is about 25% less than the upright touring position. Even better than this is to use elbow-rest handlebars, which permit a riding posture that achieves nearly the drag reduction of the hill-descent position. This is the most efficient riding technique invented to date. Not only is it better aerodynamically, but, resting on the elbows, a rider can maintain a low crouch for long periods without fatigue.

FIGURE 10.3   A carbon-composite monocoque bicycle prototype designed and built by Don Guichard and Chester Kyle for the Du Pont Company, to be used in the individual pursuit in the 1988 Olympic games. The bike was outlawed by the UCI technical commission.

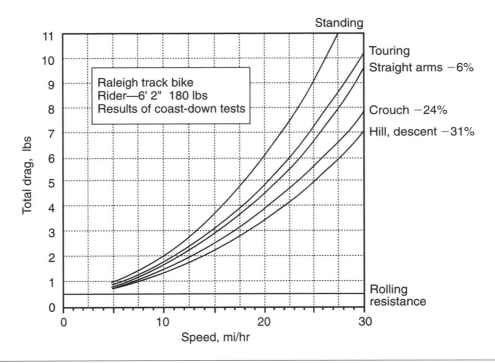

FIGURE 10.4 The effects of riding position on overall drag. The information for this graph was taken from coast-down tests at California State University, Long Beach, 1983–84. The cyclist for this chart was tall and thin, so drag and power are higher than normal for the 180-lb body weight. However, the effect on drag and power is the same. *Note.* The hill-descent position is hands on center of bars, elbows bent, chin on hands, crank at 90°, knees touching top tube, back arched.

Full-scale wind-tunnel tests, by bicycle-equipment manufacturer Steve Hed at Texas A&M in 1989, showed that Scott clip-on elbow-rest bars could lower the wind drag about 12%, compared to a full racing crouch with cowhorn time-trial bars. The best body position was with the elbow-rest bars either flat or tilted up 30° and with the rider's back as flat as possible (not arched) (see Figures 10.5 and 10.6). Hed found that it was very important to tuck the elbows in so they are inside the body contour, with the body drafting behind the upper arms. This is an important principle in decreasing aerodynamic drag: items in the airstream should be placed behind one another to benefit from drafting.

Recently, triathlon bikes have been designed with a more vertical seat tube. Moving the seat forward, or making the seat tube more vertical, may have some biomechanical advantage in increasing the pedal efficiency because it opens up the hip angle during the pedal cycle. However, Hed found that the results are inconclusive (Kyle, 1989). In any case, whenever a riding position is changed, the final verdict depends upon whether times improve.

Clothing and Helmets

Modern cycling clothing and helmets have a much lower air drag than conventional clothing and helmets. Table 10.1 shows the results of full-scale wind-tunnel tests of clothing at the California Institute of Technology (Kyle, 1987). Cyclists were placed in a fixed position on a bicycle in the low-speed wind tunnel at the California Institute of Technology, and the drag forces were measured at speeds varying from 6 m/s to 16 m/s. A cyclist with a smooth, tight skin suit had about 2.4 N less drag at 13 m/s (30 mph) than a cyclist wearing tights and a wool jersey. Table 10.2 shows that this would save about 1.86 seconds per kilometer in a long time trial and result in a 25-m lead per kilometer against an equal opponent (Kyle, 1990).

The effect of aerodynamic helmets is just as spectacular. Table 10.3 shows results of wind-tunnel tests on racing helmets (Kyle,1990). A good production aerodynamic helmet would give a racing cyclist a 19-m lead in 1 km over an equal opponent with a standard helmet. Also, a good aero helmet is better than a rider with no helmet at all: in fact, the wind-tunnel tests show that an aero helmet has a lower

FIGURE 10.5 Scott clip-on bars being tested in the Texas A&M wind tunnel, 1989. The arms are flat and the head is about halfway down in a low-drag position.

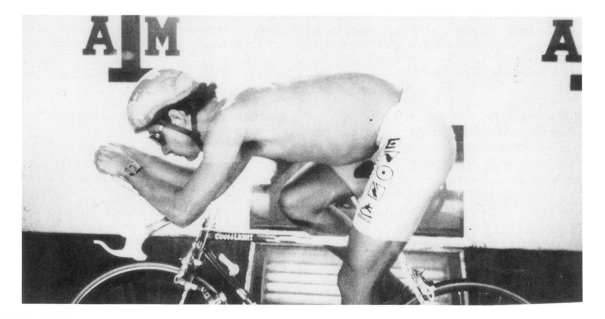

FIGURE 10.6 Clip-on bars with the arms at 30° and the head two-thirds down, also a low-drag position.

drag than a bald head. Aerodynamic racing helmets should have a glass-smooth finish: rougher surfaces gave higher drag. Figure 10.7 shows a prototype of a 1990 Specialized aero helmet.

Wind-tunnel helmet tests in 1989 by Hed at Texas A&M also showed the proper riding position for a streamlined helmet (Kyle, 1989). If the head is all the way down with the rider looking at the pavement, the tail of an aero helmet sticks up in the air

and the drag goes up. If the head is all the way up with the rider looking straight ahead, then the helmet lies on the back. This has the effect of trapping air in the tail of the helmet and increasing the drag. With the head about halfway down (the face at about 45° with the horizontal), the drag for streamlined helmets is minimum.

We also found this in our 1983 and 1986 wind-tunnel helmet tests for the U.S. Cycling Team (Kyle

Table 10.1 AERODYNAMIC DRAG OF BICYCLE CLOTHING AT 13 M/S (30 MPH)

Clothing type	Drag of bike plus rider, N
Rubberized skin suit with sleeves	25.7
Lycra suit and tights	25.89
Lycra tights, wool long-sleeved jersey	28.05
Tight polypropylene warmup suit	28.73

Note: From "The Wind Resistance of Racing Bicycles, Cyclists and Athletic Clothing" by Chester R. Kyle, 1987, *Report to the USOS Sports Equipment and Technology Committee.*

Table 10.2 THE RACING ADVANTAGE OF AERODYNAMIC DRAG REDUCTION

Drag decrease N at 13.5 m/s	Time diff. s/km	Lead dist. m/km	1000-m TT s	4000-m pursuit s
0.1	0.07	0.95	0.07	0.28
0.2	0.14	1.9	0.12	0.62
0.4	0.28	3.8	0.23	1.12
0.78	0.58	7.8	0.47	2.22
1.17	0.86	11.6	0.70	3.39
1.57	1.28	17.2	0.94	4.53
1.96	1.56	21.0	1.17	5.62
2.35	1.83	24.8	1.40	6.74

Note: From "Wind-Tunnel Tests of Bicycle Wheels and Helmets" by Chester R. Kyle, 1990, *Cycling Science,* 2(1), 27–30.

Table 10.3 THE AERODYNAMIC DRAG OF BICYCLE HELMETS

Helmet tested	Drag, N, at 13.5 m/s (30 mph)
1984 U.S. Olympic aero (rough primer finish)	−0.08[a]
1986 U.S. Team aero	−0.08[a]
Czech aero	+0[a]
Specialized prototype aero	+0.15[a]
Bell Stratos (aero)	+0.36[b]
Giro Aerohead	+0.40[a]
Mannequin, bald (no hair)	+0.53[a]
Giro Aerohead, cut off to 300 mm	+0.60[a]
OGK Aero	+0.79[a]
Mannequin, with short hair	+1.09[a]
Specialized Groundforce	+1.27[a]
Specialized Airforce	+1.32[a]
Specialized Microforce	+1.43[a]
Bell VI Pro	+1.54[a]
OGK Forza	1.59[a]
Standard leather-strap helmet	+1.78[b]
Giro Hammerhead, Lycra cover	+1.96[a]

[a]UC Irvine, February 1990, for Specialized Inc.

[b]UC Irvine, October 1985, for Bell Helmet.

Note: From "Wind-Tunnel Tests of Bicycle Wheels and Helmets" by Chester R. Kyle, 1990, *Cycling Science, 1.1.* Copyright 1990.

& Burke, 1984). Because the helmet is parallel to the airflow and because the tail is off the back and leaves a clear passage for air flowing over the shoulders, the flow is smooth and the apparent aerodynamic cross section of the helmet is a minimum. This also happens to be a very comfortable riding position for racers: It allows adequate visibility and a fairly relaxed neck position.

Bicycle Wheels

Table 10.4 shows the results of wind-tunnel tests of spinning bicycle wheels. The wheels were tested at 13 m/s (30 mph) in the wind tunnel at the University of California at Irvine. A variable-speed motor attached to the force balance rotated the wheels at a rate equivalent to the wind speed. From Tables 10.2 and 10.4, it can be seen that by using two aerodynamic wheels, such as lenticular disks or three-spoke composite wheels, a racer could gain a 30-m lead per kilometer versus an opponent with two conventional 36-spoke wheels (Kyle,1990). This is why the legalization of the disk wheel led to such spectacular increases in bicycle speed.

The disk wheels used on Moser's bike were extremely heavy, with a mass of nearly 2.7 kg (6 lb) apiece. Weight has always been considered a handicap in bicycle racing, because it retards acceleration, increases the rolling resistance, and slows the rate of ascent on climbs. However, in this case the aerodynamic improvement far overshadowed the

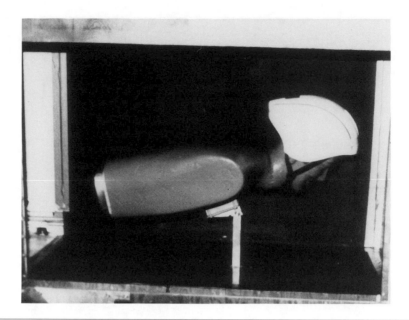

FIGURE 10.7 A plaster model of the 1990 Specialized aero helmet designed by Robert Egger. The helmet is being tuft tested in the University of California, Irvine, wind tunnel, February, 1990.

handicap of increased weight. Table 10.5 shows the effect of added weight in a time trial. Comparing the aerodynamic drag reduction in Table 10.2 with added weight in Table 10.5, it can be seen that the effect of adding 2.7 kg (6 lb) mass can be canceled by a 0.4-N aerodynamic drag reduction (Kyle, 1988). A 0.4-N aero drag decrease is quite easy to accomplish. Therefore, aero equipment, even though it weighs more, can result in substantial increases in speed.

One can draw several conclusions from the wind-tunnel tests:

- The air resistance of three-spoke composite aerodynamic wheels is equal to or better than that of the best disk wheels.

- Disk wheels or three-spoke composite aerodynamic wheels are better than any of the steel-spoked wheels tested, including a wheel with 16 aero-bladed spokes, aero rims, and narrow 18-mm tires. The drag of the best standard aluminum-rim, steel-spoke, aero wheel was about 100 to 200 mN (0.02–0.04 lb) higher at 13.4 m/s (30 mph) than disks or three-spoke composite wheels.

- Lens-shaped disks have a lower drag than flat disks.

- Narrow tires have a much lower drag then wider tires.

- Wheels with polished surfaces have a lower drag than wheels with a rougher finish.

- Smaller wheel diameters have a lower wind drag.

- With standard steel spokes, aero-bladed spokes are best, but aero-oval spokes are nearly as good. Round spokes have a very high drag. The fewer spokes in a wheel, the lower the drag.

- With standard wheels, aero rims are best. With flat rims, the turbulent flow over the trailing part of the rim creates a high cavity drag, whereas the flow over the trailing edge of an aero rim is smooth, and the apparent aerodynamic cross section is much less. The base drag of the leading part of both aero and flat rims is probably about the same.

- In a mild crosswind, the drag of disk wheels or of three-spoke wheels actually decreases, due to aerodynamic lift. When the effective wind is at an angle to the direction of bicycle travel, the airfoil shape develops some lift at right angles to the wind (see Figure 10.8). The resulting forward thrust component has the effect of lowering the drag, as shown by the wind-tunnel tests. In this case the wheel acts like a sail and actually extracts some propulsive energy from the wind. This also occurs with a bicycle frame with aero tubes. Therefore, on a circuit course with a crosswind, a bike with disk wheels and an aero frame could theoretically be faster than if there were no wind at all.

Table 10.4 THE AIR RESISTANCE OF SPINNING BICYCLE WHEELS

	Drag at 13.4 m/s (30 mph), N	10° yaw angle* N
27-in. wheels Du Pont/Specialized three-spoke composite wheel, 18-mm tire (waxed and polished)	1.1[a]	0.38[b]
27-in. wheels Du Pont/Specialized three-spoke composite wheel, unfinished surface	1.24[a]	
27-in. wheels Du Pont/Specialized composite wheel, 24-mm tire	1.64[a]	
Aerosports Kevlar lens disk, 8-mm tire	1.13[a]	0.25[b]
Campy lens disk, 18-mm tire	1.18[b]	
Trispoke, three-spoke composite, 18-mm tire	1.21[a]	1.13[b]
Aerosports carbon flat disk, 18-mm tire	1.21[a]	0.74[b]
Aerolite 16 aero-bladed spokes, aero rim, 18-mm tire	1.37[b]	
Wheelsmith 24 aero-bladed spokes, aero rim, 18-mm tire	1.44[b]	
Wheelsmith 28 aero-bladed spokes, aero rim, 18-mm tire	1.70[a]	
Wheelsmith 28 aero-Oval spokes, aero rim, 18-mm tire	1.72[a]	
USCF 18 round spokes, aero rim, 18-mm tire	2.02[c]	
Wheelsmith 36 round spokes, standard rim, 18-mm tire	2.53[b]	
26-in. wheels Aerosports carbon flat disk, 18-mm tire	1.07[c]	
Wheelsmith 32 round spokes, flat rim, 22-mm tire	2.04[a]	
24-in. wheels Huffy Special carbon flat disk, 18-mm tire	1.10[c]	
Aerosports 18 aero-bladed spokes, aero rim, 18-mm tire	1.25[c]	
USCF 16 aero-bladed spokes, aero rim, 18-mm tire	1.34[c]	
Wheelsmith 24-in., 28 round spokes, flat rim, 22-mm tire	1.78[a]	

*The apparent wind direction is at 10° to the bike axis.
[a] UC Irvine, February 1990, for Specialized.
[b] UC Irvine, June 1988, for Specialized/Du Pont.
[c] UC Irvine, December 1985, for UCSF.

Table 10.5 THE EFFECT OF MASS ON TRACK TIME-TRIAL RACES

Total mass, rider plus bicycle kg	lb	1,000-m time(s)	4,000-m time(s)	Acceleration time(s) 1,000-m 16.5 m/s	4,000-m 13.9 m/s
81.7	180	63.38	292.97	14.47	16.7
+1	+2	+0.08	+0.20	+0.17	+0.18
+2	+4	+0.16	+0.40	+0.34	+0.38
+3	+6	+0.24	+0.60	+0.50	+0.58

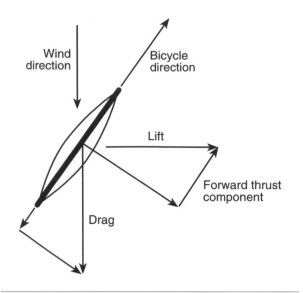

FIGURE 10.8 Wind forces on a solid aerodynamic wheel.

Front and Back Wheels

In tests (Kyle, 1988), we placed a bicycle frame and wheel in front of the test wheel and found that the drag of the rear wheel was about 40% lower than the front wheel's because it was drafting behind the frame and components. However, the drag reduction (difference in drag) was about the same regardless of whether it was a front or a rear wheel. Therefore, if one uses both front and rear disks or three-spoke composite wheels, the time saving is about double that of a single wheel. Because of its lack of sensitivity to side winds, the three-spoke composite wheel can be used on front where a disk would be too unstable to ride. Consequently, this wheel design is far more practical than a disk and will give riders an advantage over those with only one aero wheel. Three-spoke aero wheels are legal only for time trials in the U.S. at present, but they may be allowed for mass-start races in the near future.

Bicycle Frames

In 1986, we tested a variety of bicycles for the United States Cycling Federation in the low-speed wind tunnel at the California Institute of Technology. We used the same rider and made sure that in each of the tests the triangle between the seat, the handlebars, and the bottom bracket was identical; we used a streamlined chest support to make sure the rider was in the same position each time (see Figure 10.9).

FIGURE 10.9 Testing in the low-speed wind tunnel at the California Institute of Technology for the United States Cycling Federation, 1986. The bike is a prototype, designed by Chester Kyle, for the 100-km team time trial.

The bikes were also tested bare, with no rider. Table 10.6 shows the drag of several typical bikes and riders at 13.4 m/s (30 mph) wind speed. Because it was cold in the wind tunnel, the rider wore a wool jersey. The drag would be about 2 N (0.5 lb) less for each bike if the rider had worn a Lycra skin suit. The touring bikes had two 36-wire-spoke wheels. The aero track bikes had front and rear disk wheels. The standard Schwinn track bike had two 32-spoke wheels with bladed spokes and aero rims.

The bikes with aero tubing had the lowest drag, with and without riders. However, with the rider the differences were less than the differences that might be expected from the tests of the bare bikes. This might be due to induced drag caused by cross flow from the legs and body. For example, the composite monocoque bike designed for Du Pont had the lowest drag of any ever measured when tested bare, but with a rider the drag was higher than some other aero bikes. By using an aero bike frame, it should be possible to save as much as 1.5 s per kilometer compared to an equal rider on a good time-trial bike. This would be a lead of more than 19 m in 1 km (100 feet in 1 mile).

Table 10.6 THE AERODYNAMIC DRAG OF BICYCLES IN 13.4 M/S (30 MPH) WIND SPEED

Bicycle	Drag, bare bike		Drag, with rider	
	N	lb	N	lb
Touring bikes				
Kestrel[a]	11.6	2.46	31.3	7.04
Cannondale aluminum	12.1	2.72	32.2	7.25
Trek aluminum	12.1	2.71	32.7	7.36
Raleigh steel frame	11.9	2.67	32.9	7.40
4,000-m individual pursuit bikes				
Gleb composite aero[c]	6.4	1.44	28.0	6.30
Huffy U.S. team 1984[b]	7.0	1.58	28.2	6.35
Du Pont composite aero[d]	5.3	1.20	28.5	6.41
Huffy U.S. team 1986[b]	7.0	1.57	28.6	6.42
Somec production aero[a]	8.0	1.80	29.1	6.54
Schwinn standard track	10.7	2.41	31.0	6.98
100-K team time-trial bikes				
Kyle aero TTT[e]	6.45	1.45	28.1	6.31
1983–1984 Huffy Pan-Am U.S. team[b]	8.27	1.86	29.9	6.72
1986 Huffy U.S. team[b]	8.41	1.89	30.2	6.79
Rigideol aero[a]	9.00	2.02	31.2	7.02

[a]Production aero bikes.

[b]U.S. team bikes designed by Mike Melton.

[c]Composite prototype aero bike designed by Gleb Derujinski.

[d]Composite prototype aero bike designed by Don Guichard and Chet Kyle.

[e]Steel prototype aero bike designed by Chet Kyle.

Components

From Table 10.2, even a 100-mN reduction in aero-dynamic drag at 13.4 m/s (30 mph) can result in about a 1-m lead over an equal opponent in a 1,000-m race. It is relatively simple and inexpensive to achieve drag reductions of 100 mN or more in a number of ways. Table 10.7 lists typical modifica-tions and the resulting drag reduction at 30-mph wind speed. These figures come from wind-tunnel tests at California State University for the United States Cycling Federation during the period 1982 to 1984.

Table 10.8 shows the results of tests run on aero-dynamic bicycle-frame tubing. In theory, the ideal minimum-drag airfoil section has a length (chord)

Table 10.7 AERODYNAMIC DRAG OF BICYCLE COMPONENTS

CRANKS AND SPROCKETS	Drag, mN
Specially modified TA crank with 1 disk 52T sprocket (Reference)	+0
Same crank with normal 52T sprocket	+39
Shimano crank with one 42T	+108
Same crank with one 52T sprocket	+137
Same crank with two sprockets 42T/52T	+206
PEDALS	
Clipless pedals, Shimano/Look system (Reference)	+0
Shimano pedals, toe clips and straps	+235
Campagnolo pedals, toe clips and straps	+235
OTHER COMPONENTS	
Aero downtube shifters, special (Reference)	+0
Normal downtube shifter, levers up	+78
Same, levers down	+39
Sheathed cable, 0.210 in. D, crosswind	+500/m
Bare cable, 0.060 in. D, crosswind	+155/m
Aero handlebars made from helicopter strut tubing (compared to standard drop bars)	−755
Water bottle behind seat (compared to bottle on downtube)	−784
Aero bottle and cage compared to standard bottle	−127

Table 10.8 THE DRAG OF AERODYNAMIC BICYCLE TUBING

Tubing measurements	Tubing length-to-width ratio	Drag in n/m length No drafting Norm.	Reversed	Drag in n/m length Drafting Norm.	Reversed
Round 1.162 in. D	1:1	2.45	2.45	1.04	1.04
Tange 1.394 in. × 0.855 in.	1.63:1	1.81	1.47	3.59	0.59
Helicopter 2.023 in. × 0.875 in.	2.31:1	1.36	1.28	0.32	0.54
Helicopter 2.360 in. × 0.980 in.	2.41:1	1.38	1.37	0.26	0.50
Helicopter 2.832 in. × 0.930 in.	3.05:1	0.92	1.03	—	—

to width (thickness) ratio of between 3.5:1 and 5:1. Commercial aero bicycle tubes are blunt, having a ratio of less than 2:1. Normally, airfoils are placed in the windstream with the rounded edge forward and the sharp edge downstream. Tubing with a ratio below about 2.4:1 actually had a lower drag when reversed, with the sharp edge upstream, than when in normal position. However, the drag was higher when the tubing was drafting behind a wheel and fork. At ratios greater than 2.4:1, aero tubing is better in the normal position under both conditions. The best aero tubing had about one-third the drag of conventional round tubing.

Summary: *The Ideal Time-Trial Bike*

Time-trial bikes that take advantage of all of the factors mentioned in this chapter have been built. Probably the best one to date is the Hooker Elite (see Figure 10.10). Designed by Gary Hooker, Dave Spangler, and me, the bike has been tested in comparative time trials, and it is nearly a minute faster in 40 km (25 miles) than the best of the time-trial bikes currently available, either manufactured or custom (Hooker & Spangler, 1989). If a racer intends to take full advantage of aerodynamics in building a custom time-trial bike and in choosing proper clothing, the following points are important.

1. **Wheels**. A lens-shaped-disk rear wheel and a three-spoke composite front wheel give the best combination and can be ridden in almost any wind condition. The tires should have a narrow 18-mm cross section. The ridge joining the tire and the rim should be smoothed with silicone cement. Small-diameter wheels are superior in almost every way to larger wheels. They weigh less, they accelerate faster, they have a lower wind resistance, and they are stronger and stiffer. Small wheels require less frame structure to support them, for equal stiffness. However, one drawback limits the use of small wheels: the higher rolling resistance of the tires. It is possible to get high-quality racing tires for wheels from 24 in. to 27 in. A special frame using a 700C rear tire and a 24-in. front wheel (actual diameter 578 mm; 22.75 in.) seems the best combination, because most of the weight is on the rear wheel and the total rolling resistance and wind resistance

FIGURE 10.10 The Hooker Elite aerodynamic custom time-trial bike. The aluminum airfoil shaped tubing has a length-to-width ratio of 3.5:1. and was specially formed by Hooker Industries, Ontario, California. The only standard parts on the bike are the brakes, the saddle, the pedals, the derailleur, the rear cluster, the tires, and the chain.

of this combination is less at speeds above 11 m/s (24 mph). The wheels and all elements of the bicycle should be as light as possible. If the aerodynamic shape is identical, the lightest vehicle is the fastest.

2. **Frame tubing.** All elements in the frame except the top tube should be airfoil shaped with a chord-length-to-width ratio of 3:1 or higher. The top tube can be round or oval, but should be horizontal to prevent adding frontal area to the frame. The idea is to keep the number and length of the tubes facing the wind to a minimum. The strength of steel or aluminum aero tubing is perfectly adequate to give the required frame stiffness and strength, plus reasonably lightweight. In a mild crosswind (with the apparent wind angle 10° or less), the drag of such a frame is actually lower than with the wind straight ahead, since aerodynamic lift provides some forward thrust, as does a sail.

3. **Handlebars and brake levers.** Elbow-rest bars should be used and they can be built with little exposed area, and with only aero sections facing the wind. Brake levers for the Hooker Elite are custom made to be thinner than normal. The handle is horizontal and has a minimum projected cross section. All cables should be hidden inside the tubing. Center-pull brakes allow any unavoidably exposed cable to be either shielded or to provide some draft for the frame elements behind the cable. Elbow supports should be tucked inward so that the upper arms shadow the body and the air flows cleanly around the torso. The forearms should be horizontal or slightly tilted upwards (to about 30° maximum). Next, decrease the steered mass caused by the arms resting on the handlebars (this can be done either mechanically or hydraulically). If the arms could remain stationary, then the bike could steer a straighter line.

4. **Forks and wheel mounts.** The front forks should be made from very narrow aero tubing, and the wheel-mounting nuts should be recessed into the tubes, or a smoothly rounded shroud made for the head of the mounting bolt. Quick- release levers or bolts are high-drag items and should be eliminated. Hubs and wheels have to be specially made to take advantage of this design feature. On the 1984 Olympic bikes the front hubs were only 60 mm wide, and the rear was 110 mm wide, includ-

ing the sprocket cluster. Most custom disk-wheel manufacturers will make wheels to specification.

5. **Cranks, sprockets, and pedals.** In most time trials only one front sprocket is necessary since the rear gear cluster will provide an adequate number of speed changes. The front chainwheel should be a flat disk with no holes in it. Holes or cavities are harmful, because they increase the wind drag, compared to a flat surface. The cranks should be hand filed and finished to give rounded leading edges and to eliminate all sharp corners and rough surfaces. Clipless pedals should be used, with no parts being exposed as the foot goes through its normal range of motion (a flat, smooth, thin platform that is always shielded by the foot is best).

6. **Shifters.** Finger-tip shifters that can be covered by the hand should be used. The hands should be as close together as possible. Actually a praying position for the hands is most effective in decreasing aero drag (the hands form an air divider to cleanly deflect air around the arms and body).

7. **Seat tube, seat post, and water bottles.** An aero seat post should telescope inside the seat tube, and the seat tube can be extended upward from the top tube a long distance to help provide stiffness and support. This permits a frame with a minimum length of tubing and a minimum weight. The resulting tight frame triangle is very stiff. The water bottle should be mounted behind the seat, with a drinking tube to the rider's mouth. This permits drinking without reaching for the bottle, which raises the aero drag and disrupts the pedaling rhythm. Some drinking systems that use a tube can be mounted on the back.

8. **Fillets, joints, surfaces, and other components.** All joints and all elements of the frame and components should be rounded and smooth. The difference between rounded corners and square corners can mean substantially less drag. For example, the headset and bottom-bracket mounting nuts can be filed or machined to give a minimum frontal area and a rounded exposed surface. Fillets should be used at the corners of the frame to give smooth transition surfaces. Care must be taken to keep the joint within legal dimensions, since excessive shrouding and filling is illegal. The finish on the bicycle frame and wheels should be mirror smooth and waxed.

9. **Uniforms and helmets**. For short events, an aero helmet with covered vents should be used. The less the ventilation, the lower the drag of the helmet. A mirror-smooth cover or surface finish should be used. Rubberized spandex covers are acceptable, but a smoother finish is better. Skin-tight spandex suits without wrinkles or loose openings are essential. Tightly fitting short socks and shoes without exposed laces are best. Actually, clothing, especially shoes, could be better, but clothing is improving continually.

The time-trial bike described above is completely custom made, so the chance of acquiring one for the average competitor is small. However, Greg Lemond's win, by only 8 s in the 1989 Tour de France was basically due to aerodynamic equipment. In the final time-trial stage he used a bike with an aero frame, elbow-rest handlebars, and an aero helmet. With his sensational win, the sensitivity of the average cycle racer and coach to the importance of aerodynamic equipment is a quantum leap higher than it was. We have entered an era where aerodynamics is no longer viewed as an irrelevant curiosity. Its application to the sport is rapidly changing the world of cycling.

References

Hooker, G., & Spangler, D. (1989). Scientific performance testing. *Cycling Science*, **1**(1), 2–5.

Kyle, C.R. (1987, March). The wind resistance of racing bicycles, cyclists and athletic clothing. *Report to the USOC Sports Equipment and Technology Committee*.

Kyle, C.R. (1988). The mechanics and aerodynamics of cycling. In E.M. Burke & M.N. Newson (Eds.) *Medical and scientific aspects of cycling* (pp. 235–251). Champaign, IL: Human Kinetics.

Kyle, C.R. (1989). The aerodynamics of handlebars and helmets. *Cycling Science*, **1**(1), 22–25.

Kyle, C.R. (1990). Wind-tunnel tests of bicycle wheels and helmets. *Cycling Science*, **2**(1), 27–30.

Kyle, C.R., & Burke, E.M. (1984). Improving the racing bicycle. *Mechanical Engineering*, **109**(6), 35–45.

Schmitz, A. (1990). Why your bicycle hasn't changed for 106 years. *Cycling Science*, **2**(2), 3–8.

11

AERODYNAMICS VERSUS WEIGHT

Daniel Kirshner

Cyclists know that extra weight slows them down and that aerodynamic efficiency can speed them up. But increased aerodynamic efficiency often entails extra weight, for example, for fairings or recumbent frame designs. This chapter describes a method I have developed to calculate the trade-offs between aerodynamic efficiency and weight under a wide variety of riding conditions, including the power of the rider, the slope of the ground, and the frequency of stops.

One surprising result is that for a typical HPV under typical riding conditions, a small percentage reduction in the vehicle's weight is just as beneficial—in terms of overall efficiency—as the same percentage reduction in aerodynamic drag. This fact could be quite useful to designers because at this stage of HPV evolution, shaving off a few pounds of weight might be easier than improving the aerodynamic efficiency of a fully faired vehicle.

Measuring the Trade-Off

My basic assumptions are that there is no such thing as perfectly level ground and that typical

HPV riding conditions always include starts and stops. For these calculations I've assumed that the specified road course is a closed loop that includes equal distances of equal uphill and downhill slope (even nominally level ground has shallow uphills and downhills) and stop signs at regular intervals.

My criterion of overall efficiency is average velocity (on the specified closed course) for a given level of power output (i.e., muscular exertion) from the rider. To quantify the trade-off between aerodynamic efficiency and weight, I first calculate the overall average velocity, which can be obtained with a typical HPV under the specified riding conditions. Then I change the aerodynamic efficiency and find the new value for the vehicle's mass that will result in the same average velocity. For example, if the aerodynamic drag is increased (leading to a lower average velocity), the mass must be decreased to attain the same average velocity. All of these calculations are carried out using a microcomputer program written in BASIC. The actual trade-offs that result depend, of course, on the specific values of aerodynamic efficiency, mass, mechanical efficiency, and so forth that characterize the baseline typical HPV.

This chapter is adapted from an article in *Bike-Tech*, vol. 4, no. 1, 1985.

CALCULATING AVERAGE VELOCITIES BY COMPUTER

Average velocity over equally long uphill and downhill stretches is derived as follows. The time (T) to go a total distance (D) is:

Equation 11.1:

$$T = \frac{1}{2}\left(\frac{D}{V_u}+\frac{D}{V_d}\right)$$

where V_u and V_d are the average velocities uphill and downhill, respectively.

Average velocity over the total course (uphill and downhill) is given by $V = D / T$, and we can substitute T from Equation 11.1 into this expression to obtain:

Equation 11.2:

$$V = 2 \bullet V_u \bullet V_d / (V_u + V_d)$$

The uphill and downhill velocities are the result of net power input and acceleration between stop signs. Net power (P_{net}) is the power available to accelerate the vehicle after deducting power consumed by mechanical losses, aerodynamic drag, rolling resistance, and changes in potential energy (i.e., hill-climbing). Net power input is given by:

Equation 11.3:

$$P_{net} = \eta P_{in} - AC_D(\rho V^3/2) - mC_R V - mgsV$$

where

P_{in}	=	power input by rider (W)
η	=	mechanical efficiency of drive train
ρ	=	density of air (1.293 kg/m^3)
A	=	frontal area of vehicle (m^2)
C_D	=	coefficient of aerodynamic drag
V	=	velocity (m/s), either uphill or downhill
m	=	mass of vehicle plus rider (kg)
C_R	=	coefficient of rolling resistance (N/kg)
g	=	acceleration due to gravity (9.81 m/s^2)
s	=	slope (positive for uphill, negative for downhill)

The first term on the right of Equation 11.3 is the power level of the rider, adjusted for losses in the chain, bearings, and so forth. The second term is the power loss due to air resistance. The third term is power lost to rolling resistance. Finally, the last term represents the power consumed in moving the vehicle uphill or gained in moving the vehicle downhill.

Net power acts to accelerate the vehicle. Acceleration (a) as a function of net power and velocity can be derived by differentiating the equation for kinetic energy:

Equation 11.4:

$$E = m \cdot V^2 / 2$$

Equation 11.5:

$$P = dE/dt = mV(dV/dt) = mVa$$

where

$$a = dV/dt \text{ is acceleration.}$$

Thus acceleration is given by:

Equation 11.6:

$$a = P_{net}/mV$$

The computer simulation uses numerical integration to calculate the time to travel distance $D/2$ starting from a stop sign. This integration is performed for both uphill and downhill segments.

The heart of the computer program is an algorithm that calculates the velocity and position of the HPV step-by-step through time, starting from a dead stop. At each step, the net power (P_{net}, which depends on the velocity) is calculated using Equation 11.3, and then the acceleration calculated by Equation 11.6 is used to determine the velocity for the next step. A numerical integration scheme is used to estimate velocity steps in a Taylor-series expansion with two higher-order terms. The accuracy of this program was verified by comparing its results with the analytic integral, which can be solved exactly when air drag and rolling resistance are set to zero in Equation 11.3.

The program includes facilities for repeating these calculations for uphill and downhill segments for specified values of the relevant variables (e.g., total mass, drag coefficient, rider power) under the interactive control of the user. Given a value for the air-drag term and a target average velocity, the program uses a trial-and-error procedure to find the vehicle mass that will meet the target average velocity. (That is, if the velocity is too low, the mass is reduced and recalculated.) This derivation neglects the power used in increasing the rotational kinetic energy in wheel and cranks. If this were included, the form of Equation 11.5 would remain the same but the variable m in Equation 11.5 would then represent effective inertial mass which would be several percent larger than the actual gravitational mass of the vehicle.

There are a few approximations in this analysis. First, I assumed that no time is spent in slowing down to a stop. This approximation results in a slight overestimate of average velocities and thus a slight overestimate of the relative importance of aerodynamic efficiency compared to mass. The analysis also assumes that there are stop signs at the top and bottom of each uphill and downhill segment. Thus, momentum is not carried over from one segment to the next. Finally, assuming constant power input from the rider causes a numerical difficulty, because acceleration becomes infinite in Equation 11.6 when velocity is zero. This was overcome by using, for the first 0.5 s of acceleration, the analytical expression that ignores power lost to air drag, rolling resistance, and other nominal factors.

Defining a Typical HPV

In this analysis I am interested mainly in the vehicle's mass (*m*) and its aerodynamic efficiency, which is expressed by its effective frontal area: frontal area times coefficient of aerodynamic drag (*A* • C_D). Other parameters are fixed at what are hoped to be typical values. The efficiency of power transmission (chain, bearings, etc.) is set to 90%. Moulton reports three-speed efficiencies of 80%, 85%, and 90% in low gear, high gear, and direct drive, respectively (Moulton, 1982). The coefficient of rolling resistance is set to 0.05 N/kg (0.005 lbf/lbm). This value is given by Whitt and Wilson (1982) for a bicycle with 27-in. wheels.

The trade-off is calculated by varying the initial values of mass and aerodynamic drag. For the initial value of mass, assuming the rider weighs 77.3 kg (170 lb) and the vehicle weighs 22.7 kg (50 lb), the *Vector*'s approximate weight, the total mass is (our round-number goal now revealed) 100 kg (220 lb).

Although there are few published data for area and drag coefficients for HPVs, Kyle (1979) lists values which yield an *A* • C_D product ranging from 0.39 m² (4.20 ft²) for a conventional bicycle to 0.07 m² (0.75 ft²) for a fully faired upright bicycle to 0.06 m² (0.65 ft²) for a prone quadracycle with full fairing. Since practical HPVs might sacrifice some of the performance (and contortionistic requirements) of these single-purpose racing designs, I set *A* • C_D equal to 0.15 m² (1.61 ft²) as an initial value. This could be achieved by a vehicle with frontal area *A* = 0.75 m² (8.07 ft²) and a coefficient of aerodynamic drag C_D = 0.20.

I specified riding conditions (i.e., slopes, rider power output, and frequency of stops) which I felt were typical of a day trip or commuter run. For the rider's power output, I chose 100, 200, and 300 W (0.13, 0.27, and 0.40 hp, respectively). Whitt & Wilson state that an average experienced rider (a casual commuter?) can maintain 75 W (0.1 hp) power output, and a well-trained racer can maintain 200 to 300 W (0.27 to 0.40 hp) for several hours (1982, pp. 38-43). For hills, I chose slopes of 1%, 2%, and 5%. "Level ground" almost always has minor undulations with sloper greater than 1%. A 5% slope represents a substantial but bearable slope. Finally, I chose to examine stops every 0.25, 0.50, and 1 mile and no stops.

Table 11.1 summarizes, for a variety of riding conditions, the relationship between change in vehicle mass and change in aerodynamic efficiency (measured by *A* • C_D) for a constant average velocity. For the baseline conditions (*A* • C_D = 0.15 m² and vehicle mass = 50 lb) and for each combination of power, slope, and stops per mile, Table 11.1 gives the overall average velocity and, in the right-most column, the "trade-off parameter," which equals the percentage change in *A* • C_D divided by the percentage change in vehicle mass, with the average velocity constrained to remain constant. For example, at a power level of 100 W, 1% slope, and 2 stops/mile, the trade-off parameter of 0.98 indicates that changes in vehicle mass are 0.98 times as important as changes in aerodynamic efficiency.

Table 11.1 shows that at even modest rider power levels (100 W) aerodynamic efficiency is more important than mass (i.e., trade-off parameter is less than 1) for small slopes (1% or less) and infrequent stops (2 or less per mile). But with more difficult riding conditions (steeper slopes and more frequent stops) mass becomes more important. At higher rider power levels (and thus at higher speeds), however, aerodynamic efficiency reasserts its importance.

Sample Design Problem

A designer of HPVs might make use of these results in the following way. A prospective human-powered commuting vehicle might look something like the front view shown in Figure 11.1 The three-wheeler might have its wheels outside the aerodynamic shell to keep water out and for reasons of stability in cornering and crosswinds. Is it worthwhile to streamline the axle, given that a fairing for the axle increases weight? Adding an axle fairing would decrease the vehicle's *A* • C_D by 3.7% (from 0.1476 m² to 0.1421 m²) by calculations shown in Figure 11.1. The designer now selects a trade-off parameter of 1.0 which represents (as shown in Table 11.1) a typical commuting situation. Thus, the vehicle's mass could be increased by 3.7% or 1.9 lb for a 50-lb vehicle. Surely an axle fairing weighing less than 1.9 lb can be built, and this analysis shows that it is worthwhile to add it. In fact, only under severe riding conditions (slopes of 5%) does the value of adding the axle fairing become doubtful.

Conclusion

Here are some numbers that should provoke thought among HPV enthusiasts. I sent a conventional

Table 11.1	THE TRADE-OFF BETWEEN AERODYNAMIC EFFICIENCY AND MASS WHILE KEEPING AVERAGE VELOCITY CONSTANT*					
Rider power (watts—hp)	Slope	Stops / mile	**Base velocity**			$\dfrac{\%\Delta A \times C_d}{\% \,\Delta \text{vehicle mass}}$
			up	down (mph)	avrg.	
100—.13	.01	0	11.6	25.6	15.9	.47
	.02	0	7.8	32.7	12.6	1.23
	.05	0	3.7	49.8	6.9	5.40
	0	1	16.1	16.1	16.1	.35
	0	2	14.7	14.7	14.7	.58
	0	4	12.8	12.8	12.8	1.10
	.01	2	10.7	18.6	13.6	.98
	.02	2	7.6	22.0	11.3	2.29
	.05	2	3.7	30.6	6.6	10.81
200—.27	.01	0	18.7	30.5	23.2	.20
	.02	0	14.1	36.4	20.4	.50
	.05	0	7.3	51.7	12.8	2.39
	0	1	21.6	21.6	21.6	.26
	0	2	19.5	19.5	19.5	.49
	0	4	16.8	16.8	16.8	1.00
	.01	2	16.3	22.6	18.9	.62
	.02	2	13.2	25.4	17.3	1.05
	.05	2	7.2	33.1	11.9	4.45
300—.40	.01	0	23.6	34.1	27.9	.12
	.02	0	19.1	39.3	25.7	.29
	.05	0	10.7	53.4	17.9	1.42
	0	1	25.3	25.3	25.3	.23
	0	2	22.8	22.8	22.8	.45
	0	4	19.6	19.6	19.6	.93
	.01	2	20.0	25.5	22.4	.52
	.02	2	17.1	28.0	21.3	.73
	.05	2	10.5	34.7	16.1	2.70

*Example: For a rider power level of 100 W, a slope of .05, and no stops, a 5.4% change in AC_d is equal to a 1% change in a vehicle mass.

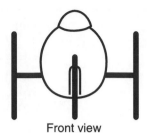

Front view

Body:
   A = 5.4 ft^2 = 0.5m^2
   C_D = 0.2

Wheels:
   A = (2) (27 in) (1 in) + (16 in) (1 in)
      = 70 in^2 = 0.0452 m^2
   C_D = 0.9

Axle:
   A = (24 in) (1.5 in)
      = 36 in^2 = 0.0232 m^2

   C_{D1} = 0.30 (for a cylinder)
   C_{D2} = 0.06 (for an optimal airfoil)-See
      Introduction to Fluid Mechanics
      by R.W. Fox and A.T. McDonald,
      John Wiley, 1973, p. 412.

Calculations:
   AC_{D1} = (.5)(.2) + (.0452)(.9) + (.0232)(.3)
         = 0.1476 m^2

   AC_{D2} = (.5)(.2) + (.0452)(.9) + (.0232)(.06)
         = 0.1421 m^2

FIGURE 11.1 Calculation of effective frontal area ($A \cdot C_D$) for a hypothetical HPV.

upright, unfaired bicycle through the calculation, under the same riding conditions that applied to the HPV in Table 11.1 (100 W rider power, 1% slope, 2 stops per mile, etc.) For the conventional bike, I assumed a vehicle mass of 12.4 kg (25 lb) with a 170-lb rider (same as for the HPV), and an $A \cdot C_D$ of

0.390 m^2 (4.20 ft^2) based on Kyle's data. The result showed that the conventional bike averages only 12.3 mph, which is more than 10% slower than the baseline HPV's 13.6 mph. The conventional bike is 50% lighter than the HPV, but it has 160% greater air resistance. Thus, the bike's penalty in air drag is far greater than its benefits in lighter weight and, in these conditions, the bike would be a poor choice compared to the typical HPV.

Practical HPVs could become popular very quickly. By all indications, modestly trained riders could average nearly 9 m/s (20 mph) under typical riding conditions, including stops and hills. These speeds should be attractive to bicycle commuters everywhere. But HPV designers have not yet developed a really attractive and practical package. I hope to see more compact vehicles in the future, because I would hate to include in the calculations of average velocity the time spent walking from the workplace to the HPV's parking space.

References

Kyle, C.R. (1979). Predicting human-powered-vehicle performance using ergometry and aerodynamic-drag measurements. *Proceedings of the International Conference on Human Powered Transportation, San Diego.* (Data are reproduced in *Bicycling*, May 1982, p. 62)

Moulton, A. (1982). Human-powered-bicycle considerations. In A.V. Abbott (Ed.) *The First Human-Powered-Vehicle Scientific Symposium Proceedings.* Indianapolis: International Human Powered Vehicle Association.

Whitt, F.R., & Wilson, D.G. (1982). *Bicycling science* (2nd ed.). Cambridge, MA: MIT Press.

12

COMPOSITE MATERIALS

T. Scott Rowe

In human-powered-vehicle (HPV) construction, composite materials have enabled racing machines and their riders to achieve new records in maximum-speed and -duration competitions (Gross, Kyle, & Malewicki, 1983). Composite materials have also been integrated into bicycles to reduce both weight and aerodynamic drag. Since 1984, when the U.S. Olympic Team pursuit bicycles were displayed with their "solid" rear wheels, a plethora of composite products for competition and sport bicycling has been marketed. Careful juxtaposition of various composite technologies in an HPV can provide extraordinary increases in machine performance. This chapter reviews composite-material technologies and their applications for land-vehicle enclosures, including recent trends in wheel and tube construction. Techniques and technologies for construction of plastic canopies (although these are not considered true composites) are also reviewed.

Composite Sandwich Construction

In many HPV designs the aerodynamic body or enclosure must also bear some or all of the vehicle loads (Rowe, 1983). To sustain these loads, the enclosure must distribute them evenly or deliver the loads to an internal frame member. Constructing the enclosure wall as a sandwich of various materials will usually do this. Typically, as shown in Figure 12.1, the sandwich consists of two face sheets bonded by an adhesive to a core material; core materials such as foam or even balsa wood could be substituted for the honeycomb shown.

Standard aerospace techniques for building this sandwich involve laminating the core material with plies of graphite or Kevlar cloth preimpregnated with epoxy, sealing the assembly in an evacuated plastic bag (for removal of air entrained in the epoxy), and baking it in a large oven. Although the costs to equip an amateur shop with the ovens and evacuation pumps are very high, various manufacturers of competition bicycle components have made the investment and now regularly turn out wheels, tubes, pedals, and cranks made out of various aerospace composite materials (Newkirk, 1989). The amateur, however, has available the techniques developed by Burt Rutan in his book, *Moldless Composite Homebuilt Sandwich Aircraft Construction*. Here, exothermic (self-curing) epoxy systems are used to laminate fiberglass, graphite, or Kevlar cloth to shaped foam cores to create stiff, lightweight, and relatively inexpensive aircraft structures without expensive shop tooling or fixtures. Such home-built-style kit aircraft as the Quickie and the VariEze use this type of construction.

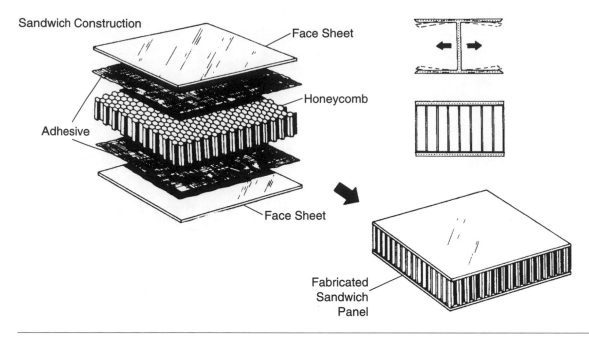

Sandwich Construction

Face Sheet

Honeycomb

Adhesive

Face Sheet

Fabricated
Sandwich
Panel

FIGURE 12.1 Sandwich construction.

HPV Composite Building Materials: Comparisons and Attributes

Table 12.1 outlines the basic design trade-offs considered when selecting a sandwich's component materials. Listed are some of the more common materials commercially available to the HPV builder. Units listed are those most commonly used in the analysis of bonded sandwich structures, and values are typical for most vendors. The workability criterion is based on the author's personal experience and judgment. As noted, the honeycomb cores were difficult to shape in the thickness dimension.

There are both advantages and disadvantages of using composite materials in HPV construction. Some of these are obvious; however, advantages such as the case in which clean aerodynamic surfaces are obtained by simple mold modifications are more subtle. Two attributes require further discussion. One is the opportunity for the HPV designer to engineer in more rider safety by the judicious use of composites. A well-designed vehicle enclosure, particularly one of monocoque shell design, acts as an entire-body helmet during an impact, cushioning the rider as the vehicle body crushes and deforms under severe shock and point loads. Equal to the shock-resistant properties of the materials is the very high abrasion resistance of Kevlar cloth. This material, when used as the outermost shell laminate, will save countless human skin grafts as the vehicle slides along the asphalt or concrete in a

crash. For the vehicle, a little automotive body filler and paint can be applied over the abraded area to restore it almost completely.

Another attribute requiring further discussion involves the inherent relationship of adhesive cure time to temperature. The exothermic epoxies currently in use require a 65 °F or greater shop temperature for a cure cycle less than 24 hours (Rowe, 1983; see Figure 12.2). This is important as many shops are not heated and night-time temperatures could prevent an epoxy-based lay-up from curing. Flameless radiant heaters can be used to elevate the shop temperature, but the shop must be ventilated well with fresh air and strong fans, as toxic fumes will be present with any lay-up.

Applications of Composites in HPVs

Composites are useful for many parts of HPVs. The qualities of light weight and strength are particularly valuable in uniquely shaped aerodynamic shells or bodies. Frames and aerodynamic wheels are increasingly being constructed of composite materials.

Shell and Body Construction

As described above, the goal in designing a vehicle enclosure is to transfer the aerodynamic loads to appropriate mechanical frame members or to

Material	Density	Strength	Workability	Cost
Cloths				
Fiberglass	12 oz/yd²	40,000 psi	good	$ 3.50/yd
Kevlar 49	5.1 oz/yd²	43,000 psi	difficult	15.00/yd
Graphite weave	5.7 oz/yd²	450,000 psi	excellent	30.00/yd
Cores				
Urethane foam	6.0 lb/ft³	150 psi shear modulus	excellent shaping	$8 / 24" × 48" × 1/4" sheet
HRH-49 honeycomb	2.1 lb/ft³	2,500 psi shear modulus	poor* shaping	$800 / 30" × 36" × 1/4" sheet
Nomex honeycomb	2.0 lb/ft³	1,900 psi shear modulus	average* shaping	$600 min. order: 42" × 96" × 1/4" sheet
HRH-78 honeycomb	2.0 lb/ft³	1,900 psi shear modulus	poor* shaping	$62 / 42" × 96" × 1/4" sheet
Epoxies				
Safe.T.Poxy	74.0 lb/ft³	5×10^5 psi tensile modulus	good wetting ability	$46 / gallon
Polyester resin	87.4 lb/ft³	1.1×10^5 psi tensile modulus	excellent wetting ability	$20 / gallon

Table 12.1 COMPOSITE MATERIALS SUITABILITY FOR HPV USE

*Thickness modification with honeycomb material

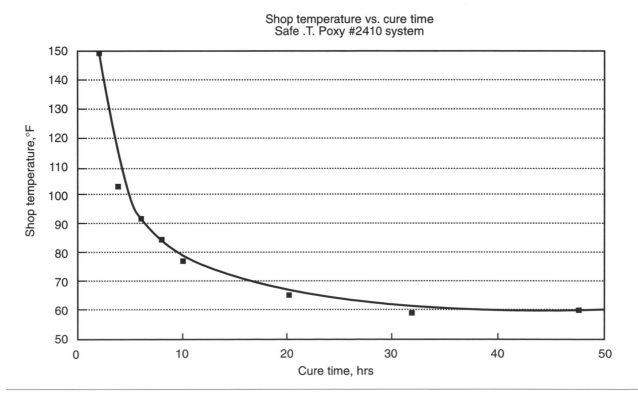

FIGURE 12.2 Shop temperature vs. cure time.

distribute them evenly in the enclosure assembly. Assuming one has a design for an aerodynamically efficient enclosure, what techniques are used to create the design? The following text explains two common methods.

Female Mold-Male Plug Technology. With this technique, the HPV builder creates a full-scale model of the vehicle, called a *plug*. The plug is commonly made on a wood frame covered with plastic foam shaped to the aerodynamic form of the vehicle, then laminated with fiberglass and relentlessly covered and sanded with automotive body filler until the surface is absolutely filled, smooth, and wave free. The importance of perfecting the male plug to the best of the builder's abilities cannot be emphasized enough, as errors made at this step are magnified all through the procedure.

Once the plug is finished and checked for conformance to aerodynamic form, it is covered with several layers of mold-release wax for releasing the female mold. The female mold is built around the male plug where the inner surface of the mold conforms exactly to the outer surface of the plug. It is constructed from coarse fiberglass soaked in polyester resin and stiffened with two-part liquid foam, poured just after mixing over the cured fiberglass, before it sets. (The foam adds rigidity to the female mold after separation from the plug.) Next, the builder must decide how to separate the female mold from the plug. Axial cuts from nose to tail work best, but the art lies in picking the locations for the cuts and determining the appropriate number of cuts. Too many cuts make the final enclosure difficult to assemble, and too few make lay up of the final enclosure in the mold difficult. The author suggests three cuts for most vehicles, at or near the vertices of the steeper curves in the vehicle-shell cross section (see Figure 12.3).

Once the cuts have been made, the most difficult step is in separating the female mold segments from the plug. Even assuming a liberal dose of mold-release wax was applied, the segments and plug will adhere with considerable strength. Assuming you do not want to destroy the male plug, the best method seems to be installing compressed-air or -water fittings into the segments and pumping air or water into the mold-plug boundary, hoping for separation. Lots of coaxing with flat pieces of sheet metal probably will also be necessary. Once the female mold segments are released, small repairs will probably be necessary on the inner surfaces. With the female segments prepared (remember to use mold release again), the final ef-

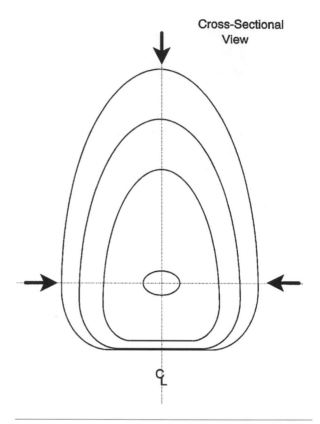

Cross-Sectional View

FIGURE 12.3 Location of incisions for female mold separation.

fort toward building the enclosure can begin. Build the enclosure from the outside in, starting with the outermost vehicle-skin material. The woven material used should be impregnated with resin prior to lay up, as you want a thin resin layer between the weave and the mold-release wax.

Enclosure-joint design is an important consideration (see Figure 12.4); leave space at the edges of the mold segments for implementing this. Once the enclosure is laid up and cured, the female mold segments may be released (this is a lot easier than in the previous step). Gentle prying should do. The reassembly of the enclosure can now begin: Refer again to the joint design. Windshields, windows, hatches, and so forth can now be cut into the enclosure; use a sabre saw with a blade designed for cutting glass. Some lightweight automotive body filler judiciously applied will finally bring you an enclosure you will be proud of!

Male-Plug-Only Technology. A second technique also involves building a male plug, but instead of making the outer covering a female mold, you can make it the actual enclosure by careful construction of the sandwich around the plug. The drawbacks to doing this are a poorer-quality outer

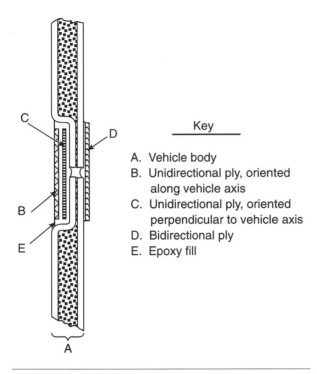

Key

A. Vehicle body
B. Unidirectional ply, oriented along vehicle axis
C. Unidirectional ply, oriented perpendicular to vehicle axis
D. Bidirectional ply
E. Epoxy fill

FIGURE 12.4 Enclosure-joint design, using raised areas in the female mold.

surface that requires much more filler (and hence weight) to smooth out, and less conformance to original aerodynamic form. One step will be saved in the process but it does not equate to one-third the time of the previous technique. The author used this second technique on the first Red Shift vehicle, where it was determined that the weight penalty incurred was unacceptable. Large panels had to be cut out of the enclosure and then recovered with Monokote, a material used to cover the wings of model aircraft. To implement this two-step technique, begin with the male plug as before. Once the mold release has been applied, begin laying up the inner laminate of the sandwich. With that layer cured, begin bonding core material to the inner skin, either in strips or using two-part foam poured over the assembly and shaped to the overall correct thickness. The outer layer is finally bonded to the shaped sandwich core in reasonably small strips, so that there will not be any folds or wrinkles in the tight-curvature areas. Release is done just as with the female mold; however, joint areas will now have to be routed out of the enclosure laminates.

Wheel and Tube Construction

With the relatively recent introduction of composite disk- and drum-type wheels, cranks, pedals, frames, and handlebars, new techniques have been developed and employed in the construction of HPVs. Drum wheels in particular are an advance in composite technology.

The Drum Wheel. The drum wheel (see Figure 12.5) starts out as one might expect, with conical plies cut out from preimpregnated, aerospace-grade Kevlar or graphite weave. These are laid into a two-part aluminum mold, machined to the final dimensions of the wheel drum. With the hub and composite rim accurately centered in the mold enclosure, the mold is clamped together and heated, both to cure the epoxy and to stretch the skins of the drum by taking advantage of the fact that the aluminum mold expands further than the composite components. Thus, a radial stress is induced in the cover plies that keeps the rim and hub coaxial and gives the wheel a natural resiliency. Completed wheel weight can be as low as 400 g.

The Disk Wheel. With the disk wheel, a true sandwich is constructed, and the disk is composed of a core of honeycomb or balsa wood laminated with plies of preimpregnated graphite or Kevlar weave. Because of the tremendous flexure and compression stresses an HPV wheel endures, delamination of the face sheets from the core could be a problem. The solution is to lay up the wheel, with accurately jigged components, in a mold that can exert high uniform pressure, forcing the epoxy in the plies to bond to all available wall surfaces in the honeycomb core. This is done by using rubber air bladders in the mold, allowing one to control the bonding pressure by filling or bleeding the bladder with compressed air. The resulting structure is also lightweight, about 1,000 g, and presents a smaller cross section to the airstream (see Figure 12.6).

Composite Tubes. These frames and handlebar structures have been attempted for many years by experienced frame builders. Only recently have composite frames seen commercial success, however. Almost all frames are built using the same techniques: spiral wrapping the preimpregnated tape around a mandrel and curing in an oven. The trick seems to be in selecting the bias of the tape weave, the weave density, and the overlap ratio. Also, air bladders encasing the spiral-wound assembly help in tape-ply bonding. The mandrel can be removed by freezing the assembly, again taking advantage of the materials' differing coefficients of expansion, or melting or chemically dissolving the mandrel away.

Composite Components. Such components as pedals or hubs are commonly machined from

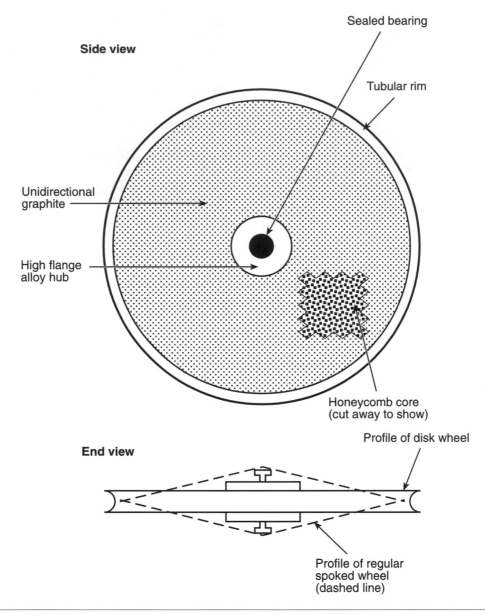

Side view

Sealed bearing

Tubular rim

Unidirectional graphite

High flange alloy hub

Honeycomb core (cut away to show)

Profile of disk wheel

End view

Profile of regular spoked wheel (dashed line)

FIGURE 12.5 Composite drum wheel construction.

composite blocks, each block consisting of many plies (typically graphite) compressed and bonded together. This is a good way to go on the smaller components since the raw material is commercially available. Carbide bits are required to work with this material; special cooling fluids and dust evacuation systems are also necessary as graphite dust is extremely irritating and toxic.

Canopy and Windshield Construction

Canopy or windshield construction is among the more difficult tasks the HPV builder has to tackle. Not only must aerodynamic and structural objec-

tives be met, but also other factors, including rider visibility and the solar-induced greenhouse effect, must also be considered. This is especially important in the practical or long-distance competition vehicle. Creating scatter-free, low-distortion optical surfaces is a topic all of its own, but the following techniques have been used by the author and others in creating successful vehicle canopies.

Canopy Materials.   Several different types of optically clear plastic exist for use in streamlined vehicles. Their workability and structural integrity differ, but the materials share some similar properties. Polymethyl methacrylate or acrylic, known by its most common trade name, Plexiglass™, is very

FIGURE 12.6 Example of composite disk wheels.

Photo by Zipp Speed Weaponry™

available and was the first material used in aircraft canopies. It is very flexible, has a low index of refraction, and has a relatively low melt temperature. It does scratch easily and has moderate impact resistance. Polycarbonate, under the trade name Lexan™, has the highest impact resistance and is used in everything from spectacle lenses to machine guards. It is relatively difficult to form, with a high forming temperature (177 °C; 350 °F) and significant shrinkage under temperature. Canopies have been formed with it, however, and in aircraft canopies it is now the preferred material. Polystyrene is also available and can be formed easily under temperature. However, it must be annealed on setting or residual stresses make the formed part very fragile. All three materials can be bought in various tints or tinted after forming, thus allowing for some solar-load regulation. If the vehicle has a canopy covering a significant portion of the top surface area, it is highly recommended to use at least a light tint. The human engine will appreciate it!

"Free-Blown" Canopy Construction. With this technology, it is possible to make high-grade optical enclosures with no waves, distortion, or optical scatter. The problem lies in forming the enclosures along a predescribed, three-dimensional aerodynamic form. Complex curvatures and curvatures that deviate significantly from spherical are difficult to form with this technique. The object is to form a bubble with the optical material and con-

form the bubble to an expected aerodynamic form. The term free-blown comes from the fact that there are no forms or molds to conform to in the third dimension.

Start with a 3/4-in. plywood sheet with the plan view of the area the canopy will cover cut out from the center. Then create a sandwich consisting from top to bottom of: plan-view cut out, canopy material, thick felt, and, finally, another sheet of 3/4-in. plywood. These should now be drilled through and bolted together around the perimeter in a fairly tight bolt pattern. In the geometrical center of the pattern a compressed air fitting should be installed, piercing both the bottom plywood and the felt, but just back of the plastic. At least two butane-fueled radiant heaters will be needed, with large-area burners. Connect the compressed-air fitting via a length of high-pressure tubing to a compressed-air scuba diving tank with a good regulator on it. These regulators have very-fine-control needle valves in them; good regulation of pressure and flow will be required. Some guidelines for controlling the third dimension is required; wire hoops bent in the correct shape and spaced on regular intervals along the canopy axis work well and should be quickly removable. This effort will require four people, two to work the heaters, one to control the regulator, and one to keep an eye on the growth of the bubble. The butane heaters, now fired up and warm, must be directed at the plastic, about 300 mm (12 in.) above the surface, and kept moving in a circular sweeping pattern. A small supply of air from the tank should be flowing into the sandwich. As the plastic gets soft, a bubble will form in the plastic, starting at the fitting and spreading outward. Control the growth of the bubble with the regulator; don't let it grow too rapidly. As the bubble enlarges, heat the areas not growing as fast more than those that are expanding. As the bubble gets near the wire hoops, throttle down the regulator to just a trickle and use the burners to heat and cool the bubble to an appropriate shape. Once at the desired form, remove all heat leaving a trickle of air flowing. The bubble will freeze rapidly. Once cool, remove from the sandwich and cut the canopy out of the shape formed. The reader may need a few tries at this to get the hang of it, but this method can produce nice, optically correct canopies.

Vacuum-Formed Canopy Construction. The vacuum technique is used to form most HPV canopies. The major attribute is that the canopy shape can be controlled precisely by the female mold in which the canopy is formed. Drawbacks include marring of the outer surface by the mold during draw, waviness of the canopy induced from the mold, and difficulty in creating sufficient vacuum to start the draw. Even the magnificent Vector vehicles of the early 1980s suffered from these problems. Surface flaws and waves can be reduced by a significant effort in finishing the female mold, or by machining the mold out of aluminum.

To start, create a female mold of the area of the vehicle to be covered by the canopy. Be careful not to have too deep a draw, or depth of the mold, as this will affect the final canopy thickness and degree of conformance to the mold. The female mold of the vehicle enclosure is a good place to start. Once the female mold has been formed to satisfaction, build a flange around the perimeter of the mold. This is where the canopy material will seat. Between the plastic and the flange, place a silicone-rubber strip or bead for sealing. Finally, set a frame piece around the flange and clamp securely. With the air fitting attached to the mold and connected to the vacuum side of an air compressor, begin heating the plastic with the butane burner. Heating the mold is recommended as well, as it will reduce sleeking, the incorporation of ultra-fine scratches on the surface, as the plastic is stretched into the mold. The canopy should form instantly when the proper combination of vacuum and material softness is achieved. Once conformance to the mold is met, allow the canopy to cool and cut it out to desired size.

One other technique may, it is hoped, be of passing interest. When the two techniques previously discussed are infeasible, the canopy can be formed from a mold using the hot-draw technique. This involves heating the canopy material and the male mold in a large (room-size) oven to 480 °F (250 °C) and sending in two or more brave individuals to grab the now-pliable sheet and draw the sheet over the mold in a forceful and rapid manner. The resulting conforming shape can now be cooled and cut out for the canopy. This technique obviously has problems, but can be a last resort for a particularly difficult shape.

Conclusion

By now readers should have an idea of the level of effort necessary to work with composite materials, but, it is hoped, are not intimidated by the uniqueness of the materials or techniques. Careful time management seems to be the biggest prerequisite for success with these materials; the best advice is to allow plenty of time for completion of each phase of the enclosure. Now that component manufacturers are using composite materials, the burden for the HPV builder has been eased somewhat with lightweight, aerodynamic wheels and tubes available off the shelf or built to specification. The success of the triathlete bicycle and the HPV Race Across America (RAAM) indicate that these advances will not be a passing fad. All HPV builders can be justifiably proud that they were and still are the leaders in the "composite revolution!"

Acknowledgments

I would like to acknowledge the technology developed by the Red Shift team, whose members include Steve Fujikawa, Gary Hoisington, Tom Milkie, Scott Rowe, and Fred Starks. I am particularly grateful to Tom for some of the photos included here. Red Shift II, as an application of the aforementioned techniques, now resides at California State University, Long Beach. Jim Horton and Scott Gordon contributed the material on triathlete machines and composite wheels, respectively. Finally, I am grateful to my patient wife Minerva, who put up with more than just foam dust during the first 2 years of our marriage so that I could pursue a dream.

References

Bicycle Guide. (1989, August).

Gross, A.C., Kyle, C.R., & Malewicki, D.J. (1983, December). The aerodynamics of human-powered land vehicles. *Scientific American*, pp. 142–152.

Newkirk, G. (1989, June). Wheels of change. *Triathlete*, p. 16.

Rowe, T.S. (1984) Construction techniques for composite human-powered vehicles. In A. Abbott (Ed.), *Proceedings of the 1983 International Human Powered Vehicle Association Symposium*. Indianapolis: International Human Powered Vehicle Association, (pp. 118–122).

13

DRIVE-TRAIN DESIGN

Rob Price

This five-part chapter attempts to evaluate the many parameters involved in HPV drive-train design. It begins with a discussion of the three rider positions, upright, supine, and prone, that may be used in HPV designs. Part 2 examines pedaling motions from a mechanical perspective and investigates various drive motions. Part 3 considers the function of the drive as it moves the vehicle and the role of variable gear ratios. Part 4 investigates oval chainwheels and similar mechanisms, which use circular pedal motion with nonconstant pedaling speed in an effort to improve efficiency. Part 5 brings the data together with some conclusions about the efficiency of converting human effort into vehicle motion.

Part 1 HPV Rider Positions

An HPV can be designed to allow a rider to propel it from one of three positions: *upright* and *crouched*, supported at the bottom of the trunk between the legs as in conventional cycling; *supine recumbent*, sitting or lying on one's back; and *prone recumbent*, lying on one's chest. The rider position selected often affects the efficiency of the drive train and its complexity and cost. For instance, a supine recumbent HPV will have a physically longer drive train than a prone recumbent HPV if the rider faces forward and the rear wheel is driven.

Upright Positions

The upright positions are the conventional bicycling positions, beginning with the full upright seating position used on utility bicycles, to the partial lean used on all-terrain bikes, to the racing-cycle positions, first with the body leaned forward to approximately a 45° angle for riding on the tops of drop-style handlebars, to the crouch used when riding on the drops. Each of these positions progressively reduces the rider's frontal area, allowing faster speed with the same power output.

Body support is provided by protrusions of the pelvis between the legs that rest against the saddle. Saddles may have springs to soften the ride, giving what is known as compliance. This type saddle is usually found on utility and some all-terrain bikes. Saddles are unsprung and get progressively narrower and harder on machines that are designed for the more leaned-over positions. As the body leans forward to the more streamlined positions, more of the rider's weight is supported by the hands, making seat compliance less important. Seat compliance also results in additional muscle motion that, because it does not contribute to propulsion, therefore contributes to energy loss. On rough terrain the rider can rise from the seat, using the arms and legs as shock absorbers, and reduce the need for saddle compliance.

Compliant seats and suspensions undergo deflection with each pedal stroke. When the leg completes a pedal stroke the torso settles onto the seat, deflecting the springs. The torso is raised again on the next stroke, slightly increasing the length of the stroke. This slight stroke-length increase robs power to the drive. A similar problem occurs with a sprung wheel. The drive tends to wind up the suspension, which then returns to a neutral point at the end of the power stroke, but the energy used to deflect the spring has been diverted from the drive. The resultant bouncing, either of the body on the seat or the whole machine on the road, can be nearly eliminated with very smooth pedaling technique and dampers (discussed in chapter 15). But energy that is better spent in turning the driving wheel is instead expended in deflecting the seat or the suspension. Shock absorbing front forks have become popular recently and when they are used on extremely rough terrain appear to be worth the power lost.

Supine Position

In the supine position the rider lies on the back, facing up or forward, supported beneath the rump and back. In the semisupine position the rider's trunk is vertical, or nearly so. The muscles of the rump and back are used in pedaling, so they raise the body slightly when they are tensed and tend to work or chafe against the seat in steeply reclined positions. This method of support can also cause rider cooling problems, already a difficulty in enclosed HPVs.

A rider can exert a greater force on the pedals with the back braced in the reclined position, as compared with the standard cycling positions. This ability to push harder on the pedals is possible only at low pedaling speeds, and does not allow a higher maximum power output, especially at higher pedaling speeds. It can also overstress the knee joints.

Prone Position

In the prone position the rider is facing downward, requiring upper-body support at the hips and shoulders. It is better not to support the chest directly, because the weight of the trunk may increase the work of breathing. This position is also uncomfortable because it requires hyperextension of the neck and it could be more dangerous in the event of a collision.

Position Effect on Efficiency

The efficiency and power produced in these positions was investigated by Kyle (Abbott, 1982) and others. He estimated the supine position to be 96% and the prone position to be 92% as efficient as the conventional upright position. This is discussed in depth in chapter 3. Because the prone and supine positions do not allow the rider to raise the body off the seat to attenuate road vibration, vehicle suspensions or sling-type seats are often used with these positions. Suspensions on smooth roads and compliant seats in any circumstances can incur losses in efficiency, because the additional motions come from muscle input. Suspensions used on rough roads can produce a reduction in the wasted kinetic energy produced by the bumps.

Rider Visibility

Part of the reason for the recent popularity of all-terrain bikes is their nearly-upright riding position, which allows riders to have the comfort and direct forward visibility of the old English three-speed, but with the technical sophistication of modern bicycles. The racing-crouch position requires the rider to crane the neck to see forward, even when resting the hands on the tops of the handlebars. Racers generally consider the resulting stiff neck to be worth the decrease in frontal area.

Adequate rider visibility is possible with the supine position to a seat-back angle of 25° to 35° from horizontal, as used on the F-16 fighter aircraft and formula racing cars respectively (Setright, 1968). The major problem with steep seat angles on HPVs is visual interference of legs and crank mechanisms of circular-drive machines with low seating positions.

Visibility is also a problem with the prone position. Greg Johnson, in his prone-position bicycle, reduced the extent of the problem by extending the shoulder support to provide a chin rest (Abbott, 1982). His neck was bent such that his eyes faced forward. Ball, in his prone-position tricycle Dragonfly, used a forehead rest with his eyes facing downward, and mirrors to allow him to see forward. Ball's machine was very low, so that the road was viewed from just a few inches off the ground (Abbott). His machine was the first to exceed 50 mph; the view from inside must have been thrilling!

Summing Up Rider Position

For a streamliner or any machine in which achieving more speed than on a conventional bicycle is important, the upright riding position is aerodynamically inefficient, and the best single way to attain more speed is better streamlining. Clearly the supine recumbent position combines good power output with reduced frontal area. Supine machines are both difficult to see and difficult to see from, but these problems can be solved with little loss in efficiency.

Part 2 HPV Pedaling Mechanisms

Conventional bicycles use circular pedaling with a chain running to a freewheel. In this section, this conventional drive train and several other drive trains are reviewed.

Freewheels

A *freewheel* is a one-way clutch. It uses pawls and a ratchet wheel to engage the drive when the two halves of the freewheel are going at the same speed. It also allows the output half to overspeed the input half when the input half is stopped or turning too slowly. Freewheels are standard equipment on the rear wheels of nearly all conventional bicycles, enabling the rider to stop pedaling and coast.

Coasting. *Coasting* occurs when the pedals are stopped or are turning slower than the freewheel portion that is connected to the drive output. Engaging the drive after coasting involves accelerating the mass of the rider's body parts doing the driving, usually the legs, and the HPV's drive system until the input and output halves of the drive reach the same speed, called *coupling speed*, and engage. This usually takes less than a half-crank revolution on standard circular-drive bicycles.

Drive Motions

The four pedaling motions discussed later in this chapter are circular, elliptical, arcuate, and linear. These motions may transmit power to the vehicle, via a drive, in only two ways, constant and intermittent. The two drive types are closely related to forced and free pedaling motions, described in part 3 of this chapter. The conventional bicycle is an excellent example of a constant drive.

An example of an intermittent drive is shown in Figure 13.5.

Constant Drives. *Constant drives* are always engaged, under normal pedaling, whether output power is low or high. Low power is inputting just sufficient power to keep the drive engaged. High power is inputting sufficient power to accelerate the machine or climb hills or overcome wind resistance.

There are places in the leg motion where power output is low, regardless of intent. These occur at the maximum and minimum leg length in each cycle. When the legs have moved beyond these low-power points, the constant drive is fully engaged, ready to transmit additional power.

Constant drives on HPVs tend to use chains and sprockets. The chain is made endless and wrapped around the sprockets, and the drive is engaged as long as the pedals are moved rapidly enough. The standard bicycle is a perfect example of a chain-driven constant drive. Inventors tend to couple circular and elliptical pedal motions to constant drives.

Intermittent Drives. *Intermittent drives* (see Figure 13.5) are engaged when power output is high and disengaged when power output is low. The drive is engaged until the pedal reaches the end of its stroke, then is disengaged until it is reengaged on the next stroke. The vehicle coasts at the end of each power stroke; accelerating the drive and the rider's legs to coupling speed must be done each stroke. This can take over half the stroke length, as on the P-4 HPV described later, severely reducing time available in each stroke for high power output.

Intermittent drives on HPVs often use cables wrapped around drums connected to freewheels, as on Steve Ball's Dragonfly (Abbott, 1982) which will be illustrated later in this chapter. Inventors tend to connect arcuate and linear pedal motions to intermittent drives.

Circular Pedaling

A conventional bicycle crank setup utilizes an axle, or spindle, mounted in bearings that are fixed to the frame of the HPV. The fixing point on a conventional bicycle is called the bottom bracket. The bearings in nearly all cases are angular-contact ball types to minimize friction. The two crank arms are phased 180° apart and the outboard ends of the cranks mount the pedals. The drive sprocket is usually mounted to the right-side crank arm, so that loads from the right pedal are fed directly into the sprocket. Loads from the left crank arm are fed torsionally through the spindle to the right crank.

Circular pedaling, simple and mechanically efficient, is a 180°-timed, forced motion drive. A *forced motion* drive is defined as connecting a rider to a linkage that requires operation at a given rate and over a given displacement. *Free motion* allows a rider to select the pedal displacement on each stroke. *Timing* is connection of one pedal to the other. Timing of 0° forces the feet to operate together and timing of 180°, as on a conventional bicycle, forces the feet to oppose each other. *Untimed* drives allow each foot to operate independently. Modifying the velocity of the pedal as it orbits the spindle offers promise of small increases in leg power output, as will be discussed in part 4 of this chapter.

Elliptical Pedaling

Differential cranks or variable-length cranks may be used to obtain elliptical pedal motions, but have not been widely applied. Wilson sketched a differential cranking mechanism, reproduced in Figure 13.1, which by tailoring the lengths of the arms gave ellipses with different major-to-minor axis ratios (see Figure 13.2) (Abbott, 1982).

Differential cranks, where each crank is constructed in two parts, use an additional bearing set where they are connected by an intermediate shaft partway out the full crank length. The outer crank part is timed to the inner part using a 2:1 ratio chain or three-gear step-up from the bottom bracket. The step-up is required because the sprocket or gear at

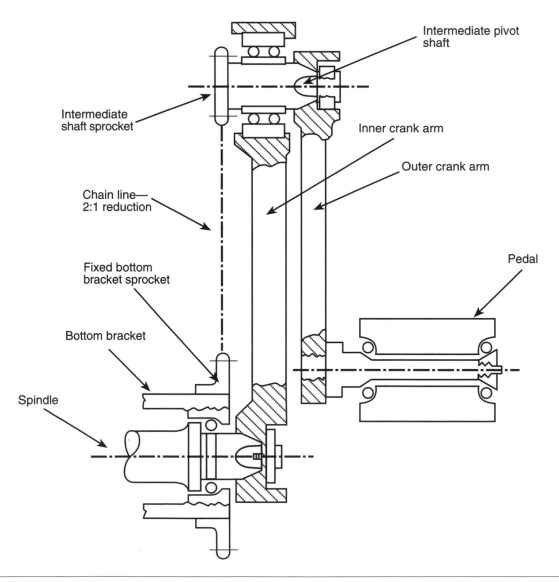

FIGURE 13.1 Differential crank. Patented by Magus Patent ver wertungs-Genossenschaft, Swiss patent 553,055, 1943.

Ratios shown are inner to outer crank lengths

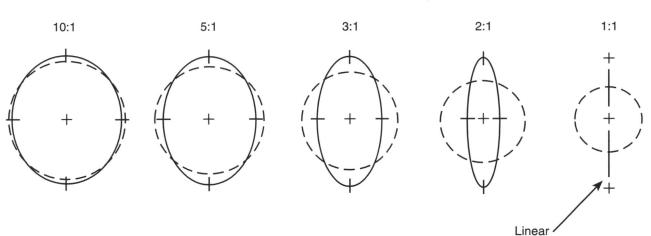

FIGURE 13.2 Elliptical pedaling ratios.

the bottom bracket is fixed, and the sprocket or gear at the intermediate shaft is connected to the outer portion of the crank arm. The outer portion then rotates in the reverse direction of the inner portion.

Another method of obtaining an elliptical pedaling path is to vary the length of the cranks, by sliding one piece within the other, as shown in Figure 13.3. The 2:1 ratio is required to obtain an elliptical pedal path. The ovality of the ellipse is twice the length of the "crank arm for oscillation" in the figure. A similar design was built by Mairag (DeLong, 1978) using a 1:1 ratio in the gear set so that the pedal path was circular, but offset from the spindle center, to obtain a longer crank length on the downstroke and shorter length on the return stroke. This is discussed later in this chapter in the section on advance-retard mechanisms.

The 1983 Swiss Z-Traction unit (Hugaud, 1983) was an adapter designed to be added to a standard bicycle. As shown in Figure 13.4, it used L-shaped arms mounted to each crank arm at the elbow. The lower, short end extended forward and the pedal mounted to that end in standard fashion. The upper portion of the arm contained a bearing sliding in a track fastened to the bicycle seat tube. The resultant pedal path was elliptical, with the long axis oriented about 30° forward of vertical. The manufacturer claimed a 30% performance increase, presumably from increased human output, because the mechanisms added friction over that for regular cranks. Because the pedals were moved forward about 4 in., the seat and handlebars would need to be moved a like distance to maintain their relative locations.

Arcuate Pedaling

Many examples of arcuate-pedaling bicycles have been marketed over the years and never heard from again. Several examples of untimed and timed intermittent drives and a timed constant drive were examined. Most of these machines could utilize shorter wheelbases than standard bicycles because the pedals did not move as far forward as on conventional bicycles. Only selected machine drives are sketched in the list that follows.

- **Kallander:** An interesting untimed free-motion machine, built by Charles Kallander in 1975 (DeLong, 1975), is shown in Figure 13.5. This machine used belts with thick blocks attached to space the belt wraps as they wound up on drums, one drum for each pedal. The drive was taken out through freewheels and a standard chain drive to the rear wheel. It had a continuously varying gear ratio, and the effective gear ratio increased as the pedal was pushed and the belt pulled on a smaller radius. Kallander designed the gear increase because he contended that the leg provides maximum thrust when it approaches the fully extended position. The pedals were spring returned and the lever pivot was under the rear-wheel hub. The maximum pedal travel was through about a 45° arc with half above horizontal; partial travel, free motion, could be used at the rider's option.

- **Creative Motion:** This 1982 machine ("Cable," 1982) was untimed, cable-driven to freewheels

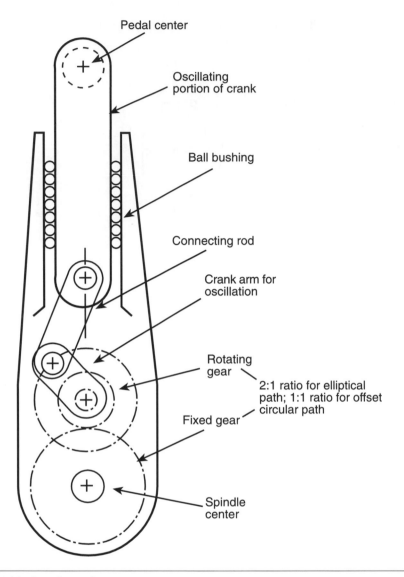

FIGURE 13.3   Variable-length crank.

on both sides of the rear hub, single speed, spring pedal return, lever pivot forward of the pedal, and crank travel was from horizontal to about 30° below horizontal.

- **EFROS:** The Boris Efros machine, also introduced in 1982 ("Peddling," 1982) was untimed, chain-driven to freewheels on both sides of the rear hub, and multiple speed, using spring pedal return, with the lever pivot aft of the pedal. Crank travel was from slightly above horizontal down nearly 90°.
- **Alenax:** Shown in Figure 13.6 (Alenax Co., 1983) the Alenax "Transbar Power" bicycle used chain drive, which also timed the pedals 180°. However, lifting the returning pedal did not input power to the drive, that is, there was

no *retractile input*. The location where the chain attached to the crank could be varied for different gear ratios. The levers were approximately 50% longer than standard bicycle cranks, pivoted aft of the pedals, and were nearly vertical at the bottom of the 120° stroke. Similar drives have been produced by many previous manufacturers.

- **Harris:** This machine, designed by race car designer Trevor Harris (Anson, 1973), had the lever pivots below the rear wheel and included a linkage to time the pedals 180°. Like the Kallander machine, Harris used about a 45° arc for the lever arms, centered at horizontal. The arms were also pivoted below the rear-wheel hub. He also used rebound springs to

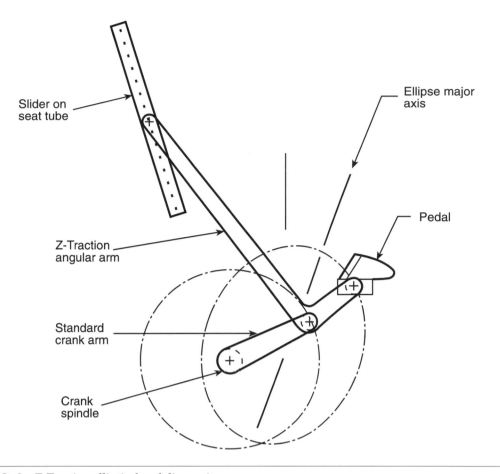

FIGURE 13.4 Z-Traction elliptical pedaling unit.

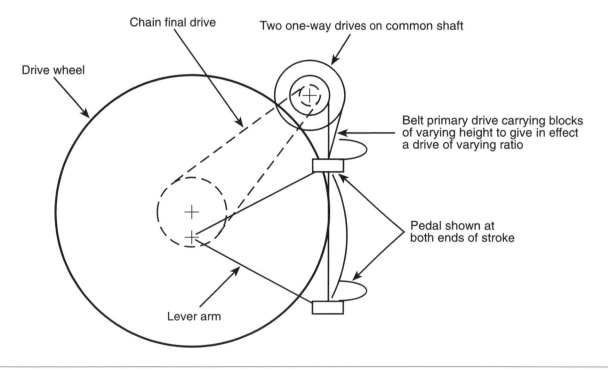

FIGURE 13.5 Kallander drive.

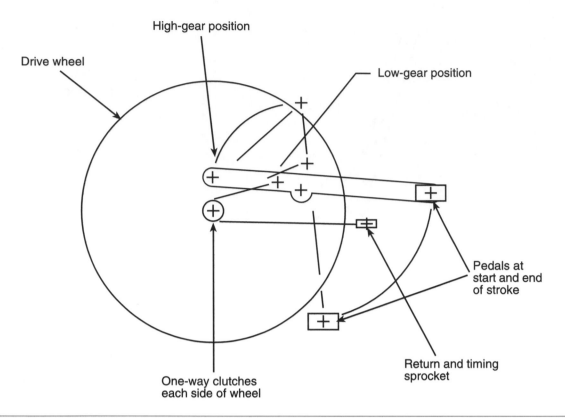

High-gear position

Drive wheel

Low-gear position

Pedals at
start and end
of stroke

Return and timing
sprocket

One-way clutches
each side of wheel

FIGURE 13.6   Alenax lever drive.

absorb energy at the pedal stops. A cable drive for each pedal drove both sides of the wheel and a variable pulley location allowed gear-ratio changes. Retractile input was featured, but at low efficiency, due to an involved mechanical path.

- **Klopfenstein:** This tricycle design by King L. Klopfenstein (Hogan, 1986) used timed cranks to turn crank arms via levers through an arc of 165°. The track of the pedals moved through an arc of about 30°, starting at horizontal so the pedals moved aft as the crank moved down, making it easier for elderly people to use, due to reduced knee bending. As on the Harris machine, retractile input was possible but not efficient. Final drive was through a five-speed derailleur to the single rear wheel.

- **Land Scull:** The only example reviewed of lever-motion constant drive was this arm-and-leg-powered recumbent machine built for the 1982 IHPVA Speed Championships. The motion was similar to sliding-seat rowing. In this drive the arms moved together and the feet moved together but the drive was timed so that when the arms were extended the legs

were retracted. All four limbs were in the power stroke at the same time. Pedal motion was in arcs, and the pivot point for the feet was *pendant* (above the pedals) while the hands were opposite. The stroke of the arms was about 600 mm (24 in.) and the legs 450 mm (18 in.).

Linear Pedaling

Linear-pedaling machines may feed power into a rotary crank-and-connecting-rod mechanism, much like a gasoline engine or a railroad steam engine, for forced motion. The drive may also feed into a one-way clutch, for free motion.

Ball's Dragonfly (Abbott, 1982), and the author's P-4 were both free-motion machines. In both drives the feet, and in Ball's case, the hands, were timed and retractile input was possible. The output of Ball's drive connected to a standard derailleur mechanism for multiple gears. P-4 used a variable location for a cable drive, giving continuously variable gears between the limits (Price, 1981). As stated previously, Dragonfly was the first machine to exceed 50 mph.

Slider Mechanisms.   Arcuate drives have arms that add only a few ball bearings to the friction-adding components in a drive train. Linear drives require what engineers call moment connections to locate the drive elements. These have always been difficult to design. Steam engines used hardened ways and brass or iron inserts and plenty of heavy grease, but the friction levels were unimportant because of high engine outputs. The puny human requires lightweight and efficient bearings. Ball bearings that roll on flat surfaces or utilize V-shaped guides are used to minimize slider friction, but many such bearings are needed to fully constrain the mechanisms.

Ball's mechanism for the hands had to be able to twist to accommodate the Dragonfly steering mechanism. P-4 used a pedal stroke of 350 mm (14 in.) and Dragonfly used a stroke of 530 mm (21 in.) for both hands and feet (Price, 1981, 1983).

Reducing Coupling Time.   As discussed earlier, an intermittent drive must be brought up to coupling speed on each stroke before additional power can be applied. The faster a machine is going, the greater the part of the stroke it will take to spin up and couple the drive. On P-4 the drive was coupled about 50% of the available time at moderate vehicle speeds and gears. Dragonfly used a variable pul-

ley, shown in Figure 13.7, to quickly spin up the drive at the beginning of the stroke. In Ball's first design the initial ratio was 2.5 times the final ratio, 19 mm (0.75 in.) radius to 48 mm (1.88 in.) radius. This coupled too quickly. His second design started with a ratio 1.5 times the final ratio, 32 mm (1.25 in.) radius to the 48 mm (1.88 in.) radius. The eccentric portion of the pulley, a half turn, brought the drive up to speed within 20% of the full stroke of 2.5 turns (Price, 1983).

Rebound Springs.   Rebound springs are compressed when the pedal nears the end of its stroke and return the energy to the pedals after they reverse direction. They were tried by Ball with poor results (Price, 1982). Another 1982 IHPVA Speed Championships competitor said that they were the only way to get back the kinetic energy lost in direction reversals in unforced motion drives (Price, 1982). Joe Mastropaolo did tests for the *Gossamer Albatross* (Abbott, 1982), stretching a spring and varying the phasing with the pedal stroke, as an energy-storage device. In 60-min tests the advantages were less than 4%, so the concept was abandoned.

Cable Tensioners.   Some designers use springs to return intermittent drives to the beginning of the power stroke. The springs need to be strong enough

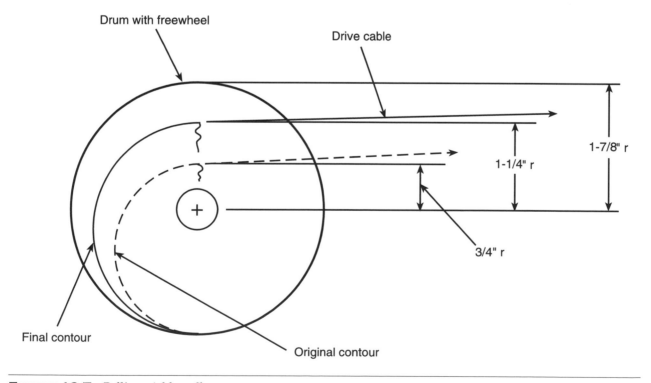

FIGURE 13.7   Ball's variable pulley.

to lift the leg and the mechanisms or require the rider to pull up to assist the return. When the drive is actuated, work goes into flexing the spring, which is not recovered during the undriven return stroke. P-4 used a second cable around each drive drum and interconnected them, so that as the cables wound off one drum they wound onto the other. A small tensioning spring was used to maintain preload and compensate for drive-cable-length differences due to gear changes, but absorbed no energy. The chain-tensioning spring on a derailleur cage is another example of a tensioner that is not part of the energy path.

Slider Offset.   In recumbent designs linear pedaling reduces the frontal-area problems of arcuate or circular drives. If connected to a crank mechanism for forced motion and if low-friction slide bearings are found, the designer may then be able to look at improving efficiency by offsetting the slider from the crank pivot. Several possibilities are shown in Figure 13.8. Offsetting the slider affects the pedal velocity, assuming constant rotational speed of the crank. This is shown in Figure 13.9. A close look at nonconstant pedal velocity in part 4 of this chapter will show that these subtle shifts in pedal speed may be advantageous.

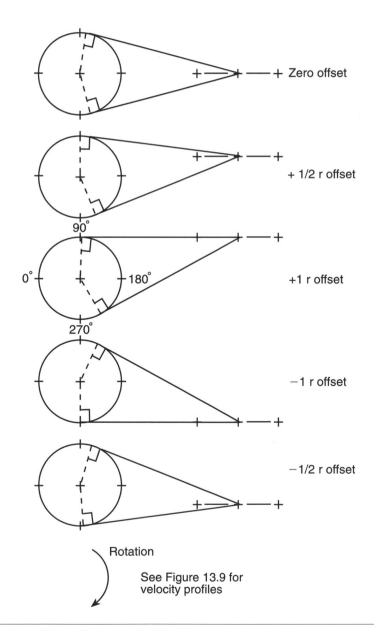

FIGURE 13.8   Linear drive slider offsets.

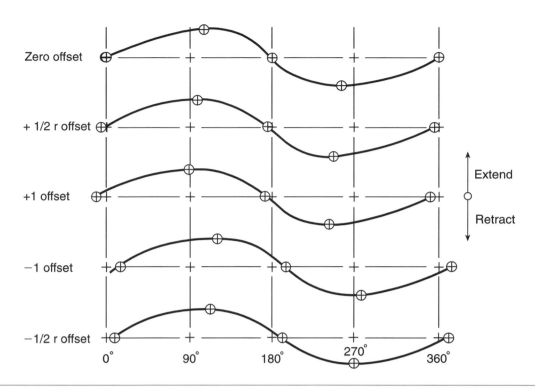

FIGURE 13.9 Offset slider velocity profiles.

Summing Up Pedaling Mechanisms

Circular pedaling is customary, mechanically simple, and parts are readily available for use in HPVs. Elliptical pedaling is mechanically more complex, but that limitation may be outweighed by a more efficient power-input pattern. Extreme ellipses might offer advantages on a recumbent machine requiring small frontal area and unobstructed rider visibility. The elliptical linkage with equal-length arms giving linear motion might cure the slider-bearing problem. Arcuate pedaling has few additional friction points, but the length of the crank arm required to keep the sweep angle small probably requires as much frontal area on a recumbent as does circular pedaling. Linear pedaling's great liability is slider friction. If that is cured linear pedaling offers promise, if connected to cranks for efficient forced motion.

Part 3 HPV Driving Mechanisms

Although conventional bicycles use hub gears and derailleur gears as alternatives to single-speed drives, there are many other possibilities, although few are commercially available. The conventional design and the alternatives are reviewed here.

Variable-Drive Ratios

An important part of HPV drive-train design is the ability to vary the drive ratio to allow the rider to pedal at a comfortable or sustainable rate. Both constant- and intermittent-drive types can be connected to the machine output via fixed or variable ratios. An example of a fixed ratio is a single-speed track racing bicycle, which does not even have a freewheel for coasting.

Step-type gear changes make a discrete change in the ratio when a gear is shifted. Examples are hub- or derailleur-type multiple-speed machines. Some variable-speed drives where the ratio was infinitely variable between the high and low limits have already been reviewed. To complete the subject some common and unusual gear shifters are discussed. These unusual designs were intended not to add to efficiency, but to make gear shifting easier or automatic. None have been well received by consumers.

Hub Gears. Hub gears use an epicyclic gear train consisting of a nonrotating sun gear, or pinion, fixed to the hub axle, planet gears with their axles fixed to a cage but rotating in contact with the pinion, and a ring gear, internally toothed to engage the planet gear teeth.

A selector mechanism mounted on the frame or handlebar allows a choice of step-down, direct, or step-up gearing in the usual three-speed gearbox. When the drive is input to the ring gear, the planet-gear cage revolves at a lower speed, resulting in a step-down. Drive into the planet cage results in a step-up of the ring gear. Direct drive bypasses the gear train, locking the wheel hub to the input sprocket. Varying the number of teeth on the gears allows different ratio sets to be chosen.

The original manufacturer of these gearboxes, Sturmey-Archer, produced several models, including four- and five-speed versions, which used two epicyclic gear trains. Generally bicycle gear-ratio steps get closer as the ratios get higher. With the epicyclic gear train the step-up from direct is much wider than the step-down, which is not advantageous. (As a guide, the ratio between neighboring gears should be similar.) Alex Moulton (Abbott, 1982) measured efficiency through the most common three-speed (Type AW) hub and found 80% efficiency in low gear (25% step-down), 96% efficiency in direct drive, and 85% efficiency in high gear (33% step-up).

Hub gearboxes are compact, fairly well sealed against road grime, and if adjusted properly are unbreakable. They are also easy to shift, but the limited ratio availability, high weight, and low efficiency are drawbacks. Use of aluminum for the housing and needle bearings in the planet gears could reduce weight and improve efficiency, but the benefits would be slight, certainly insufficient to displace derailleur gears from their near-universal usage.

Derailleurs. In 1959 derailleurs were rare in the U.S. That year the Benelux derailleur was introduced with two sprockets on a special hub that mounted onto a three-speed Sturmey-Archer to obtain six ratios! Today derailleurs are the standard. Front sprockets or chainwheels seem to be topping out at three chain rings on mountain bikes and two on road bikes. On the rear, freewheels are standardizing at seven sprockets or cogs. This gives 14 or 21 ratios and often involves many near-duplicate ratios.

Advantages of derailleurs are that ratios are easily altered by changing cogs, and once the gear change is made the changing mechanism consumes no more energy than a direct drive, except for the chain offset due to the driver and driven sprockets not being in line, and the friction in the small idlers on the tensioning arm.

These tiny idler pulleys, too small to have proper teeth on them, usually run in sleeve-type bearings and revolve at high speed. Roger Durham (Durham Bicycles, 1981) marketed a ball-bearing replacement unit for the idlers with which he claimed an efficiency increase of 5%.

A drawback of derailleur gears is chain offset. Seldom is the chain ring chosen in line with the rear cog chosen. Particularly bad are the extreme gears, such as the inner small chain ring driving the outer small cog, a combination that should be avoided. Power losses in the transmission due to offset are very low, because a derailleur-type chain is designed to accommodate sideward flexure. An additional problem is dirt thrown up from the road, but how much this affects efficiency is not known and is a problem shared with many other drives. Derailleur shifting once was a high art because of the need to fine-tune the location of the derailleur cages to prevent clattering of the chain on the edges of the cogs or rubbing on the cages. The advent of self-centering and shifters with detents has corrected this major drawback for the recreational rider. Shift levers can also be mounted on the handlebars, hub-gear style, eliminating the need to remove hands and reach down to shift.

Other Drives. Following is a list of drives that, except for the Deal drive, had in common the need for a derailleur-style chain-tensioning mechanism, but had the advantage that all maintained a fixed chain alignment. No comparative tests were made, so it is not possible to accurately identify relative advantages and disadvantages.

- **Cambiogear:** An expanding chainwheel was utilized that increased in two-tooth increments from 24 to 54 teeth, giving 16 steps. This 1983 design is similar to the Deal automatic discussed below ("Cambiogear," 1983).

- **Hagen:** Continuously variable ratios were available in this 1974 design by moving six small jockey pulleys axially outward to raise the ratio. The jockey pulleys ran on one-way clutches to compensate for differences in chain centers and tooth location. Minimum-to-maximum ratio range was 3:1 (Van Cleave, 1974).

- **Moritsch:** The chainwheel center was shifted relative to the spindle, which engaged a segment of the chainwheel via pawls and ratchets, the ratio being determined by the distance of the engaged pawl from the spindle in this 1982 design (Stengel, 1981).

- **Tokheim:** Two-tooth segments were moved radially outward in a carrier plate and into alignment with the chain. This 1972 design used five ratios over a 3:1 span ("Revolutionary," 1972).

- **Deal:** This automatic transmission from 1984 provided 16 ratios, similar to the Cambiogear above, that changed ratios due to changes in pedal force. Toothed elements and guide units contracted to select lower ratios, and it was possible to go from top to bottom gear in two revolutions. No chain tensioner was required. Force required to effect gear changes was adjustable for different-strength riders (Bak, 1984).

All but the Moritsch drive shared an effectively noncircular chain ring resulting in a variation in ratio, or chordal action, as the chain ring rotated and the chain spanned the gap between sprocket segments. The maximum range of ratios in these variable-chainwheel-diameter drives was about 3:1. This is adequate for a utility rider, but not for a touring, or recumbent bicycle, for which riders generally want a 4:1 range. Thus, as designed these drives would need to be used with a supplemental rear-wheel derailleur.

Drive Elements

As mentioned previously, HPV drives are usually transmitted via roller chain or cable. Both are discussed along with differentials and universal joints in the following pages.

Roller Chain. Standard bicycle derailleur roller chain is 0.5 in. (12.7 mm) between link centers with a roller width of .093 in. (2.3 mm) (Campagnolo, 1960). Whitt and Wilson (1982) discussed use of chains of shorter pitch, 8 mm (0.32 in.) and 0.25 in. (6.4 mm), and Shimano (1978) marketed a chain of 10 mm (0.39 in.) pitch on single-speed track racing bicycles. Many readily available industrial chain sizes, both inch and metric, could be substituted for 0.5 in. pitch. Whitt and Wilson stated that 0.5 in. pitch is larger than needed from a strength standpoint. Miles Kingsbury (1989) used 8-mm industrial chain and found it no lighter than 0.5 in. pitch, but said that it made the chain rings and sprockets more compact on his Bean HPV. Several human-powered, propeller-driven aircraft and boats have successfully used 0.25-in.-pitch chain for weight and size advantages.

Roller-chain drive efficiencies run in the high 90% range according to Whitt and Wilson (1982). Sprockets for circular-drive machines in 0.5-in. pitch are available in a wide variety of materials and tooth quantities. Chain rings, available in steel and aluminum, run from 24 to 55 teeth. On speed-record machines chainwheels with 100 or more teeth are often used. Freewheel or rear-cluster sprockets are steel or, if you are very rich, titanium, and run from 38 down to 11 teeth.

Frank Berto (1982) found that 11-tooth cogs gave a 4.5% chordal action. The effective ratio is lowest when the roller is about to leave the sprocket and highest when the link plates are in line with the departing chain line. Chain manufacturers (Boston Gear, 1985; Browning, 1986) do not recommend sprockets smaller than 17 teeth, but make them down to 8 teeth! They also do not recommend ratios greater than 7:1.

Cable. Wire rope, or cable, is sometimes used for drives, usually in conjunction with untimed machines. Steve Ball used 0.06 in. (1.6 mm) diameter cable on Dragonfly and Price used 0.09 in. (2.4 mm) on P-4.

Cable is made up of wire strands, and a 7 x 19 cable is 7 strands of 19 wires per strand. Single strands should not be used in moving applications, such as HPV drives. Wilson (1989) quoted cable manufacturers' requirements that minimum pulley diameter should optimally be 72 times the cable diameter, and 40 is a minimum to avoid fatigue failure. Machinery's Handbook (Schubert, 1979) recommends 72 and 31, depending on construction. More wires in a cable makes the cable more flexible and a smaller pulley may be safely used. A wire rope company that specializes in small cables recommended 50 and 15, also dependent on cable construction (Sava Industries, 1989).

Sava Industries indicated that pulley diameters less than 16 rope diameters severely reduce cable life, that doubling pulley diameter can increase cable life up to 13 times, and that plastic coatings increase cable life by 3 to 10 times (1989). Cable construction is a high art; use of cable in HPV drives and to energize brakes requires careful design and large safety factors to ensure reliable operation.

Differentials. HPVs that are driven by more than one wheel usually need a differential to allow the outside wheel in a turn to roll faster or farther than the inside wheel, because the wheels roll about different radii. The drive load is shared equally between the wheels until one lifts off the ground or hits a slippery spot. Then power is transmitted to the unloaded wheel and the vehicle is not being driven. In automobiles this problem has been solved by differentials that lock up or reduce slippage after a certain speed difference between the axles is reached (Baumeister, 1967). The low power levels of HPVs make limited-slip differentials unnecessary.

Differentials are available for adult tricycles, but because HPVs have a coasting mechanism (that is, the wheels do not need to "back-drive" the drive mechanism as they do on a car), two freewheels (the driver halves tied together) and each driven half connected to each axle could give the same results as a locking differential as well as providing the coasting mechanism. In a turn the inside wheel would be driven, and the outer, faster, wheel would overspeed. If the inside wheel lifted off the ground the drive would increase speed until it coupled with the outer-wheel freewheel, then the drive would continue.

Universal Joints.   In an HPV with suspension on the driven wheel(s) the drive may utilize U-joints, or universal joints, to transmit power while the wheel is moving relative to the chassis. Most U-joints are of the Hooke design, which uses two yokes displaced 90° and a connecting crosspiece to allow variable angular locations between the two shafts. A single Hooke joint has a cyclic speed change between the input shaft and the output shaft because of the velocities of the joint parts, which can lead to annoying vibration in turns (Schubert, 1979). To avoid this problem U-joints should always be used in pairs, the angles at both joints should be the same, and the axes of the crosses should be parallel.

Summing Up HPV Driving Mechanisms

Although many inventors and manufacturers have seen advantages in alternatives to the conventional multispeed hub and derailleur gears, few alternatives have reached commercial production and none have been commercially successful.

Part 4 Nonconstant Pedaling

Much work has been done to improve the efficiency of traditional-bicycle circular drives by modifying the pedal velocity as the crank revolves, assuming a steady vehicle speed. This is an effort to maximize the efficient use of the rider's leg muscles as the pedals are moved.

Noncircular Chainwheels

These simple devices have been around since the beginning of bicycling. Archibald Sharp (1977) described elliptical chainwheels as having been in use in the 1880s. Whitt and Wilson (1982) stated that sprockets of high ovality, over 1.3:1 ratio, were used in racing in the 1890s, but fell out of favor. DeLong (1975) used a 1.08:1-ratio Thetic chainwheel, which was popular briefly in the 1930s, with excellent results.

A noncircular chainwheel is a sprocket having teeth the standard 0.5 in. (12.7 mm) distance apart to accept a standard chain, but instead of all the teeth being equidistant from the crank spindle, the tooth pattern moves closer and farther from the spindle around the periphery of the chainwheel. Thus there is a variation in pitch diameter or drive ratio as the pedals are turned. *Pitch diameter* is the distance across the sprocket, chainwheel, or chain ring, measured from the middle of the chain rollers. There are three types of noncircular chain rings: elliptical, skewed elliptical, and oval, as shown in Figure 13.10.

As the chainwheel is turned the drive ratio is dependent on the distance from the spindle to where the drive chain runs onto the sprocket. In a single revolution of the crank the chain encounters two maximum ratios and two minimums, one for the power stroke of each leg. If the vehicle's speed is constant the rider's feet will move fastest at the minimum pitch diameters, where the teeth are closest to the spindle.

Elliptical Chainwheels.   This chainwheel describes a true ellipse, in that the minimum pitch diameter is 90° from the maximum pitch diameter, and the transition from minimum to maximum is mathematically smooth.

Skewed Chainwheels.   If the minimum and maximum pitch diameter on a chain ring are not 90° apart, the sprocket is a skewed ellipse. On a skewed ellipse the transitions from minimums to maximums are still very smooth. Skewed chain rings can be mounted on the crank arm in two ways, making the transition from large to small either quickly or slowly, giving different foot-velocity patterns.

Oval Chainwheels.   With an oval chainwheel the sprocket teeth vary in distance from the spindle, as

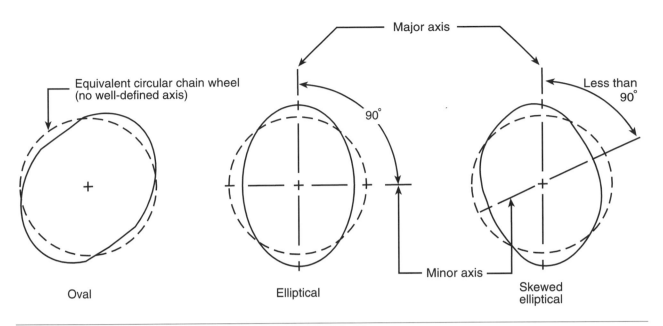

FIGURE 13.10 Noncircular chainwheels.

on elliptical chainwheels, but not as smoothly and to no rigorous mathematical formula. The chainwheel is still symmetrical so that the ratios for both legs are the same. Ovals are sometimes called cam shaped (Dailey & Dailey, 1975). *Ovality* is the ratio of maximum pitch diameter (p.d.) to minimum p.d. An 8 in. maximum p.d. by 5 in. minimum p.d. would be an 8:5 ratio and may be expressed as 1:6:1, or just 1.6. Some people express ovality as a percentage, 62% in this example.

Axis-to-Crank Orientation. On noncircular chainwheels the maximum chain-ring pitch diameter location relative to the crank arm determines the speed characteristics of the leg. As mentioned in the discussion of skewed chainwheels, the relative orientation of the minimum and maximum pitch diameters is also an important determinant of leg velocity.

On most bikes the upper, power side of the drive chain is nearly horizontal to the ground, which places the maximum gear point with the pedal horizontal if the long axis is perpendicular to the crank arm. A bike's seat tube roughly corresponds to the rider's lower body axis, modified somewhat by the seat location atop the tube. Assuming a 72° seat-tube angle from horizontal, this makes the high gear at 108° to the seat tube. As shown in Figure 13.11, the 108° maximum gear point is beyond the mid-point of the leg stroke and may not be optimum.

Many studies have been done on the merits of various ovalities, skew angles, and axis orientations.

Those discussed in the list that follows were done on flywheel ergometers, except the Biopace (Okajima, 1983), which was done with bicycles on a treadmill or rollers. The studies compared like numbers of teeth on the circular and noncircular sprockets; there was no compensation for higher peak ratios. Here is a short summary of the history and theory behind noncircular design.

- **Sharp:** Sharp's description dates from 1896, before the invention of multiple-speed derailleur gears, so the elliptical chain rings were used with single-speed bikes. Chain-length requirements varied only slightly, and so were not a problem. Though not stated, the ovality shown in Sketch 428 in his book is 1.6:1, and the major axis was perpendicular to the cranks (Sharp, 1977).

- **Harrison:** John Harrison's studies (1970) compared elliptical 1.5 ovality chainwheels with circular. He found that all subjects preferred the ellipse for heavy loads and low speed, because under those conditions it enabled a more steady speed to be maintained. Harrison aligned the major axis perpendicular to the crank. He showed virtually identical outputs for both chainwheel types.

- **Durham:** Roger Durham marketed an elliptical ring 1.6 ovality (Dailey & Dailey, 1975) and reported favorable comment from users (Price, 1980). Durham followed Sharp and Harrison

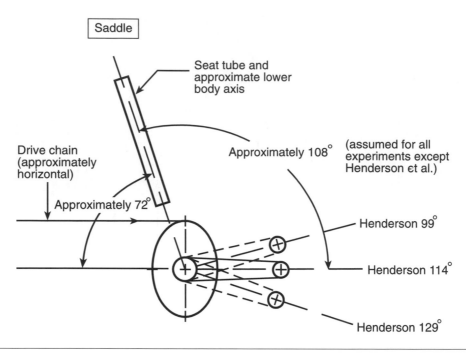

FIGURE 13.11　Crank, chain ring, and body orientation.

by setting the crank arm perpendicular to the long axis of the ellipse, making the highest gear slightly after the midpoint of the leg stroke. The Daileys did comparative testing of this unit.

- **Henderson:** Scott Henderson, Raymond Ellis, Geraldine Klimovitch, and George Brooks (1977) used an elliptical wheel with eccentricity of .714, assumed to mean 1.4 ovality. They used three orientations of the sprocket to the seat tube: 99°, 114°, and 129°, as shown in Figure 13.15. Their results showed the crank at 114° to be most efficient, followed by 129°, then circular, and worst, 99°. The previous experiments had the maximum gear at about 108°. Their data indicated the best position showed a 2.4% reduction of caloric cost over circular pedaling, a differential that could be significant in a long race.

- **Dailey:** Patrick and Gary Dailey (1975) performed short-duration tests on circular, Durham 1.6, 1.2, and 1.1 ellipses, and 1.2 and 1.1 skewed elliptical chainwheels. The skew angles were between 60° and 85°, but not specified, and the skewed sprockets made the transition from the low ratio to the high ratio more quickly than high to low. They noted pedaling seemed smoother on the skewed chain rings but gave no further results. They tried various axis-to-crank angles, but did not indicate the most favorable. The Daileys found that, overall, the circular chainwheel did best, followed closely by the 1.1, then the 1.2, ellipses. All outputs were within 5% of each other. They found the Durham 1.6 ellipse was 11% less efficient than the average of the other sprockets.

- **Thetic:** DeLong (1975) used a Thetic 1.08:1 chain ring successfully in racing and touring. He felt it was definitely advantageous, but took no data. He mentioned a New Zealand study showing the same results, and he wished for 1.08 to 1.1 ovality availability as double or triple chain ring sets.

- **Biopace:** DeLong's wish was answered in 1983 when Shimano introduced the Biopace oval chain ring set with 48, 38, and 28 teeth and ovalities of 1.07, 1.12, and 1.17, respectively (Shimano Industrial Company, 1983). The designs were tailored so that the three chain rings had slightly different ovalities, skew angles, and axis-to-crank orientations, as shown in Figure 13.15. These rings were mounted to the standard 5-arm crank spider so that the maximum gear was approximately in line with the crank arms, 90° out-of-phase to the others. The designs were rigorously studied and tested, and they proved to be successful in the marketplace on many all-terrain bikes for several years.

I used a set of Biopace chain rings for about a year (1991), then rotated them 72° to obtain the high point near the mid-power stroke, as the previous experimenters had done. Even with the low 1.12 ovality of the center ring used predominantly, the low-gear in mid-power stroke condition caused an instantaneous uncoupling of the drive, in the middle of the power stroke. In the high-gear in mid-power stroke condition, the increase in knee joint strain was evident in the middle of the power stroke, but the rapid traverse of top and bottom center was welcome.

Noncircular Chainwheel Comparisons

Ovalities greater than 1.2 appear to reduce cyclist power output. On the Biopace system, the major axes are nearly in line with the crank arm, increasing time at the dead centers, in opposition to the popular wisdom. Shimano's literature indicated that this was to lighten the burden on the muscles during the power stroke. In addition, the transition from low to high was done slowly, opposite to the Daileys' tests. In all cases the efficiency or power increase was small, under 5%, but Shimano has published no comparative data. A power increase,

even a small one, could give a commanding advantage in a close race.

Advance-Retard Mechanisms

The same or similar variations of pedaling speed around a circular path as obtained with oval chainwheels can be achieved using mechanisms such as the Selectocam, the Hollandaise, the Mairag, and the Biocam, all of which are reviewed below.

Selectocam (Powercam). The Selectocam (Schubert, 1980) drive was invented by Lawrence Brown, who had earlier designed the Biocam drive (Whitt & Wilson, 1982), which is reviewed later in this chapter. The Selectocam was later marketed under the name Powercam (Weaver, 1984). This drive utilized an advance-retard mechanism configured as shown in Figure 13.12. A stationary cam was mounted to the bicycle's bottom bracket and a roller connected to a small arm moved onto the cam lobe and retarded the crank relative to the sprocket as the crank reached the top or bottom of the stroke. Given constant bicycle speed, the gear was thus reduced through most of the power stroke, from 25° to 160° after top center (Bicycle Business Journal, 1983). The

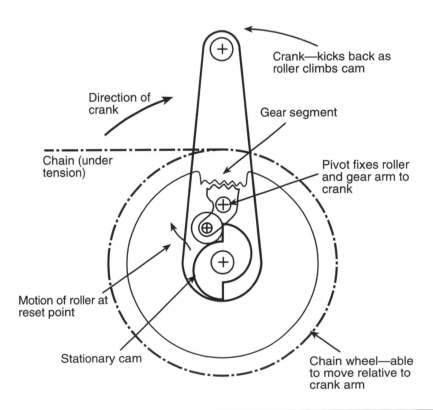

FIGURE 13.12 Selectocam (Powercam) mechanism.

relative ratios are shown in Figure 13.13. This drive was unique in that it could be switched off.

Brown said that Selectocam was good for cruising, but not very good for sprinting (Schubert, 1980). This was confirmed by user Jim Delaney (Price, 1984), who said in an interview that spinning made the unit rattle, evidence that the cam follower was floating off the cam. Brown also advocated gear ratios 30% to 50% higher than standard, coupled with a lower cadence of 50 to 80 RPM versus racers' common 100 to 115 RPM. The lowered effective ratio would account for 15% of the overall ratio increase. Delaney found an increase in speed of up to 10%, and Brown claimed an increase in efficiency of 25% when cruising (Schubert).

Hollandaise. This Dutch design from an unknown inventor (Hugaud, 1983) used a mechanism within the chainwheel to vary the timing of the crank arms relative to the chainwheel and to each other. The pedals moved slower on the descent and faster on the return, effectively raising the gear ratio. The crank arms were timed to vary by a maximum of about 15° in each direction from the

standard 180°, with the maximums occurring at the ends of the stroke.

Mairag. This variable-length crank unit (DeLong, 1978) was mentioned in the section on elliptical pedaling and is shown in Figure 13.3. Pedaling is circular, but the center is moved forward and upward by 15 mm in each direction. Thus, the effective crank length is 190 mm at 45° after top center, 176 mm at 135° and 305°, and 160 mm at 225° on the low-power return stroke. The increased length on the power (down) stroke increases the lever arm nearly 10%, allowing riders to turn higher gear ratios without injury. Seat and handlebar locations were altered.

Biocam. Brown invented the Biocam drive before the Selectocam (Powercam) . As shown in Figure 13.14, the chainwheel was replaced with a slotted cam (Facet Enterprises, c. 1979) which was duplicated on the opposite crank. Arms were located behind the crank spindle, with a pivot slightly above and behind the spindle. A roller ran in the cam slot, which varied the distance from the spindle. The

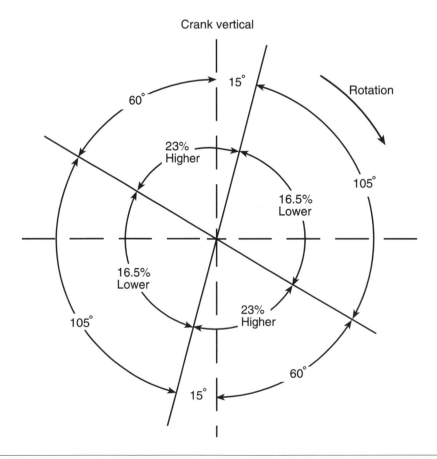

FIGURE 13.13 Selectocam (Powercam) data.

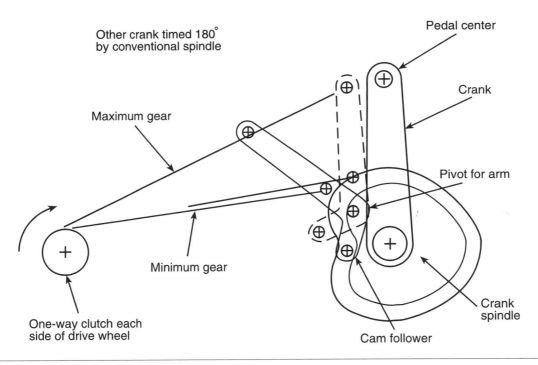

FIGURE 13.14   Biocam crank mechanism.

other end of the arm mounted a drive chain at variable radii from the pivot. The chains ran over freewheels on both sides of the rear hub. The drive was used to set 1977 time-trial records for 10, 60, 90, and 150 miles. Wormley (1978) indicated that the effective ratio was greatest when the larger leg muscles were applying force.

The Biocam pedals were timed 180°. Lifting on the return stroke inputted efficiently into the drive on the opposite side and the arms returned without spring loading. However, the chains required tensioning springs. All the drives reviewed here met the criteria for efficient drives, including the cam-and-lever drive.

Comparison of Pedaling Speeds

Many experimenters have used elliptical and oval chainwheel shapes to vary the pedal speed as the cranks are turned through a circular path. Conventional circular pedaling is mechanically simple, efficient forced motion. Modifying pedal velocity as the pedal orbits the spindle offers promise of improved efficiency, but evidence is inconclusive. The Mairag variable-length crank and the Biocam suffered from complexity and their benefits could be realized using noncircular chainwheels. The Powercam was simple and light, but had a limited rotational-speed (RPM) range.

Noncircular chain rings with ovality under 1.2 can utilize standard front derailleurs and require no further changes to the bicycle. Axis-crank orientation is an area of much controversy. The positions of maximum and minimum pitch diameters for each drive are charted in Figure 13.15. Sharp, Harrison, Durham, Harrington, and Dailey favored the high gear in mid-power stroke, whereas Shimano, Mairag, and Brown favored low gear in mid-power stroke.

Figure 13.15 charts the relative locations of the maximum and minimum ratios of the drives discussed relative to the top center of the crank. The maximum and minimum gear location in the rider's foot stroke must be corrected for any deviation of the taut (drive side) of the chain from horizontal where the chain is tangent to the chainwheel, the location of the rider's leg axis due to differing seat-tube angles, and the seat location relative to the seat tube. Figure 13.16 charts relative pedal velocities for each of the drives.

Summing Up Nonconstant Pedaling

Records have been set with mechanisms using nonconstant pedaling. Research results are not unanimous on such factors as the optimum angle of the major axis of elliptical chainwheels with the cranks or even on the benefit of nonconstant over constant

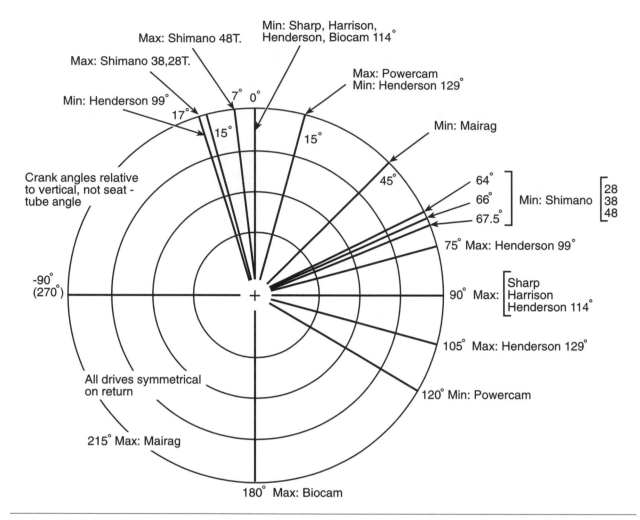

FIGURE 13.15   Crank angles compared.

pedaling. Few bicycle racers use even the simplest of these systems, even though the predominance of research findings show 2% to 5% improvement in either power output or metabolic energy-production efficiency. This range in improvement would give competitors a significant advantage.

Part 5 Conclusion

Reducing the time the leg spends at the low-power points at the top and bottom of the crank revolution indicates that the lowest gears should be there. The highest gears for extended high power input would appear to be best handled by the leg near the 70° point, from top center, or approximately 90° from the seat tube. This is the output Harrison (1963) was working toward when he modified the sinusoidal simple-harmonic-motion curve, filling it out into a square wave.

However, the leg could be injured from pushing too hard or could expend too much energy at the stroke midpoint if the high ratio is there. It may be more beneficial to extend the low-power point, that is to make the high gear at the top and bottom of the stroke to allow a longer rest time for the leg muscles, as Shimano did (Okajima, 1983). Though the peak power output is lower, the endurance may be increased greatly.

Comparing Efficiencies

Efficiency may be defined in several ways, such as the distance an HPV will travel given a fixed rider output and a fixed vehicle speed, or the speed an HPV can be made to go given a fixed rider output over a fixed distance. Two vehicles may be compared using the same or equivalent rider outputs and the same course or the speed and then recording

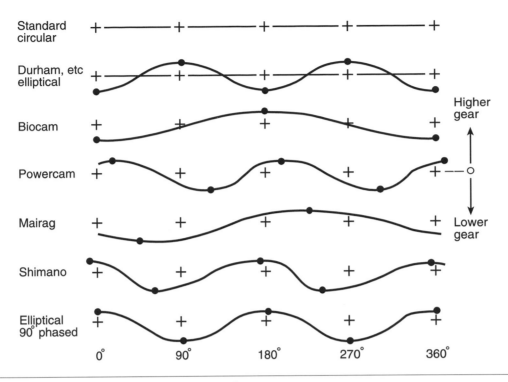

FIGURE 13.16 Circular pedaling speeds compared.

which machine is faster or goes farther. However, many of the variables that are to be fixed for testing purposes, such as rider output, wind speed, and traffic, may not cooperate to allow accurate determination of the better machine, so to a certain extent feelings can modify the results.

Table 13.1 compares the various efficiencies of the positions, motions, and drives reviewed in this chapter. The table lists the important areas of efficiency gain and loss that were reviewed and are quantifiable.

Maximizing Efficiency

The overall efficiency of a human-powered vehicle is dependent on many factors. The rider must be able to maximize output comfortably, the pedaling movements must be mechanically efficient, and the drive must minimize power losses.

In Table 13.1 standard bicycle designs were assigned a rating of 100%, because that is the norm against which all improvements must be judged. The standard bicycle is highly efficient, being the beneficiary of more than a hundred years of detailed refinement, and other drive trains must show improvement over this standard, much as the Wankel automobile engine had to overcome nearly 100 years of detailed development of the piston engine.

The analysis reported here began as a search for undiscovered mechanisms that might make efficient HPV drives. Figure 13.17 shows the combinations reviewed and several possibilities not found. Those no-example combinations may not be worth inventing around—or one may be the way to a major efficiency increase.

Of the methods reviewed, noncircular chainwheels appear to be the most promising way to more efficiently convert muscle power to machine motion. It appears the most efficient motion can be trained into the body without losses, given sufficient training time and a positive attitude on the part of the rider. Comparison testing to determine which drives improve output should use cycles, not ergometers, preferably on indoor tracks to eliminate random wind effects. Test subjects should be worked at sustainable outputs rather than to exhaustion.

Ultimately, any practical HPV drive revolves a shaft to propel the machine, requiring rotary motion. Other motion eventually must be converted into rotary motion in the end. Given the low sustainable power output of the human engine, the most practical drives will make that conversion early in the overall system or will begin with circular motion to eliminate conversion inefficiencies.

	Estimated efficiency %*	Source
Table 13.1 EFFICIENCY COMPARISON		
Rider positions:		
Upright and racing crouch	100	Standard*
Supine recumbent	97 to 100	Kyle, others
Prone recumbent	92	Kyle
Pedaling movements:		
Circular pedaling, circular chainwheel	100	Standard*
Combined arm and leg pedaling	121	Kyle
Elliptical sprockets	89 to 105	Sharp, Harrison, Durham, Henderson, Dailey, Thetic, Biopace
Hub gears	80 to 96	Moulton
Rebound springs	104	Mastropaolo
Drive motions:		
Standard circular constant drive	100	Standard*
Forced, seat fixed, constant drive	110	Harrison
Free motion, intermittent, nonvariable pulley	50	Price
Free motion, intermittent, variable pulley	80	Ball

*Estimated efficiency is defined as maximum output relative to that obtained with legs-only cycling.

References

Abbott, A.V. (Ed.). (1982). *Proceedings of the First Human-Powered-Vehicle Symposium.* Indianapolis: International Human Powered Vehicle Association.

Alenax Corporation. (1983). Transbar power bicycles. Rochester, NY: Author.

Anson, M. (1973, October). Pedal up and down? The Harris vertical bicycle. *Bicycling,* pp. 39–40.

Bak, D.J. (1984, March). Expanding chain wheel forms bicycle drive. *Design News,* pp. 182–183.

Baumeister, T.C. (Ed.). (1967). *Standard handbook for mechanical engineers* (7th ed.). New York: McGraw-Hill.

Berto, F. (1982, March). The workshop: Today's freewheels. *Bicycling,* p. 126.

Boston Gear Works. (1985). Catalog 100. Quincy, MA: Author.

Browning Manufacturing Company. (1986). Catalog 100. Maysville, KY: Author.

Cable-driven commuter bike optimizes pedal power. (1982, May 6). *Machine Design,* p. 44.

Cambiogear: Innovative transmission. (1983, January). *Bicycle Journal,* p. 25.

Campagnolo, B.I. (c. 1960). Catalog No. 14. Vicenza, Italy: Author.

Dailey, P., & Dailey, G. (1975, December). Elliptical sprockets: Power plus or minus? *The 49er Engineer,* pp. 2, 4–5.

DeLong, F. (1975, October). Unconventional drives. *Bicycling,* pp. 10–11.

DeLong, F. (1978, March). The Mairag variable-geometry crank (FB system). *Bicycling,* pp. 74–75.

Durham Bicycles. (1981) Bullseye catalog. Burbank, CA: Author.

Facet Enterprises. (c. 1979). Biocam catalog. Tulsa, OK: Author.

Harrison, J.Y. (1963). The effect of various motion cycles on human power output. *Human Factors, 5,* 453–465.

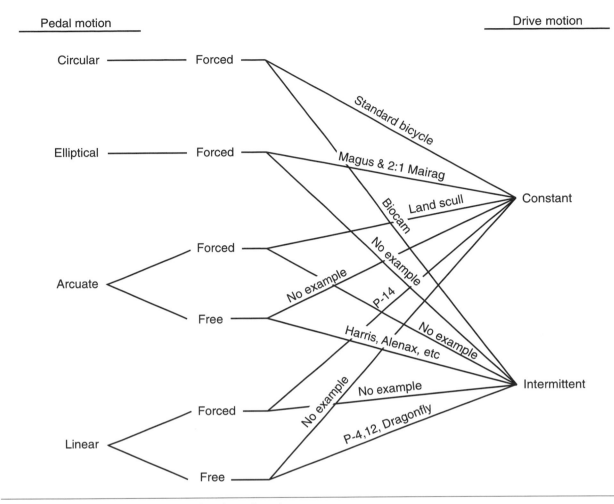

FIGURE 13.17 Drive types found and not found.

Harrison, J.Y. (1970). Maximizing human power output by suitable selection of motion cycle and load. *Human Factors, 3,* 315–329.

Henderson, S.C., Ellis, R.W., Klimovitch, G., & Brooks, G.A. (1977). The effects of circular and elliptical chainwheels on steady-rate cycle ergometer work efficiency. *Medicine and Science in Sports, 4,* 202–207.

Hogan, Brian J. (1986, November 17). Reciprocating pedal motion propels bicycle. *Design News,* pp. 126–127.

Hugaud, P.G. (1983, September). Recherche sur le pedalage [Research on pedaling]. *Le Cycle,* pp. 35, 37

Kingsbury, M. (1989, Summer) The baking of the Bean. *Human Power,* pp. 11–15.

Mechanics Corner. (1983, May). *Bicycle Business Journal,* pp. 26–27.

Okajima, S. (1983, August). Designing chainwheels to optimize the human engine. *Bike Tech,* pp. 1–7.

Peddling his wares. (1982, April 12). San Luis Obispo County Telegram-Tribune.

Price, R.L. (1980). [Interview with Mrs. Roger Durham].

Price, R.L. (1981). [P-4 design notes]. Unpublished raw data.

Price, R.L. (1982). [1982 IHPVA Speed Championships notes]. Unpublished raw data.

Price, R.L. (1983). [Interview with Steven Ball].

Price, R.L. (1984). [Interview with Dr. James Delaney].

Price, R.L. (1991). [Biopace user notes]. Unpublished raw data.

Revolutionary new transmission. (1972, August). *Bicycling,* pp. 78–79.

Sava Industries, Inc. (1989). Catalog 14A. Riverdale, NJ: Author.

Schubert, J. (1980, March). Beating Europe's best. *Bicycling,* pp. 38–39.

Schubert, P.B. (Ed.). (1979). Machinery's handbook (21st ed.). New York: Industrial Press.

Setright, L.J.K. (1968). *The Grand Prix car 1954–1966.* New York: Norton.

Sharp, A. (1977). *Bicycles & tricycles.* Cambridge, MA: MIT Press. (Original work published 1886)

Shimano Industrial Co., Ltd. (1978). Bicycle system components catalog. Osaka: Author.

Shimano Industrial Co., Ltd. (1983). Biopace service instructions. Osaka: Author.

Stengel, R.F. (1981, February). Mechanical transmission has infinitely variable ratio. *Design News,* pp. 177–178.

Van Cleave, D. (1974, May). New transmissions: More push-power for your bike. *Popular Science,* pp. 98–99.

Weaver, S. (1984, September–October). Powercam! *Bicycling,* pp. 38–40, 42, 44, 138–142.

Whitt, F.R., & Wilson, D.G. (1982). *Bicycling science* (2nd ed). Cambridge, MA: MIT Press.

Wormley, S. (1978, March). New time-trial records with IPD bicycles. *Bicycling,* p. 72.

Wilson, D.G. (1989, Summer). Editorial. *Human Power,* p. 2.

14

STEERING DESIGN

Rob Price

This chapter explains the basics of steering in human-powered vehicles. Many articles, the most famous being "The Stability of the Bicycle" (Jones, 1970), have presented the theory of bicycle steering in exhaustive detail, so I will simply illustrate some basic principles to allow HPV builders to design stable machines. After reviewing bicycle-steering geometry, I discuss steering with two wheels, using automotive steering as a model and comparing bicycle and automotive steering. Chapter 15 looks at HPV suspensions, again using motorcycles and cars as models.

Bicycle Steering

Figure 14.1 shows the bicycle steering geometry. *Head-tube angle* is the angle the steering tube makes, as measured from a horizontal axis. Typical values are 68° to 75°. *Fork rake,* or offset, is measured from the center line of the fork-tube bearings to the center of the wheel axle. Usual values are 30 mm to 60 mm (1.25 in. to 2.5 in.). *Trail* is the distance from the intersection of the fork-tube bearing center line and the ground to the point where the center of the tire patch touches the road. Common values for the trail are 12 mm to 50 mm (0.5 in. to 2 in.). These three factors are interdependent in the design of a stable bicycle.

Trail, where the tire patch tends to follow the point at which the steering axis intersects the road,

is the primary stabilizing element in well-designed bicycles. This is known as *caster* in the automotive industry, and it can be observed on grocery-store shopping carts. These have vertical steering axes on their castering wheels, which can often be seen oscillating as the cart is rolled down the aisle. The angled steering or fork axis on bicycles tends to dampen these oscillations.

Bicycles use fork rake to reduce the amount of trail. This increases the sensitivity of the steering. When the fork has too much rake for the head-tube angle, trail approaches zero and the machine becomes unstable. When the fork has too little rake or is installed backward (as was popular a few decades ago) there is plenty of trail, which leads to an increase in steering effort.

Shallower (lower numerical) head-tube angles generally give more directional stability. However, coupling very shallow angles with large fork offsets to reduce trail, as is done on some recumbent machines, may lead to oversteer, where the steered wheel tends to continue steering farther into the turn.

Automotive Steering

With the basic principles of bicycle steering as a backdrop, we can look at how automobile designers solved the problems of two-wheel-steering geometry. Figure 14.2 illustrates *camber,* the angular

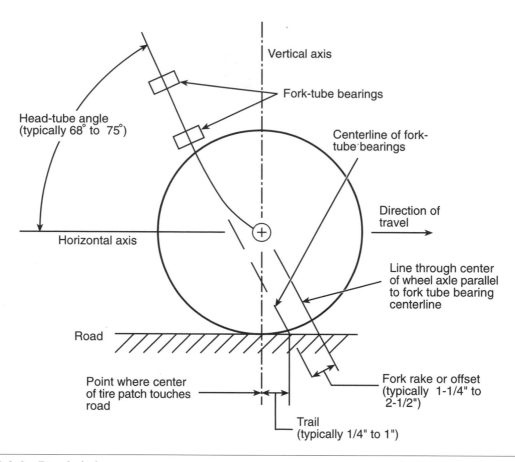

FIGURE 14.1 Bicycle fork geometry.

offset of the wheel disk from the vertical axis. Positive camber splays the wheels out at the top. Wheels on horse-drawn wagons had positive camber because of the built-up construction of their conical wooden-spoked wheels. The outside wheel in a turn carries greater load, so the sideward force tended to push the spokes into their sockets in the hub and rim, keeping the wheel together. Cars continued using positive camber long past the wooden-spoke days until increased tire widths forced the wheels to be more nearly perpendicular to the road. HPVs that are cornered hard can benefit from negative camber, where the tires are farther apart at the bottom for better wheel loading, as is discussed in the next chapter on suspension. However, an orientation perpendicular to the road, zero camber, minimizes both tire wear and rolling friction.

Steering-axis inclination is illustrated in Figure 14.3, which also shows how the intersection of the kingpin, or steering axis, and the ground relative to the center of the tire patch can result in positive or negative offset. Positive offset is most common on cars. This gives the driver an expected reaction, al-

though small, at the steering wheel when a tire encounters resistance.

If the offset used with the narrow tires typical of HPVs is large, it can lead to "bump steer," where the steering handle is constantly kicked about when riding on rough roads. Both positive and negative offset will result in bump steer, but the direction of the turn induced by the bump hitting one wheel can be partially offset by the tendency of negative offset to steer the wheel in the opposite direction. Steering offset is best kept close to zero, with the axis intersection inside the tire-patch area. On HPVs that is within 6 mm (0.25 in.) of the wheel center line on narrow-tired machines.

Caster angle is illustrated in Figure 14.4. Positive caster causes the center line of the steering axis to intersect the road ahead of the center of the wheel, analogous to trail on a bicycle. As on a bicycle, positive caster helps the vehicle to track, or tend to travel straight.

Figure 14.5 shows *toe-in*, where the front of the wheels are slightly closer together than the rear of the wheels. This is from 0 to 3 mm (0.125 in.) on cars, less than 1°. A slight amount of toe-in helps a

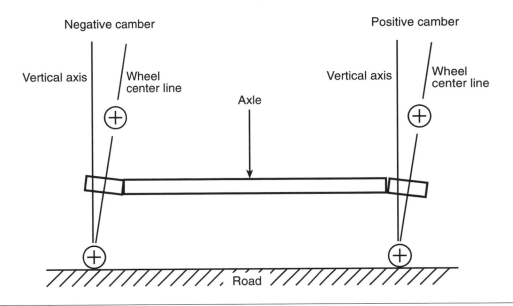

FIGURE 14.2 Wheel camber.

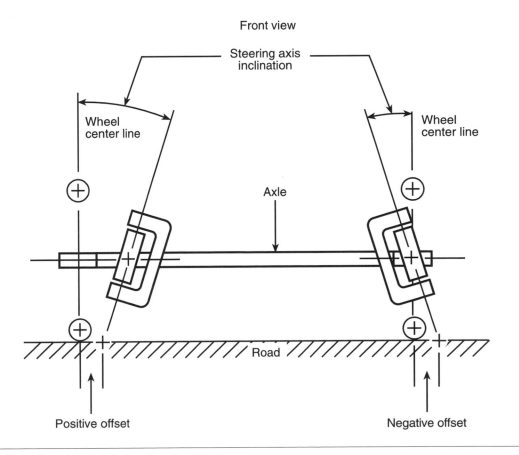

FIGURE 14.3 Steering-axis inclination.

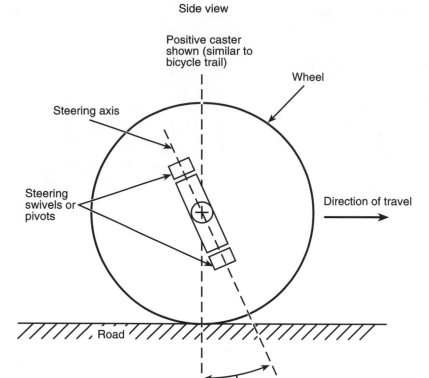

FIGURE 14.4   Caster angle.

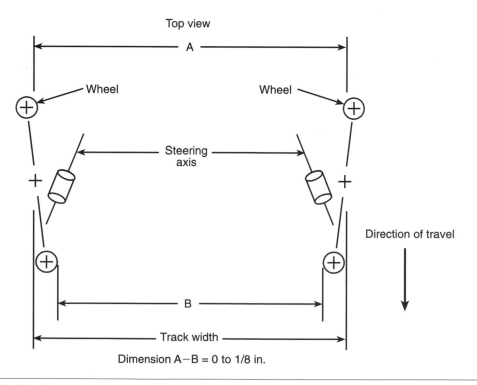

FIGURE 14.5   Toe-in.

machine track straight, but too much causes tires to scrub sideways, increasing tire wear and reducing coasting distances. A car with *toe-out* tends to swoop, or oversteer, into a turn, which can be unnerving. Also shown in Figure 14.5 is *track width*, the distance between the centers of the tire patches.

Steering Linkages

Figures 14.6 and 14.7 show the two most common linkages used to steer automobiles, rack-and-pinion steering and recirculating-ball, or worm-type, steering. The fine points of the design of these linkages are complex, but one major feature common to both

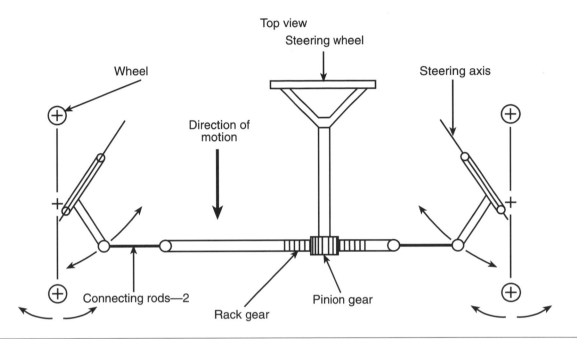

FIGURE 14.6 Rack-and-pinion steering.

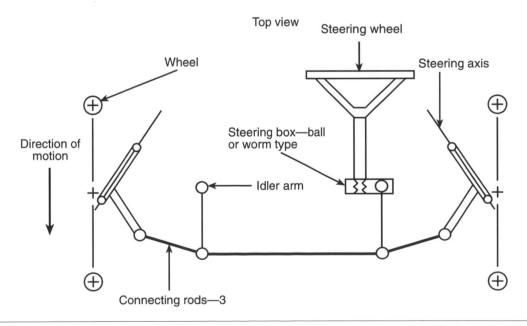

FIGURE 14.7 Worm-and-roller steering.

is important. This is Ackerman compensation, which causes the wheel on the inside of the turn to steer through a greater angle than the wheel on the outside of the turn, resulting in a toe-out condition. This is described in Baumeister (1967). Ackerman geometry causes the wheel axles to point to a common pivot point, as shown in Figure 14.8, and is accomplished by angling the steering arms inward from the fore-aft plane of the steering axis. This also

illustrates why two driven wheels on a common axle need a differential unit, discussed in chapter 13, to compensate for the different radii along which the wheels travel.

In the real world of freeway travel at 30 m/s (65 mph), cars round turns pivoting about a point extended inward from between the center of gravity and the rear axle. The tires all slip at different angles to the pivot point, as in Figure 14.9, eliminating the

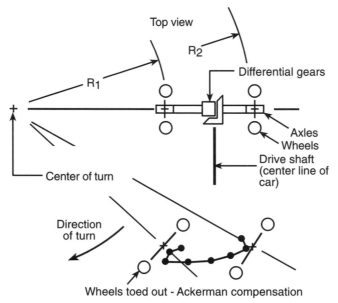

R_1 = Turning radius of wheel on the inside of the turn
R_2 = Turning radius of wheel on the outside of the turn

FIGURE 14.8 Ackerman compensation.

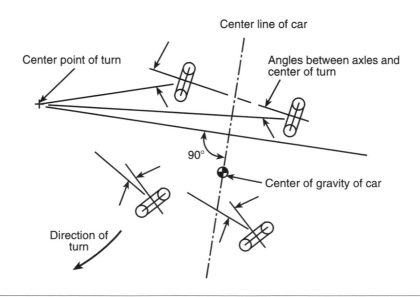

FIGURE 14.9 Tire slippage in turns.

importance of Ackerman compensation, as noted by Setright (1968). HPVs with small tire-contact patches and high cornering loads are similar to high-performance cars, so geometries that keep the steering wheels parallel are best for simplicity of design, efficiency in cornering from reduced tire scrub, and minimizing steering effort.

Just where the car pivot point will be at any instant is dependent primarily on sideward tire loading, which is a function of vehicle speed and the radius of the turn. Above speeds of about 10 m/s (20 mph) the steering pivot point moves forward from between the center of gravity and the rear-axle center line, as shown in Figure 14.9. Generally, when the pivot point moves forward of the front axle the driver has established what is known in automobile racing as a *four-wheel drift*, or just *drift*. It requires careful power regulation and skillful minute steering inputs to maintain this condition through a turn. It takes considerably more power than can be generated by a human to maintain a drift, unless on ice or loose dirt, so this does not need to be designed for in HPVs.

Rear-Wheel Steering

The last topic to be discussed here has to do with which end of the machine to steer. HPVs have been built with front or rear steering. As shown in Figure 14.10 for the conventional case, the front wheel is steered in the desired direction and the rear wheel tracks slightly inside the front. This illustrates the slow-speed case for the bicycle. The rear wheel tracks with or outside the front wheel during hard cornering, but if the steering pivot point moves forward of the front-wheel center line, establishing the machine in a drift as described previously for cars, chances are great that the bicycle is about to crash! Figure 14.11 illustrates the rear-steer-bicycle case where the rear wheel is initially steered to aim the front, then partially unsteered to maintain the turn. Like tail-wheel aircraft, there is a tendency for rear-steering machines to do a ground loop—that is, the rear end tends to swing outward due to centrifugal force. This is the probable reason that all modern aircraft have tricycle landing gear despite its higher weight and stowage complexity. Successful rear steerers have conventional fork angle, rake, and caster dimensions, but navigating them precisely is an acquired skill.

The forces required to steer an HPV are dependent on the angle through which the wheels turn, the angle through which the steering bar moves, the steering mechanism bearing types, and the motion of the hand on the steering lever. One of my designs combined a large wheel-steer angle and short hand levers that required wrist-twisting motion, a movement where humans can exert little force, to steer the vehicle. Another design used a tiller between the legs that interfered with pedaling at extreme steering angles. With careful

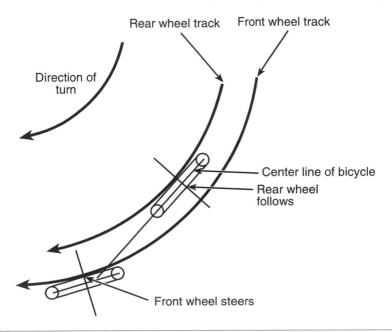

FIGURE 14.10 Front-wheel steering.

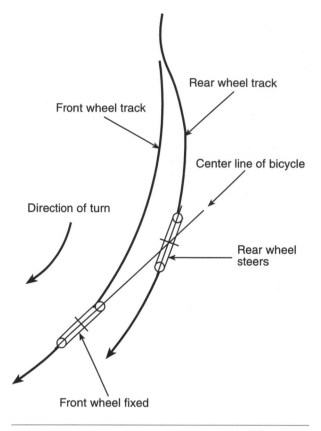

FIGURE 14.11   Rear-wheel steering.

attention to detail, an HPV can be designed to utilize the concepts presented here, which will result in a more precise steering and a more comfortable machine. These principles have been used successfully on cycles and automobiles for more than a hundred years.

Conclusion

Good steering behavior of single-track vehicles is given principally by appropriate choices of the head-tube angle and the trail. Front-steered four-wheel vehicles require choices of many more steering design angles and relative distances.

References

Baumeister, T.C. (Ed.) (1967). *Standard handbook for mechanical engineers* (7th ed.). New York: McGraw-Hill.

Jones, D.E.H. (1970, April). The stability of the bicycle. *Physics Today*, pp. 34–40.

Setright, L.J.K. (1968). *The Grand Prix car 1954–1966.* New York: Norton.

15

SUSPENSION DESIGN

Rob Price

This chapter gives guidance on the choice of the overall configuration of suspensions and of the components of suspension systems. Some bicycles have featured suspensions over the years, but cushioning over the worst bumps can be obtained, on conventional bikes, by rising off the saddle and using the legs to absorb shocks. Bicycle suspensions, when used, also add weight and absorb that precious commodity, power. However, a well-designed suspension system may absorb less power on a rough road surface than would a bicycle or HPV without a suspension. HPV designs often do not allow the rider to use the raised-body technique of damping and can benefit from the addition of suspensions because of reduced rolling resistance in certain circumstances, better road holding, reduced structural loads, and greater comfort.

Springs support the weight of a vehicle, but once set in motion, a spring mass can oscillate for many cycles before the motion ceases. Springs are constantly excited when the vehicle is moving, so shock absorbers or dampers are associated with each suspension member to eliminate the oscillations within a few cycles.

Pneumatic tires are the first part of any suspension. Even the very narrow and very-high-pressure tires common today on road and racing bikes provide some attenuation of road irregularities. Springs and dampers are the next parts of suspensions that this chapter examines.

Springs and Dampers

Springs come in many varieties, but today shock absorbers, or dampers, are telescopic hydraulic cylinders, although friction dampers have been used in the past. Figure 15.1 shows the three varieties of shock absorbers. The friction damper uses a spring clamping against a friction-material disk which is attached to the chassis. The actuating arm is connected via linkage to the suspension, or it may be one of the links in the suspension. Hydraulic dampers are closed, two-chamber systems usually filled with a noncompressible liquid with valves that meter the rate at which fluid moves from one chamber to the other. Sometimes a gas (air or nitrogen) augments or replaces the liquid. The piston is connected to the suspension via a rod on the telescopic type or an arm on the lever type. As in the friction damper, this may be a link of the suspension. The valves may be adjustable to vary the *ride*, or amount of dissipation available as the piston moves.

Figure 15.2 shows several varieties of springs. Torsion bars, which twist to provide spring force are similar to coil springs, which can be considered cylindrically wound torsion bars. Elastomer or rubber springs have the advantage of being small and lightweight, so are well suited for use on HPVs and are used on some Moulton bicycles.

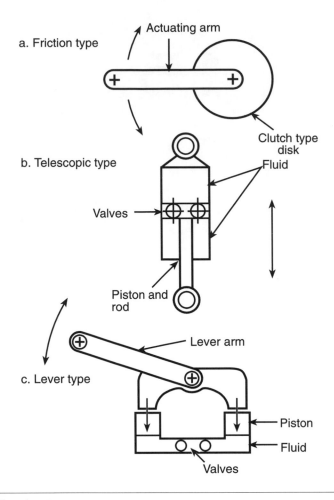

FIGURE 15.1　Shock absorber types.

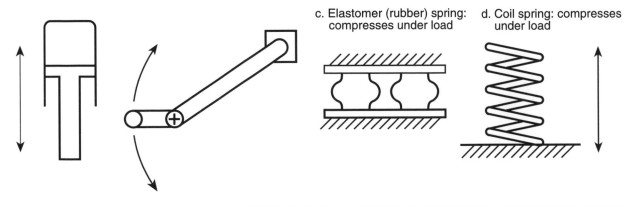

FIGURE 15.2　Spring types.

Pneumatic springs are another possibility; air or nitrogen acts as the suspending medium. An advantage here is that the spring may be combined with the damper, as is done on some cars that add air to shock absorbers to control ride height.

Leaf springs (see Figure 15.3) may be built up of several leaves or may be made of a single leaf. The usual material is steel, but in recent years fiber-reinforced composites have been used in automotive applications. Multiple leaves provide some internal friction damping. Semielliptical springs were universal on cars for decades, but require a shackle to compensate for the variable length under deflection. Quarter ellipticals have the advantage of requiring neither a shackle nor a chassis mount aft of the axle.

Semielliptical and quarter-elliptical springs mounted to live, or beam, axles are excellent at locating the vehicle wheels, as shown in Figure 15.4. A disadvantage of elliptical leaf springs is that they require additional struts to locate the wheels relative to the chassis. Coil springs in connection with a beam axle need location arms for fore-and-aft location and a transverse, or Panhard, rod for lateral location. These are shown in Figure 15.5.

Motorcycle Suspensions

Currently variations of motorcycle suspensions are used as off-road bicycle suspensions. Motorcycles use coil springs as a suspension medium because they can allow long suspension strokes and they fit well within the mechanical parts of the motorcycle. Bicycles favor elastomers because they are lighter and more compact than metal springs. A motorcycle's front suspension is set up much like a bicycle's, but the fork is compressible, wrapped with coil springs and with internal telescopic shock absorbers. Figure 15.6 shows that trail increases slightly under bump and braking.

A short swing arm, Figure 15.7, known as a *leading link,* can also be used on front suspensions, and in this case trail will vary under bump as the fork rake varies.

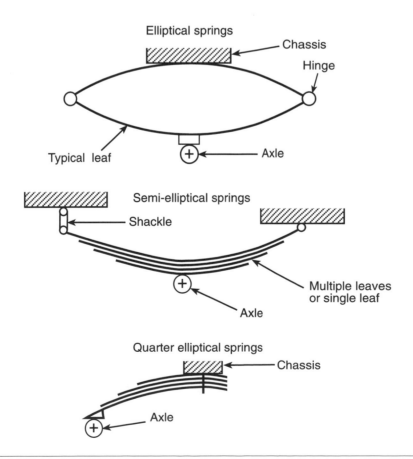

FIGURE 15.3 Leaf-type springs.

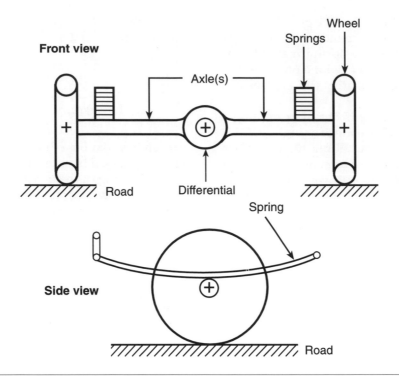

FIGURE 15.4 Beam axle leaf spring suspension.

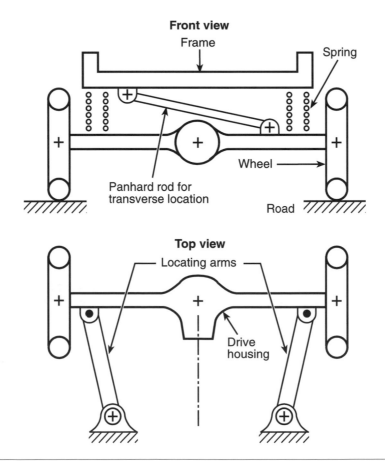

FIGURE 15.5 Beam axle coil spring suspension.

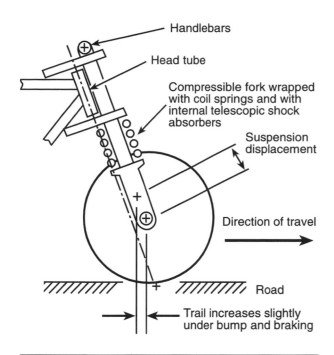

FIGURE 15.6 Piston-type front suspension.

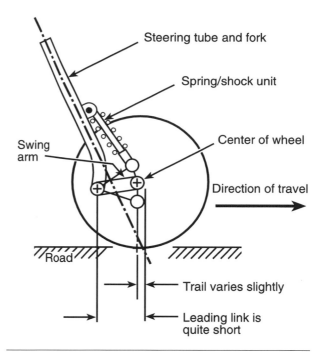

FIGURE 15.7 Leading-link front suspension.

Figure 15.8 shows a rear swing-arm suspension. Location of the arm pivot point below the drive-side chain line results in some suspension compression under power. A pivot above the chain line results in some unloading of the suspension, which, though slight, can partially compensate for the compressive effects of a strong pedaling down stroke on an HPV. It is difficult to achieve the neutral condition, where the chain line passes through the suspension pivot, on a derailleur-gear bike, because the chain location varies with sprocket combinations.

Automobile Suspensions

Many cars have independent suspensions and, unlike with beam axles, each wheel can move independently of the others. A few variants are illustrated in Baumeister (1967). A common front suspension of this type uses two A-shaped arms at each wheel to locate the upper and lower pivots on the steering axis, as shown in Figure 15.9.

An inexpensive variant of the A-arm suspension is the MacPherson strut (see Figure 15.10), which utilizes the lower A-arm but substitutes the telescoping strut of the shock absorber for the upper arm. This strut, surrounded by a coil spring, twists to allow for steering.

The swing-arm suspension is simple and effective (see Figure 15.11). It is primarily used on rear suspensions of the older Volkswagen automobiles. A universal joint on the drive shaft near the differential is the pivot point for the axle and attached rear wheel. As the suspension travels through its full stroke, the wheel camber changes considerably. Universal joints are discussed in chapter 13.

Cars tend to roll axially about the center of gravity in a turn, making them lean outward at the top. A machine that rolls excessively is uncomfortable to ride in, and large resultant camber changes reduce cornering ability. Excessive roll is compensated for by linking the two sides of the vehicle with an antiroll, or sway, bar, shown in Figure 15.12. The bar is fastened to the sides of the chassis and at the outboard ends to the suspensions, so that when the suspension compresses on the side of the car in the outside of a turn, it lifts the inside wheel, causing the car to corner with less axial roll. Of course, an independent suspension so equipped is no longer completely independent. Antiroll bars are common on front suspensions, and they are being used more on the rear as independent rear suspensions become more popular. An exhaustive discussion of suspensions and their characteristics is found in Setright (1968).

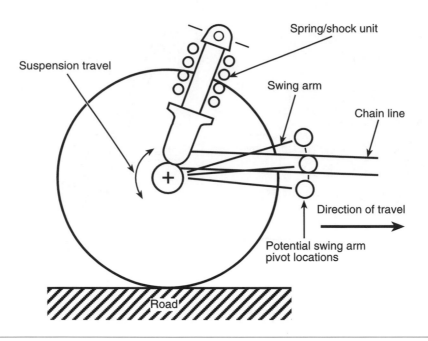

FIGURE 15.8 Rear swing-arm suspension.

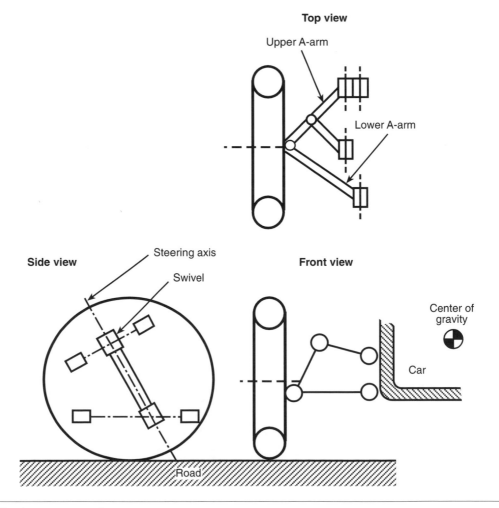

FIGURE 15.9 A-arm suspension.

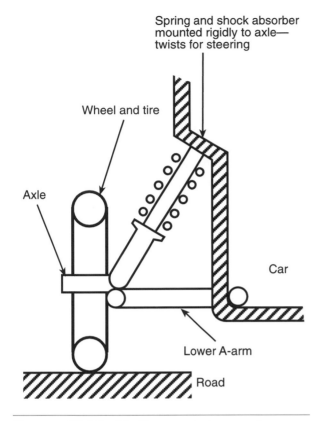

FIGURE 15.10 MacPherson strut suspension.

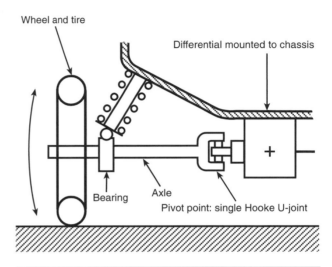

FIGURE 15.11 Swing arm suspension.

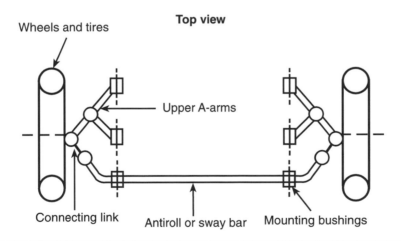

FIGURE 15.12 Antiroll bar.

Wheel Design

Part of the trick of bicycle balance is leaning into a turn, which balances the inward radial-force vector and the vertical weight vector into a resultant vector that acts straight down through the inclined bicycle. In this way the bicycle's wheels do not receive sideward loading. Many HPVs have three or more bicycle-style wheels, so do not lean in a turn,

causing the wheels to receive side loads for which they are not designed. A bicycle wheel is only about 15% as strong in side loading as in downward loading. A bicycle wheel overloaded sideways will often snap into a second unwanted stable state in which the rim bends out of its plane to resemble a potato chip. Many HPVs also have narrow tracks which makes them easy to roll onto their sides. So it is desirable to make HPVs lean in a corner, if that can be arranged in the suspension design, by having the wheels cant over to take the cornering loads in as near to a radial, in-plane, direction as possible. Lean-steer has been used experimentally on railroad cars and in automobiles, but it is heavy and complex in those applications. The example below illustrates one concept for achieving lean-steer in an HPV.

Applying Suspension and Wheel Design Concepts to HPV Design

The concepts explained in this chapter were used to develop a suspended lean-and-steer mechanism for an HPV. The lean-steer mechanism, illustrated in Figure 15.13, uses a fixed tubular steering axis inclined at the proper caster and offset angles. The wheel hub moves up the tube on the inside of the turn and down the tube on the outside. A roller, which is connected to the wheel hub, rides in a vertical track behind the steering tube, forcing the hub

to rotate as it moves along the tube, making the machine steer as it leans.

The steering linkage on this HPV is shown in Figure 15.14. It uses telescopic dampers to reduce bump-steer forces transmitted to the control stick. The twisting shafts act as torsion springs, and the linkage is set up to raise the outer wheel more than the inner wheel falls, to provide a tracking well.

Designing and building human-powered vehicles can be a lot of fun, and a little attention to the basics of suspension design (and steering design, as shown in chapter 14) can make them easy and fun to ride as well.

References

Baumeister, T.C. (Ed.) (1967). *Standard handbook for mechanical engineers* (7th ed.). New York: McGraw-Hill.

Setright, L.J.K. (1968). *The Grand Prix car 1954–1966.* New York: Norton.

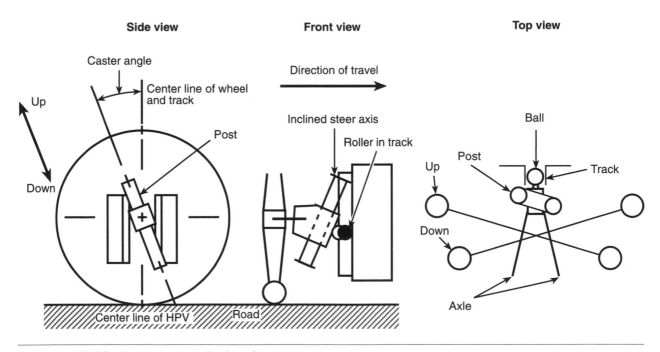

FIGURE 15.13   Lean steering wheel configuration.

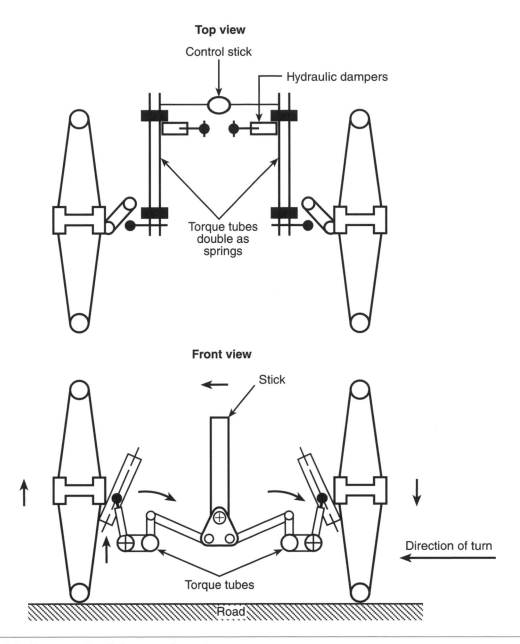

FIGURE 15.14   Lean steering linkage configuration.

IV

AIRCRAFT

Throughout history humans have dreamed of flying like the birds. Daedalus, a character in Greek mythology, was an architect and sculptor. To escape from King Minos's disfavor, Daedalus made wings of feathers and wax for himself and his son, Icarus. Daedalus's flight was successful, but Icarus's wings melted when he flew too close to the sun, and he fell into the Icarian sea and drowned. Amazingly, this ancient quest for flight was realized in 1988, when a team from the Massachusetts Institute of Technology retraced the mythological flight with their *Daedalus* human-powered aircraft and flew from the Greek island of Crete to the island of Santorin.

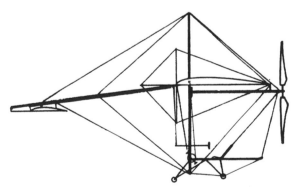

In 1903 the Wright Brothers achieved the first flight of an airplane by using the power from an internal-combustion engine. However, it was not until late in the 20th century that human-powered flight became a reality. In 1959 British industrialist Henry Kremer offered a remarkable challenge: a significant prize (the largest in aviation history at that time) for human-powered flight. A team in

California led by Paul MacCready won the Kremer Prize in 1977 with the *Gossamer Condor*. Thus, a chapter in human history has been completed—humans have finally flown through the air under their own power, like the birds, and Paul MacCready is recognized as the father of human-powered flight. These feats will be preserved in history among humans' greatest accomplishments.

This part begins with an invaluable historical review of human-powered flight, a review that is also an expert commentary on design choices and evolution by a pioneer in human-powered aircraft, Chris Roper. There follows Paul MacCready's commentary, partly engineering, partly philosophic, on the breakthrough Gossamer designs and the influence they had on later development. The last chapter in this part is a scientific commentary, with guidelines and forecasts by a leader in human-powered flight, Ernest Schoberl, who performed much of the aerodynamic design and optimization of the magnificent Musculair aircraft.

16

HISTORY AND PRESENT STATUS OF HUMAN-POWERED FLIGHT

Chris Roper

This short history of human-powered flight (HPF) and human-powered aircraft (HPA) is in four parts. The first covers 1783 to 1808, in which two lighter-than-air craft were fitted with crude human-powered devices. The second section covers 1912 to 1959, in which prizes catalyzed the development of heavier-than-air HPAs. The third section covers 1959 to 1985, when a series of later Kremer Prizes was offered and won. The fourth section covers 1985 to the present, during which time HPF activity has been stimulated principally by enthusiasts who set their own goals. (Even in this period, prize competitions seem likely to bring about further breakthroughs, particularly in Japan.)

This breakdown implicitly acknowledges the catalytic role of the prizes financed by Henry Kremer, a British industrialist, and organized by the Man Powered Aircraft Group (now renamed the Human Powered Aircraft Group) of the Royal Aeronautical Society (RAeS). At first, only British efforts were eligible, and a great deal of work on several HPAs was undertaken in the U.K., result-

ing in successful takeoffs, controlled flight, and landing of heavier-than-air HPAs. When eligibility for the Kremer Prize was extended worldwide, energetic efforts started in several countries. The principal Kremer prizes were won by teams from the U.S. and West Germany: Paul MacCready, leader of many of the most successful efforts, gives his personal views in the next chapter.

This chapter reviews the most significant HPF projects that have led to the recent remarkable performances. This progress has required new materials. Another essential breakthrough was the utilization (by the MacCready *Gossamer* team) of much simpler, more radical designs that could be built, tested, crashed, rebuilt and retested in days, rather than the months or years of the earlier efforts. HPAs since the *Gossamers* have benefited from the knowledge of all of these innovations and have frequently adopted them.

The story starts with crude attempts to add human power to balloons and to propel an airplane with wheel thrust alone.

Part 1 Human-Power-Assisted Balloons, 1783 to 1808

Jean-Pierre Blanchard built and flew what could be called the first human-powered airship. Shortly after the Montgolfier brothers' first balloon (1783), Blanchard fitted a hand-driven propeller to a balloon. To a certain extent he could influence the course taken by the vehicle (Reay, 1977).

Jakob Degen of Vienna obtained lift from a balloon beneath which he and a pair of umbrella-like devices were suspended (1808) (see Figure 16.1). By the use of levers he could move these up and down and thereby produce some control of altitude.

It is said that reports of Degen's flights reached Sir George Cayley without mention of the balloon. This encouraged Cayley, whose 28 m² glider carried a man several yards in 1809. In 1799 he had sketched a plane with oars. He theorized that each kilogram of resistance to motion (drag) would need as much power as 30 kg of weight (Roper, 1991). Similarly systematic and persevering were the Wright brothers, who built several gliders before building their own engine for the first engine-powered flight in 1904.

FIGURE 16.1 Degen's balloon, 1808.

From *Transportation, a pictorial archive*, Jim Harter, Dover, NY, 1984.

Part 2 HPF 1912 to 1959: The Pursuit of Prizes

In 1912 Robert Peugeot of France and others offered prizes for the first HPA to fly at least 10 m (33 ft). There were several consolation prizes for "flights" of less than the then long-jump record, 7.61 m. The main Peugeot Prize was eventually won 9 years later by the Farman Company. It built an HPA that was pedaled by Gabriel Poulain, a racing bicyclist and an experienced pilot, on the morning of July 9, 1921, yielding a flight of 11.98 m. The craft was a biplane with a span of 6.1 m (20 ft) and a wing area of 12.3 m² (132 ft²). A fairing enclosed the pilot. The plane had no propeller and, apparently, no aerodynamic controls. With Poulain aboard, the all-up weight was 91 kg (201 lb).

Dr. Alexander Lippisch, a prolific designer of sailplanes and other aircraft, built an ornithopter in 1929. This was always launched as is a glider. The wings were designed to twist as they flapped (Shenstone, 1960). With pilot Hans Werner Krause, results were poor until Lippisch offered to pay Krause's rail fare to see his girlfriend for the weekend if Krause were to fly 300 m. Krause completed the course on the first attempt.

Muskelflug-Institut

In 1935 the Muskelflug-Institut (Institute of Muscle-Powered Flight) was set up within the Polytechnische Gesellschaft, Frankfurt, and a prize was offered for the first flight of 1 km in Germany. The institute's director, Oskar Ursinus, carried out tests of the power developed by humans and made the data available in 1936.

The *Mufli* was built by two Junkers workers, Helmut Haessler and Franz Villinger, in 1935. It had an airframe similar to, but lighter than, gliders of the period, and bicycle-type pedals. The general approach, including the pylon-mounted propeller, influenced several HPA designers during the 1960s; however, most reverted to ailerons, rejecting the *Mufli's* all-moving wing. The *Mufli*, which flew 712 m, was designed to be catapult-launched as permitted by competition rules. Its wingspan was 13.5 m, and it weighed 34 kg plus 10 kg of launching gear.

Hans Seehase also built an aircraft for the Muskelflug competition. There is no record of it taking off, but it had several interesting design features. The wing had an aluminum-alloy tube spar, widely spaced ribs, and fabric covering, similar to modern hang gliders. His aim was to reduce weight even at the expense of more drag. No other designer applied this principle to such an extent for 42 years.

The power transmission mechanism was also unique. The pedals drove a two-throw crankshaft through a chain. This was coupled through light connecting rods to a similar crankshaft on the propeller shaft, at right angles to the first. Compliant rubber bearings were used to take up the small changes in length and angle setting of the rods that such an unorthodox arrangement in theory requires.

Pedaliante

In the 1930s Enea Bossi, an Italian aircraft designer, started his research into HPF by fitting a propeller to a tricycle. It was unstable, and Bossi concluded that two wing-mounted counterrotating propellers would be required for an HPA. Hence his drive train was complex and heavy. The *Pedaliante* was of conventional glider construction, weighed 99 kg (220 lb), and had a wingspan of 17.7 m (58 ft) and area of 23.2 m² (250 ft²).

The *Pedaliante* made dozens of flights after towed launches. There has been much dispute as to whether it ever took off under the pedal power of the pilot alone. If it did, it would have been a world first, preceding *SUMPAC* (q.v.) by 35 years.

Part 3 In Pursuit of the Kremer Prizes: 1959 to 1985

Just as the developments in HPF between the world wars were encouraged by offers of prizes, so were the later developments. After World War II, most of the prizes were offered by Henry Kremer, through the RAeS. They were the figure-eight, the cross-Channel, and the speed prizes. Two later prizes, one for an HPF involving a water takeoff, had been announced before Kremer's death in 1992, but as this is written no attempt has been made.

The Kremer Figure-Eight Prize

In the U.K. in the late 1950s, Daniel Perkins (q.v.) and other enthusiasts were trying to build HPAs. Professor Geoffrey Lilley (q.v.) and other senior academics and engineers formed a group to investigate HPF, which became the aforementioned Man Powered Aircraft Group. This group soon became part of the RAeS. They decided that true HPF must include right and left turns, unassisted takeoff, and at least a modest climb. They agreed that flight around a half-mile (804 m) figure eight after climbing to 10 ft (3 m) defined this. Group member Robert Graham introduced the subject of HPF to Henry Kremer, a hard-headed businessman. Mr. Kremer promptly offered £5,000 to the group, who decided to award it as a prize for a flight as they had defined.

SUMPAC. Alan Lassiere, Anne Marsden, and David Williams (three students at Southampton University), decided in their last term (spring 1960) to attempt to build a man-powered aircraft (Southampton University Man-Powered Aircraft, or *SUMPAC*). The first Kremer Prize competition had been announced the previous November. Other students soon joined the three. Tests of human physical power were first carried out by timing people of known weight running up stairs, but after a recumbent position was chosen for the single pilot, an ergometer rig was built for more relevant power measurements (Marsden, 1961).

Wherever possible, design and construction followed conventions of the bicycle, the glider, or the *Mufli*. For instance, they used ailerons, because they were the accepted method of lateral control. The airfoil section was modeled after one designed by the National Advisory Committee for Aeronautics (NACA, now known as the National Aeronautics and Space Administration, or NASA). The span chosen was 24 m (80 ft). Analysis had shown that a larger span would require less power, but the aircraft would be more difficult to turn. The propeller and the main wheel were driven, with the ratio between them chosen daily to match the prevailing wind speed.

Wind-tunnel tests were made of the wing section, the propeller, and a model of the complete aircraft. The model showed excessive drag (almost 30% of the total) at the junction of the wing and the propeller pylon. A compromise reshaping of the pylon was adopted, because by that time the plane was nearly complete.

Starting in January 1961, the *SUMPAC* team packed an enormous amount of work into a short time. Their effort paid off on November 9th when, with Derek Piggott as pilot, their HPA became the first to fly in Britain, beating their nearest competitors by a week. However, the Kremer Prize was not won for another 16 years.

Just as it is important for bicyclists to efficiently get the power from their legs into wheel thrust, so it is important for HPA pilots to efficiently convert leg power into propeller thrust, with the propeller

shaft at right angles to the pedal shaft. The team had accomplished this, but realized that their drive system was unreliable. In an attempt to improve the drive reliability and solve the pylon-drag problem, Alan Lassiere modified the plane at Imperial College, London. The numerous modifications took longer to accomplish than the building of the plane. Unfortunately, in 1965, on its first flight, under the pedaling of a strong bicyclist the plane went steeply up to 10 m (30 ft), stalled, and crashed, breaking the wing and fuselage beyond repair. The *SUMPAC* (in its modified form) is now displayed at Southampton Aircraft Museum in the U.K.

Puffin I, Puffin II, and Liverpuffin. This second HPA in Britain was flying on November 16, 1961, a week after *SUMPAC's* first flight. *Puffin I* (see Figure 16.2) was built by the Hatfield Man-Powered Aircraft Club (largely by employees of the De Havilland Aircraft Company), including John Wimpenny, aerodynamicist, and Frank Vann, structural engineer. Like *SUMPAC*, *Puffin I* was a single-seat monoplane made principally of wood, with a drive to a bicycle-type wheel and the propeller. Conventional controls were used. The wingspan and wing area were larger than those of *SUMPAC*: 25.6 m (84 ft) and 30.6 m² (330 ft²), although the empty weight was less, 53.2 kg (118 lb). The pilot position was, however, upright rather than recumbent, and transmission was by shaft and bevel gears rather than by belt. The airfoil section at the center of the wing was a Hatfield design with a flat underside, and the tip had an NACA section.

Most of the *Puffin I* structure was like an enormous balsa model (spars, ribs, and skin). The need to assemble large panels led to the use of excessive glue, which accounted for most of an extra 10 kg that the pilot had to lift and propel.

The plane was built in just over a year and rolled out on the evening of November 15, 1961; it was flown the next day on the first attempt. The power required was apparently less than that needed for *SUMPAC*. However, measurements made by towing the plane showed that the drag was 30% greater than predictions. The balsa wing covering had warped in places, so soft foam strip (sold for home draft exclusion) was stuck around the outside of the profile of each rib, and an entire new polyester film covering was attached outside this foam. This step reduced the drag considerably, even though the wing was now a half-inch thicker.

A straight-line flight of 908 m was made fairly easily by John Wimpenny; however, sustained turns remained elusive, except with the assistance of a

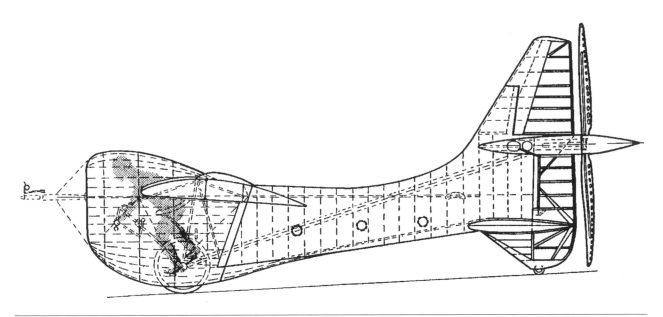

FIGURE 16.2 A view of the *Puffin I* showing the short coupled fuselage, small tail area, and large vertical surfaces. (Courtesy *Aeromodeller Annual* and R. Moulton)

model-airplane engine. Another method of increasing power was to use a racing cyclist rather than merely a muscular pilot. This step led to disaster in April 1962, when a crash destroyed the entire wing and fuselage.

Puffin II was constructed (using the propeller and gearbox of *Puffin I*) with a wingspan of 28 m and a wing area of 36 m². The new wing had an airfoil section designed especially for *Puffin II* by Dr. Wortmann of Stuttgart University, designated as FX-63137. Because the previous model had splintered when it crashed, this time they opted for a wing spar built of sturdy spruce and balsa strips like a crane-gantry. The lightweight, shape-forming balsa was built onto this stronger spar. The 64-kg craft had its first flight on August 27, 1965.

The performance was disappointing, little better than with *Puffin I*. With the Kremer figure-eight course in mind, the engineers at Hatfield devised and fitted many ingenious aerodynamic controls to try to make *Puffin II* fly around turns. But no official entry was made for the competition. Later studies indicated that the airfoil section might have had a higher drag than expected.

Puffin II hit a concrete runway-lightpost in April 1969, but the strong wing spar, the transmission, and the propeller (itself salvaged from *Puffin I*) survived and were handed over to Dr. Keith Sherwin, on the faculty of Liverpool University. The same wing section was built up on the salvaged spar from blocks of hot-wire-cut rigid polystyrene foam, pioneering a system later used on *Light Eagle* and *Daedalus*. The

span was reduced to 19.5 m, with the aim of producing a simple (rather than a record-breaking) HPA, called the *Liverpuffin*. Its first, short, flight was in March 1972. No long flights were recorded.

Mayfly: A Two-Person HPA. The original *Mayfly* was designed by Brian Kerry, an aerodynamicist, in 1960, but it was modified by others in the group that formed in and around Southend, Essex, U.K. In its final form it had a rectangular nose to accommodate the crew of two side by side. The wingspan was 27 m (90 ft), and the wing area 37.6 m² (405 ft²). Construction started in summer 1961, and was supposed to have been completed by May 1962. The first attempted flight, however, was in July 1965. *Mayfly* may never have flown, although some claimed to have seen light occasionally under the wheels.

Mayfly had conventional glider layout and control surfaces, and a propeller on a pylon at the nose. The wing structure was similar to others of its period. Drive to the propeller from the two-person recumbent crew (an airline pilot and a racing cyclist) was by twisted chain. *Mayfly* had a nosewheel, and the main wheel was driven. The skin was aluminized Melinex polyester film.

There was no one reason for the lack of success of the *Mayfly*, but the many modifications, for example, the widening of the cabin during building, precluded a neat result. The transmission involved three bearings in line with insufficient rigidity to maintain alignment; weight distribution was not as the designers had expected; the wing was warped and there was insufficient spirit left after all the delays for the group to rebuild it. In 1967 the end of the storage shed collapsed, damaging all three wing sections and providing the final discouragement. The propeller was salvaged and used on another two-seater HPA called the *Toucan* (q.v.).

Jupiter: Flying Straight From the Drawing Board to the Long-Distance Record.

In 1961, the author, a newly qualified engineer, designed a plane called the *Hodgess Roper*, which had a simple tube for the rear fuselage. The tube was 6 m long, 63.5 mm in diameter, and 0.56 mm thick, and later some of it became the propeller pylon structure of *Jupiter*. The author designed *Jupiter* in 1963, after the experiences of *SUMPAC* and *Puffin I* were made known. Construction began in Woodford, Essex, U.K., with Susan Roper and others (see Figure 16.3). Financial help came from a grant from the RAeS MPAG. Construction continued at Woodford until February 1968. Morale had diminished, and after a series of disasters the decision was made to hand over the plane. (An unintentional benefit of this decision was that during the flying stage, the person in charge was a professional pilot.) In 1970, the hardware was handed over to John Potter, then in the RAF, who led the project and a team of 99, in-cluding the author. *Jupiter* was completed at Halton and flew many times in 1972 and later (see Figure 16.4). Some significant design data are: wingspan 24 m (80 ft); wing area 27.9 m² (300 ft²); wing section NACA 65_3618; aircraft weight 66.3 kg (146 lb) (original estimated weight 52.6 kg; 116 lb). Compared to other HPAs, *Jupiter* was heavy but had a very smooth wing.

Jupiter flew without needing any alterations, straight from the drawing board. After the first flight a chain tensioner, ventilation holes, and instrumentation were added. John Potter achieved a high usage of the plane, unusual for HPA at that period. He was able to claim the world long-distance record more by training himself than by modifying the plane. *Jupiter* is now displayed at the Filching Manor Museum in Polegate, England.

Linnets, I, II, III and IV: The First Takeoffs From Propeller Thrust Alone.

This series of early successful aircraft were student projects built at Nihon University, Japan, under the leadership of Professor Hidemasa Kimura, after news of the flights of *SUMPAC* and *Puffin I* was received. The first flight was on February 25, 1966, with Munetaka Okamiya at the controls. The *Linnet I* was the first HPA to take off under propeller thrust alone—there was no drive to the wheels. The longest flight was only 43 m

FIGURE 16.3 Chris and Susan Roper working on the *Jupiter* (photo by Ken Bray).

FIGURE 16.4 *Jupiter* airborne at Benson, U.K., flown by Squadron Leader John Potter (photo by R. Moulton).

because pilots found that keeping the nose level distracted from piloting. The wing surface was covered with 0.5-mm styrene paper, which Kimura felt was far superior to polyester film. Subsequent Linnets were produced at almost one per year. Work at Nihon University following the Linnets is discussed later in this chapter.

Malliga.   Josef Malliga, a pilot in the Austrian Air Force, designed and built an HPA on his own in 1967. He even drew his own airfoil sections. It resembled the Linnets in having styrene covering and bevel-gear transmissions, but in this case the propeller axis was the same height as the pilot's feet, a layout dictating a tall undercarriage. The first human-powered flights, in autumn 1967, were up to 140 m. The original wingspan was 20 m and the weight 51 kg. The propeller diameter was increased from about 2 m to nearly 3 m, the span was increased to 26 m, and the flight lengths then increased to 350 m. Malliga tried out various lateral-control devices.

Ottawa: The Birth of a New Construction System.   Czerwinski (1967), working in Ottawa, developed a new method of strong lightweight construction for HPA: a framework of aluminum tubes lashed together with glass fibers. Almost all subsequent craft used this system, using, later, Kevlar or

carbon fibers for both lashings and tubes. He designed a two-seater aircraft with two propellers using this system; records of flight trials are unknown to the author.

Dumbo (Mercury): Chemically Milled Tubes. The *Dumbo* project was started in early 1966 by P.K. Green, W.F. Ball, and M.J. Rudd, all employed at the British Aircraft Corporation (BAC), Weybridge. One aim was to increase wingspan 50% above that of previous HPAs without increasing weight. The group felt that this could be done by not using ailerons (thus avoiding the stress on the wings caused by ailerons); instead the entire wing was made to be rotatable on each side. The spar was built curved so that it would straighten out in flight; the tubes were etch-milled (chemically) to a thickness of 0.25 mm. It appeared to the author that not as much loving care had been put into the shaping of the front wing as had gone into construction elsewhere on the machine. This would cause extra drag and partially offset the advantage of the enormous span of 37 m (120 ft). Also, weight had to be added at the front of the fuselage to restore balance to the design position. The first flight, with Chris Lovell, a cyclist and glider pilot, in *Dumbo's* rather cramped cockpit, was on September 18, 1971. The performance was disappointing; the aircraft was directionally unstable. Only a few short flights were attempted, partly for lack of people eager to fly it.

The plane was taken over in 1974 by John Potter, who had gained experience restoring and flying *Jupiter*. He refurbished the wing and renamed the plane *Mercury*. But performance was not greatly improved.

Toucan I: The First Two-Person HPA to Fly.

Martyn Pressnell, who had been with the Southend group, became the leader of a group based at the Handley Page Aircraft Company in Radlett, U.K. They felt in 1965 that the current generation of single-seat HPA was not going to be able to complete the Kremer figure-eight course, so they decided that a two-person machine was required. The wingspan eventually chosen was 42.4 m (139 ft), and the aircraft was 8.8 m (29 ft) long. It was powered by two people in tandem. The construction effort required more than 20,000 man-hours. They coped with problems arising from the liquidation of Handley Page in February 1970. On December 23, 1972 *Toucan I* made the world's first flight of a two-seat HPA, covering a distance of 62 m (68 yd). After a series of modifications to the wing mounting system, *Toucan I* flew again on July 3, 1973, and with a slight head wind of about 1 m/s (3 ft/s) flew about 700 m in a stable and well-controlled manner, land-ing safely on the runway after being airborne for 80 s. A second flight of about 330 m was made that evening. Later, however, serious damage occurred to the starboard wing in an accident, and repairs were undertaken during the remainder of 1973 and most of 1974.

The opportunity was taken to increase the wing-span by inserting a central 4.9 m (16 ft) addition and to make other smaller changes (see Figure 16.5). The craft was renamed the *Toucan II*, and flight test-ing continued until September 1978. Several dozen flights of lengths up to 500 m were achieved. The aircraft was stable in straight flight, but turns were not attempted because of the probable damage that would occur if it were to land off the runway. When the group had to vacate the airfield in October 1978, they presented the plane to an aircraft museum. The machine was disposed of in 1982. Now only the seat frame and the propeller remain, and they are in the care of Martyn Pressnell.

Wright: Carbon Fiber in a One-Person Effort.

Of the three HPA to fly in the spring of 1972, only the *Wright*, the first successful British one-person project, was not the result of a takeover. Peter Wright, trained in carbon-fiber fabrication at Rolls-Royce, was an active glider pilot. He believes that he spent 500 hours constructing the *Wright*. He

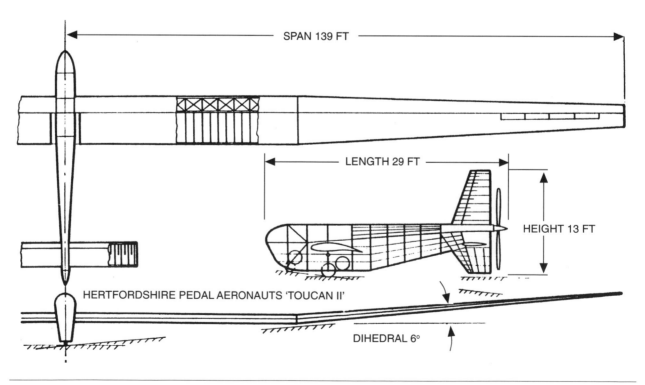

FIGURE 16.5   The Hertfordshire Pedal Aeronauts *Toucan II*.

started to design in October 1969, aiming for quick construction. He pioneered the HPA use of carbon fiber for diagonal taping and for reinforcing plastic foam. The seat frame was welded mild-steel tube. The wing area was the largest of all HPAs up to then: 45 m² (486 ft²), increased in 1973 (by extending the wingtips) to 48.4m². Wright had plans to improve the performance by increasing the diameter of the three-bladed propeller to 3 m (10 ft) and to move it from behind the tail to a nose-mounted pylon.

The Post-Linnet Nihon University Series: Egrets, the Stork, Ibis, and Milan, and a New Distance Record. The *Egret* series was built at Nihon University after a well-equipped runway of 620 m length and 30 m width and an adequate hangar were completed in 1972. The transmission was made shorter than that of the *Linnet* by using a belt and by mounting the propeller on a pylon right behind the cockpit, similar to *SUMPAC* and *Jupiter*. Three *Egrets* were built following the established pattern of one HPA each year. Professor Kimura wrote: "The 1975 student team was com-

posed wholly of enthusiasts who had been helping their seniors with the manufacture of HPA since their freshman days. The [*Stork*] team had an expert designer named Junji Ishii as its leader. I decided that I could entrust them with the task of undertaking drastic model changes" (Kimura, 1977).

The *Stork* (see Figure 16.6) flew a distance of ten times anything previously flown at Nihon, and almost twice the distance of its predecessor, the *Jupiter*. Ishii made admirable improvements on *Jupiter's* design. Its wing spar, made using balsa plywood like *Jupiter*, was much lighter and neater; the ventilation was better; and it was easier to rig and derig. The *Stork* made one 180° turn, but crashed on that flight while still turning. After repairs and modifications, *Stork* flew 2,094 m on January 2, 1977, thereby gaining the world distance record for HPA flight.

Nihon's 1978 airplane, the *Ibis*, followed the same general configuration as the *Stork* except that the wing was mounted lower and the *Ibis* was a slightly smaller plane. Its performance was also reduced.

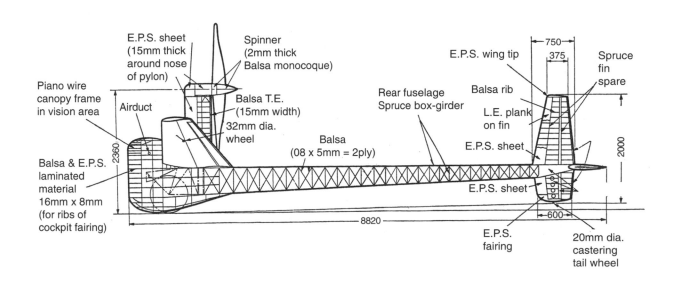

E.P.S. = expanded polystyrene

FIGURE 16.6 A portion of the plan for the *Stork*, a successor to the *Jupiter*, designed and built at Nihon University, Japan. It flew 2,094 m on January 2, 1977, thus gaining the world distance record. (Courtesy *Aeromodeller*, R. Moulton, editor)

The *Milan* flew in December 1981, the first new aircraft from Nihon University since March 1978. The configuration was also totally new, having an almost rectangular high wing from which twin tail booms projected on each side of the propeller, which was behind the pod. The pilot position was upright. The plane flew 590 m. A similar plane, *MiLan '82*, flew on October 16, 1982. The cruising speed was 5.4 m/s and the propeller diameter 4.3 m.

The Aviette: Aerodynamic Restraints to Wing Warp.

Aviette, meaning "small airplane," usually refers to the class of 1920s flying bicycles that typically had ground drive only. Maurice Hurel's 1976 plane of the same name had a span of 42 m and a propeller of 4 m diameter.

He used an aerodynamic solution to a structural problem: that of keeping the wings from warping or twisting. He attached stabilizing surfaces to mini tail booms behind each outer wing. Thus, on the principle of a weathercock, the outer wings were held at an appropriate angle to the airflow. Spruce, balsa, and polyester film, conventional construction materials of the time, were used. The *Aviette* flew at France's premier international commercial airfield, Le Bourget, largely through national recognition of Hurel's lifelong contribution to industry, and achieved flights of about a kilometer.

Verstraete and the Masschelin Brothers.

Paul and Stephan Masschelin and Eric Verstraete, an expert bicyclist, built several elegant machines at the time the *Aviette* was being developed. One of these was transported to France to fly at Calais-Marck airport, because the Belgian authorities would not grant a permit for them to fly. The flights were remarkable for the altitude gained (about 5 m) and the location, a base adjacent to the sea where wind is both fierce and gusting. Wingspan was 26 m and weight 53 kg. Ron Moulton, later the chair of the RAeS HPAG, visited the brothers in 1974 and found them working, with little support or equipment, in their chicory-roasting shed.

Olympian ZB-1: The First American HPA to Fly.

This first HPA to fly in North America, the *Olympian ZB-1*, was a one-man venture by Joe Zinno, an ex-pilot. It made its first officially observed flight on April 21, 1976. It used rudder-only lateral control, a pod-and-boom fuselage, and treadles rather than rotary pedals for power input. The 24-m wooden wing framework had rigid foam-plastic nose skinning.

Bliesner Series: Totally Solo HPAs.

Wayne Bliesner has designed, built, and flown a bewildering number of HPAs, producing about one new aircraft or variant each year.

Bliesner's first three aircraft made flights only under tow. After the successful flight of the fourth, there followed a series of planes using the same elliptic planform spruce-spar-wing. Various propeller positions and tail arrangements were tried during this time.

Bliesner was a student at the University of Washington in 1975 when he built his first HPA, *Bliesner 1*, a flying-wing design. The spar was a girder of brazed aluminum tubes, and the ribs were balsa. The propeller was on a pylon above the pod. The plane was designed to fly at 5.4 m/s (12 mph) as indeed it did—but only when towed. Before further flight tests could be made, a storm destroyed the temporary hangar and the aircraft with it. The propeller was salvaged, and a new plane, *Bliesner 2*, was designed and built, having a glider-type rear fuselage and a recumbent pilot position, using a spar and a propeller pylon similar to those of the first plane. The plane flew in 1977, but, again, only under tow.

A new elliptic planform wing with a spruce spar and foam ribs was built for *Bliesner 3*. The fuselage was designed for the possibility of a water landing, with pilot access from the top. The plane made many tow-assisted flights in 1978, but crashed after stalling at 6 m. For *Bliesner 4*, the wing was rebuilt to its original shape and a new fuselage with a better contoured surface was constructed. The wing was left low, with the pilot sitting on the wooden spar. Drive-train problems on the previous aircraft led to the decision to run the propeller on a short pylon at the front of the fuselage. The configuration was moved to Arlington airport, where a hangar allowed partial assembly. A large, unused runway was available for flight tests. This proved to be an ideal site for straight-line flight. This aircraft became the first configuration to be pedaled off the ground without tow assistance, and several short flights of up to 90 m were achieved.

The 1980 *Bliesner 5* fuselage incorporated a carbon structure, two wheels in front, a new propeller, and an upright seat. Flight-distance increases up to a mile (1.6 km) were attributed mainly to the new propeller. There were many occasions when the aircraft was assembled, taxied out to the field, and flown with only the pilot around. Bliesner had not expected to have this capability but, once achieved, decided to retain this aspect in later designs. The upright pilot position was considered to be the major factor in a noseover when the aircraft was blown into a ditch while taxiing. It was decided to revert to a recumbent position for pilot safety.

A high wing was used for his later aircraft. *Bliesner 6* made only a few short hops before the failure of a hastily made wing-to-fuselage joint destroyed much of the craft. The 1981 *Bliesner 7* was the last to use a wooden wing. Several steps were taken to reduce interference drag, including the use of a V-tail. However, tail-boom flexibility considerably reduced its effectiveness. Flight tests were terminated so that a new wing could be fitted for the *Bliesner 8*, or *Man-Eagle*.

The *Man-Eagle I* was made in 1982. The span, optimized on a computer, was 33.5 m. However, the wingtip deflection turned out to be nearly 5 m, and Bliesner cut the span progressively to 19 m. With the announcement of the Kremer speed competition, described later in this chapter, Bliesner decided to tailor his next plane for the competition and accordingly abandoned the V-tail. Instead, he used a propeller capable of absorbing peak power output (560 W or 0.75 hp) without stalling, and mounted it at the front. He added a rubber energy-storage system, which he later changed to an electrical system.

Bliesner often took the *Man-Eagle* out of the hangar alone, climbed in, and flew and landed single-handedly, as he had done with his fifth aircraft. A ground crew of two or three was, however, optimum. He made hundreds of flights in 1985, with a total flight time of more than 3 hours, and on one occasion completed 90% of the Kremer speed course (q.v.) in 125 s at a time when 136 s was required for the prize. He made eight attempts on the course.

Newbury Manflier: A Two-Person, Two-Pod HPA.

In the mid-1970s, after the first few British HPA had flown but had failed to win the figure-eight prize, people were looking for new concepts. Rear Admiral H.C.N. (Nick) Goodhart, a champion glider pilot, proposed distributing load along a long wing by having two pilots 21 m (70 ft) apart, each pedaling one propeller. To yaw, each pilot would pedal harder; to roll, one would apply elevator. But with two pilots, who is in charge? Surprisingly, what worked best was for each pilot to look after his own end. With the widest-ever undercarriage, the *Newbury Manflier* could operate only from a very wide runway. It first flew in 1979 from Greenham Common, U.K., its longest flight being 69 s. Torsional oscillations, perhaps due to localized gusts, resulted in a wing spar fracture. In a letter to the author, Goodhart wrote: "After repair, the wing spar proved entirely satisfactory and took up exactly the predicted shape in flight, indicating that the loadings were as anticipated. The project was terminated soon after the first two flights had been achieved as the hangar and runway at Greenham Common became unavailable."

Inflatable HPAs.

In 1957, Daniel Perkins, who worked for the Royal Aircraft Establishment at Cardington, Britain's largest experimental airship facility, decided to build an inflatable-wing HPA with a pod-and-boom fuselage. All his varied tests came up against a strange speed barrier of 6.3 m/s (14 mph). In 1965, he achieved success with his design of the *Reluctant Phoenix*, the first ever inflatable heavier-than-air HPA to fly.

The aircraft was a delta flying wing with a wingspan of 31 ft (9.4 m) and an empty weight of 39 lb (18 kg). The envelope of the wing was made of polyurethane-coated nylon fabric. Because of the high power requirement for cruise, the aircraft was limited to short hops under human power as it was being flight tested inside an 800-ft-long (240-m) airship hangar. About 90 flights were made. *Reluctant Phoenix* was successful in that it could be folded away and transported in the back of a small station wagon. It also survived many crashes without requiring repairs as the aircraft merely bounced when in collision with the ground. Shortly after Perkins' death the *Reluctant Phoenix* was handed over to Frederick To who immediately recognized the advantages of the system (To, 1985).

Frederick To was an architect who had made a 1974 film about HPF called *The Last Challenge*, and, with David Williams of *SUMPAC* (q.v.), created *Solar One*, the world's first solar-powered aircraft. Starting in 1978, he designed and built a new inflatable, the *Phoenix*, with 30-m wingspan and 5-m chord. The weight was 48 kg, but the takeoff run involved accelerating this weight, the pilot's own weight, and the 90 kg of air enclosed by the enormous wing. He used radio-controlled model-aircraft servos, four on each elevon. Eventually the plane could be inflated in 20 min and deflated in 30, and could be carried on the roof of a small car. (The propeller was the most awkward component to transport.) The first flight was on March 28, 1982, with Ian Parker as pilot; eventually, all group members flew the plane, but none covered any considerable distance.

Icarus: A Gossamer Condor Relative?

Taras Kiceniuk's *Icarus* HPA was flying in the Mojave desert of southern California in the same year that the MacCready team was flying its *Gossamer Condor* in the same area; at one time the planes shared a hangar. They were both constructed from aluminum tubing, foam, and polyester film. The *Icarus* had the propeller concentric with the tail boom, the first use of this scheme. Kiceniuk later helped with the *Gossamer Albatross* and then the *Bionic Bat*, which had a propeller position similar to the *Icarus*. The arrangement was considered and rejected for the *Daedalus*, but adopted for the *Airglow*.

The *Icarus* had a very low wing, the ribs of which were fabricated by the technique used on the *Liverpuffin*, and later the *Light Eagle* and *Daedalus*— by hot-wire cutting of solid blocks of rigid foam. Takeoff was possible only with towing.

Gossamer Condor: Winner of the First Kremer Prize.
Before the Gossamers, aircraft had followed the patterns of the glider and the bicycle. There had been little real change since the 1935 *Mufli* of Haessler and Villinger. The *Stork* had flown 2,094 m in a straight line, compared with the 712 m of the *Mufli*. No HPA could repeatedly demonstrate controlled sustainable turns.

The quantum leap in HPA progress made by the Gossamer series occurred through a combination of novel ideas and thorough analysis, as well as through iteration in flight testing and modifica-

tions. In 1976 Paul MacCready, former world-champion glider pilot and aerodynamicist, decided to follow the hang glider concept. His first calculations showed that with a much larger wing area than other HPAs, flying speed could be brought so low that the drag of wire bracing would be allowable. Also, wheel drive would not be needed for takeoff.

There were three *Gossamer Condors*. The first, called the Pasadena version, was built by Jack Lambie from 12-ft lengths of 2-in. diameter (51 mm) aluminum tube and a web of wires, and flew just once in the parking lot of the Pasadena Rose Bowl. The second, the Mojave version, was the first true *Gossamer*. It had a single-surface Mylar-covered airfoil of 29-m span and 102-m² area, an aluminum-tube spar at the leading edge and a second tube near the trailing edge, and no pilot fairing (see Figure 16.7). Tyler MacCready (Paul MacCready's son) powered it on its first (40-s) flight, at midday on December 26, 1976. Many subsequent flights were made. It was basically unstable, but its motions were so slow that all pilots could handle it. The aircraft also could not turn. The canard stabilizer worked only as an elevator to control pitch. Later this was made to bank, so that it would, as Paul MacCready described it, "pull the plane around by the nose."

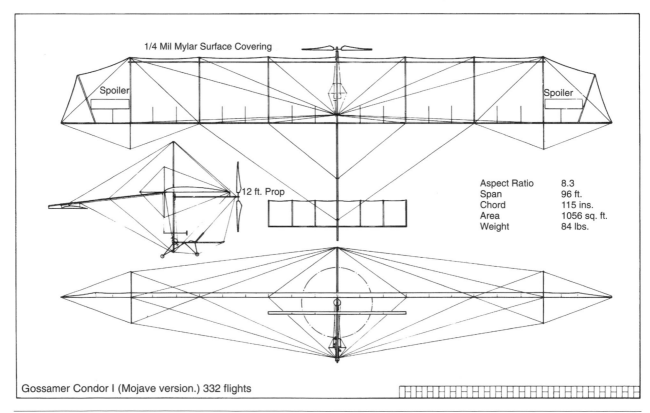

FIGURE 16.7   *Gossamer Condor I*, winner of the first Kremer Prize, 1977.

An improved *Condor*, the Shafter version, used a new airfoil designed by Peter Lissaman and flew in March 1977 at Shafter airport, in California. A variety of lateral-control surfaces, including spoilers, a forward rudder, and an aft rudder, were tried out, because the banking canard stabilizer was by itself insufficient. Soon the *Gossamer Condor's* total time in the air exceeded that of all other HPA put together. Minor crashes were frequent. If the spar broke the pilot would jump out so as to land feet-first and reduce crash impact on the aircraft. Failed parts were rebuilt and improved, and the *Condor* evolved from a contraption to a sophisticated flying machine. However, a particularly severe crash during an attempted turn produced damage so extensive that a rebuild was necessary.

The new plane incorporated wing twist in addition to the banking canard stabilizer to assist in sustained turns. This performed as planned. In the first flight after the rebuild, the wake from a passing crop-duster plane cause the *Condor* to crash, but after repairs Bryan Allen flew the figure eight on August 23, 1977. The Kremer Prize was won after 18 years.

Many people subsequently flew the *Gossamer Condor*, from athletes to grandmothers, before it was hung in the Smithsonian Institution in Washington.

The New Kremer Prizes

Henry Kremer promptly proposed that there be a new challenge, and the RAeS HPAG drew up the rules for a cross-Channel flight. He also offered a new figure-eight prize for entrants from any country other than that of the first winner.

The Gossamer Albatross. It was generally thought that the time before the English Channel was crossed would be much longer than the 18 years it took for the figure-eight prize to be won. However, the MacCready team that produced the *Gossamer Condor* started work on the *Gossamer Albatross* in 1977 and made the first flight in July 1978. It differed from the *Condor* in using carbon-fiber spars, a wing surface improved by closer spacing of the ribs, a smaller wing area to suit a higher cruising speed, and a conventional cycling position for the pilot. Du Pont's Kevlar fiber and Mylar polyester film were used extensively, and in March 1979 Du Pont agreed to be chief sponsor of the attempt.

At a time when Allen's maximum duration flight was 18 min, MacCready met with Eugene Larrabee of MIT, who was supervising design of propellers, and asked for help. The MIT *Chrysalis* team designed a new propeller for the *Gossamer Albatross*. Allen's flights immediately went from 18 to 69 min; after that duration he landed merely to give a backup pilot a flight. The team planned to make some practice flights over water, but the next day the RAF offered transport to the U.K. for the *Gossamer Albatross* and two spare planes, and the overwater flights were skipped.

The weather was not good in England until June 12, 1979 when at 5:51 a.m. Bryan Allen headed out to sea in the *Gossamer Albatross*. All went well until a head wind sprung up half way across the Channel. It became stronger until, 10 km from his destination, Cape Gris Nez, Allen prepared to give up. This entailed climbing to the height of a fishing rod to be hooked up for a tow from a boat. Surprisingly, he found that at this greater height he could keep going, and did so, arriving in complete exhaustion at 8:40 a.m., an hour after his last food and drink were consumed.

Chrysalis: A Recreational Biplane. In the 1970s, two HPAs called *BURD I* and *BURD II* had been built. These never flew, but a later attempt by John Langford and other students to fly *BURD II* inspired them to build their own craft. In November 1978 the team set forth 5 goals (Chrysalis Flight Team, 1982) (see Figure 16.8):

1. The aircraft should be ready to fly in 6 months.
2. The aircraft should be easy for anyone to fly.
3. The aircraft should be buildable in the available space.
4. The aircraft should be easy to build and repair.
5. The aircraft should be an improvement over the *BURDs*.

The designers, after consulting a Czerwinski article on joining tubes and the plans of the *Gossamer Condor*, decided on a biplane built of tubes and foam plastic. The team cooperated with MacCready, trading propeller design for polyester film. They met all their aims, and *Chrysalis* was flown by 44 people, including Bryan Allen on his return from France. He found that *Chrysalis* required more power for climb but less power for cruise and had greater stability than the *Gossamer Albatross*.

Figure-Eight Competitions Continue

A prize of £10,000 was still available in 1980 for this course, first flown in the U.S. The rules stated that

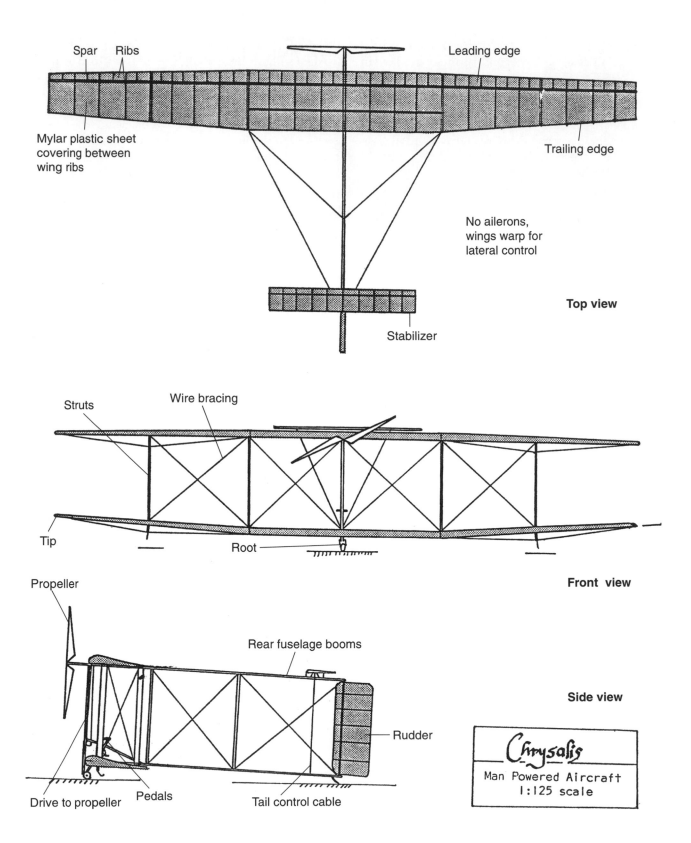

FIGURE 16.8 A preliminary sketch of the *Chrysalis*, built by MIT students in 91 days in early 1979 and subsequently flown by 44 people, including Bryan Allen and one of this book's editors (from the proposal; drawing believed to be by Mark Drela).

the second winner must be from a different country than the U.S., and the competition was to close in June 1984. Three teams raced to beat this date.

HVS: A Plane for All Seasons. Franz Villinger, co-designer of the 1935 *Mufli*, teamed with two other mature aircraft workers to produce *HVS* (Hunter-Villinger-Schule), a small, sleek craft with a sophisticated carbon structure packed with ingenious mechanisms (Moulton, 1983) (see Figure 16.9). Its design approach was very different from that of the *Condor* series, yet it similarly had many innovations. The entire wing lifted off for pilot access. Pedals used treadle action to minimize cockpit size. Wing position was the lowest ever. Its first flight was in June 1982, but performance was disappointing and it did not compete for any of the three Kremer prizes for which it was eligible. What it did achieve was flight in wind speeds greater than its own cruising speed of 10 m/s.

Pelargos 2. Max Horlacher, head of his own composites company in Mohlin, Switzerland, built *Pelargos 1* so that his 11-year-old son could try to win the remaining Kremer figure-eight prize. *Pelargos 1* did not fly, and *Pelargos 2* was designed

with help from Zurich aerodynamicist Fritz Dubs and the firm of Reichhold Chemie AG. The firm's techniques and materials were, perhaps excessively, used in construction, and the plane was exhibited on the Horlacher stall at a trade show. *Pelargos 2* first flew in December 1983, and later covered 1,000 m with Peer Frank (q.v.) as pilot.

Musculair I: A non-U.S. Kremer Prize Winner. The *Musculair I* was designed with the intention of winning two Kremer prizes, but won three (see Figure 16.10). It was built by the father-and-son team of Gunter and Holger Rochelt and designed by Gunter Rochelt, Ernst Schöberl, and Heinz Eder. The elder Rochelt had previously built a successful and radical solar-powered aircraft. Schöberl aimed to find a configuration that would be suitable both for the figure-eight course and for the triangular mile (see the explanation of the Kremer speed prizes below), with the piloting and pedaling of Holger Rochelt, who was not particularly athletic. The wing area of 16 m² was one of the smallest used on an HPA; the only other plane to have completed the figure eight had 71 m². *Musculair I* was a conventional high-wing monoplane with the propeller behind the tail, the drive shaft having the length of

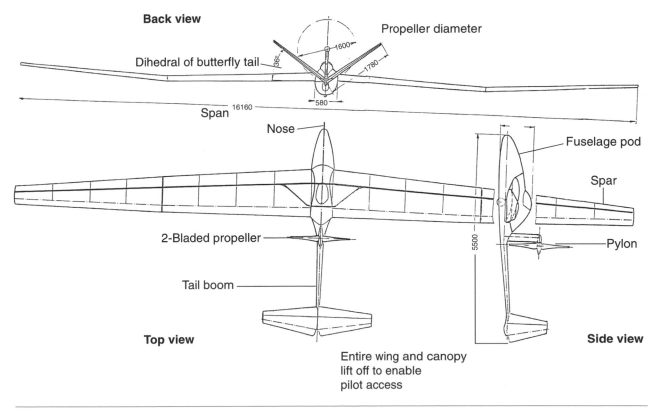

FIGURE 16.9 HVS (Hutter-Villinger-Schule) general arrangement. This plane probably flew in the highest winds, over 10 m/s of any HPA. (Courtesy *Aeromodeller*, R. Moulton, editor)

FIGURE 16.10   The *Musculair I* won the non-U.S. figure-eight Kremer Prize and the third Kremer Prize (photo © E. Schöberl).

the tail boom. It was built in 3 months and made its first flight in May 1984. On June 18 of that year Holger Rochelt flew a figure eight and won the team's first Kremer Prize.

A seat was taped to the main fuselage vertical tube for Holger's young sister, Katrina, who weighed 28 kg. Holger took off, reaching 5-m altitude, and flew 500 m, thereby achieving the first HPA passenger flight.

The Kremer World Speed Competition (Triangular Mile)

The RAeS and Henry Kremer had been working on another prize for HPF, one that would encourage the development of HPAs that could be used in other than unusually calm conditions. The rules for the Kremer Speed Competition, published May 4, 1983, were considered to be just beyond the current state of the art. The prize was for flight around a triangular course of 1,500 m (slightly less than a mile) in less than 3 min. Subsequent prizes would be awarded for speed improvements of 5% or greater. Energy stored purely by pilot effort during the 10 min immediately preceding the flight would be allowed. Entrants could do this by twisting strands of rubber as in model planes, using dynamos to charge batteries, or in whatever way they chose.

The competition for this prize was intense, principally among four contenders: the MacCready team with *Bionic Bat*; the MIT team with *Monarch*; Wayne Bliesner with *Man-Eagle*; and the Rochelt family with *Musculair*. That month the MacCready and MIT teams started design work on new aircraft, and Wayne Bliesner began adding twisted-rubber energy storage to his *Man-Eagle*, which had been fast and controllable in its first flights in 1982.

Monarch A and Monarch B: The First Kremer Speed Prize. At MIT Mark Drela and John Langford designed a successor to *Chrysalis* named, logically, *Monarch* (after the monarch butterfly). Its structure was simple, following *Chrysalis*, but Steve Finberg added a highly sophisticated electric battery energy-storage system. It flew on August 14, 1983, 88 days after start of construction. It crashed, seriously damaging the fuselage, on September 23, 1983, just before MacCready apparently won the first Kremer Speed Prize. (The claim was, however, disallowed by the RAeS on November 23.) During the winter, the team redesigned the fuselage and renamed the plane *Monarch B*. The new fuselage had a recumbent pilot position (it had been upright on *Monarch A*), giving relaxed arms for easier control, decreasing the chances of a noseover, and making a more streamlined cockpit; and a variable-pitch propeller (see Figure 16.11). It was built in secrecy

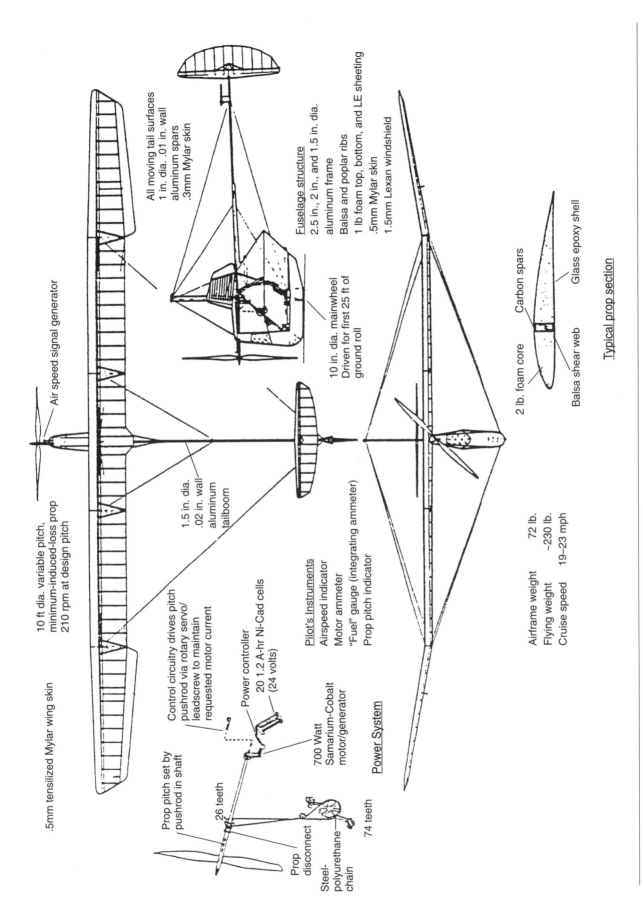

.5mm tensilized Mylar wing skin

10 ft dia. variable pitch,
minimum-induced-loss prop
210 rpm at design pitch

Air speed signal generator

All moving tail surfaces
1 in. dia. .01 in. wall
aluminum spars
.3mm Mylar skin

Fuselage structure
2.5 in., 2 in., and 1.5 in. dia.
aluminum frame
Balsa and poplar ribs
1 lb foam top, bottom, and LE sheeting
.5mm Mylar skin
1.5mm Lexan windshield

10 in. dia. mainwheel
Driven for first 25 ft of
ground roll

1.5 in. dia.
.02 in. wall
aluminum
tailboom

Carbon spars

Glass epoxy shell

2 lb. foam core

Balsa shear web

Typical prop section

Prop pitch set by
pushrod in shaft

Control circuitry drives pitch
pushrod via rotary servo/
leadscrew to maintain
requested motor current

Power controller

20 1.2 A-hr Ni-Cad cells
(24 volts)

Pilot's Instruments
Airspeed indicator
Motor ammeter
"Fuel" gauge (integrating ammeter)
Prop pitch indicator

700 Watt
Samarium–Cobalt
motor/generator

Power System

Prop
disconnect

Steel-
polyurethane
chain

26 teeth

74 teeth

Airframe weight   72 lb.
Flying weight   ~230 lb.
Cruise speed   19–23 mph

FIGURE 16.11 The *Monarch B*, built by an MIT student team, won the first Kremer Speed Prize on May 11, 1984 (drawing by M. Drela).

because the team knew that California's mild weather gave the MacCready group a substantial advantage. *Monarch B* first flew on April 4, 1984. Attempts on the prize were made on May 3, 5, 6, and 7, and success came with an officially certified 175-s flight on May 11, 1984. The *Monarch* team received its prize of £20,000 and retired from the competition, knowing that their plane was incapable of a substantial increase in performance.

The Bionic Bat and the Gossamer Swift: The MacCreadys' Entry for the Triangular Mile. This aircraft went through many changes, including a change of name, but the configuration remained a recumbent pilot under a high wing. The propeller was concentric with the tail boom and just behind the pod (as in the *Icarus* q.v.), an arrangement that was credited with achieving a drag lower than estimated. In contrast to the *Monarch*, this was a sophisticated plane, and a departure from the earlier MacCready designs. Various battery systems were used, but the best, a nickel-cadmium battery plus a DC motor-generator, gave an overall efficiency of only 22%. Large-diameter carbon-fiber tubes were used. The plane was designed to withstand crashes, a 4-g landing load and a 6-g head-on load. After modifications, the span was 17 m, the wing area 13.8 m² and the weight 33 kg.

The *Bionic Bat* (see Figure 17.3) made its first flight on August 20, 1983. On September 25, 1983, Parker MacCready flew the course in 159 s and the team claimed the Kremer Speed Prize. The MIT *Monarch* team knew that it could not beat this speed. However, the RAeS HPAG committee disallowed the claim because it could not be shown that the battery was completely discharged prior to the 10-min pilot charging period.

Paul MacCready decided to dispense with stored energy, and his plane, now renamed the *Gossamer Swift*, flew in April 1984. However, in June 1984, after the *Monarch B* had won the first prize, MacCready returned to the use of stored energy, and on July 18 Parker MacCready flew the course in 163 s. This improved on the *Monarch B* time by considerably more than 5%, and the team won the second prize of £5,000. Speed based on a nominal mile was 22 mph.

Holger Rochelt took *Musculair I* (without energy storage) (Rochelt, 1984) around the speed course in 165 s on August 3, 1984, and, unaware of the *Bionic Bat's* success on July 18, thought that he had won the second Prize. On August 21 he improved on both times to finish in 151 s. Thus he won the third Kremer Speed Prize, and his second Kremer Prize.

With no major changes to the *Bionic Bat*, Bryan Allen covered the course in 143 s on December 2, 1984, improving on the previous time by 5.8% and winning the fourth Kremer Speed Prize. Speed based on a nominal mile was 25 mph.

Musculair II. In February 1985 *Musculair I* was severely damaged in a highway accident. The Rochelts and Schöberl decided to design and build *Musculair II* specifically for the speed course (Schöberl, 1986). No energy storage would be used. To win another prize, the time now had to be improved to 135 s. On October 1, 1985, Holger Rochelt flew the *Musculair II* around the course in 141 s, and on October 2, in 122 s. Thus he won the team's third Kremer Prize with a 15% improvement on the previous winner, at a nominal speed of 30 mph, 50% faster than the original target at the start of the competition just over two years earlier. The RAeS closed the competition shortly afterwards, although the same course is still recognized by the FAI for speed records.

Swift Series. A series of three aircraft were built by students at Nihon University to compete for the Kremer Speed Prize. *Swift A* and *Swift B* had the configuration of a high-performance sailplane, a recumbent pilot, and a propeller on a pylon above the wing. *Swift C* was similar to *Musculair I*. All had about 6 kg of twisted rubber inside the tail boom. The transmission was a twisted Shimano bicycle chain. Pilot Kouichi Nakamura said in 1992 that these aircraft were easy to fly; however, no official entry for the speed competition was made (Nakamura, 1992).

Part 4 HPF With Other Goals: 1985 to Present

Although later Kremer prizes were announced before Kremer's death in 1992, the most significant activities in HPF since 1985 have been carried out with individually set objectives.

The Light Eagle, the Daedalus, and Mythic Flight

After the Kremer-Prize-winning flight of *Monarch B* on May 11, 1984, the team of MIT current and former students wondered if their involvement in HPF was over. And then someone conceived of the idea of retracing the mythical flight of Daedalus from Crete to the Greek mainland, a distance 3 times the width of the English Channel. In February 1985 the Smithsonian Institution gave the group some initial backing after they made a proposal based on preliminary studies by Juan Cruz, Mark Drela, Steve Finberg, and Barbara and John Langford. The official first phase of the project was, then, from April 1985 to April 1986. The conclusion of the study was that the Aegean could indeed by crossed by an HPA. Pilot selection would be important. Drela calculated that for this trip (and generally on a typical HPA), the power needed would be directly proportional to the weight of the pilot producing it. Hence, suitability equated, in round terms, to how fast one could run upstairs, or (in SI units) watts/kg. Later, physiologist Ethan Nadel of Yale University and Steve Bussolari of MIT were responsible for pilot selection and training, using a sophisticated dynamometer.

The next phase was sponsored by Anheuser Busch, and the plane on which construction started was called the *Michelob Light Eagle*. The group was a little embarrassed at being sponsored by a beer company, and referred to the plane by the last two names whenever possible. Eighteen members of the MIT group devoted 15,000 hours to build the plane. The first flight was in October 1986 at Hanscom Field, Bedford, Massachusetts. The wingspan was increased to 34.7 m for test flights at NASA's Dryden Flight Research Facility (CA) in January 1987. On January 22, Glenn Tremml surpassed the *Gossamer Albatross* long-distance record by flying 58.7 km (36.5 mi). Lois McCallin's flight of 15.44 km (10 mi) in 37 min 38 s established feminine records for duration and closed-course distance recognized by the FAI.

A separate series of flight tests were made with *Light Eagle* from December 1987 to March 1988. This research was aided by J.E. Murray of NASA-Dryden, who was interested in the relevance of the data to the design of high-altitude pilotless drones. The flights were also invaluable pilot training for all five *Daedalus* pilots: Erik Schmidt, Frank Scioscia, Glenn Tremml, Greg Zack, and Kanellos Kanellopoulos. A video recorder and a pair of mirrors were fitted to the plane so that both wing tips and the tail could be seen in one picture. The airframe was fitted with accelerometers, rate gyros, and strain gauges to measure aircraft motion and wing and tail-boom bending. The computer that polled these sources 20 times per second weighed 1 kg (2 lb) and had a half-megabyte memory. The data were processed on a NASA computer the same day to give useful results for the next day's flying.

The *Light Eagle* was the precursor to the *Daedalus* (see Figure 16.12), which was considerably lighter because it was designed to a lower load factor, and

because a higher grade of carbon was used for the spar. There were no ailerons on *Daedalus*, whereas on the *Light Eagle* the outer 4 m of the wing could rotate. The weight thus saved more than offset the slightly heavier wing-skinning foam used. Parts for two airframes were made simultaneously. United Technologies Corporation backed *Daedalus* with $500,000, and there were many other smaller sponsors.

The first flight of the first Daedalus airframe, *Daedalus-87*, was in November 1987. Flight trials were satisfactory until a loss of control leading to spiral divergence resulted in a crash in February, 1988. This was attributed to insufficient dihedral and to the rudder cable stretching. Construction of *Daedalus-88* was stepped up, and *Daedalus-87* was repaired. On March 26, 1988, the Hellenic Air Force transported all three aircraft to their Heraklion base on Crete. This conveniently had a runway pointing straight out to sea. The group received magnificent support from several organizations in Greece, both governmental and private.

Weather data indicated that there were maybe 3 or 4 days a year when the weather would be suitable for the flight, and two had already occurred just before arrival. The team had to wait until April 23 for the weather along the whole flight path to be suitable. The pilots were on rotation, and that day it was the turn of the Greek national cycling champion Kanellos Kanellopoulos. He took off, glided from the 40-m cliff, and pedaled out over the escort boats. His airspeed was 7 m/s, compared with the 5 m/s of the *Gossamer Albatross*. He was blessed with a tail wind, whereas Bryan Allen had to pedal into a head wind. At his destination, the island of Santorin, there was turbulence close to the hot beach, and gusts snapped first the tail boom and then the starboard wing 6 m from land. Kanellopoulos swam to shore, completing the trip under his own power. His astonishing distance record of 119 km seemed likely to stand for a considerable time, but is currently being challenged by the Raven project in Seattle (Illian, 1994).

Velair 88 and Velair 89: Use of Model-Aircraft Servo Control

Peer Frank of Stuttgart was a former glider pilot and racing cyclist. He had flown the *Pelargos 2*, *Pelargos 3*, and the *Musculair II*, and he had contributed to the aerodynamic design of the *Pelargos 3*. He started design on his own plane after graduating from college in 1986 and began building it with two friends in May 1987. Named *Velair 88*, it first

Empty weight:	70 lbs.
All up weight:	229 lbs.
Span:	112 ft.
Length:	28 ft. 9 ins.
Prop diam:	11.3 ft.
Wing area:	332 sq. ft.
Design speed:	14-17 m.p.h.
Power:	0-27 hp.
Prop R.P.M.:	108

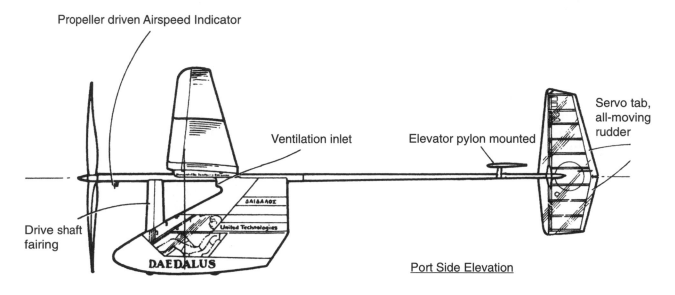

Propeller driven Airspeed Indicator

Ventilation inlet

Elevator pylon mounted

Servo tab, all-moving rudder

Drive shaft fairing

DAEDALUS

Port Side Elevation

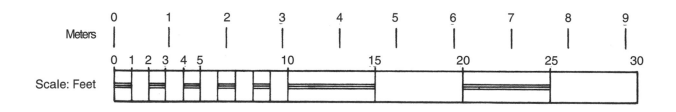

Meters

Scale: Feet

FIGURE 16.12 *Daedalus*, built by an MIT student-faculty team (the faculty being former student members of earlier HPA teams) flew from Crete to Santorin, 119 km, on April 23, 1988, piloted by Greek national cycling champion Kanellos Kanellopoulos.

Drawn by A.A.P. Lloyd

flew on August 9, 1988, and in 1989, he could fly the 3,100-m length of the runway.

The subsequent sophisticated aircraft, *Velair 89*, had the usual pod-and-boom layout of the period, but was distinguished by the bean-shaped pod slung low from the wing to reduce interference drag. Lateral control was by rotating wing tips actuated by model-aircraft servos. The plane first flew on September 24, 1989.

Japan International Birdman Rally

This annual one-day rally is organized and sponsored by the Yomiuri Telecasting Corporation as a spectator event on Lake Biwa, Japan's biggest lake. There have been many similar events in other parts of the world, and their object is more to entertain the audience with comical falls into the water than to promote HPF. The Japan International Birdman Rally does both.

The event was first held in 1977. Entrant Number 1 covered 2.02 m, and the best in the contest that year was 82.44 m. In the mid-eighties, however, a few people started taking it seriously and in 1985 the winner covered 290 m, competing alongside jokers with big funny hats for extra wing area who covered distances of only 4 or 5 m.

Since then, the character of the Rally has been transformed, and it now takes a respected place in the calendar of HPF events. Building and test flying for this event now dominates worldwide over all other HPA work. The great public interest is testimony to the value Japan puts on engineering and engineering education. Individuals and teams from schools, universities, and companies build aircraft in two categories: true human-powered aircraft and human-launched gliders. A large ramp is built out into a bay, and the aircraft are carried up and launched from a height of 10 m off a 10-m-long runway inclined at 3.5°. Many craft are beautifully made; many also break up on launch and the pilot is plucked unceremoniously from the water. The aircraft have to cope with whatever wind and weather conditions occur at the time of launch. They have to be built, also, to be assembled on land and carried up the narrow track of the ramp. Craft are sacrificed as they plunge, either directly or after a glorious celebrated flight, into the lake.

In 1993 previous winners *Aeroscepsy* were the favorite with pro cyclist Kazuo Ohishi as pilot in their *Gokuraku Tonbo*, which had flown 4,436 m from an ordinary takeoff (Kataoka, 1993).

They were competing against Motoki Noro in Nihon University's *Möwe X*, a sophisticated machine with bevel gears and a variable-pitch propeller. *Aeroscepsy* was allocated to fly first, and Ohishi gave it all he could. He reached a speed greater than that which the wings of this high-performance plane were designed to withstand, and the plane broke up after only 44 m.

Möwe X's wheel drive failed during takeoff, and the craft flopped off the edge of the platform. But with a burst of power, the pilot was able to pull out of the dive and continue to fly for 2,180 m, thereby gaining the Birdman Cup for that year.

There is still a prize for the "Funniest Birdman," but others are planning to cross 17-km-wide Lake Biwa rather than fall into it.

American Helicopter Society's Sikorsky Prize

In May 1980, the American Helicopter Society (AHS) announced the Igor I. Sikorsky Human-Powered Helicopter Competition. The object was to hover for 1 min and reach a height of 3 m (Drees, 1993).

It is much harder to get airborne using rotating wings rather than fixed wings. A dozen or so HPH have been built and tested indoors, usually in sports halls. The only serious U.K. machine was experienced helicopter engineer Andrew Cranfield's 4-bladed *Vertigo*, which had a rotor diameter of 24 m (79 ft) and structure typical of a fixed-wing HPA. Occasionally, it has been claimed that an HPH has hovered. Nihon University named one of their machines *A Day Fly* because it was thought that one day in December 1985 it did fly.

Since the mid-1980s, students at California Polytechnic State University at San Luis Obispo, with project manager Neal Saiki, have been working on the Da Vinci helicopter project. On December 10, 1989, the *Da Vinci 3* took off and hovered for 7 s, reaching a height of 200 mm, powered by pilot Greg McNeil, an Olympic-standard cyclist.

One-rotor operation is made possible by the propulsion system, consisting of a small propeller on each helicopter blade that pulls the blade around. The propellers are spool driven, thus putting a limit on the duration of the pilot effort. The weight of the craft had been reduced to 44 kg.

Toshio Kataoka and Kouichi Nakamura have been working on their 24-m, 36-kg *Mitsubachi* HPH since 1988 (Nakamura, 1992). The rotors, which revolve once every 12 s, are driven by legs and hands via chain and cord.

Later Nihon University HPHs have been the 1985 *Papillon A, Papillon B,* and *Papillon C,* the first two having counterrotating concentric rotors like those of *A Day Fly.* All were supervised by Akira Naito who, since his retirement in 1991, had been personally developing a four-rotor HPH, *YURI I,* with each rotor at one end of a girder. Each 10-m rotor has a *Daedalus* design aerofoil, DAE 11, and revolves once every 5 s. On March 7, 1994, with Norikatsu Ikeuchi piloting, *YURI I* was officially observed hovering above the Nihon University gym floor for 19.46 s. Since then, the *YURI I* has hovered several times. Ward Griffiths, an American woman with no special training, became the first female HPH pilot with her August 1994 flight in *YURI I.* On her second attempt, she hovered the *YURI I* for 8.6 s, observed by delegates at an HPF symposium.

Kremer Seaplane Competition

This competition involves takeoff from water, flight in a figure-eight pattern, and landing on water. No HPA has taken off from water, but recent developments in human-powered boats have shown that the required speed may be attainable.

Kremer Marathon Competition

For this competition, the craft must complete a figure-eight flight of standard marathon distance within an hour. One likely contender for the marathon prize is Wayne Bliesner with *Marathon Eagle,* a very sophisticated plane. The wing is made in a mold, meaning that the shape can be the optimum double curvature. Also, the skin can carry load, thus saving spar weight. *Marathon Eagle* will be the first HPA to have a retractable undercarriage. To avoid the adverse effects of sideslip, Bliesner is hinging the rear part of the pod like a rudder, following a similar system proposed for a road HPV.

The Future

The dream of having a vehicle in a shed that you can wheel out and pedal into the air has been real-ized by a very few people on a very few days of exceptionally calm weather. The challenge now is to design more weatherworthy and practical craft that might stimulate wider participation in human-powered flight.

References

Czerwinski, W. (1967, January). Structural tests in the development of man-powered aircraft. *Journal of the Royal Aeronautical Society,* pp. 9–13.

Drees. (1993). HP challenge. *Vertiflight,* **39**(1), 32–34.

Illian, P.R. (1994, August). Human-powered airplane simulator. In *Proceedings of the Human-Powered Flight International Symposium.* Bellevue, WA.

Kataoka, T. (1993). HPH *YURI I. HPV news of Japan,* p. 1.

Kimura, H. (1977). Development of MPA in Nihon University. *AeroModeller Annual,* pp. 25–32.

Marsden, A., Williams, D., & Lassière, A. (1961). Southampton's man-powered aircraft. *Flight,* **23,** 787–788.

Moulton, R.G. (1983, August). New MPA speed competition. *AeroModeller,* pp. 366–388.

Nakamura, K. (1992, January). *Human powered aircraft of Japan.* Paper presented at the RAeS HPAG Symposium, London.

Reay, D.A. (1977). *The history of man-powered flight.* Oxford: Pergamon Press.

Rochelt, G. (1984, July). Musculair Fliegen mit Muskelkraft. *Aerokurier,* pp. 794–795.

Roper, C. (1991). *Review of human powered flight to 1990.* London: Author.

Schöberl, E. (1986, Summer). *Musculair I & II. Human Power,* pp. 1–6.

Shenstone, B.S. (1960, August). Engineering aspects in man-powered flight. *Journal of the Royal Aeronautical Society,* pp.471–477.

Sherwin, K. (1976). *To fly like a bird.* Folkestone, UK: Bailey Brothers and Swinfen.

To, F.E. (1985, June). *Phoenix. Aerospace,* pp. 6–12.

17

GOSSAMER AIRCRAFT AND WHERE THEY LEAD

Paul B. MacCready

Winning the first Kremer Prize in 1977 (the largest in aviation history at that time) with the *Gossamer Condor* started the Gossamer team on a series of unusual developments that are still continuing. Working in relatively unexplored areas stimulates innovation, and the results broaden perspectives of everyone who learns about them. When the developments involve doing more with less, and emphasize the interface between nature and technology, one even finds oneself developing insights about the serious issues of civilization's global survival. This chapter gives a personalized view of the various vehicle developments, with special attention to viewing them in a larger context.

By his large prize, Kremer assured that humankind's oldest aviation dream would be achieved—a dream that everyone understood to be of no direct practical value once we began flying with engines. Offering a substantial prize can indeed foster various technological developments. However, when one tries to concoct prize rules one quickly realizes how special Kremer's challenge was: technologically just barely achievable, and with winning based solely on easily quantified performance, for a development that would not have high priority were it not for the prize.

Kremer's challenge was far different than that which ordinarily confronts vehicle designers in the U.S. Conventionally, to make a new vehicle we incorporate an existing fossil-fuel engine or develop a new one and operate with hundreds of horsepower. However, Kremer asked, in effect, that we fly on 250 W (1/3 hp). His prize was far more important than is widely appreciated. I consider that civilization's primary challenge now is to reach a comfortable accommodation with the flora and fauna and resources of this limited earth. Kremer inspired us to pay attention to getting by with the puny power of a human, as had been the case when our ancestors coexisted with the natural world instead of taking it over.

The Aircraft

The focus here is on the primary Gossamer aircraft, the *Gossamer Condor* and the *Gossamer Albatross*. *Gossamer* is a noun denoting spider threads that occasionally drift and alight in such profusion that they cover a grassy field; the word has come to mean something fragile, flimsy, tenuous, cobweblike—

and so is appropriate for these transparent wire-braced, human-powered airplanes. We chose *condor* in honor of the giant, ugly, slow flying, impractical (and nearly extinct) California condor. *Albatross* was chosen because it represents the large, slender-winged bird that soars for long distances just over the waves.

We also mention here the *Gossamer Penguin*—a three-quarter-size backup version of the *Gossamer Albatross* that was pressed into service as a research tool for solar-powered flight. The transparent *Bionic Bat* that won two Kremer speed prizes was somewhat analogous to the *Gossamer Condor* and the *Gossamer Albatross*, in being fragile and thus, for safety, limited to flight no higher than 5 to 7 m (15 to 20 ft). It melded an electrical power system with human muscle, thus perfectly fitting the word *bionic*. *Bat* seemed an appropriate name: a mammal that flies silently close to the ground in the still air of dusk.

The Gossamer Condor

Many authors describe the *Gossamer Condor*, its development, and the remarkable team that built it (Brown, 1988; Burke, 1980; Grosser, 1981; and MacCready, 1978, 1979). A 28-min video by Ben Shedd, "Flight of the Gossamer Condor" (that won the Academy Award for short documentaries in 1979) is available from Direct Cinema Ltd. (P.O. Box 69699, Los Angeles, CA 90069, 213-652-8000). Here we will not provide details that are covered more completely elsewhere, but rather give comments about some special aspects of the program.

The primary principle underlying the *Gossamer Condor* was to get power requirements low by making the vehicle large and light rather than by making it elegant and efficient like a sailplane.

Ignoring propeller efficiency (which can always be kept high by proper shaping and sizing), the minimum power to fly (*P*) for an airplane of a given shape (hence characterized by a particular glide ratio or *L/D*, where *L* is the lift and *D* is the drag), weight *W*, and size (say wing span, *b*, although any other dimension would suffice), is simply

$$P \sim \frac{1}{(L/D)} \cdot W^{3/2} \cdot b^{-1}$$

This formula is equivalent to a statement that power is weight times descent speed during gliding, noting that forward speed is proportional to the square root of wing loading, weight per unit area. Prior to 1976, the conventional approach to

human-powered flight had been to make the $1/(L/D)$ term small, in other words a large *L/D*, by using the efficient sailplane as a role model. However, the required elegance of construction made *W* large (and, when there were the inevitable crashes, made repairs difficult). *P* is extra sensitive to *W* because *W* appears in this equation with a bigger exponent than the $1/(L/D)$ term. My approach was essentially to ignore glide ratio, (using a simple hang glider rather than a sailplane as the role model), to keep *W* as small as possible (of course the pilot is the main contributor to *W*), and then simply to make *b* as large as needed to get power down sufficiently. Exterior wire bracing, basically 0.03-in. diameter piano wire, was the structural key permitting *b* to be large while *W* remained small.

Every vehicle development discussed here was the result of an evolving team of innovative dedicated people—too many to list, except to note that Peter Lissaman, AeroVironment vice president for aerosciences, filled a senior aerodynamist role for every project. The *Gossamer Condor* project, being the first one, was especially memorable—a remarkable year-long happening for all of us. As I look back at it from the perspective of an additional 17 years, I am amazed to see that the systems-management and systems-engineering approach still make sense, in spite of the fact that as the project was proceeding we made plenty of mistakes and went up various blind alleys. Many factors deserve mention here, starting with the matter of our having more than our share of good luck; other factors included the following:

- My background included familiarity with hang gliders and fragile indoor model airplanes, aircraft that provided valuable insights for the Gossamer aircraft. Although my academic background featured aerodynamics, I had essentially no background in aircraft structures and so found it easier than more experienced aeronautical engineers to draw on the unique structural features of these role models. (However, I am happy that the structure of the airliners in which I fly are designed by engineers with appropriate experience.)

- The need for the prize to pay off a large debt provided a continuing stimulus to me to keep the project at high priority. This helped us focus clearly on the goal: Win the prize as quickly and inexpensively as possible. We did not have the distraction of goals that some other teams held high: having fun, being excited by pioneering, being interested in historical significance, or developing technical publications. For example, we never drew detailed vehicle plans until after the prize was won; we did only the drawings essential to winning. In spite of our focus, the project turned out to have many unexpected wonderful aspects. It brought the family closer together, as everyone pitched in. It got us acquainted with wonderful new friends and reacquainted with old ones. It opened up new opportunities.

- Where precedent is unavailable, getting a simple test vehicle into action early is vital to let you start acquiring some intuition about the dominant phenomena. What you learn could always have been figured out easily by just some clear thinking, without experiment—except that unfortunately such thinking becomes obvious only in hindsight. Also helpful is simple construction, which allows repairs and changes to be made quickly, and simple, safe flight-test procedures that also make obtaining experimental information convenient. This is the wrong approach for creating a standard vehicle, such as a new light plane; theory and experience are already available, and you can confidently handle design for performance, stability and control, and structural integrity.

- Being in southern California was a significant plus. Here, in the world's center of aviation developments, you can readily locate low-wind conditions, airports, hangars, helpers, consultants, and suppliers. For example, a short drive lets you pick up any size and heat treatment of aluminum tubing you want, and in a day or two you can get it chemically milled to the desired wall thickness.

A performance-oriented project such as this can be boiled down to three main rules—so simple they seem trivial, yet they are rarely obeyed. They were followed for the *Gossamer Condor* program, although I was not consciously analyzing our efforts from this perspective at the time.

1. Understand the project goal.

2. Start with a clean sheet of paper (i.e., no preconceived notions). Pretend you have never seen an airplane before—but of course be respectful of the unbreakable laws of conservation of energy and conservation of momentum, which frame aerodynamic theory.

3. Draw on all appropriate technologies. This means using simple techniques when they are suitable, but not being afraid to use advanced techniques when needed, and leaning on others for special expertise when required.

As to Rule 1, for all our projects the goal was to achieve some specific performance (with safety) with as small an investment of time and money as possible. With more work, every vehicle could have been made still more efficient, but that would have been directed toward a different goal.

As to Rule 2, aerodynamic theory defined the approximate size of the wing, and structural considerations dictated exterior wire bracing with spars in compression. Thereafter, every configurational aspect was assessed based on whether or not the feature was essential to propel or control the wing. We always took the simple approach for every challenge and were surprised how often that proved adequate (saving time to focus on the few areas that emerged as especially troublesome).

As to Rule 3, we did a lot of mechanical engineering by crude calculation and then testing. There was no point in careful calculations because the aeroelastic complexities of the vehicle meant it was easier or quicker to establish by experiment what did or didn't work. We employed the latest stability-and-control theory and computer models when these seemed necessary, but we also fell back on a number of arm-waving discussions when the modeling proved confusing or irrelevant.

On August 23, 1977, Bryan Allen piloted and pedaled the *Gossamer Condor* around the Kremer course we had set up at Shafter Airport (see Figure 17.1). The prize, which had stood for 18 years, was won. Then everyone on the project team and many of their friends and relatives got to fly the vehicle (for a short flight you do not need to be a pilot or athlete). A few months later a number of us attended the impressive award ceremony in London. In early 1978 the airplane was put on permanent display at the Smithsonian National Air and Space Museum, near the 1903 Wright Brothers plane and Charles Lindbergh's *Spirit of St. Louis*. This was an honor that none of us had even dreamed about as we were single mindedly working toward winning the prize. The *Gossamer Condor* was the first of five vehicles we developed that are now the property of the Smithsonian.

FIGURE 17.1 Bryan Allen pilots the final *Gossamer Condor* to win the Kremer Prize at Shafter, California, August 23, 1977 (photo by Judy MacCready).

The Gossamer Albatross

The *Gossamer Albatross* was a cleaned-up *Condor*. The aerodynamic principles were the same, but by improving the structure we ended up with a much more accurately contoured configuration. The new plane operated on a third less power, and so we were sure the cyclist (again Bryan Allen) could greatly increase the duration. The plane cruised at about 5.4 m/s (12 mph), as opposed to 4.5 m/s (10 mph) for the *Condor*. Carbon-fiber tubing was substituted for the *Condor*'s aluminum, and the wing shape was refined by using many ribs, a foam leading edge, and tensioned Mylar covering that under heat treatment tightened more in the spanwise than in the chordwise direction. The final propeller was optimized for the cruise condition, using a procedure developed by Eugene Larrabee of MIT.

The Albatross program is described by Allen (1979), Burke (1980), and Grosser (1981). The effort included some new aerodynamic and structures developments, but was not really pioneering in the sense of the Condor program. The big challenges were economic, managerial, and logistic. We built the *Albatross* in the spring of 1978, in response to the announcement of Henry Kremer's new £100,000 prize for a flight across the Channel from England to France. The airplane worked fine right from the beginning, although in its stability and control it was more "squirrelly" than the *Condor*.

After the plane was damaged in a crash in the fall, we had to do some serious thinking about the business aspects of the event. We concluded that sponsorship was required if we were to prepare backup vehicles, perform lots of testing, establish a headquarters in England, rent boats and radios, and in general turn the program into a serious venture with a high probability of success. The Du Pont Company agreed to sponsor us; the *Gossamer Albatross* provided a good example of the use of some of their advanced materials, and it fitted their spirit of pioneering.

By late spring of 1979 we had done many tests on the improved (and often repaired) original vehicle, and had two backup vehicles in advanced stages of preparation. The three vehicles, and all our development facilities, were miraculously transported to England in an RAF C-130, and we set up shop at Manston RAF Base. Six weeks later on June 12, 1979, Bryan Allen piloted the plane across the Channel on the first try (see Figure 17.2).

FIGURE 17.2 The *Gossamer Albatross* enroute from Folkestone to Cape Gris Nez, June 12, 1979 (photo by Don Monroe).

There were many reasons why we were sure this first try could not succeed. We were confident in our pessimism when, some 2 hours into the flight, Bryan was out of drinking water and getting cramps from dehydration. The increasing head wind had added another hour to the needed flight time, and the wind and waves caused turbulence that greatly increased the power required to fly. Bryan logically decided to give up; it was hopeless. But during the hookup maneuver when the team was required to fasten a tow line from the chase boat to the plane, he flew a bit higher, found less turbulence and less power required, and decided to stick it out another 5 min, then another 5 min, and eventually, with both legs cramping, somehow just reached the beach in France. For the first 2 hours it had been a team project, with Bryan a key team member. For the last hour it was a solo performance by Bryan, a virtually impossible feat of human stamina.

The Bionic Bat

Kremer's new prizes for a speed event were small, so one had to have some motive other than economic to participate. We decided the *Bionic Bat* could be justified by serving as a stepping stone for extending the technology of our *Solar Challenger* (a cantilever wing aircraft powered solely by electricity from photovoltaic cells) toward a high-altitude drone airplane or an ultra-low-speed sailplane. The prize rules permitted the pilot to store energy for 10 min immediately prior to flight (say, in a battery), and then use the stored energy to assist the muscles during flight. This flight had to take less than 3 min to circumnavigate around pylons a half mile apart. The next winner had to complete the course at least 5% faster than the previous record holder.

The *Bionic Bat* (see Figure 17.3) won the second and fourth speed prizes: July 18, 1984, piloted by Parker MacCready, time 163 s; December 2, 1984, piloted by Bryan Allen, 143 s. Our battery system was quite inefficient, returning to the propeller only some 25% of the energy extracted from the pilot before the flight. The gears, the motor-generator, and the nicad battery all contributed to the low value. If you just wanted to win the prize you could have omitted the power system, which probably depleted the pilot's energy potential more than it delivered energy; Gunter Rochelt, who won the third and fifth Kremer prizes in Germany, did just that. The first prize was won by MIT with a gossamer-type plane called the *Monarch B*, using battery storage of energy.

FIGURE 17.3 The *Bionic Bat* evolved through many minor configuration changes. In this final form, span was 18 m (60 ft) and weight 28 kg (62 lb) when two Kremer Speed Prizes were won in 1984. The airplane appeared in the Omnimax film "A Freedom to Move," the theme movie for the international Expo 86 in Vancouver.

Conclusion

A practical airplane must be structurally sound, must be controllable, and must have some climbing capability—all adequate to permit routine, safe flight in the real atmosphere well above the ground. Looking realistically at sizes and weights of modern composite aircraft that would be deemed practical for carrying one person aloft, one is forced to the conclusion that a practical airplane must have 2 kW (3 hp) or more available occasionally, and at least half that much continuously. Human power falls far short of this power requirement, and so I believe that human-powered aircraft will not achieve practicality, at least in the ordinary sense of the word. If you define practical in a more unusual way—as winning giant prizes or competitions, as providing enjoyable educational experience, as serving as a catalyst for broadening perspectives about efficient transportation or the nature-technology interface, or as stimulating innovation—then human-powered aircraft can be practical.

If you want to fly, use an engine. For the price of a dinner for four at a good restaurant, you can purchase a small model-airplane engine that, with 2% of the weight of a human, can continuously put out 5 to 10 times the power of a human and permit safe, versatile flight. Even a small electric drive can do much better than a person, while offering the advantage of quietness compared to a reciprocating engine. The realm of gliding offers a different approach. In still air, an efficient hang glider or lightweight sailplane consumes 1 to 1.5 kW (1.5 to 2 hp), this power being derived from the potential energy represented by its weight times its height. With good up currents, the glider may acquire energy in rising air at rates of 4 to 8 kW (5 to 10 hp) and consume energy at comparable power rates when dashing rapidly to the next up current. Human power is thus negligible compared to the power that gliding vehicles use.

In comparing the speeds obtainable with human-powered vehicles operating in the air or on a smooth road, the advantage goes to the land vehicle. In contrast to the land machine, power for the airborne machine is converted to a wake of disturbed air: moving backward to provide thrust and downward to provide lift. With land and air human-powered vehicles of comparable elegance, the land vehicle does not waste the energy in such wakes (one does not have to carry along a giant wing) and so will achieve a speed appreciably (say, 20%) higher than the air vehicle. However, with a nonsmooth road or beach or swamp, of course the aerial traveler is not limited, whereas the ground traveler is greatly slowed.

For surface vehicles, no minimum power is required inasmuch as no minimum speed is necessary. Thus, human power can be deemed practical for bikes and boats. This emphasis on low speed for some bicycle applications means there is no concern for aerodynamics, but at higher speeds, as with racing, aerodynamics looms large. Paradoxically, bicycle-racing rules permit some aerodynamic features, but prohibit others, in an evolving, arbitrary manner. Rules thwart technological innovation, but they are needed to make competitions between riders fair—and competitions stimulate a sport and thus permit the economic benefits of mass production (MacCready, 1987). As more attention is paid to aerodynamics for conventional bikes as well as for the vehicles racing in IHPVA events, the effects of wind get more priority—effects on vehicle stability, on vehicle drag, and on vehicle propulsion. Surface vehicles can operate solely on human power, can operate far better with motors (and then can also be heavier, more rugged, and safer), and in some cases can benefit significantly from wind.

In summary, for all human-powered vehicles of land, sea, and air, there is a need to define the goal and decide what is practical. Health, fun, competition, design, experience, pioneering, and transportation are all reasonable goals. Human-powered airplanes are so complex to build, so large to transport and assemble, and require such special flying sites and weather conditions that a critical assessment shows they are precluded from aiming at most of the goals that inspire human-powered land vehicle developments. There will be continuing developments, as demonstrated dramatically by the elegant *Daedalus* program of MIT, but I feel that IHPVA's future excitement rests with surface vehicles. For flight, there is still an exciting potential for animal power (meaning an animal other than human and not using its wings for propulsion)

(MacCready, 1986). Having a hamster keep itself aloft for 3 min represents a significant technological challenge that would not be expensive but would require researchers to explore new, broad aspects of the nature-technology interface.

References

Allen, B. (1979). Winged victory of the *Gossamer Albatross*. *National Geographic*, **156**, 640–651.

Brown, K.A. (1988). *Inventors at work*. Redmond, WA: Tempus Books.

Burke, J.D. (1980). *The Gossamer Condor and Albatross: A case study in aircraft design* (Report No. AV-R-80/540). Simi Valley, CA: AeroVironment, Inc.

Grosser, M. (1981). *Gossamer odyssey*. Boston: Houghton Mifflin.

MacCready, P.B. (1978, February). *Flight on 0.33 horsepower: The Gossamer Condor*. Paper presented at the American Institute of Aeronautics and Astronautics 14th Annual Meeting and Technical Display, Washington, D.C.

MacCready, P.B. (1979). Flight of the *Gossamer Condor*. In *Science Year 1979* (pp. 85–99). Chicago: WorldBook-Childcraft International.

MacCready, P.B. (1986). Muscle-powered flight. In A. Abbott (Ed.), *Proceedings of the Third International Human-Powered Vehicle Symposium*. Indianapolis: International Human Powered Vehicle Association.

MacCready, P.B. (1987). Goals, rules, and technological innovation. In E.R. Burke & M.M. Newson (Eds.), *Medical and scientific aspects of cycling* (pp. 253–263). Champaign, IL: Human Kinetics.

MacCready, P.B., Lissaman, P.B.S., & Jex, H.R. (1979, February). Aerodynamics of flight at speeds under 5 m/s. In *Proceedings of the Third Man Powered Aircraft Group Symposium*. London: Royal Aeronautical Society.

18

CONCEPTION AND OPTIMIZATION OF HUMAN-POWERED AIRCRAFT[1]

Ernst Schöberl

The progress made in fiber-reinforced composites and the resulting advanced aerodynamic design (especially in laminar-flow airflows[2]) over the past 20 years has made it possible to build sophisticated human-powered airplanes with half the weight of earlier human-powered aircraft (HPA). The optimum configuration seems to be a conventional high-wing monoplane with a faired hanging cockpit and an all-moving rudder. At a flying speed of about 8.5 m/s this configuration would have a wing span of about 25 m and a power requirement of slightly below 200 W (near the ground). This chapter provides guidance to designers of HPA by considering the design of a future HPA which we will call the *Cyclair*.

The Cyclair Optimum HPA

The *Cyclair* can be built at a weight of slightly more than 30 kg with the following design characteristics:

- Fully sandwich-covered[3] wings with a laminar-flow airfoil
- A carbon-fiber-reinforced epoxy main spar in four sections designed for 3 times the static load
- A sandwich-covered cabin with semirecumbent pilot position
- An all-moving elevator
- An all-moving rudder with auxiliary rudder
- A rear propeller to protect the plane from avoidable turbulence

The *Cyclair* is similar to the MIT-designed *Daedalus*, but is a little smaller and lighter and is optimized for a higher flying speed. It would also have dimensions similar to the Musculair series. The data on size and weight for the two Musculairs are shown below.

Musculair 1	Musculair 2
span: 22 m	span: 19.5 m
empty weight: 28 kg	empty weight: 25 kg

Canard[4] Versus Conventional Configuration

Although many pioneers have achieved success with canard-type planes (e.g., the Wright Brothers, Focke, MacCready, and Burt Rutan and Jeana Yeager with their *Voyager*), this concept, despite its stall safety, has some disadvantages:

- The fuselage surfaces located far in front of the center of gravity make yaw control difficult (sometimes a power-consuming swept-back main-wing design is necessary).

- The lift of the canard wing is usually generated with too much induced drag because of its low aspect ratio (aspect ratio is span ÷ chord).

- The main wing usually cannot operate at the best glide ratio or minimum sinking velocity, as its angle of attack cannot be adjusted as with the canard wing.

- The canard wing affects the field of vision.

These disadvantages can be avoided by using a conventional high-wing-monoplane configuration with faired hanging cabins and all-moving rudders. Although the high-wing configuration does not benefit from the increased lift from an aerodynamic phenomenon called *ground effect*[5], it has been found that contribution of ground effect from the use of low-winged monoplanes has been generally overestimated.

Cantilevered Versus Wire-Braced Construction

As experience is accumulated in high-strength ultralight construction, there are increasing advantages in using cantilevered structures (those in which there are no external bracing wires supporting the wings and fuselage). Rough estimates at the early design stage of *Musculair 1* showed that the increased power demand due to the higher structural weight of a design without bracing wires is outweighed by the lower drag of a cantilevered design.

Recommended Elevators and Rudders

Spring-compensated, all-moving elevators and rudders have turned out to be both lightweight and effective. An all-moving vertical tail plane with auxiliary rudder seems to be better for lateral control. Airfoils with 9% to 10% thickness, like the NACA 0009 or the FX100 MP, are favorable, as they work well, even at low Reynolds numbers[6] (below 300,000). Although elliptical tail wings are best aerodynamically, the trapezoid shape is advantageous as it can be built easier and lighter. The positioning of the elevator must avoid the down-wash turbulence of the wing at all flight positions and angles of attack. (This caused considerable problems in *Musculair 2*.)

Recommended Wing-Section Shape and Structure

Only the best laminar-flow airfoils that could operate in the range of Reynolds numbers from 300,000 to 800,000 should be considered, such as the FX 76 MP, designed in 1976 by F.X. Wortmann especially for HPAs.

Though, as with elevators and rudders, an elliptically shaped wing seems aerodynamically the best, a trapezoid wing is preferred for design and aerodynamic reasons. A trapezoid wing can be built to be simpler, lighter in weight and more accurate in shape, and the airfoil operates better at the wing tips because of the larger chord length and higher Reynolds numbers there.

The increase in induced drag near the ground from not following the ideal elliptical lift distribution is small. More important are well-shaped and profiled wing tips. With semicircular wing tips, the effective wing span is increased and hence the induced drag is slightly reduced.

To build a lightweight, strong wing that is stiff torsionally and in bending, with the necessary accuracy required for laminar-flow airfoils, carbon-fiber-reinforced spar and foam-fiberglass sandwich covering should be used (see Figure 18.1). For aerodynamic reasons the sandwich has to cover at least the whole laminar area on the upper side and from the nose to the curvature inflection on the lower side. To get the wing torsionally stiff enough the nose covering and the spar should form a closed tube. However, the sandwich covering and the carbon spar deform differently under load. On the wings of the *Musculair 2* boundary-layer transition occurred nearer the leading edge than desired—just behind the spar on the upper side. This can be avoided in future aircraft by using a slightly flexible skin covering the spar. The best solution seems to be a wing structure as shown in Figure 18.1 with an integral flexible aileron connection. These flexible connections have been tested successfully in gliders (*Speed Astir*) and model aircraft.

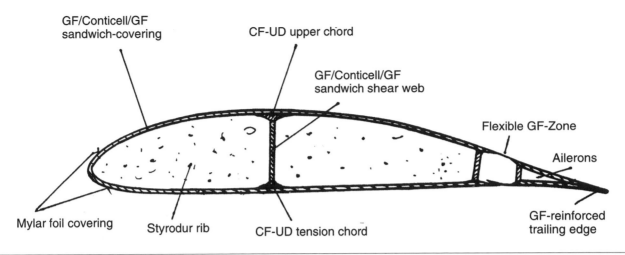

FIGURE 18.1 Wing structure with Wortmann airfoil FX MP 160. GF = glass-fiber web; CF-UD = carbon-fiber unidirectional rovings.

Fuselage

Tests have shown that the pilot delivers about the same power output in the semirecumbent position as in the upright position. In the semirecumbent position the cabin can be made smaller. The aerodynamic drag can be further reduced by using an extremely light fiberglass sandwich fairing, at least in the front, which ensures a more accurate shape and surface finish. The supporting fuselage structure with the wing connections and the stabilizer strut in which the propeller shaft rotates are preferably made of carbon-sandwich tubes.

Drive and Propulsion

Although the flapping wing can in theory be made highly efficient, the propeller is by far the most efficient means of propulsion. A maximum efficiency of 90% can be reached in HPA through the use of relatively large slowly running propellers designed for minimum induced losses by, for instance, Larrabee's (1984) elegant method.

A large propeller adds weight and beyond a certain size the tips are likely to strike the ground when the aircraft is taking off or landing. The diameters required for good efficiency (89%) and medium efficiency (85%) are given in Figure 18.2.

The chain drive is highly efficient, lightweight, and reliable when carefully designed and built. In HPA projects in Japan and Germany, it was found that the pedal power output could be improved by about 5% through the use of an elliptical chainwheel.[7]

The propeller often has been located behind the wings (MacCready's *Bionic Bat*) or behind the tail plane (Rochelt's *Musculair 1* and *Musculair 2*) to protect fuselage and wings from the turbulent slipstream. The middle and rear arrangements are aerodynamically better. Although it requires a long propeller shaft, a pusher propeller seems best as the tail plane works more effectively in the accelerated air flow before a propeller and the power demand of the HPA can be slightly reduced.

Controls

Most HPA designers have arrived at elegant and ergonomic controls. Because precise control with steering handlebars (Figure 18.3 shows the MIT design) is very important, the pilot must remain almost immobile above the hips to allow the controls to be handled sensitively, while cycling with high power output.

In this design the pilot has only to imagine holding the wingtips and moving the controls will cause the plane to perform the desired maneuvers. Sideways tilting of the control bar operates the ailerons, rotation around the vertical axis operates the main rudder, and tilting the handgrips around the horizontal axis operates the elevator. As the aerodynamic control forces are rather small, it is practical to install self-centering spring units.

For long-distance flights it is desirable to install an automatic control system to reduce the pilot's mental work load. Such an autopilot can improve the system performance by maintaining flight near minimum power requirement. For the *Daedalus*

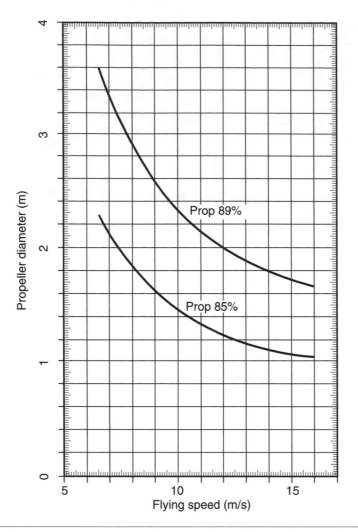

FIGURE 18.2 Propeller diameters required for efficiencies of 85% and 89%.

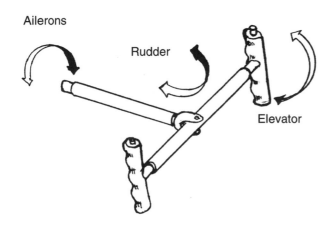

FIGURE 18.3 MIT design of three-axis control stick.

project the MIT team designed an autopilot that weighed only a few hundred grams; this allowed the pilot to concentrate more on power performance and navigation.

The Resulting Cyclair Concept

The result of these recommendations is an aircraft combining minimum power demand and good-natured flying behavior: the cantilevered high-wing monoplane, *Cyclair* (see Figure 18.4), with laminar-flow airfoils, hanging faired cabin with the pilot in a semirecumbent position, all-moving elevator, all-moving rudder with auxiliary rudder, and pusher propeller. This basic aircraft can be designed for different cruising speeds and flight durations.

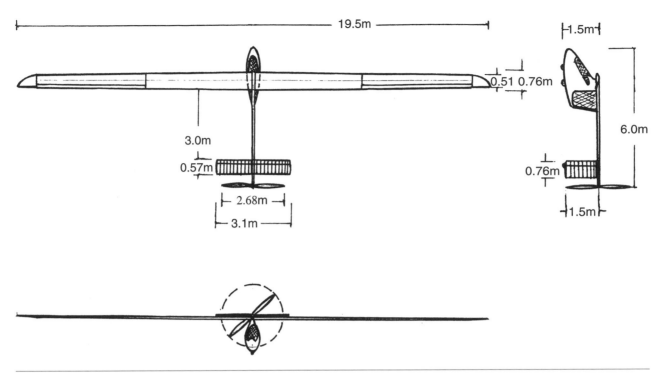

FIGURE 18.4 The cantilevered high-wing monoplane *Cyclair* combines minimum power demand with good-natured flying behavior.

Aircraft Optimization for Various Flight Conditions

HPAs can be optimized for any point in a range from long-distance flight with minimum power requirement to short-duration, high-speed flight.

In designing the *Cyclair*, we used the following guidelines in making the optimizations:

- Ground-effect factor of 0.8[8] (for flying at an altitude of about one-fourth wing span)

- Lift coefficient not over 1.1 to ensure enough reserve lift for stability and control

- Reynolds numbers not below 300,000 to avoid unexpected laminar-bubble separation with hysteresis effects[9]

- Minimum wing chord length of 700 mm for a low-speed, long-distance plane, and 400 mm for a high-speed plane

Both the chord and span of wings decrease with increasing flight speed, resulting in the rapid decrease in wing area shown in Figure 18.5.

The optimum wing span and chord length of a trapezoid wing with the corresponding sinking velocity and power requirement are given in Figure 18.6 for the whole flying-speed range.

The most important results of the optimization are shown in the velocity polars, Figure 18.7. The minimum power requirement of HPA at the present state of the art is slightly more than 150 W (near the ground), achievable with a low-speed plane (about 6 m/s) of more than 25-m wing span. The author believes that wing spans larger than 25 m are not practical, because little further reduction in power requirement is possible and the aircraft becomes hard to control because of the increased moment of inertia, even with extremely lightweight construction. In addition, very low speed aircraft are sensitive to gusts.

For a low-speed plane we have chosen, therefore, a wing of 25-m span (18 m² wing area), with a maximum glide ratio of 44[10] and a power requirement of only 190 W. Such a wing can be satisfactorily handled and controlled by an experienced pilot.

This plane would be capable of covering long-distance flights, even against light head winds, and would not react sensitively to gusts, because of the relatively high flying speed of 6 m/s. At a flight speed of more than 13 m/s, high power is required with an airplane of smaller wingspan. The high-speed aircraft *Musculair 2* showed that first-class athletes are capable of maintaining speeds of over 13 m/s for a few minutes only. With such an airplane it seems possible to fly the

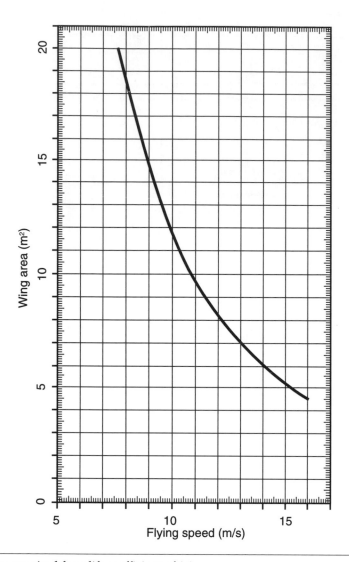

FIGURE 18.5 Wing area required for a lift coefficient of 1.1.

1,500-m speed course in about 100 s without energy storage; this means a flight speed of 54 km/hr (15 m/s). A new speed record could be set with such an airplane.

Technological Outlook

The pinnacle of present HPF might be the 119-km flight of the MIT *Daedalus* from Crete to Santorin. The highly sophisticated technology required and the high degree of athleticism and flying effort of the pilot restricts competitive HPF to a few dedi-

cated enthusiasts and to university teams. With their efforts some improvements in present records are undoubtedly possible.

Other benefits will result from HPF projects. The precise design of high-strength ultralight construction developed for HPA has spurred work in the unusual range of Reynolds numbers between those for model aircraft and those for gliders. The technology developed will also benefit unmanned high-altitude aircraft powered with solar or hybrid energy, used, for example, for communication relays that can remain aloft in the stratosphere for weeks or months.

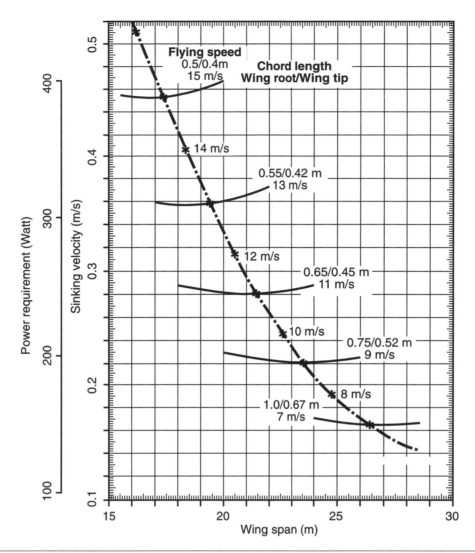

FIGURE 18.6 Minimum sinking velocity, power requirements, and optimum wing configuration of human-powered planes.

Notes

[1]This is an edited and shortened version of a paper presented at the 20th OSTIV Congress at Benalla, Australia in January 1987. It is both a summary of and a sequel to the article on the *Musculair 1* and *Musculair 2* by the same author in the Summer 1986 issue of *Human Power*. It is adapted by permission of *Human Power* (Spring 1987, vol. 6, no. 1).

[2]*Laminar flow* is smooth and steady. On most wings, the flow in the *boundary layer*—the thin layer of air on the surface—is turbulent, which greatly increases the resistance, or drag.

[3]This means that the wing surface is made of a sandwich of a foam core between two film surfaces, instead of only the usual thin, flexible film.

[4]A *canard configuration* is one in which the elevator, and often the rudder, is placed ahead of the main wing, instead of the conventional position on the tail plane.

[5]*Ground effect* is the increased pressure on the underside of a wing flying near the ground. It

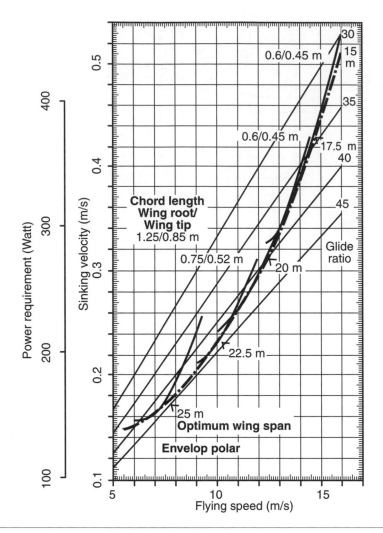

FIGURE 18.7 Velocity polar of human-powered planes with optimum wing configurations.

results from the deflection of the down wash (the downward flow of air) by the ground.

[6]The *Reynolds number* is an inverse measure of flow viscosity. It is defined as (velocity of air relative to wing) × (air density) × (wing chord) ÷ (kinematic air viscosity).

[7]This improvement is larger than found for the use of elliptical chainwheels in bicycles; see chapter 13. However, it is possible that the lower inertia of a propeller versus a bicycle and rider endows an elliptical chainwheel with especially favorable attributes.

[8]The *ground-effect factor* is the ratio of the induced drag near the ground to the induced drag far from

the ground, and is a function only of the altitude-to-span ratio.

[9]*Laminar-bubble separation* is a type of local stalling, or separation of the flow from the wing, that is difficult to eliminate once it occurs.

[10]The *glide ratio* is the ratio of the forward distance divided by the height lost in a glide in still air.

References

Larrabee, E.E. (1984). Propellers for human-powered vehicles. *Human Power*, **3** (2), 10.

V

THE FUTURE

This book focuses on the recent developments in HPV design that have resulted in greatly improved performance; however, improvements in our understanding of the human engine have also contributed to this progress. The future of HPVs will be determined by continued advances in science and engineering, but perhaps more importantly by economic forces.

Human-powered vehicles are now used for three overlapping purposes: utility and transportation, sport and recreation, and physical exercise and health. In today's world the largest use of HPVs occurs in underdeveloped countries where people move themselves and their possessions under their own power. In industrialized countries, where most people can afford internal-combustion engines or other power sources to provide power for most of their transportation needs, HPVs are used prima-

rily for sporting purposes. Many of these people regard HPVs as exercise machines and use them to maintain mental and physical health.

Will HPVs continue to be used primarily for utility in some parts of the world and for sport and recreation in other parts? Will HPVs return to popularity for transportation as a result of technological innovation? In chapter 19 David Gordon Wilson suggests that future roles of HPVs will be determined more by economic forces than by engineering. He gives insight into the real costs and subsidies of automobile travel. In chapter 20 Paul B. MacCready provides some stimulating perspectives on HPV technology and predicts that people will continue to focus on lifestyles that do more with less. He envisions more hybrid technology that balances mechanical devices and nature, mingling human power with solar, wind, or other power sources.

19

POTENTIAL FOR A MAJOR INCREASE IN THE USE OF HPVS[1]

David Gordon Wilson

Before human-powered vehicles (HPVs) are adopted for everyday commuting, shopping, and recreation, they need to become safer and more convenient to use. Even these design developments will not suffice without improvement in highways and the economics of transportation.

The transportation patterns we have in most Western countries have developed largely because of large subsidies. Fully justifiable in most cases at the time of their introduction, these subsidies are anachronistic in today's changed circumstances. In general they have led to congestion, pollution, and environmental degradation. If there is a positive side to these problems, it is that people and politicians now are contemplating radical measures that only a short while ago were unthinkable. By removing even the subsidies for automobiles, a substantial portion of the population might freely choose HPVs for commuting. For this change to occur there should be a concomitant change in the design of HPVs.

The Past: Prologue or Epilogue?

Three distinct revolutions in human-powered land vehicles occurred in the 19th century. In 1817 Karl von Drais introduced the hobbyhorse, or Draisienne. In 1862 to 1866 Pierre Michaux and/or Pierre Lallement brought out the pedaled velocipede, which evolved into the ordinary, or high, bicycle. And the chain-driven "safety" bicycle, developed principally by John Kemp Starley, was very close to the modern configuration of the "standard" bicycle (although Dunlop's pneumatic tires did not become available until 2 years later).

The enthusiasm these early HPVs engendered was amplified because there were so few personal-transportation alternatives other than walking and horseback. Widespread use of the safety bicycle continued long into the automobile age. It is easy to look back longingly to those past days. During my postgraduate apprenticeship I lived in Loughborough, a market town in the English Midlands overlooking the rolling hills of Charnwood Forest. I would bicycle in less than 10 min to the other side of town, where I worked at an engineering company. The firm employed about 5,000 people. A single-lane road led to the parking lot, where there were racks for 2,000 bicycles, spaces for about 10 cars, and a shelter for 10 motorcycles. The bike racks were always full; the car and motorcycle slots were often half empty. The town was small enough for many employees to walk to work, and a large proportion came by bus. Commuting was hassle-free, with lots of banter and greetings shouted to friends on all sides. For longer journeys, buses and trains were readily available and went almost everywhere. You could be in London, a hundred miles away, in an hour and a half. The reason this delightful, even idyllic, arrangement survived was that buying and using a motor vehicle was too expensive an alternative.

Today, not only are automobiles relatively inexpensive, but the inflation-adjusted prices of fuel and oil are almost at their historically lowest levels. Parking curbside at one's place of employment is also priced low. If these prices represented the true costs to society, the laws of economics would produce an optimal system for the nation and the locality. In *The Going Rate: What It Really Costs to Drive* MacKenzie, Dower, and Chen state, however, "Together, the market and external costs of motor-vehicle use that are not reflected directly in user charges amount to almost $300 billion per year, more than 5 percent of the gross domestic product" (1992, p. 23). They account for these unmet costs in these categories: roadway capital and maintenance, highway services, air pollution and climate change, congestion, accidents, noise, damage from vibration, land loss, and the security costs of importing oil. Therefore, motor vehicle use, including parking, is in general highly subsidized.

The result is a very different modern version of the town and plant I described earlier. With automobile subsidies in Loughborough most people would have automobiles and use them for most trips. The plant would have to be out of town to have space for parking and approach roads. Gas stations, repair shops, auto-sales lots, and wrecking yards also would occupy considerable space. Most bus services would disappear, along with railroad branch lines and much of the main-line rail service. An airport would be nearby, by which one could reach central London in more time than formerly by train.

Modern technology is not all bad, of course. Most HPV enthusiasts use automobiles and planes to travel long distances. These and other powered vehicles endow us with unparalleled freedom to travel to visit friends and relatives, to enjoy the beauty of nature, and to make efficient work and production arrangements.

However, the transportation mix in many countries is the result of economic distortions that overwhelmingly favor automobile use. Although improvements in vehicles and roads may increase the use of HPVs somewhat, a large shift in the methods and patterns of transportation would require aligning the costs and benefits of alternative forms of transportation to more closely represent actual economics. Modern technology could use a variation of the earlier system of charging motorists about what actual costs are. Before we discuss these weighty matters, let us review some alternatives for HPVs.

Improved Human-Powered Vehicles

The best future commuting HPV is very likely to be a recumbent bicycle. There may be special cases where tricycles and four-wheeled designs have advantages (for instance, in retirement communities), but the increased width required makes them difficult to use on existing roads. And although we may wish for an entirely separate HPV road network, we will have to put up with the present highway system for almost all our journeys.

The track width required of a four-wheeled HPV to prevent it rolling over in a tight turn is very large. It is desirable in a vehicle designed for use on our general highways that the rider's eye level be similar to that of most automobile drivers—about 1.2 m above the ground. The height of the center of gravity of the vehicle and driver is then around 700 mm. Tires in dry conditions have a coefficient of friction of 0.8 to 0.9, and we must allow for a slight slope in the roadway and for the rider to be sitting a little off center. The required track width for stability then becomes about 1.4 m (55 in.), giving a vehicle that would have to occupy a full highway lane. In contrast, bicycles of any type can use a small fraction of a lane alongside, if necessary, other traffic in the same lane. In these circumstances motor vehicle users find bicycles acceptable.

Recumbents Need Fairings

Recumbent bicycles need further major development. Weather protection is generally poor. It is not possible in reasonable comfort to wear a poncho, under which one can propel an upright bicycle all day in a downpour. We need full or partial fairings, like those on the Lightnings described in chapter 9. Fairings must not cause wandering steering in crosswinds. A fairing must not make the recumbent too heavy or awkward to carry into an upstairs apartment at the end of a ride. In hot weather a fairing should be a layer of insulation and a duct for cool air, not an ovenlike enclosure; it should also, of course, reduce drag from air resistance.

If a rigid fairing is used it should be attached to the frame or chassis. On normal (i.e., bumpy) roads, a rigid fairing may need to be attached firmly to a "sprung" frame (one with a suspension system for the two wheels). This would be an unfortunate complication, because otherwise a long-wheelbase recumbent with a tensioned-fabric seat is extremely comfortable without any additional suspension, even on bumpy roadways. Other technology, such as that of the pop out umbrella, should be examined for possible application to unsprung recumbents. Paul Van Valkenburgh made some lightweight inflatable fairings that were fitted more to the rider than to the vehicle. This approach has very attractive features.

Recumbent Wheelbase

With regard to the wheelbase of recumbent bicycles, the ideal seems to be somewhere between that of the long wheelbase, which gives safe and comfortable riding but greater weight in a vehicle that is difficult to carry and to store, and that of the short wheelbase, which can have steering and braking characteristics that require getting used to. Some builders have put the cranks high over the front wheel to produce an intermediate wheelbase. I believe that this pedaling position is acceptable to enthusiasts but would be an obstacle to the conversion of many members of the public to recumbent riding. An ideal would be a lightweight, efficient linkage giving an oscillating or long-oval pedaling motion over the front wheel. The mechanism probably has already been invented, but not yet applied to this task. This intermediate wheelbase would unload the rear wheel a little and add a little load to the front wheel, thus improving slow-speed balancing and reducing the frontal and side-wind drag, compared with a faired long-wheelbase vehicle. Another alternative would be an easily folded long-wheelbase recumbent.

Improved Roadways

The position of John Forester (1983) and many others in the "effective cycling" movement is that we do not need "separate but unequal" roadways for HPVs. We need improvements to the regular roads. In particular, we need the recognition by the authorities, by other road users, and by the riders themselves, that HPVs are full vehicles, with (almost) all the rights and responsibilities of engine-powered vehicles. In general, this is the law, but not yet accepted in practice, in the U.S. (Almost all bicyclists welcome additional bike trails, but fear being *required* to use them and being denied the use of regular roads.)

If attitudes are changed, we should work to advocate the redefining of lanes on roads. Often the full road width is divided into equal lanes. An HPV in one lane can slow traffic and cause hostility. Yet in many states in the U.S. the lanes are marked in widths that are even for trucks and buses and extremely wide for today's smaller cars. Therefore it would be safer for all road users if the roads were laid out with somewhat narrower lanes and marked half-width in curbside lanes for HPVs. This approach has been followed with great success in many areas and needs to be made universal wherever it is practicable.

The Potential for Power-Assist and for HPV Guideways

Even the most enthusiastic supporter of HPVs acknowledges that the general public will not switch to such vehicles in very hilly areas, nor in places where extreme weather prevents all but the hardiest people from bicycling. An 1892 solution to some of these problems was the Mt. Holly & Smithville [New Jersey] Bicycle Railroad (see Figure 19.1), a monorail that was designed by Arthur Hotchkiss to provide a low rolling resistance and easy grades to riders who supplied their own power through a treadle mechanism taken from the Star bicycle (Wilson, 1992). This and other schemes were started at around this time and failed for many reasons: the lines were short; they could not take the users' regular bicycles; passing was not possible so the travel speed was that of the slowest user; and for a time at least one line was used for traffic in two directions, leading to much dismounting and waiting.

FIGURE 19.1 Mt. Holly and Smithville Bicycle Railroad. (From "Transportation," Jim Harter, Dover, 1984)

In many areas bicycles could be carried on trains and on streetcars (see Figure 19.2), giving the user faster line travel coupled with the freedom of using one's own bicycle to start and finish the journey. Some communities are equipping buses to give the same capability of carrying bicycles today.

Another form of power assist could be supplied from an escalator-type of moving hand-rail alongside a regular highway on steep-uphill sections (see Figure 19.3) (Whitt & Wilson, 1982). Riders of bicycles and of appropriate HPVs would steer close to the belt at the bottom of the hill, grasp the hand-rail, and proceed at a steady speed (perhaps 5 m/s). Because all users would be going the same speed, there would be no danger of collisions. Parking would have to be banned on such hills.

Enclosed HPV-dedicated powered and possibly air-conditioned guideways have been proposed by several people, usually from places where winters are harsh. The Syracuse University Research Corporation partly developed its Crusway concept, in which bicycles and other HPVs took traction from a cable-pulled hook on short, steep, uphill segments and coasted down long descents of 2.5% grade at 7.5 to 9 m/s (17 to 20 mph). This ingenious arrangement meant that entrances and exits

and overtaking could be carried out under normal manual control. An HPV guideway proposal originating in Canada is the Skyway Project (Kor, 1992), in which the power assist would be provided by a continuous flow of air in the direction of vehicle movement.

These and other proposals for HPV guideways are reviewed by Wilson (1992). Western societies may be approaching the time when some of these have a high likelihood of successful implementation when it is shown how great would be the resulting reduction of energy use and of ozone-destroying emissions. The next section has, however, shorter range objectives: to show how present-day HPVs, principally bicycles, would come into far greater use if motor vehicle subsidies were reduced.

Bringing Economic Realities Home

In its history, human society has followed some strange and often cruel practices. It is, for instance, not too long ago that small children were sent down into British coal mines to pull coal carts on their

FIGURE 19.2   Proposal for bike trailers on buses. (By David M. Eggleston, Cal State, San Diego)

FIGURE 19.3   Power assistance from a moving handrail. (Proposed by D. G. Wilson in *Bicycling Science*)

hands and knees; until only recently, slavery was common in the U.S.; and women in most countries were, and in some cases still are, virtual slaves of their husbands. We now regard these practices as barbaric. Human beings are not stupid, but at the time these practices were regarded as right and proper, even, hard though it is to believe, by some of their victims.

There is no doubt that future generations will find our treatment of automobile use similarly hard to believe. We have allowed a system to grow up that has given free reign to selfishness. Close-knit communities have been destroyed and have been replaced by sprawling messes of often indescribable ugliness. It is no longer possible to walk to stores in a community converted to automobile living; moreover, often, unless heavily subsidized, bus and other transportation means formerly available to the old and the poor have also disappeared in such communities. U.S. and Western foreign policy and defense expenditures are largely based on ensuring that "our" oil supplies are not interrupted. These expenditures are paid by the general taxpayers, not by the users of motor vehicles. The same is true for most of the motor-vehicle-related expenditures by cities and towns.

Parable of the Shared Lunch

The reader might want to point out that most taxpayers are simultaneously drivers. However, even if all taxpayers were drivers, large individually incurred costs should not be distributed to all, as overhead. The serious effects that result from the failure to charge something approaching the full cost of activities are illustrated by the economic parable of the shared lunch. If thirty thrifty people have lunch together, regularly choosing inexpensive meals, and then decide to save the time of the restaurant employees by having a common bill and dividing it equally, each person will have an incentive to order the most expensive meal, because the incremental cost will be shared by all thirty people. The inevitable result after a few days is that the total costs of lunch are far higher than they would be if each person ordered individually, and the burden falls particularly hard on poorer people. They might order inexpensive meals, but would pay just as much as those eating lobster and caviar. This is a close analogy to our automobile-dominated society. It also points the way to bringing about a more rational situation.

Transportation Subsidies

The indictment against overreliance on the automobile can be summed up in one statement: Use of the automobile, particularly in urban areas, imposes costs on others. The fact that these costs are not paid directly by the users means that, in effect, the use of automobiles is heavily subsidized. The response of the political community in the U.S. and in most other developed countries is to counter one subsidy with others: The politicians subsidize public transportation by bus, subway, railroad, and even by air. One result is that government is involved in transportation to a much greater extent than it need be. Many enthusiasts for human-powered transportation join these other disadvantaged modes in looking in turn for their subsidies. We should urge the

opposite: that the subsidies for automobile use should be removed.

There have been generations of economists and political scientists in favor of removing these subsidies, and they have proposed a wide range of alternatives. We will describe one of these, a system to equip all vehicles, public and private, with road-use meters.

Road-Use Charging: A Model for Removing Subsidies

The origin of the proposal is usually attributed to the Smeed Report (1964), published by the U.K. Ministry of Transport, in which the delay costs alone of adding a vehicle to the traffic in central London were assessed at the present equivalent of $5 to $10 per mile. It recommended that a system of charging motorists for use of the roads be developed. The recommendations became known by the title of a popular paperback, *Paying for Roads*, written by one of the panel members, Gabriel Roth (1967). It was proposed that the road-use charges change with location and with time of day, as with telephone charges. The British government commissioned the development of three vehicle-mounted meters by which the charges could be assessed. Adams (1984), in an undergraduate thesis at MIT, worked on a modern realization of these meters that could be implemented now. The system would work in the following way.

The meters would be like large, flexible credit-card calculators, displaying a single row of large, easily visible digits with a maximum value of, say, 10,000. Motorists would be required to buy them at designated places. The meters themselves would cost about $3.00, and the cost of prepurchased "road-use units" displayed on the meters would be perhaps a cent each. One displaying 10,000 units on purchase would therefore cost $103. It would be attached with adhesive, perhaps under a vacuum, to the inside corner of the windshield. Any tampering would cause the display to fall to zero, and watchful inspectors would ticket any car used with a zeroed meter.

Highway Treatment

The roads would be grooved to carry sets of loop antennas. When a vehicle passed over an activated loop, its meter display would be lowered by one unit. The loops could be as close as 100 m apart in congested areas, or 1 km apart in suburban areas. All loops would be activated at rush hours, but many would be switched off at other times. Signs would inform road users of loop status. Drivers would see their costs adding as they drove, as do passengers in taxi-cabs, and most would change their driving patterns to avoid rush hours and congested streets.

If such a system were instituted, driving an automobile in a congested area, which is where most of the external costs are incurred, would become much more expensive. Many people would decide to use other forms of transportation. For maximum effectiveness, the charge rates would be gradually increased until traffic jams completely disappeared. Buses would then travel much faster and become more attractive as transportation alternatives on this account alone. All public transportation services would then become more frequent and reliable. Subsidies could be removed, and private-enterprise buses, jitneys, rail services, and modern guideway systems would compete for the public's patronage.

Parking meters could be replaced by curbside focused antennas, which would be pulsed to impose parking charges through the same on-vehicle meters. The pulsing frequency would be very high near fire hydrants, and would vary elsewhere according to demand. The economist William Vickrey (1963) maintained that parking charges should be set so that there is always one place in five or ten free.

A Popular Tax?

Vickrey (1963) also claimed that increased parking charges and other fees that eliminate traffic jams and the frustrating search for parking should be the most popular of taxes. The increased cost of driving would, he calculated, be more than offset by the drivers' valuations of their time saved. Road use by all, including the nonmotorists, would be much more enjoyable. The motorists would be sure of getting to a destination fast and of finding a nearby place to park. The users of public transportation would have a frequent, reliable, and competitive service. Pedestrians would no longer have to get through jams of fuming vehicles carrying fuming drivers.

Cities would have a large, new source of income being, one hopes, cheerfully paid by the more well-to-do. Other taxes would be reduced, again helping the more-affluent section of the population. It would be highly desirable, also, that the less afflu-

ent share in this wealth through some form of rebate or negative income tax. The money collected from congestion taxes (including those on parking) would result from and eliminate much of the inefficiency of the present anarchy on our urban roads, and the money should be shared among all members of society.

And, of course, human-powered vehicles would become much more viable and much more attractive. They would be used by more people, whose rights would become more recognized. The absence of traffic jams would be almost as beneficial for them as for the motorists.

We HPV enthusiasts should be ready to advocate the establishment of a new era of enlightenment, to the benefit of everyone in all countries.

The Future

The reader will have perceived a case of role reversal. The author is an engineer with an agenda for some of the engineering improvements desirable in HPVs. Yet he believes that the future pattern of HPV use will be determined more by economics than by improvements in HPVs alone. If the authors of the World Resources Institute report (MacKenzie, et al., 1992) and their many sources are even approximately correct in their assessment that the use of motor vehicles imposes costs on others of $300 billion per year in the U.S., an amount corresponding to over $2.50 per mile per driver, and if means were devised to charge only $1.00 per mile in some equitable way and to redistribute the collected funds, there would indeed be a major change not only in the patterns of transportation, but also in housing, working, merchandising, and recreation. Irrational economic arrangements become more difficult and more expensive to maintain as time goes on (communism being a prime example). Therefore the signs point to, but do not guarantee, a greatly increased role for HPVs in the future.

Note

[1]This chapter was adapted from Wilson, D.G. (1986). A blueprint for an HPV revolution. In A.V. Abbott (Ed.), *Proceedings of the Third International Human-Powered-Vehicle Scientific Symposium* (pp. 79–83). Indianapolis: International Human Powered Vehicle Association.

References

Adams, R.L., Jr. (1984). *Study of a road-use-charging system in the United States*. Unpublished bachelor's thesis, Massachusetts Institute of Technology, Cambridge, MA.

Forester, J. (1983). *Bicycle transportation*. Cambridge, MA: MIT Press.

Kor, J. (1992). The Skyway Project, an HPV alternative city transport plan. *Proceedings of the Fourth International Human-Powered-Vehicle Scientific Symposium* (p. 27). Indianapolis: International Human Powered Vehicle Association.

MacKenzie, J.J., Dower, R.C., & Chen, D.D.T. (1992). *The going rate*. Washington, DC: World Resources Institute.

Roth, G. (1967). *Paying for roads: The economics of traffic congestion*. London: Penguin Books.

Smeed, R.J. (1964). *Road pricing: The economics and technical possibilities*. London: Her Majesty's Stationery Office.

Vickrey, W.S. (1963). Pricing in urban and suburban transportation. *American Economic Review, 8*, 452–465.

Whitt, F.R., & Wilson, D.G. (1982). *Bicycling science*. Cambridge, MA: MIT Press.

Wilson, D.G. (1992). Transportation systems based on HPVs, past, present, and prospective. In A. Abbott (Ed.), *Proceedings of the Fourth International Human-Powered-Vehicle Scientific Symposium* (pp. 11–16). Indianapolis: International Human Powered Vehicle Association.

20

THE VALUE AND FUTURE OF HUMAN-POWERED VEHICLES

Paul B. MacCready

You started reading this book with the expectation that it would introduce you to the history and technology of devices that help humans power themselves on land, sea, and air—and your expectations were fulfilled. As you read on, you may have begun realizing that you were exploring a subject with much greater breadth and significance than you had expected.

Human-powered vehicles inhabit the interface where technology impacts human physiology and psychology. Thus they connect to some of the most serious issues facing humanity: the meaning of life, the future of civilization, and the impact of humans on the environment, as well as lesser issues of lifestyle, health and recreation, safety, and education. Let's look at what underlies human-powered vehicles, how they involve us in the present, and then speculate where they may be in 30 to 50 years.

Human-Powered Vehicles in Perspective

As the human race evolved into its present form some hundred thousand years ago, we, as a part of nature, were closely integrated with our natural surroundings. We used our muscles to move around, and we were continually aware of our surroundings and the way wind and terrain affected our travels. Even a short century ago most of our personal travel was still that intimate; we were connected to our biological roots. Then power from fossil fuel (oil) became convenient—cheap and ubiquitous—and in advanced countries human muscles started to become irrelevant. Previously, coal and wood, via steam, augmented the natural power of muscles, water, and wind, but with the advent of gasoline suddenly an individual could command great power. Now we drive in a car, insulated from our surroundings. With a push of the foot on the accelerator we release the energy of fossil fuel, the stored energy of sunlight captured millions of years ago.

Bicycling grew rapidly in the late 1800s when the modern bike (tension spokes, two similar-size wheels, pneumatic tires, and chain drive) emerged. It served roles in recreation and transportation; also, racing and record setting became popular, which helped make the bicycle itself better designed and more popular and economical. The peculiar specialty of paced racing with a bike drafting behind some higher powered vehicle attracted wide attention and stimulated the development of motorcycles as lead vehicles. Early aircraft builders honed their skills in the engineering and innovation of bicycles, the Wright Brothers and Glen Curtis being the most famous. Bicycling technology was not just an end in itself; it affected other fields.

Then cars took over, and in the U.S. cars have, to a large extent, created our culture. It has often been suggested that a galactic explorer observing this country from space might perceptively conclude that cars are the dominant life form, being serviced by lesser two-legged slave devices. (Perhaps batteries that enter charged and are removed discharged?) Certainly our city designs, industry, habits, social patterns, and recreation are determined by cars. Bicycle racing continued, but on a diminishing basis. Bicycling for sport and transportation grew slowly as the population grew, but always in an uncomfortable accommodation with the dominant cars. Thus bicycles are prohibited on freeways and on some streets, and safety factors greatly reduce their use for commuting.

Beginning in the mid-1970s, the International Human Powered Vehicle Association disconnected human-powered land vehicles from the design constraints imposed in racing—the rule that all bikes had to look like the bikes of the late 1800s. IHPVA put a strong focus on low drag, especially aerodynamic drag, and made innovation fashionable. The races sponsored by IHPVA also grew through college competitions organized by the American Society of Mechanical Engineers.

In 1959 Henry Kremer initiated the large prize for human-powered flight that was won in 1977 by the *Gossamer Condor*. Other prizes, and sometimes just the challenge, stimulated later human-power aircraft developments. However, the vehicles are so complex to build and so limited in safe flight to such low altitudes and rare, benign weather conditions that this branch of human power does not seem to offer the potential for exciting growth. Water vehicles have a somewhat more enticing future. The Du Pont Water Vehicle Prize in the late 1980s has strongly stimulated innovation. Nevertheless, it is with the land vehicles that the primary excitement and potential lies—for human-powered vehicles, and for other vehicles that rely on extremely low power but may use other weak energy sources to supplement, or even completely substitute for, human muscles.

The solar car race in Australia in 1987 melded bicycle and IHPVA technology with some car technology ideas. The lessons about efficiency, about doing more with less, began infecting the serious car field a bit as green movements put some priority on efficiency (a priority previously neglected because gasoline was so effective and, at least for the U.S. consumer, so cheap). Without IHPVA there would have been no *GM Sunraycer*, that won the 1987 solar car race, and then no subsequent *GM Impact* car—the prototype of a vehicle now entering mass production, a vehicle made possible only by the strict application of efficiency engendered by the IHPVA philosophy.

In 1990 General Motors sponsored the *GM Sunrayce* competition for 32 university teams to make vehicles that would race from Florida to Michigan. Everyone involved found that the competition served as a wonderful stimulus to education, as students had to work in teams, in subject areas well beyond their normal academic training, to tight deadlines. Lives were changed, graduates became more valuable to employers and hence to society at large, and more races were planned for the future. Now more of the educational institutions are giving college credit for the work on such vehicles, and many engineering schools find such hands-on work and competition experience so valuable that they are incorporating equivalent projects into their curriculum.

In summary, we see how human-powered land vehicles evolved to fill niches for recreation, transportation, and competition. They also helped advance other fields where lightweight construction was vital (early airplanes), where carrying more people faster was needed (early motorcycles and cars), and where the whole philosophy of efficiency needed a higher priority for conserving energy and decreasing pollution (cars of the future).

gy.

The Future

My crystal ball presents only hazy images. Since I am an engineer aware of many of the physical and economic constraints on new devices, I am inhibited from unleashing a vision of the future unfettered by present practices. Also, the role of human power in the future depends on the unknown future role of humans as civilization grows and consumes—while the earth does not get bigger and while the rest of nature and resources diminish.

Human physiology, as discerned from paleontological studies of our ancestors as evolutionary pressures were selecting the form of Homo sapiens—inferences supported by recent glimpses of the remnants of primitive gatherer-hunter peoples—indicate we are sturdy physical creatures, with a natural state of strength and endurance. Now in technologically advanced countries, we can avail ourselves of energy in the form of engines powered by fossil fuel and devices drawing on electricity. The result is a large number of couch potatoes; a large number of athletes, joggers, and health enthusiasts; and a still larger number of persons who fall between these two groups.

In just the last 5 years there has been a huge increase in our attention to fitness. Now, throughout the U.S., much energy goes into human-powered exercise bikes, stair steppers, treadmills, cross-country ski analogs, and rowing machines—all connecting to our physiology, all disconnecting us from the outside world. (There are, of course, some indoor exercisers that make a tenuous connection to surrounding nature by sometimes even employing video tapes depicting countryside scenes tied to a bicycling path.) The people who operate these machines now often find themselves doing the real thing outdoors, for recreation: bike riding, mountain climbing, jogging, skiing, and rowing. One has to question where all this will lead. As the population grows (250,000 more people on earth every day) and nature declines (we cause the extinction of numerous species of flora and fauna each day) will we be emphasizing the exercise indoors but relying more on video or more sophisticated virtual-reality techniques to substitute for nature?

I suspect that there will be increasing use of low-powered vehicles for practical transportation—in advanced countries because of green influence relating to resources, energy, and pollution, and in developing countries more because of economic necessity. It seems both desirable and inevitable that many of these vehicles will be hybrid, mingling human power with solar, wind, battery, or some other power source. An average fit human can continually put out 100 or 150 W. One square meter of modern terrestrial-grade photovoltaic cells can, in bright sunlight, do as well. A sail with only 0.1 m^2 of sail area can, in a 5 to 7 m/s crosswind, deliver thrust to a vehicle going 30 m/s that produces the equivalent of this same range of power. (At lower vehicle speeds the power falls off rapidly; at 20 m/s vehicle speed the full square meter sail area is needed.) A 4-kg, lead-acid or nickel-cadmium battery can deliver 100 to 150 W for an hour. In other words, if the philosophy of efficiency engendered by human-power devices prevails, there are many other energy sources that become convenient for transportation.

I do not foresee streamlined bikes, or hybrid devices, on highway races. The speeds are already too fast for safety. The most exciting developments may be in practical vehicles limited for safety to 10 to 15 m/s. These serve for transportation as well as exercise, but not for racing. Even collapsible, portable bikes have a role, permitting people to have a convenient way of traveling to mass transit vehicles without having to store outside or lock their tiny wheeled devices.

Technological and societal changes are now coming so fast (and the rate of change will continue to increase) that any 30-year prediction of the future of human-powered vehicles is an exercise in naivete. Most predictions of technology will certainly be wrong. But I can predict with some confidence that people will continually be putting more focus on lifestyles that involve doing more with less, including use of human-powered vehicles. Also, because human-powered vehicles illuminate some perspectives about balancing nature and technology, they have a special value. We all share the goal of a desirable, sustainable world. Human-powered vehicles will help move us in that direction.

INDEX

269

Hyper-Cycle, 117

I

IHPVA. *See* International Human Powered Vehicle Association
Illian, P.R., 235, 238
Inbar, O., 38, 44
Inflatable human-powered aircraft, 227
Internal-combustion engine, 13
    invention of, vii-viii, 1, 11, 50
International Human-Powered Speed Championships, 104, 111, 123, 124, 142, 180
International Human-Powered Submarine Race, First, 64
International Human Powered Vehicle Association, vii, 79, 93, 106, 109
    design criteria of, 130
    founding of, 62, 104, 105
    future of, 245
    international competitions and, 110, 125, 129, 181
    racing design constraints and, 266
    recumbents revival and, 113
Ishii, Junji, 225
Izumi, Pearl, 143

J

J-Rad recumbent bicycle, 114, 115
Japan International Birdman Rally, 237
Jarey, Paul, 114
Jex, H.R., 245
Johnson, Greg, 174
Johnson, R.E., 17, 27
Jones, D.E.H., 197, 204
Jones, N.L., 31, 45
Jupiter, 222, 223

K

Kallander, Charles, 177, 178
    diagram of his drive, 179
Kanellopoulos, Kanellos, 24, 235, 236
Kataoka, Toshio, 237, 238
Katch, F.I., 13, 15, 28, 35, 44
Katch, V.L., 13, 15, 28, 35, 44
Kautz, S.A., 27, 36, 41, 44
Kayaks, vii
Kemp, P., 5, 11, 63, 66
Kerry, Brian, 221
Kevlar by DuPont, 109, 110, 163, 164, 165, 167, 223, 229
Kiceniuk's Icarus, Taras, 227-228
Kimura, Hidemasa, 222, 223, 225, 238
Kingsbury, Miles, 185, 195
Kirshner, Daniel, 157, 278
Klein, Gary, 93
Klimovitch, Geraldine, 40, 44, 188, 195
Klopfenstein, King L., 180
Knapp, Jon, 60
    Sea Saber and, 82
Kor, J., 260, 264
Kremer, Henry
    Figure-Eight prize and, 219-229
    prizes (1959-1985) and, 215, 217, 219-234, 239, 266
Ktesibios, 5
Kurke, J.D., 245
Kyle, Chester R., vii, 19, 20, 22, 27, 28, 30, 32, 33, 34, 35, 36, 37, 40, 44, 45, 95, 103, 104, 111, 124, 141, 145, 146, 147, 148, 150, 151, 153, 155, 160, 162, 163, 171, 174
    carbon-composite monocoque bicycle prototype and, 144
    Streamliner and, 103, 104

L

Lallement, Pierre, 114, 257
Lamb, D.R., 28, 44
Lambie, Jack, vii, 104, 143, 228
Land Scull, 180
Land Shark, 108, 109
Land vehicles, 93-213
    heyday of, vii
    overview of, 93-94
Landry, F., 44
Langford, John, 229, 232, 235
Larrabee, Eugene E., 57, 82, 91, 229, 242, 249, 254
Lassière, Alan, 220, 238
Lawrence, R.A., 33, 44
Lawson, H.J., 95
Leg cranking, 2, 29, 31
    muscles used in, 10-11
    oxygen cost of, 20
Legs on treadles, 9-10
Levaseur, C., 64, 66
Levers actuated by arms and back muscles, 5, 7
Lewis, S.E., 28
Lightning models case history, 106-107, 125, 126, 129-140
    analysis of, 139-140
    braking and, 137, 138
    climbing speed and, 135, 136
    costs of, 138-139
    cruising speed and, 133, 134-135
    future of, 140
    performance and cost comparisons of, 132, 133-139
    racing and, 108, 109, 110
    rider cooling and comfort of, 137, 138
    top speed and, 133, 134
    turning radius and handling of, 136
    vehicle descriptions of, 130-132
    visibility of, 136, 137
Lilley, Geoffrey, 219
Linnets I, II, III, and IV, 222, 223, 225
Lippisch, Dr. Alexander, 219
Lissaman, Peter B.S., 229, 240, 245

M

MacCready, Parker, 60, 66, 91, 234, 243
    Preposterous Pogo Foil and, 59
MacCready, Paul B., 143, 215, 217, 227, 228, 229, 232, 234, 239, 240, 245, 248, 249, 255, 265, 278
Machine versus muscle power, 30, 31
Maciejewski, Harald, 118
Mack, G.W., 28
MacKenzie, J.J., 258, 263, 264
Macmillan, Kirkpatrick, 9, 10, 114
Malewicki, D.J., 163, 171
Malina, R.M., 4, 11
Mallard, 60
Malliga, Josef, 223
Manuped, 108
Margaria, R., 28
Marsden, Anne, 220, 238
Martin, Gardner, 105, 106, 108, 109, 122-123
    and dominance of his Easy Racer team, 124-126
Masschelin, Paul, 226
Masschelin, Stephan, 226
Mastropaolo, J., 36, 44, 181
Matthies, A., 8, 11
Mayfly, 221-222

About the Editors

Allan V. Abbott has held four world records for speed in human-powered vehicles of his own design and construction: unlimited paced bicycle (1973–1985), streamlined bicycle (1976–1977), 2,000-meter human-powered watercraft (1986–1987), and 100-meter human-powered watercraft (1987–1988). Along with Alec Brooks, he designed and competed on the first successful human-powered hydrofoil. He was founding president of the International Human Powered Vehicle Association (IHPVA) and has served on its Board of Directors since 1977.

Abbott is a professor of family medicine at the University of Southern California School of Medicine and a board-certified sports medicine physician. He, his wife, Colony, and their two children live in San Marino, California.

David Gordon Wilson, coauthor of the popular book *Bicycling Science*, is the co-designer of the Avatar 1000 and 2000 recumbent bicycles. The Avatar 2000, on which the world bicycle speed record for 1982–1983 was set, became the archetype for recumbent bicycle design. Wilson organized and sponsored the first modern design contest for human-powered vehicles from 1967 to 1969, an event that led to the modern interest in recumbent bicycles. He was a founding board member of the IHPVA and later served as its president. Wilson has been the editor of *Human Power*, the IHPVA journal, since 1984 and a professor of mechanical engineering at the Massachusetts Institute of Technology since 1971.

ABOUT THE CONTRIBUTORS

Alec Brooks is the co-developer of the Flying Fish series of human-powered hydrofoil watercraft. He has also developed several streamlined human-powered land vehicles, starting while he was in college. He studied civil engineering at the University of California, Berkeley, and the California Institute of Technology, receiving his PhD in 1981. He is now a Vice President at AeroVironment Inc., in Monrovia, CA, where he has led the teams that created the *Quetzalcoatlus northropi* flying pterodactyl replica, the GM *Sunraycer* solar-powered car, and the GM Impact electric vehicle prototype.

Tim Brummer has been involved with HPVs since 1977 when he designed the White Lightning, the first in his Lightning series of HPVs. The White Lightning was the first HPV to break the 55-mph barrier and thus win the Abbott Prize. Other Lightning models include the X-2, which enjoyed considerable racing success and was at one time the world's fastest bicycle. In 1988, Brummer introduced the world's first commercially available fully-faired HPV, the Lightning F-40. This model also set a record by winning the HPV Race Across America in a time of 5 days, 1 hour. Brummer has a BS in aerospace engineering from Northrop University and an MS in systems management from the University of Southern California. He is the founder and chief engineer of Lightning Cycle Dynamics and lives in Lompoc, California.

Daniel Kirshner lives in Berkeley, CA, where he is a Senior Economic Analyst in the California office of the Environmental Defense Fund, a national not-for-profit environmental organization. He works on electric energy conservation and alternative energy options, and can be seen most days attempting to conserve energy by commuting on a medium-wheelbase recumbent bicycle of his own design.

Chet Kyle is an independent consultant and former professor of mechanical engineering at the University of California, Long Beach. With Jackie Lambie he started the open-rules races that became the International Human Power Speed Championships and then founded the International Human-Powered Vehicle Association. He has carried out a great deal of research on the aerodynamics and rolling resistance of human-powered vehicles, and was a member of the team that developed the "funny bikes" that were used by the US Olympic Cycling Team.

Paul B. MacCready is considered the "father of human-powered flight" because he led the *Gossamer Condor* team that in 1977 won the Kremer Prize, and the *Gossamer Albatross* team that in 1979 took the next Kremer Prize (aviation's largest cash award) for a flight across the English Channel. He is the International President of the IHPVA and the founder and Chairman of the Board of AeroVironment Inc., a Monrovia, CA, services and products company renown for pioneering developments in energy-efficient vehicles. He has received the 1982 Lindbergh Award for contributing "significantly to achieving a balance between technology and the environment," and numerous awards including the Collier Trophy, Reed Aeronautical Award, Guggenheim Medal, SAE Cole Award for Automotive Engineering, and the Chrysler Award for Innovation in Design.

Robert L. Price is an electronics packaging Staff Engineer at Lockheed Martin Marietta Astronautics in Denver, Colorado, where the air is thin and dry. He has two Bachelors of Science degrees, in Mechanical Engineering and Organization Management. He is a Senior Member of the American Institute of Aeronautics and Astronautics and an early member of the IHPVA. He designs and builds HPVs and spacecraft that utilize aluminum monocoque construction. To keep his mind in a practical orientation within a ridiculously complex work environment, he has a complete basement workshop. Amazingly, his wife still keeps him around and his kids still talk to him, probably because he keeps their bikes in tune.

Chris Roper has been an enthusiast for human-powered flight since the 1950's when he was told "A man would need arm muscles 6-foot thick in order to fly." He started work in the aircraft industry in 1953 and studied at City University, London, UK, being awarded an HNC in aeronautical engineering in 1958. In 1960, before anyone had taken off using either arm or leg muscles, he designed his first HPA. In 1963 he designed the *Jupiter*, which later held the distance record for HPAs. Since 1982 he has been a member of the Human-Powered Aircraft Group Committee of the Royal Aeronautical Society, and in 1990 became the Vice President-Air of the IHPVA. His other interests include cycling and canoeing. He paddled from England across to France in a canoe of his own design in 1958. He maintains an interest in HPA worldwide and has helped to build HPA in three continents.

T. Scott Rowe is currently a Principal Engineer with Alcon Laboratories in Irvine, CA. He has been interested in HPV systems, and in particular the application of composite materials, since 1980. He helped design and build the two Red Shift vehicles under contract with the Schwinn Bicycle Company, with *Red Shift I* finishing third in the 1981 International Human-Powered Speed Championships road race. The Red Shift vehicles have made numerous appearances in TV and film, including *Discovery: The World of Science*, *CHiPs*, and the IMAX motion picture *Speed*. His work has been published in the proceedings of the second IHPVA Scientific Symposium.

Theodor Schmidt was born in Switzerland in 1954, grew up in the USA, and was educated in Switzerland and Great Britain, where he graduated (BSC, Wales) and lived for a number of years, working mainly on kite-sails for marine propulsion. He developed extremely light inflatable hulls with Keith Stewart, propellers for human-powered watercraft, and a number of highly portable and amphibious cruising boats. Theodor now lives in Switzerland and, having designed and raced a number of human/solar-powered vehicles in the Tour de Sol, works as a consultant for solar and hybrid drive technology and safety.

Ernst Schöberl has been building model aircraft since the age of 12. After studying mechanical and chemical engineering at Technical University Munich, he helped design and build the HPA *Musculair I* and *Musculair II*, as well as a solar-powered aircraft, the *Solair I*. His contributions to human- and solar-powered aircraft have earned him several awards, including the Environmental Prize at the International Berblinger Aviation Competition. Ernst is currently a professor at Fachhochschule Würzburg Schweinfurt in Germany.

Ted Van Dusen is president and founder of Composite Engineering. Human-powered craft designed by Van Dusen have earned more than fifty gold, silver, and bronze medals in World Championship and Olympic competitions. A former National Team rower, he received a PhD in ocean engineering from the University of Massachusetts; a marine mechanical engineering degree and MS in naval architecture from the Massachusetts Institute of Technology; and a BS in naval architecture from Webb Institute. Van Dusen's other compelling professional interest is wind-powered craft and wind turbines. In the early 1970s, he helped found US Windpower, and he continues to design and manufacture composite wind turbine blades and composite spans for wind-powered boats from small dinghies to BOC and TransPac competitors. He currently lives in Concord, Massachusetts, rows competitively at the Masters' level, and sails whenever he can.

Related books from Human Kinetics

1994 • Cloth • 560 pp
Item BWIL0693
ISBN 0-87322-693-3
$49.00 ($68.50 Canadian)

Logically organized, superbly written, and beautifully illustrated, this top-seller has become the new standard by which exercise physiology texts are measured.

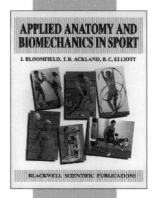

1995 • Paper
Approx 344 pp
Item PBUR0535
ISBN 0-87322-535-X
$19.95 ($29.95 Canadian)

Cutting-edge science applied to cycling. Provides insights and practical applications to improve cycling training and performance.

1995 • Paper • 272 pp
Item PBUR0759
ISBN 0-87322-759-X
$18.95 ($26.50 Canadian)

Take your cycling to the next level with year-round training programs to improve speed and endurance.

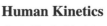

1994 • Paper • 392 pp
Item BBLO0305
ISBN 0-86793-305-4
$35.00 ($48.95 Canadian)

Explains how state of the art advances in sport science can be used in coaching to achieve optimal skill performance.